AQA Science
Biology

New GCSE

Ann Fullick

Bev Cox

Niva Miles

Series Editor
Lawrie Ryan

Nelson Thornes

Published in 2011 by:
Nelson Thornes Ltd
Delta Place
27 Bath Road
CHELTENHAM
GL53 7TH
United Kingdom

12 13 14 15 / 10 9 8 7 6 5 4

A catalogue record for this book is available from the British Library

ISBN 978 1 4085 0826 8

Cover photograph: Bloom Works Inc./Alamy

Illustrations include artwork drawn by Wearset Ltd and David Russell Illustration

Page make-up by Wearset Ltd, Boldon, Tyne and Wear

Index created by Indexing Specialists(UK) Ltd

Printed in China

Biology Contents

Welcome to AQA GCSE Biology!

Learning objectives

Each topic begins with key questions that you should be able to answer by the end of the lesson.

Examiner's tip

Hints from the examiners who will mark your exams, giving you important advice on things to remember and what to watch out for.

Did you know ... ?

There are lots of interesting, and often strange, facts about science. This feature tells you about many of them.

∞ links

Links will tell you where you can find more information about what you are learning.

Activity

An activity is linked to a main lesson and could be a discussion or task in pairs, groups or by yourself.

Maths skills

This feature highlights the maths skills that you will need for your GCSE Biology exams with short, visual explanations.

This book has been written for you by the people who will be marking your exams, very experienced teachers and subject experts. It covers everything you need to know for your exams and is packed full of features to help you achieve the very best that you can.

Questions in yellow boxes check that you understand what you are learning as you go along. The answers are all within the text so if you don't know the answer, you can go back and reread the relevant section.

Figure 1 Many diagrams are as important for you to learn as the text, so make sure you revise them carefully.

Key words are highlighted in the text. You can look them up in the glossary at the back of the book if you are not sure what they mean.

 Where you see this icon, you will know that this part of the topic involves How Science Works – a really important part of your GCSE and an interesting way to understand 'how science works' in real life.

(k) Where you see this icon, there are supporting electronic resources in our Kerboodle online service.

Practical

This feature helps you become familiar with key practicals. It may be a simple introduction, a reminder or the basis for a practical in the classroom.

Anything in the Higher Tier boxes must be learned by those sitting the Higher Tier exam. If you'll be sitting the Foundation Tier, these boxes can be missed out.

The same is true for any other places which are marked Higher or [H].

Summary questions

These questions give you the chance to test whether you have learned and understood everything in the topic. If you get any wrong, go back and have another look.

And at the end of each chapter you will find …

Summary questions

These will test you on what you have learned throughout the whole chapter, helping you to work out what you have understood and where you need to go back and revise.

Examination-style questions

These questions are examples of the types of questions you will answer in your actual GCSE exam, so you can get lots of practice during your course.

Key points

At the end of the topic are the important points that you must remember. They can be used to help with revision and summarising your knowledge.

Higher

How does science work? ⓚ

Learning objectives

- What is meant by 'How Science Works'?
- What is a hypothesis?
- What is a prediction and why should you make one?
- How can you investigate a problem scientifically?

This first chapter looks at 'How Science Works'. It is an important part of your GCSE because the ideas introduced here will crop up throughout your course. You will be expected to collect scientific **evidence** and to understand how we use evidence. These concepts will be assessed as the major part of your internal school assessment.

You will take one or more 45-minute tests. These tests are based on **data** you have collected previously plus data supplied for you in the test. They are called Investigative Skills Assignments (ISA). The ideas in 'How Science Works' will also be assessed in your examinations.

How science works for us

Science works for us all day, every day. You do not need to know how a mobile phone works to enjoy sending text messages. But, think about how you started to use your mobile phone or your television remote control. Did you work through pages of instructions? Probably not!

You knew that pressing the buttons would change something on the screen (**knowledge**). You played around with the buttons, to see what would happen (**observation**). You had a guess based on your knowledge and observations at what you thought might be happening (**prediction**) and then tested your idea (**experiment**).

Perhaps 'How Science Works' should really be called 'How Scientists Work'.

Science moves forward by slow, steady steps. When a genius such as Einstein comes along, it takes a giant leap. Those small steps build on knowledge and experience that we already have.

The steps don't always lead in a straight line, starting with an observation and ending with a conclusion. More often than not you find yourself going round in circles, but each time you go around the loop you gain more knowledge and so can make better predictions.

 links
You can find out more about your ISA by looking at H10 The ISA at the end of this chapter.

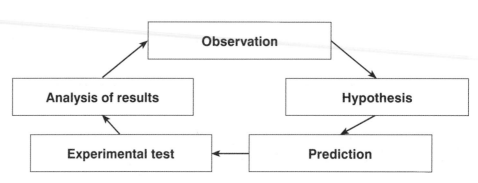

Each small step is important in its own way. It builds on the body of knowledge that we have, but observation is usually the starting point. In 1796, Edward Jenner observed that people who worked with cows did not catch smallpox but did catch a very similar disease called cowpox. This observation led him to develop a system of inoculating people with cowpox to prevent them from catching smallpox. Jenner called this process vaccination, from the Latin word for cow, *vacca*.

Figure 1 Albert Einstein was a genius, but he worked through scientific problems in the same way as you will in your GCSE

Activity

Coconut seeds

Once you have got the idea of holidays out of your mind, look at the photograph in Figure 2 with your scientific brain.

Work in groups to *observe* the beach and the plants growing on it. Then you can start to think about why the plants can grow (*knowledge*) so close to the beach.

One idea could be that the seeds can float for a long while in the sea, without taking in any water.

You can use the following headings to discuss your investigation. One person should be writing your ideas down, so that you can discuss them with the rest of your class.

- What prediction can you make about the mass of the coconut seed and the time it spends in the sea water?
- How could you test your prediction?
- What would you have to control?
- Write a plan for your investigation.
- How could you make sure your results were repeatable?

Figure 2 Tropical beach

Key points

- **Observations** are often the starting point for an investigation.

- **A hypothesis** is a proposal intended to explain certain facts or observations.

- **A prediction** is an intelligent guess, based on some **knowledge**.

- **An experiment** is a way of testing your prediction.

Summary questions

1 Copy and complete this paragraph using the following words:

   experiment   knowledge   conclusion   prediction   observation

   You have learned before that a cup of tea loses energy if it is left standing. This is a piece of .... You make an .... that dark-coloured cups will cool faster. So you make a .... that if you have a black cup, this will cool fastest of all. You carry out an .... to get some results, and from these you make a ....

Fundamental ideas about how science works

- How do you spot when an opinion is not based on good science?
- What is the importance of continuous and categoric variables?
- What does it mean to say that evidence is valid?
- What is the difference between a result being repeatable and a result being reproducible?
- How can two sets of data be linked?

AQA Examiner's tip

Read a newspaper article or watch the news on TV. Ask yourself whether any research presented is valid. Ask yourself whether you can trust that person's opinion and why.

Science is too important for us to get it wrong

Sometimes it is easy to spot when people try to use science poorly. Sometimes it can be funny. You might have seen adverts claiming to give your hair 'body' or sprays that give your feet 'lift'!

On the other hand, poor scientific practice can cost lives.

Some years ago a company sold the drug thalidomide to people as a sleeping pill. Research was carried out on animals to see if it was safe. The research did not include work on pregnant animals. The **opinion** of the people in charge was that the animal research showed the drug could be used safely with humans.

Then the drug was also found to help ease morning sickness in pregnant women. Unfortunately, doctors prescribed it to many women, resulting in thousands of babies being born with deformed limbs. It was far from safe.

These are very difficult decisions to make. You need to be absolutely certain of what the science is telling you.

a Why was the opinion of the people in charge of developing thalidomide based on poor science?

Deciding on what to measure: variables

Variables are physical, chemical or biological quantities or characteristics.

In an investigation, you normally choose one thing to change or vary. This is called the **independent variable**.

When you change the independent variable, it may cause something else to change. This is called the **dependent variable**.

A **control variable** is one that is kept the same and is not changed during the investigation.

You need to know about two different types of these variables:

- A **categoric variable** is one that is best described by a label (usually a word). The 'colour of eyes' is a categoric variable, e.g. blue or brown eyes.
- A **continuous variable** is one that we measure, so its value could be any number. Temperature (as measured by a thermometer or temperature sensor) is a continuous variable, e.g. 37.6 °C, 45.2 °C. Continuous variables can have values (called quantities) that can be found by making measurements (e.g. light intensity, flow rate, etc.).

b Imagine you were growing seedlings in different volumes of water. Would it be better to say that some were tall and some were short, or some were taller than others, or to measure the heights of all the seedlings?

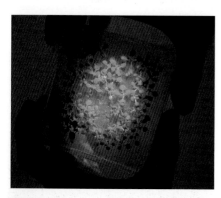

Figure 1 Cress seedlings growing in a Petri dish

Making your evidence repeatable, reproducible and valid

When you are designing an investigation you must make sure that other people can get the same results as you. This makes the evidence you collect **reproducible**.

A measurement is **repeatable** if the original experimenter repeats the investigation using the same method and equipment and obtains the same results.

A measurement is reproducible if the investigation is repeated by another person, or by using different equipment or techniques, and the same results are obtained.

You must also make sure you are measuring the actual thing you want to measure. If you don't, your data can't be used to answer your original question. This seems very obvious but it is not always quite so easy. You need to make sure that you have controlled as many other variables as you can, so that no one can say that your investigation is not **valid**. A measurement is valid if it measures what it is supposed to measure with an appropriate level of performance.

   c State one way in which you can show that your results are repeatable.

How might an independent variable be linked to a dependent variable?

Looking for a link between your independent and dependent variables is very important. The pattern of your graph or bar chart can often help you to see if there is a link.

But beware! There may not be a link! If your results seem to show that there is no link, don't be afraid to say so. Look at Figure 2.

The points on the top graph show a clear pattern, but the bottom graph shows random scatter.

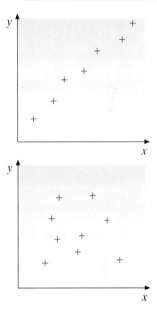

Figure 2 Which graph shows that there might be a link between *x* and *y*?

Summary questions

1 Copy and complete this paragraph using the following words:

   continuous   independent   categoric   dependent

   Stefan wanted to find out which was the strongest supermarket plastic carrier bag. He tested five different bags by adding weight to them until they broke. The type of bag he used was the .... variable and the weight that it took to break it was the .... variable. The 'type of bag' is called a .... variable and the 'weight needed to break' it was a .... variable.

2 A researcher claimed that the metal tungsten 'alters the growth of leukaemia cells' in laboratory tests. A newspaper wrote that they would 'wait until other scientists had reviewed the research before giving their opinion'. Why is this a good idea?

H3 Starting an investigation

Learning objectives

- How can you use your scientific knowledge to observe the world around you?
- How can you use your observations to make a hypothesis?
- How can you make predictions and start to design an investigation?

Figure 1 Plant showing positive phototropism

Observation

As humans we are sensitive to the world around us. We can use our many senses to detect what is happening. As scientists we use observations to ask questions. We can only ask useful questions if we know something about the observed event. We will not have all of the answers, but we know enough to start asking relevant questions.

If we observe that the weather has been hot today, we would not ask whether it was due to global warming. If the weather was hotter than normal for several years, we could ask that question. We know that global warming takes many years to show its effect.

When you are designing an investigation you have to observe carefully which variables are likely to have an effect.

> **a** Would it be reasonable to ask whether the plant in Figure 1 is 'growing towards the glass'? Explain your answer.

A farmer noticed that her corn was much smaller at the edge of the field than in the middle (observation). She noticed that the trees were quite large on that side of the field. She came up with the following ideas that might explain why this is happening:

- The trees at the edge of the field were blocking out the light.
- The trees were taking too many nutrients out of the soil.
- The leaves from the tree had covered the young corn plants in the spring.
- The trees had taken too much water out of the soil.
- The seeds at the edge of the field were genetically small plants.
- The drill had planted fewer seeds on that side of the field.
- The fertiliser spray had not reached the side of the field.
- The wind had been too strong over winter and had moved the roots of the plants.
- The plants at the edge of the field had a disease.

> **b** Discuss each of these ideas and use your knowledge of science to decide which four are the most likely to have caused the poor growth of the corn.

Observations, backed up by really creative thinking and good scientific knowledge, can lead to a **hypothesis**.

Testing scientific ideas

Scientists always try to think of ways to explain how things work or why they behave in the way that they do.

After their observations, they use their understanding of science to come up with an idea that could explain what is going on. This idea is sometimes called a hypothesis. They use this idea to make a prediction. A prediction is like a guess, but it is not just a wild guess – it is based on previous understanding.

A scientist will say, 'If it works the way I think it does, I should be able to change **this** (the independent variable) and **that** will happen (the dependent variable).'

Predictions are what make science so powerful. They mean that we can work out rules that tell us what will happen in the future. For example, electricians can predict how much current will flow through a wire when an electric cooker is connected. Knowing this, they can choose the right thickness of cable to use.

Knowledge of energy transfer could lead to an idea that the insides of chips cook by energy being conducted from the outside. You might predict that small, thinly sliced chips will cook faster than large, fat chips.

c Look at the photograph of a frog in Figure 2. Note down anything you find interesting. Use your knowledge and some creative thought to suggest a hypothesis based on your observations.

Not all predictions are correct. If scientists find that the prediction doesn't work, it's back to the drawing board! They either amend their original idea or think of a completely new one.

Figure 2 A frog

Starting to design a valid investigation

observation ✚ **knowledge** ➡ **hypothesis** ➡ **prediction** ➡ **investigation**

We can test a prediction by carrying out an **investigation**. You, as the scientist, predict that there is a relationship between two variables.

The independent variable is one that is selected and changed by you, the investigator. The dependent variable is measured for each change in your independent variable. Then all other variables become control variables, kept constant so that your investigation is a fair test.

If your measurements are going to be accepted by other people, they must be valid. Part of this is making sure that you are really measuring the effect of changing your chosen variable. For example, if other variables aren't controlled properly, they might be affecting the data collected.

d Look at Figure 3. When investigating his heart rate before and after exercise, Darren got his girlfriend to measure his pulse. Would Darren's investigation be valid? Explain your answer.

Figure 3 Measuring a pulse

Summary questions

1 Copy and complete this paragraph using the following words:
   controlled   dependent   independent   knowledge
   prediction   hypothesis
   An observation linked with scientific .... can be used to make a
   .... A .... links an .... variable to a .... variable. All other
   variables need to be ....

2 What is the difference between a prediction and a guess?

3 Imagine you were testing how an enzyme affects the rate of reaction. The reaction might cause the solution to get hot.
   a How could you monitor the temperature?
   b What other control variables can you think of that might affect the results?

Key points

- Observation is often the starting point for an investigation.

- Testing predictions can lead to new scientific understanding.

- You must design investigations that produce valid results if you are to be believed.

H4

Planning an investigation

Learning objectives

- How do you design a fair test?
- How do you set up a survey?
- How do you set up a control group or control experiment?
- How do you reduce risks in hazardous situations?

Fair testing

A **fair test** is one in which only the independent variable affects the dependent variable. All other variables (called control variables) should be kept the same. If the test is not fair, the results of your investigation will not be valid.

Sometimes it is very difficult to keep control variables the same. However, at least you can **monitor** them, so that you know whether they have changed or not.

Figure 1 Corn being examined

a   Imagine you were testing how close together you could plant corn to get the most cobs. You would plant five different plots, with different numbers of plants in each plot. List some of the variables that you could not control.

Surveys

Not all scientific investigations involve deliberately changing the independent variable.

Imagine you were investigating the effect of diet on diabetes. You might conduct a survey. You would have to choose people of the same age and same family history to test. The larger the sample size you test, the better your results will be.

Control group

Control groups are used in investigations to try to make sure that you are measuring the variable that you intend to measure. When investigating the effects of a new drug, the control group will be given a **placebo**. This is a 'pretend' drug that actually has no effect on the patient at all. The control group think they are taking a drug but the placebo does not contain the drug. This way you can control the variable of 'thinking that the drug is working' and separate out the effect of the actual drug.

Usually neither the patient nor the doctor knows until after the trials have been completed which of the patients were given the placebo. This is known as a **double-blind trial**.

Risks and hazards

One of the first things you must do is to think about any potential **hazards** and then assess the **risk**.

Everything you do in life presents a hazard. What you have to do is to identify the hazard and then decide the degree of risk that it gives. If the risk is very high, you must do something to reduce it.

For example, if you decide to go out in the pouring rain, lightning is a possible hazard. However, you decide that the risk is so small that you will ignore it and go out anyway.

If you decide to cross a busy road, the cars travelling along it at high speed represent a hazard. You decide to reduce the risk by crossing at a pedestrian crossing.

Figure 2 The hazard is the busy road. We reduce the risk by using a pedestrian crossing.

Activity

Burning foods

Imagine you were testing crisps to see how much energy they give out when burned.

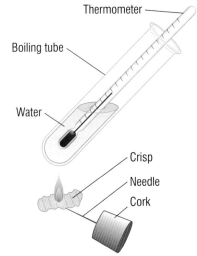

- What are the **hazards** that are present?
- What could you do to reduce the **risk** from these hazards?

Key points

- Care must be taken to ensure fair testing – as far as is possible.
- Control variables must be kept the same during an investigation.
- Surveys are often used when it is impossible to carry out an experiment in which the independent variable is changed.
- Control groups allow you to make a comparison.
- A risk assessment must be made when planning a practical investigation.

Summary questions

1 Copy and complete this paragraph using the following words:

   investigation   hazards   assessment   risks

   Before you carry out any practical ...., you need to carry out a risk .... You can do this by looking for any potential .... and making sure that the .... are as small as possible.

2 Explain the difference between a control group and a control variable.

3 Briefly describe how you would go about setting up a fair test in a laboratory investigation. Give your answer as general advice.

H5

Designing an investigation

Learning objectives

- How do you make sure that you choose the best values for your variables?
- How do you decide on a suitable range?
- How do you decide on a suitable interval?
- How do you ensure accuracy and precision?

Choosing values of a variable

Trial runs will tell you a lot about how your early thoughts are going to work out.

Do you have the correct conditions?

A photosynthesis investigation that produces tiny amounts of oxygen might not have enough light, pondweed or carbon dioxide. Alternatively, the temperature might not be high enough.

Have you chosen a sensible range?

Range means the maximum and minimum values of the independent or dependent variables. It is important to choose a suitable range for the independent variable, otherwise you may not be able to see any change in the dependent variable.

For example, if the results are all very similar, you might not have chosen a wide enough range of light intensities.

Have you got enough readings that are close together?

The gap between the readings is known as the **interval**.

For example, you might alter the light intensity by moving a lamp to different distances from the pondweed. A set of 11 readings equally spaced over a distance of 1 metre would give an interval of 10 centimetres.

If the results are very different from each other, you might not see a pattern if you have large gaps between readings over the important part of the range.

Accuracy

Accurate measurements are very close to the **true value**.

Your investigation should provide data that is accurate enough to answer your original question.

However, it is not always possible to know what that the true value is.

How do you get accurate data?

- You can repeat your measurements and your **mean** is more likely to be accurate.
- Try repeating your measurements with a different instrument and see whether you get the same readings.
- Use high-quality instruments that measure accurately.
- The more carefully you use the measuring instruments, the more accuracy you will get.

Precision, resolution, repeatability and reproducibility

A **precise** measurement is one in which there is very little spread about the mean value.

If your repeated measurements are closely grouped together, you have precision. Your measurements must be made with an instrument that has a suitable **resolution**. Resolution of a measuring instrument is the smallest change in the quantity being measured (input) that gives a perceptible change in the reading.

It's no use measuring the time for a fast reaction to finish using the seconds hand on a clock! If there are big differences within sets of repeat readings, you will not be able to make a valid conclusion. You won't be able to trust your data!

How do you get precise data?

- You have to use measuring instruments with sufficiently small scale divisions.
- You have to repeat your tests as often as necessary.
- You have to repeat your tests in exactly the same way each time.

If you repeat your investigation using the same method and equipment and obtain the same results, your results are said to be **repeatable**.

If someone else repeats your investigation in the same way, or if you repeat it by using different equipment or techniques, and the same results are obtained, it is said to be **reproducible**.

You may be asked to compare your results with those of others in your group, or with data from other scientists. Research like this is a good way of checking your results.

A word of caution!

Precision depends only on the extent of random errors – it gives no indication of how close results are to the true value. Just because your results show precision does not mean they are accurate.

a Draw a thermometer scale reading 49.5 °C, showing four results that are both accurate and precise.

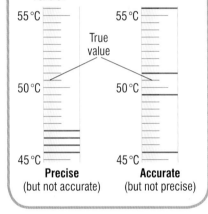
Summary questions

1 Copy and complete this paragraph using the following words:

range   repeat   conditions   readings

Trial runs give you a good idea of whether you have the correct .... to collect any data; whether you have chosen the correct .... for the independent variable, whether you have enough ...., and whether you need to do .... readings.

2 Use an example to explain how a set of repeat measurements could be accurate, but not precise.

3 Explain the difference between a set of results that are reproducible and a set of results that are repeatable.

H6   Making measurements

- Why do results always vary?
- How do you choose instruments that will give you accurate results?
- What do we mean by the resolution of an instrument?
- What is the difference between a systematic error and a random error?
- How does human error affect results and what do you do with anomalies?

Figure 1 Student testing the rate at which oxygen is produced using an enzyme

Using instruments

Try measuring the temperature of a beaker of water using a digital thermometer. Do you always get the same result? Probably not! So can we say that any measurement is absolutely correct?

In any experiment there will be doubts about actual measurements.

> **a** Look at Figure 1. Suppose, like this student, you tested the rate at which oxygen was produced using an enzyme. It is unlikely that you would get two readings exactly the same. Discuss all the possible reasons why.

When you choose an instrument you need to know that it will give you the accuracy that you want. You need to be confident that it is giving a true reading.

If you have used an electric water bath, would you trust the temperature on the dial? How do you know it is the true temperature? You could use a very expensive thermometer to calibrate your water bath. The expensive thermometer is more likely to show the true temperature. But can you really be sure it is accurate?

You also need to be able to use an instrument properly.

> **b** In Figure 1 the student is reading the amount of gas in the measuring cylinder. Why is the student unlikely to get a true measurement?

Instruments that measure the same thing can have different sensitivities. The **resolution** of an instrument refers to the smallest change in a value that can be detected. This is one factor that determines the precision of your measurements.

Choosing the wrong scale can cause you to miss important data or make silly conclusions. We would not measure the weight of a prescription drug in kilograms, we would use milligrams.

> **c** Match the following scales to their best use:

Used to measure	Resolution of scale
Size of a cell	millimetres
Human height	metres
Length of a running race to test fitness	micrometres
Growth of seedlings	centimetres

Errors

Even when an instrument is used correctly, the results can still show differences.

Results may differ because of **random error**. This is most likely to be due to a poor measurement being made. It could be due to not carrying out the method consistently.

If you repeat your measurements several times and then calculate a mean, you will reduce the effect of random errors.

The **error** might be a **systematic error**. This means that the method was carried out consistently but an error was being repeated. A systematic error will make your readings be spread about some value other than the true value. This is because your results will differ from the true value by a consistent amount each time a measurement is made.

No number of repeats can do anything about systematic errors. If you think that you have a systematic error, you need to repeat using a different set of equipment or a different technique. Then compare your results and spot the difference!

A **zero error** is one kind of systematic error. Suppose that you were trying to measure the length of your desk with a metre rule, but you hadn't noticed that someone had sawn off half a centimetre from the end of the ruler. It wouldn't matter how many times you repeated the measurement, you would never get any nearer to the true value.

Look at the table. It shows the two sets of data that were taken from the investigation that Sara did. She tested five different volumes of enzyme.

Sara's investigation into the volumes of enzymes

Amount of enzyme used (cm³)	1	2	3	4	5
Oxygen produced (cm³)	3.2	8.9	9.5	12.7	75.9
Volume of oxygen expected (cm³)	3.1	6.4	9.7	12.5	76.1
Calculated oxygen production (cm³)	4.2	8.4	12.5	16.6	20.7

d Discuss whether there is any evidence of random error in these results.
e Discuss whether there is any evidence of systematic error in these results.

Anomalies

Anomalous results are clearly out of line. They are not those that are due to the natural variation you get from any measurement. These should be looked at carefully. There might be a very interesting reason why they are so different. You should always look for anomalous results and discard them before you calculate a mean, if necessary.

- If anomalies can be identified while you are doing an investigation, it is best to repeat that part of the investigation.
- If you find anomalies after you have finished collecting data for an investigation, they must be discarded.

Summary questions

1 Copy and complete this paragraph using the following words:

accurate   discarded   random   resolution   systematic use   variation

There will always be some .... in results. You should always choose the best instruments that you can in order to get the most .... results. You must know how to .... the instrument properly. The .... of an instrument refers to the smallest change that can be detected. There are two types of error – .... and .... Anomalies due to random error should be ....

2 What kind of error will most likely occur in the following situations?
  a Asking everyone in the class to measure the length of the bench.
  b Using a ruler that has a piece missing from the zero end.

Did you know ...?

Sir Alexander Fleming had grown bacteria on agar plates. He noticed an anomaly. There was some mould growing on one of the plates and around it there were no bacteria. He decided to investigate further and grew more of the mould. Only because Fleming checked out his anomaly did it lead to the discovery of penicillin.

Key points

- Results will nearly always vary.
- Better quality instruments give more accurate results.
- The resolution of an instrument refers to the smallest change that it can detect.
- Human error can produce random and/or systematic errors.
- We examine anomalies; they might give us some interesting ideas. If they are due to a random error, we repeat the measurements. If there is no time to repeat them, we discard them.

<table>
<tr><td>**H7**</td><td># Presenting data</td></tr>
</table>

Learning objectives

- How do you calculate the mean from a set of data?
- How do you use tables of results?
- What is the range of the data?
- How do you display your data?

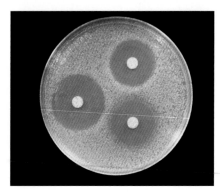

Figure 1 Petri dish with discs showing growth inhibition of bacteria

For this section you will be working with data from this investigation:

Mel spread some bacteria onto a dish containing nutrient jelly. She also placed some discs onto the jelly. The discs contained different concentrations of an antibiotic. The dish was sealed and then left for a couple of days.

Then she measured the diameter of the clear part around each disc. The clear part is where the bacteria have not been able to grow. The bacteria grew all over the rest of the dish.

Tables

Tables are really good for getting your results down quickly and clearly. You should design your table **before** you start your investigation.

Your table should be constructed to fit in all the data to be collected. It should be fully labelled, including units.

You may want to have extra columns for repeats, calculations of means or calculated values.

Checking for anomalies

While filling in your table of results you should be constantly looking for anomalies.

- Check to see whether any reading in a set of repeat readings is significantly different from the others.
- Check to see whether the pattern you are getting as you change the independent variable is what you expected.

Remember, a result that looks anomalous should be checked out to see if it really is a poor reading.

Planning your table

Mel had decided on the values for her independent variable. We always put these in the first column of a table. The dependent variable goes in the second column. Mel will find its values as she carries out the investigation.

So she could plan a table like this:

Concentration of antibiotic (µg/ml)	Size of clear zone (mm)
4	
8	
16	
32	
64	

Or like this:

Concentration of antibiotic (µg/ml)	4	8	16	32	64
Size of clear zone (mm)					

All she had to do in the investigation was to write the correct numbers in the second column to complete the top table.

Mel's results are shown in the alternative format in the table below:

Concentration of antibiotic (µg/ml)	4	8	16	32	64
Size of clear zone (mm)	4	16	22	26	28

The range of the data

Pick out the maximum and the minimum values and you have the range of a variable. You should always quote these two numbers when asked for a range. For example, the range of the dependent variable is between 4 mm (the lowest value) and 28 mm (the highest value) – and don't forget to include the units!

a What is the range for the independent variable and for the dependent variable in Mel's set of data?

 Maths skills

The mean of the data

Often you have to find the **mean** of each repeated set of measurements. The first thing you should do is to look for any anomalous results. If you find any, miss these out of the calculation. Then add together the remaining measurements and divide by how many there are.

For example:
- Mel takes four readings, 15 mm, 18 mm, 29 mm, 15 mm
- 29 mm is an anomalous result and so is missed out. So 15 + 18 + 15 = 48
- 48 divided by three (the number of valid results) = **16 mm**

The repeat values and mean can be recorded as shown below:

Concentration of antibiotic (µg/ml)	Size of clear zone (mm)			
	First test	Second test	Third test	Mean
8	15	18	15	16

Displaying your results

Bar charts

If one of your variables is categoric, you should use a **bar chart**.

Line graphs

If you have a continuous independent and a continuous dependent variable, a **line graph** should be used. Plot the points as small 'plus' signs (+).

Summary questions

1 Copy and complete this paragraph using the following words:

categoric   continuous   mean   range

The maximum and minimum values show the .... of the data. The sum of the values in a set of repeat readings divided by the total number of these repeat values gives the .... Bar charts are used when you have a .... independent variable and a continuous dependent variable. Line graphs are used when you have .... independent and dependent variables.

2 Draw a graph of Mel's results from the top of this page.

H8 | Using data to draw conclusions

Learning objectives

- How do you best use charts and graphs to identify patterns?
- What are the possible relationships you can identify from charts and graphs?
- How do you draw conclusions from relationships?
- How can you decide whether your conclusions are valid?

Identifying patterns and relationships

Now that you have a bar chart or a line graph of your results you can begin to look for patterns. You must have an open mind at this point.

First, there could still be some anomalous results. You might not have picked these out earlier. How do you spot an anomaly? It must be a significant distance away from the pattern, not just within normal variation. If you do have any anomalous results plotted on your graph, circle these and ignore them when drawing the **line of best fit**.

Now look at your graph. Is there a pattern that you can see? When you have decided, draw a line of best fit that shows this pattern.

A line of best fit is a kind of visual averaging process. You should draw the line so that it leaves as many points slightly above the line as there are points below. In other words it is a line that steers a middle course through the field of points.

The vast majority of results that you get from continuous data require a line of best fit.

Remember, a line of best fit can be a straight line or it can be a curve – you have to decide from your results.

You need to consider whether your graph shows a **linear relationship**. This simply means, can you be confident about drawing a straight line of best fit on your graph? If the answer is yes – is this line positive or negative?

a   Say whether graphs **i** and **ii** in Figure 1 show a positive or a negative linear relationship.

Look at the graph in Figure 2. It shows a positive linear relationship. It also goes through the origin (0,0). We call this a **directly proportional** relationship.

Your results might also show a curved line of best fit. These can be predictable, complex or very complex! Look at Figure 3 below.

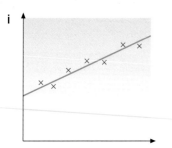
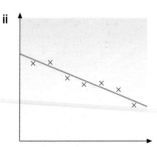

Figure 1 Graphs showing linear relationships

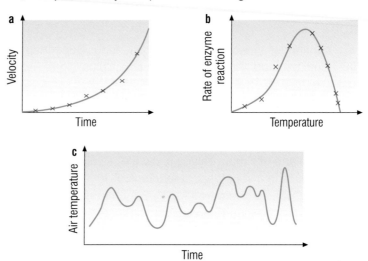

Figure 3 a Graph showing predictable results **b** Graph showing complex results **c** Graph showing very complex results

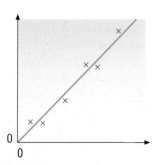

Figure 2 Graph showing a directly proportional relationship

Drawing conclusions

If there is a pattern to be seen (for example as one variable gets bigger the other also gets bigger), it may be that:

● changing one has caused the other to change

● the two are related, but one is not necessarily the cause of the other.

Your conclusion must go no further than the evidence that you have.

Activity

Looking at relationships

Some people think that watching too much television can cause an increase in violence.

The table shows the number of television sets in the UK for four different years, and the number of murders committed in those years.

Year	Number of televisions (millions)	Number of murders
1970	15	310
1980	25	500
1990	42	550
2000	60	750

Plot a graph to show the relationship. Do you think this proves that watching television causes violence? Explain your answer.

AQA Examiner's tip

When you read scientific claims, think carefully about the evidence that should be there to back up the claim.

Poor science can often happen if a wrong decision is made here. Newspapers have said that living near electricity substations can cause cancer. All that scientists would say is that there is possibly an association.

Evaluation

You will often be asked to evaluate either the method of the investigation or the conclusion that has been reached. Ask yourself: Could the method have been improved? Is the conclusion that has been made a valid one?

Summary questions

1 Copy and complete this paragraph using the following words:

anomalous complex directly negative positive

Lines of best fit can be used to identify .... results. Linear relationships can be .... or .... If a straight line goes through the origin of a graph, the relationship is .... proportional. Often a line of best fit is a curve which can be predictable or ....

2 Nasma knew about the possible link between cancer and living near to electricity substations. She found a quote from a National Grid Company survey of substations:

Measurements of the magnetic field were taken at 0.5 metres above ground level within 1 metre of fences and revealed 1.9 microteslas. After 5 metres this dropped to the normal levels measured in any house.

Discuss the type of experiment and the data you would expect to see to support a conclusion that it is safe to build houses over 5 metres from an electricity substation.

Key points

● Drawing lines of best fit helps us to study the relationship between variables.

● The possible relationships are linear, positive and negative, directly proportional, predictable and complex curves.

● Conclusions must go no further than the data available.

● The reproducibility of data can be checked by looking at other similar work done by others, perhaps on the internet. It can also be checked by using a different method or by others checking your method.

H9 Scientific evidence and society

Learning objectives

- How can science encourage people to trust its research?
- How might bias affect people's judgement of science?
- Can politics influence judgements about science?
- Do you have to be a professor to be believed?

MOBILE PHONE TUMOUR RISK?

Swedish researchers found that the risk of developing an ear tumour increased if you used a mobile phone. The study was of 750 people. This type of tumour affects one in 100 000 people and the risk increased four times if you used the phone for more than 10 years.

A spokes...
...that...

STAR IN SCANDAL SHOCK
We Find Out What They Don't Want You To Know... And WE TELL YOU!

??? Did you know ... ?

A scientist who rejected the idea of a causal link between smoking and lung cancer was later found to be being paid by a tobacco company.

AQA Examiner's tip

If you are asked about bias in scientific evidence, there are two types:

- the measuring instruments may have introduced a bias because they were not calibrated correctly
- the scientists themselves may have a biased opinion (e.g. if they are paid by a company to promote their product).

Now you have reached a conclusion about a piece of scientific research. So what is next? If it is pure research, your fellow scientists will want to look at it very carefully. If it affects the lives of ordinary people, society will also want to examine it closely.

You can help your cause by giving a balanced account of what you have found out. It is much the same as any argument you might have. If you make ridiculous claims, nobody will believe anything you have to say.

Be open and honest. If you only tell part of the story, someone will want to know why! Equally, if somebody is only telling you part of the truth, you cannot be confident about anything they say.

a A disinfectant claims that it kills 99.9% of germs on surfaces that you come in contact with every day. What is missing? Is it important?

You must be on the lookout for people who might be biased when presenting scientific evidence. Some scientists are paid by companies to do research. When you are told that a certain product is harmless, just check out who is telling you.

b Bottles of perfume spray contain this advice: 'This finished product has not been tested on animals.' Why might you mistrust this statement?

Suppose you wanted to know about how to slim. Who would you be more likely to believe? Would it be a scientist working for 'Slim Kwik', or an independent scientist? Sometimes the differences are not quite so obvious.

We also have to be very careful in reaching judgements according to who is presenting scientific evidence to us. For example, if the evidence might provoke public or political problems, it might be played down.

Equally, others might want to exaggerate the findings. They might make more of the results than the evidence suggests. Take as an example the data available on animal research. Animal liberation followers may well present the *same* evidence completely differently to pharmaceutical companies wishing to develop new drugs.

c Check out some websites on smoking and lung cancer. Do a balanced review looking at tobacco manufacturers as well as anti-smoking lobbies such as ASH. You might also check out government websites.

The status of the experimenter may place more weight on evidence. Suppose a lawyer wants to convince a jury enquiry that a particular piece of scientific evidence is valid. The lawyer will choose the most eminent scientist in that field who is likely to support them. Cot deaths are a particularly difficult problem for the police. If the medical evidence suggests that the baby might have been murdered, the prosecution and the defence get the most eminent scientists to argue the validity of the evidence. Who does the jury believe?

EXPERT WITNESS IN COT DEATH COURT CASE MISLED THE JURY

A child abuse expert was struck off as a doctor today for giving seriously misleading evidence in a court case. The court case led to a woman being wrongly convicted of murdering her two children.   Full report – Page 6

The limitations of science

Science can help us in many ways but it cannot supply all the answers. We are still finding out about things and developing our scientific knowledge. For example, the Hubble telescope has helped us to revise our ideas about the beginnings of the universe.

There are some questions that we cannot answer, maybe because we do not have enough reproducible, repeatable and valid evidence. For example, research into the causes of cancer still needs much work to be done to provide data.

There are some questions that science cannot answer at all. These tend to be questions where beliefs, opinions and ethics are important. For example, science can suggest what the universe was like when it was first formed, but cannot answer the question of why it was formed.

 Did you know ...?

Science can often lead to the development of new materials or techniques. Sometimes these cause a problem for society where hard choices have to be made.

Scientists can give us the answers to many questions, but not to every question. Scientists have a contribution to make to a debate, but so do others such as environmentalists, economists and politicians.

Figure 1 The Hubble space telescope can look deep into space and tell us things about the Universe's beginning from the formations of early galaxies

Summary questions

1 Copy and complete this paragraph using the following words:

   status   balanced   bias   political

   Evidence from scientific investigations should be given in a .... way. It must be checked for any .... from the experimenter. Evidence can be given too little or too much weight if it is of .... significance. The .... of the experimenter is likely to influence people in their judgement of the evidence.

2 Collect some newspaper articles to show how scientific evidence is used. Discuss in groups whether these articles are honest and fair representations of the science. Consider whether they carry any bias.

3 This is the opening paragraph from a review of GM foods.

   The UK government has been promoting ... a review of the science of GM, led by Sir David King (the Government's Chief Scientific Adviser) working with Professor Howard Dalton (the Chief Scientific Adviser to the Secretary of State for the Environment, Food and Rural Affairs), with independent advice from the Food Standards Agency.

   Discuss this paragraph and decide which parts of it make you want to believe the evidence they might give. Next, consider which parts make you mistrust any conclusions they might reach.

Key points

- Scientific evidence must be presented in a balanced way that points out clearly how valid the evidence is.

- The evidence must not contain any bias from the experimenter.

- The evidence must be checked to appreciate whether there has been any political influence.

- The status of the experimenter can influence the weight placed on the evidence.

H10 | The ISA

Learning objectives

- How do you write a plan?
- How do you make a risk assessment?
- What is a hypothesis?
- How do you arrive at a conclusion?

When you are making a blank table or drawing a graph or bar chart, make sure that you use full headings, e.g.

- the length of the leaf', **not** just 'length'
- the time taken for the reaction', **not** just 'time'
- the height from which the ball was dropped', **not** just 'height'

and don't forget to include any units.

There are several different stages to the ISA (Investigate Skills Assignment) that you will complete for your Controlled Assessment. This will make up 25% of your GCSE marks.

Stage 1

Your teacher will tell you the problem that you are going to investigate, and you will have to develop your own hypothesis. They will also set the problem in a context – in other words, where in real life your investigation could be useful. You should have a discussion about it, and talk about different ways in which you might solve the problem. Your teacher should show you the equipment that you can use, and you should research one or two possible methods for carrying out an experiment to test the hypothesis. You should also research the context and do a risk assessment for your practical work. You will be allowed to make one side of notes on this research, which you can take into the written part of the ISA.

Figure 1 Doing practical work allows you to develop the skills needed to do well in the ISA

You should be allowed to handle the equipment and you may be allowed to carry out a preliminary experiment.

Make sure that you understand what you have to do – now is the time to ask questions if you are not sure.

How Science Works

Section 1 of the ISA

At the end of this stage, you will answer Section 1 of the ISA. You will need to:

- develop a hypothesis
- identify one or more variables that you need to control
- describe how you would carry out the main experiment
- identify possible hazards and say what you would do to reduce any risk
- make a blank table ready for your results.

a What features should you include in your written plan?
b What should you include in your blank table?

Stage 2

This is where you carry out the experiment and get some results. Don't worry too much about spending a long time getting fantastically accurate results – it is more important to get some results that you can analyse.

After you have got results, you will have to compare your results with those of others. You will also have to draw a graph or a bar chart.

c How do you decide whether you should draw a bar chart or a line graph?

Stage 3

This is where you answer Section 2 of the ISA. Section 2 of the ISA is all about your own results, so make sure that you look at your table and graph when you are answering this section. To get the best marks you will need to quote some data from your results.

How Science Works

Section 2 of the ISA

In this section you will need to:

- say what you were trying to find out
- compare your results with those of others, saying whether you think they are similar or different
- analyse data that is given in the paper. This data will be in the same topic area as your investigation
- use ideas from your own investigation to answer questions about this data
- write a conclusion
- compare your conclusion with the hypothesis you have tested.

You may need to change or even reject your hypothesis in response to your findings.

Key points

- When you are writing the plan make sure that you include details about:
  - the range and interval of the independent variable
  - the control variables
  - the number of repeats.
- Try to put down at least two possible hazards, and say how you are going to minimise the risk from them.
- Look carefully at the hypothesis that you are given – this should give you a good clue about how to do the experiment.
- Always refer back to the hypothesis when you are writing your conclusion.

Summary questions

1 Copy and complete the paragraph using the words below:

control independent dependent

When writing a plan, you need to state the variable that you are deliberately going to change, called the .... variable. You also need to say what you expect will change because of this; this is called the .... variable. You must also say what .... variables you will keep constant in order to make it a fair test.

Summary questions

1 a Put these words into order. They should be in the order that you might use them in an investigation.

design; prediction; conclusion; method; repeat; controls; graph; results; table; improve; safety; hypothesis

2 a How would you tell the difference between an opinion that was scientific and a biased or prejudiced opinion?

b Suppose you were describing the height of plants for some fieldwork. What type of variable would you choose and why?

3 You might have observed that lichens do not grow where there is air pollution. You ask the question why. You use some theory to answer the question.

a Explain what you understand by the term 'hypothesis'.

b Sulfur dioxide in the air forms acids that attack the lichens. This is a hypothesis. Develop this into a prediction.

c Explain why a prediction is more useful than a hypothesis.

d Suppose you have tested your prediction and have some data. What might this do for your hypothesis?

e Suppose the data does not support the hypothesis. What should you do to the theory that gave you the hypothesis?

4 a What do you understand by a 'fair test'?

b Explain why setting up a fair test in fieldwork is difficult.

c Describe how you can make your results valid in fieldwork.

d Suppose you were carrying out an investigation into how pulse rates vary with exercise. You would need to carry out a trial. Describe what a trial would tell you about how to plan your method.

5 Suppose you were watching a friend carry out an investigation measuring the carbon dioxide produced by yeast cells. You have to mark your friend on how accurately she is making her measurements. Make a list of points that you would be looking for.

6 a How do you decide on the range of a set of data?

b How do you calculate the mean?

c When should you use a bar chart?

d When should you use a line graph?

7 a What should happen to anomalous results?

b What does a line of best fit allow you to do?

c When making a conclusion, what must you take into consideration?

d How can you check on the repeatability and reproducibility of your results?

8 a Why is it important when reporting science to 'tell the truth, the whole truth and nothing but the truth'?

b Why might some people be tempted not to be completely fair when reporting their opinions on scientific data?

9 a 'Science can advance technology and technology can advance science.' What do you think is meant by this statement?

b Who should answer the questions that start with 'Should we ... '?

10 Look at the electron micrograph image below. Stomata are very small holes in the leaves of plants. They allow carbon dioxide to diffuse into the leaf cells for photosynthesis. The size of the hole is controlled by guard cells. It was suggested that the size of the hole might affect the rate at which carbon dioxide diffused through the hole.

Stomata are very small holes (when fully open they are 10–20 μm in diameter). The question was:

Are small holes better than large holes? This would seem reasonable as plants have very small stomata. The hypothesis was that small holes would allow more carbon dioxide to pass through than large holes.

It was decided to use much larger holes than the stomata because it would be easier to get accurate measurements. The investigation was carried out and the results were as follows.

Diameter of hole (mm)	Volume of CO_2 diffusing per hour (cm³)
22.7	0.24
12.1	0.10
6.0	0.06
3.2	0.04
2.0	0.02

a What was the observation on which this investigation was based?

b What was the original hypothesis?

c What was the likely prediction?

d What was the independent variable?

e What was the dependent variable?

f What is the range for the diameter of the hole?

g Why was the temperature kept the same during the investigation?

h Was this a sensible range of size of holes to use? Explain your answer.

i How could the investigation be made more repeatable and reproducible?

j Was the sensitivity of the instrument measuring volumes of CO_2 satisfactory? Provide some evidence for your answer from the data in the table.

k Draw a graph of the results in the table above.

l Describe the pattern in these results.

m What conclusion can you make?

n Does your conclusion support the prediction?

B1 1.1

Diet and exercise

Learning objectives

- What does a healthy diet contain?
- Why can some people eat lots of food without getting fat?
- How does an athlete's diet differ from yours?

Did you know ... ?

Whether you prefer sushi, dahl, or roast chicken, you need to eat a varied diet that includes everything you need to keep your body healthy.

What makes a healthy diet? k

A balanced diet contains the correct amounts of:

- carbohydrates
- proteins
- fats
- vitamins
- minerals
- fibre
- water.

Your body uses carbohydrates, proteins and fats to release the energy you need to live and to build new cells. You need small amounts of vitamins and minerals for your body to work healthily. Without them you will suffer deficiency diseases. If you don't have a balanced diet then you will end up **malnourished**.

Figure 1 A balanced diet provides everything you need to survive, including plenty of energy

Fortunately, in countries like the UK, most of us take in all the minerals and vitamins we need from the food we eat. However, our diet can easily be unbalanced in terms of the amount of energy we take in. If we take in too much energy we put on weight. If we don't take in enough we become underweight.

It isn't always easy to get it right because different people need different amounts of energy. Even if you eat a lot, you can still lack vitamins and minerals if you don't eat the right food.

a Why do you need to eat food?

How much energy do you need?

The amount of energy you need to live depends on lots of different things. Some of these things you can change and some you can't.

Males need to take in more energy than a female of the same age – unless she is pregnant.

If you are a teenager, you will need more energy than if you are in your 70s.

b Why does a pregnant woman need more energy than a woman who isn't pregnant?

Your food supplies energy to your muscles as they work. So the amount of exercise you do affects the amount of energy you need. If you do very little exercise, then you don't need as much food. The more you exercise the more food you need to take in.

Figure 2 Athletes have a great deal of muscle tissue so they have to eat a lot of food to supply the energy they need

People who exercise regularly are usually much fitter than people who take little exercise. They make bigger muscles – up to 40% of their body mass. Muscle tissue transfers much more energy than fat. But exercise doesn't always mean time spent training or 'working out' in the gym. Walking to school, running around the house looking after small children or doing a physically active job all count as exercise too.

c Why do athletes need to eat more food than the average person?

The temperature where you live affects how much energy you need as well. In warmer countries you need to eat less food. This is because you use less energy keeping your body temperature at a steady level.

The metabolic rate

Think of a friend who is very similar in age, gender and size to you. Despite these similarities, you may need quite different amounts of energy in your diet. This is because the rate of chemical reactions in your cells (the **metabolic rate**) varies from person to person.

Men generally have a higher metabolic rate than women. The proportion of muscle to fat in your body affects your metabolic rate. Men often have a higher proportion of muscle to fat than women. You can change the proportion of muscle to fat in your body by exercising. This will build up more muscle.

Your metabolic rate is also affected by the amount of activity you do. Exercise increases your metabolic rate for a time even after you stop exercising.

Scientists think that your basic metabolic rate may be affected by genetic factors you inherit from your parents. This is an example of how **inherited** factors can affect our health.

Did you know ...?

Between 60–75% of your daily energy needs are used up in the basic reactions needed to keep you alive. About 10% is needed to digest your food – and only the final 15–30% is affected by your physical activity!

AQA Examiner's tip

'Metabolic rate' refers to the chemical reactions which take place in cells.

Figure 3 If you work somewhere really cold your metabolic rate will go up to keep you warm. You will need lots of fat in your diet to supply the energy you need.

Summary questions

1 What is 'a balanced diet'?

2 **a** Why do you need more energy in your diet when you are 18 than when you are 80?
  b Why does a top athlete need more energy in their diet than you do? Where does the energy in the diet come from?

3 **a** What is the 'metabolic rate'?
  b Explain why some people put on weight more easily than others.

Key points

● Most people eat a varied diet, which includes everything needed to keep the body healthy.

● Different people need different amounts of energy.

● The metabolic rate varies from person to person.

● The more exercise you take, the more food you need.

B1 1.2 Weight problems

Learning objectives

- What health problems are linked to being overweight?
- Why is it unhealthy to be too thin?
- Why are people who do exercise usually healthier than those who do not?

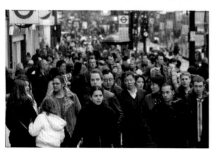

Figure 1 In spite of some of the media hype, most people are not obese – but the amount of weight people carry varies a great deal!

Obesity

If you take in more energy than you use, the excess is stored as fat. You need some body fat to cushion your internal organs. Your fat also acts as an energy store for when you don't feel like eating. But if someone eats a lot more food than they need, this is a form of malnourishment. Over time they could become **overweight** or even **obese**.

Carrying too much weight is often inconvenient and uncomfortable. Obesity can also lead to serious health problems such as arthritis, type 2 diabetes (high blood sugar levels which are hard to control), high blood pressure and heart disease. Obese people are more likely to die at an earlier age than non-obese people.

a What health problems are linked to obesity?

Losing weight

Many people want to be thinner. This might be for their health or just to look better. You gain fat by taking in more energy than you need. You lose **mass** when the energy content of your food is less than the energy you use in your daily life. There are three main ways you can lose mass.

- You can reduce the amount of energy you take in by cutting back the amount of food you eat. In particular, you can cut down on energy-rich foods like biscuits, crisps and chips.
- You can increase the amount of energy you use by doing more exercise.
- The best way to lose weight is to do both – reduce your energy intake and exercise more!

Scientists talk about 'mass', but most people talk about losing weight. Many people find it easier to lose weight by attending slimming groups. At these weekly meetings they get lots of advice and support from other slimmers. All slimming programmes involve eating fewer energy-rich foods and/or taking more exercise.

Exercise can make you healthier by helping to control your weight. It increases the amount of energy used by your body and increases the proportion of muscle to fat. It can make your heart healthier too. However, you need to take care. If you suddenly start taking vigorous exercise, you can cause other health problems.

Fitness instructors can measure the proportion of your body that is made up of fat. They can advise on the right food to eat and the exercise you need to become thinner, fitter, or both.

Figure 2 Fitness instructors can help with improving health and fitness

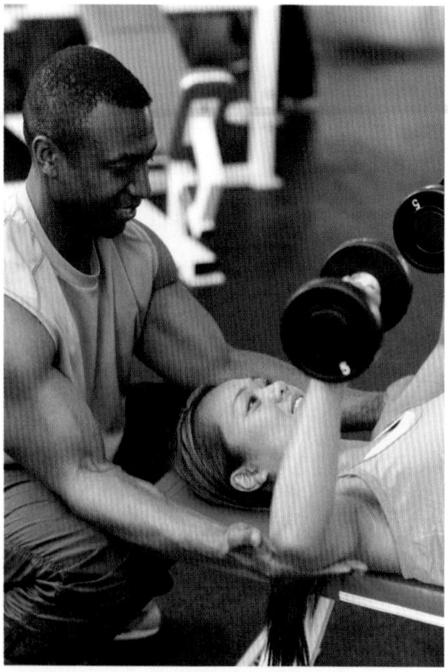

Different slimming programmes approach weight loss in different ways. Many simply give advice on healthy living. They advise lots of fruit and vegetables, avoiding too much fat or too many calories and plenty of exercise. Some are more extreme and suggest that you cut out almost all of the fat or the carbohydrates from your diet.

b What must you do to lose weight?

Figure 3 Slimming products can help you lose weight, but only if you control the total amount of energy you take in

Lack of food

In some parts of the world many people are underweight and malnourished because there is not enough food to eat. Civil wars, droughts and pests can all destroy local crops.

Deficiency diseases, due to lack of mineral **ions** and vitamins, are common in both children and adults when they never have enough food. Deficiency diseases can also occur if you do not have a balanced diet.

Summary questions

1 Copy and complete using the words below:

energy fat less more obese

If you take in more .... than you use, the excess is stored as .... If you eat too much over a long period of time, you will eventually become .... To lose weight you need to eat .... and exercise ....

2 Why do people who are very thin, and some people who are obese, suffer from deficiency diseases?

3 One slimming programme controls your food intake. Another controls your food intake but also has an exercise programme. Which do you think would be the most effective? Explain your answer.

Key points

● If you take in more energy than you use, you will store the excess as fat.

● Obese people have more health problems than others.

● People who do not have enough to eat can develop serious health problems.

● Exercise helps reduce weight and maintain health.

B1 1.3   Inheritance, exercise and health

∞ **links**

For information on metabolic rate, look back at B1 1.1 Diet and exercise.

Inheriting health

Inherited factors from your parents affect your appearance, such as the colour of your eyes. They also have a big effect on your health. They affect your metabolic rate, which affects how easily you lose and gain mass. Being overweight has a bad effect on your health. Inherited factors affect the proportion of muscle to fat in your body. They also affect your risk of heart disease, partly because they influence the levels of cholesterol in your blood.

Figure 1 Lots of things affect your health – your diet, how much exercise you take and what you inherit from your parents

Controlling cholesterol

The way your body balances cholesterol is an example of how an inherited factor can affect your health. You need cholesterol for your cell membranes and to make vital hormones. There are two forms of cholesterol carried around your body in your blood. One form is healthy but the other can cause health problems. If the balance of your cholesterol levels is wrong, your risk of getting heart disease increases.

a Why do you need cholesterol in your body?

The way your liver deals with the fat in your diet and makes the different types of cholesterol is inherited from your parents. For most people, eating a balanced diet means your liver can keep the balance of cholesterol right.

Eating lots of high-fat food means you are likely to have raised levels of harmful cholesterol and an increased risk of heart disease. But 1 in every 500 people inherit factors which mean they will have high levels of harmful cholesterol and an increased risk of heart disease whatever they eat. This is an example of how an inherited factor can affect your health.

?? **Did you know ...?**

The maximum healthy blood cholesterol is given as 6 mmol/l, 5 mmol/l and 4 mmol/l on different medical websites.

Scientists don't always agree!

Figure 2 Next time you eat a burger and fries, think about all the fat you are taking in. Will your body be able to deal with it, or are your blood cholesterol levels about to go up?

Exercise and health

Scientists have collected lots of evidence about exercise and health. It shows that people who exercise regularly are generally healthier than people who don't do much exercise. The graph in Figure 3 shows the results of an American study published in the journal *Circulation*. 6213 men were studied. The least active men were 4.5 times more likely to die early than the fittest, most active men.

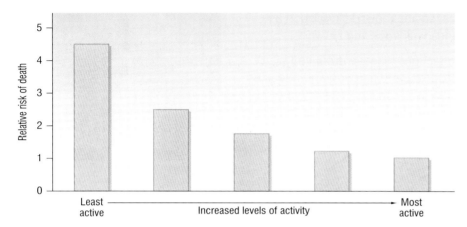

Figure 3 The effect of exercise on risk of death (Source: Jonathan Myers, *Circulation*, 2003)

These are some of the scientific explanations why exercise helps to keep you healthy.

- You are less likely to be overweight if you exercise regularly. This is partly because you will be using more energy.
- You will have more muscle tissue, which will increase your metabolic rate. If you can control your weight, you are less likely to be affected by problems such as arthritis, diabetes and high blood pressure.
- Your cholesterol levels are affected by exercise. Regular exercise lowers your blood cholesterol levels. It also helps the balance of the different types of cholesterol. When you exercise, your good cholesterol level goes up and the harmful cholesterol level goes down. This lowers your risk of heart disease and other health problems.

  b How could you change your cholesterol levels?

Summary questions

1 Copy and complete using the words below:

   heart   metabolic   inherited   cholesterol   balance

   There are .... factors such as your .... rate that can affect your health. The way your liver makes .... is inherited and if the .... of cholesterol is wrong it can increase your risk of .... disease.

2 Why are people who exercise regularly usually healthier than people who take little exercise?

3 Using the data in Figure 3, which group of people do you think are most at risk of death? Why do you think this might be? What could they do to reduce the risk?

Key points

- Inherited factors affect our health. These include our metabolic rate and cholesterol level.

- People who exercise regularly are usually healthier than people who take little exercise.

B1 1.4

Pathogens and disease

Learning objectives

- What are pathogens?
- How do pathogens cause disease?
- How did Ignaz Semmelweis change the way we look at disease?

Infectious diseases are found all over the world, in every country. Some diseases are fairly mild ones, such as the common cold and tonsillitis. Other diseases are known killers, such as tetanus, influenza and HIV/Aids.

An infectious disease is caused by a **microorganism** entering and attacking your body. People can pass these microorganisms from one person to another. This is what we mean by **infectious**.

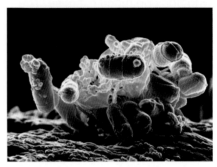

Figure 1 Many bacteria are very useful but some, like these *E. coli*, can cause disease

Microorganisms which cause disease are called **pathogens**. Common pathogens are bacteria and viruses.

a What causes infectious diseases?

The differences between bacteria and viruses

Bacteria are single-celled living organisms that are much smaller than animal and plant cells.

Although some bacteria cause disease, many are harmless and some are really useful to us. We use them to make food like yoghurt and cheese, to treat sewage and to make medicines.

Viruses are even smaller than bacteria. They usually have regular shapes. Viruses cause diseases in every type of living organism from people to bacteria.

Figure 2 These tobacco mosaic viruses cause disease in plants

b How do viruses differ from bacteria?

How pathogens cause disease

Once bacteria and viruses are inside your body they reproduce rapidly. This is how they make you ill. Bacteria simply split in two – they often produce toxins (poisons) which affect your body. Sometimes they directly damage your cells. Viruses take over the cells of your body as they reproduce, damaging and destroying the cells. They very rarely produce toxins.

Common disease symptoms are a high temperature, headaches and rashes. These are caused by the damage and toxins produced by the pathogens. The symptoms also appear as a result of the way your body responds to the damage and toxins.

You catch an infectious disease when you pick up a pathogen from someone else who is infected with the disease.

⚬⚬ **links**

For more information on bacteria that are resistant to antibiotics, see B1 1.8 Changing pathogens.

c How do pathogens make you feel ill?

How Science Works

The work of Ignaz Semmelweis

Ignaz Philipp Semmelweis was a doctor in the mid-1850s. At the time, many women in hospital died from childbed fever a few days after giving birth. However, no one knew what caused it.

Semmelweis noticed something about his medical students. They went straight from dissecting a dead body to delivering a baby without washing their hands. He wondered if they were carrying the cause of disease from the corpses to their patients.

Then another doctor cut himself while working on a body. He died from symptoms which were identical to childbed fever. Semmelweis was sure that the fever was caused by something that could be passed on – some kind of infectious agent.

He insisted that his medical students wash their hands before delivering babies. Immediately, fewer mothers died from the fever.

Getting his ideas accepted

Semmelweis talked to other doctors. He thought his evidence would prove to them that childbed fever was spread by doctors. But his ideas were mocked.

Many doctors thought that childbed fever was God's punishment to women. No one had ever seen bacteria or viruses. So it was hard to believe that disease was caused by something invisible passed from person to person. Doctors didn't like the idea that they might have been spreading disease. They were being told that their actions had killed patients instead of curing them.

In hospitals today, bacteria such as MRSA, which are resistant to antibiotics, are causing lots of problems. Getting doctors, nurses and visitors to wash their hands more often is part of the answer – just as it was in Semmelweis's time!

Semmelweis couldn't bear to think of the thousands of women who died because other doctors ignored his findings. By the 1860s he suffered a major breakdown and in 1865, aged only 47, he died – from an infection picked up from a patient during an operation.

Figure 3 Ignaz Semmelweis – his battle to get medical staff to wash their hands to prevent infections is still going on today

Summary questions

1   Copy and complete using the words below:

    toxins   viruses   microorganisms   reproduce   pathogens   damage symptoms   bacteria

    The .... which cause infectious diseases are known as .... Once .... and .... get inside your body they .... rapidly. They .... your tissues and may produce .... which cause the .... of disease.

2   Give five examples of things we now know we can do to reduce the spread of pathogens to lower the risk of disease, e.g. hand-washing in hospitals.

3   Write a letter by Ignaz Semmelweis to a friend explaining how he formed his ideas and the struggle to get them accepted.

Key points

- Infectious diseases are caused by microorganisms called pathogens, such as bacteria and viruses.

- Bacteria and viruses reproduce rapidly inside your body. Bacteria can produce toxins which make you feel ill.

- Viruses damage your cells as they reproduce. This can also make you feel ill.

- Semmelweis recognised the importance of hand-washing in preventing the spread of infectious diseases in hospital.

B1 1.6

Using drugs to treat disease

Learning objectives

- What is a medicine?

- How do medicines work?

- Why can't we use antibiotics to treat diseases caused by viruses?

When you have an infectious disease, you generally take medicines which contain useful drugs. Often the medicine doesn't affect the pathogen that is causing the problems. It just eases the symptoms and makes you feel better.

Drugs like aspirin and paracetamol are very useful as painkillers. When you have a cold they will help relieve your headache and sore throat. On the other hand, they will have no effect on the viruses which have entered your tissues and made you feel ill.

Many of the medicines you can buy at a chemist's or supermarket are like this. They relieve your symptoms but do not kill the pathogens. They do not cure you any faster. You have to wait for your immune system to overcome the pathogens.

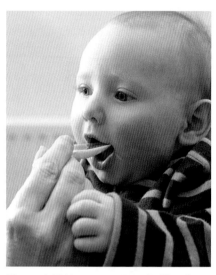

Figure 1 Taking paracetamol will make this child feel better, but she will not actually get well any faster as a result

a Why don't medicines like aspirin actually cure your illness?

Antibiotics

Drugs that make us feel better are useful but what we really need are drugs that can cure us. We use antiseptics and disinfectants to kill bacteria outside the body. But they are far too poisonous to use inside your body. They would kill you and your pathogens at the same time!

The drugs that have really changed the way we treat infectious diseases are **antibiotics**. These are medicines that can work inside your body to kill the bacteria that cause diseases.

b What is an antibiotic?

How antibiotics work

Antibiotics like penicillin work by killing the bacteria that cause disease while they are inside your body. They damage the bacterial cells without harming your own cells. They have had an enormous effect on our society. We can now cure bacterial diseases that killed millions of people in the past.

Unfortunately antibiotics are not the complete answer to the problem of infectious diseases. They have no effect on diseases caused by viruses.

The problem with viral pathogens is that they reproduce inside the cells of your body. It is extremely difficult to develop drugs that kill the viruses without damaging the cells and tissues of your body at the same time.

Figure 2 Penicillin was the first antibiotic. Now we have many different ones which kill different types of bacterium. Scientists are always on the look out for new antibiotics to keep us ahead in the battle against pathogens.

c How do antibiotics work?

Discovering penicillin

Alexander Fleming was a scientist who studied bacteria and wanted to find ways of killing them. In 1928, he was growing lots of bacteria on agar plates. Alexander was rather careless, and his lab was quite untidy. He often left the lids off his plates for a long time and forgot about experiments he had set up!

After one holiday, Fleming saw that lots of his culture plates had mould growing on them. He noticed a clear ring in the jelly around some of the spots of mould. Something had killed the bacteria covering the jelly.

Fleming saw how important this was. He called the mould 'penicillin'. He worked hard to extract a juice from the mould. But he couldn't get much penicillin and he couldn't make it survive, even in a fridge. So Fleming couldn't prove it would actually kill bacteria and make people better. By 1934 he gave up on penicillin and went on to do different work.

About 10 years after penicillin was first discovered, Ernst Chain and Howard Florey set about trying to use it on people. They gave some penicillin they extracted to Albert Alexander, who was dying of a blood infection. The effect was amazing and Albert recovered. But then the penicillin ran out. Florey and Chain even tried to collect unused penicillin from Albert's urine, but it was no good. The infection came back and sadly Albert died.

They kept working and eventually they managed to make penicillin on an industrial scale. The process was able to produce enough penicillin to supply the demands of the Second World War. We have used it as a medicine ever since.

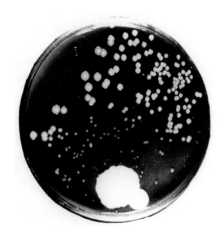

Figure 3 Alexander Fleming was on the lookout for something that would kill bacteria. As a result of him noticing the effect of this mould on his cultures, millions of lives have been saved around the world.

d Who was the first person to discover penicillin?

Summary questions

1 What is the main difference between drugs such as paracetamol and drugs such as penicillin?

2 **a** How did Alexander Fleming discover penicillin?
  b Why was it so difficult to make a medicine out of penicillin?
  c Who developed the industrial process which made it possible to mass-produce penicillin?

3 Explain why it is so much more difficult to develop medicines against viruses than it has been to develop antibacterial drugs.

Key points

- Some medicines relieve the symptoms of disease but do not kill the pathogens which cause it.

- Antibiotics cure bacterial diseases by killing the bacteria inside your body.

- Antibiotics do not destroy viruses because viruses reproduce inside the cells. It is difficult to develop drugs that can destroy viruses without damaging your body cells.

B1 1.7 Growing and investigating bacteria

To find out more about microorganisms we need to culture them. This means we grow very large numbers of them so that we can see all of the bacteria (the colony) as a whole. Many microorganisms can be grown in the laboratory. This helps us to learn more about them. We can find out what nutrients they need to grow and investigate which chemicals are best at killing them. Bacteria are the most commonly cultured microorganisms.

Growing microorganisms in the lab

To culture (grow) microorganisms you must provide them with everything they need. This means giving them a liquid or gel containing nutrients – a **culture medium**. It contains carbohydrate as an energy source along with various minerals and sometimes other chemicals. Most microorganisms also need warmth and oxygen to grow.

You usually provide the nutrients in **agar** jelly. Hot agar containing all the nutrients your bacteria will need is poured into a Petri dish. It is then left to cool and set before you add the microorganisms.

You must take great care when you are culturing microorganisms. The bacteria you want to grow may be harmless. However, there is always the risk that a **mutation** (a change in the DNA) will take place and produce a new and dangerous pathogen.

You also want to keep the pure strains of bacteria you are culturing free from any other microorganisms. Such contamination might come from your skin, the air, the soil or the water around you. Investigations need uncontaminated cultures of microorganism. Whenever you are culturing microorganisms you must carry out strict health and safety procedures to protect yourself and others.

Figure 1 Culturing microorganisms like bacteria makes it possible for us to observe them and see how different chemicals affect them

a What is agar jelly?

Growing useful organisms

You can prepare an uncontaminated culture of microorganisms in the laboratory by following a number of steps.

The Petri dishes on which you will grow your microorganisms must be sterilised before using them. The nutrient agar, which will provide their food, must also be sterilised. This kills off any unwanted microorganisms. You can use heat to sterilise glass dishes. A special oven called an autoclave is often used. It sterilises by using steam at high pressure. Plastic Petri dishes are often bought ready-sterilised. UV light or gamma radiation is used to kill the bacteria.

Figure 2 When working with the most dangerous pathogens, scientists need to be very careful. Sensible safety precautions are needed when working with microorganisms.

b Why must everything be sterilised before you start a culture?

The next step is to **inoculate** the sterile agar with the microorganisms you want to grow.

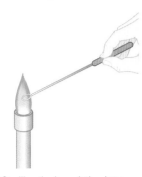 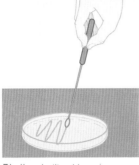 

Sterilise the inoculating loop used to transfer micro-organisms to the agar by heating it until it is red hot in the flame of a Bunsen and then letting it cool. Do not put the loop down or blow on it as it cools.

Dip the sterilised loop in a suspension of the bacteria you want to grow and use it to make zigzag streaks across the surface of the agar. Replace the lid on the dish as quickly as possible to avoid contamination.

Seal the lid of the Petri dish with adhesive tape to prevent microorganisms from the air contaminating the culture – or microorganisms from the culture escaping. Do not seal all the way around the edge so oxygen can get into the dish and harmful anaerobic bacteria do not grow.

Figure 3 Culturing microorganisms safely in the laboratory

Once you have inoculated your plates, the sealed Petri dishes need to be incubated (kept warm) for several days so the microorganisms can grow. In school and college laboratories the maximum temperature at which cultures are incubated is 25 °C. This greatly reduces the likelihood that you will grow pathogens that might be harmful to people. In industrial conditions, bacterial cultures are often grown at higher temperatures, which allow the microorganisms to grow more rapidly.

Practical

Investigating the action of disinfectants and antibiotics

You can use cultures you set up yourself or pre-inoculated agar to investigate the effect of disinfectants and antibiotics on the growth of bacteria. An area of clear jelly indicates that the bacteria have been killed or cannot grow.

- What are the safety issues in this investigation and how will you manage any risks?

Summary questions

1 Why do we culture microorganisms in the laboratory?

2 Why don't we culture bacteria at 37 °C in the school lab?

3 When you set up a culture of bacteria in a Petri dish (see Figure 3) you give the bacteria everything they need to grow as fast as possible. However these ideal conditions do not last forever. What might limit the growth of the bacteria in a culture on a Petri dish?

Key points

- An uncontaminated culture of microorganisms can be grown using sterilised Petri dishes and agar. You sterilise the inoculating loop before use and seal the lid of the Petri dish to prevent unwanted microorganisms getting in. The culture is left at about 25 °C for a few days.

- Uncontaminated cultures are needed so we can investigate the effect of chemicals such as disinfectants and antibiotics on microorganisms.

- Cultures should be incubated at a maximum temperature of 25 °C in schools and colleges to reduce the likelihood of harmful pathogens growing.

B1 1.8 Changing pathogens

Learning objectives

● What is antibiotic resistance?

● How can we prevent antibiotic resistance developing? [H]

● Why is mutation in bacteria and viruses such a problem?

If you are given an antibiotic and use it properly, the bacteria that have made you ill are killed off. However some bacteria develop resistance to antibiotics. They have a natural mutation (change in the genetic material) that means they are not affected by the antibiotic. These mutations happen by chance and they produce new strains of bacteria by **natural selection**.

More types of bacteria are becoming resistant to more antibiotics. Diseases caused by bacteria are becoming more difficult to treat. Over the years antibiotics have been overused and used when they are not really needed. This increases the rate at which antibiotic-resistant strains have developed.

Antibiotic-resistant bacteria

Normally an antibiotic kills the bacteria of a non-resistant strain. However individual resistant bacteria survive and reproduce, so the population of **resistant** bacteria increases.

Antibiotics are no longer used to treat non-serious infections such as mild throat infections, which are often caused by viruses. Hopefully this will slow down the rate of development of resistant strains.

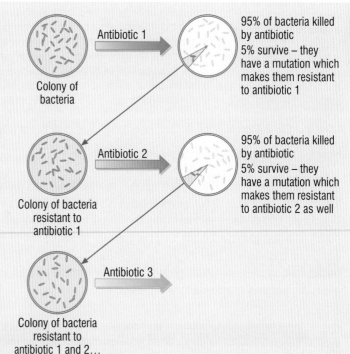

Higher

Colony of bacteria

Antibiotic 1

95% of bacteria killed by antibiotic
5% survive – they have a mutation which makes them resistant to antibiotic 1

Colony of bacteria resistant to antibiotic 1

Antibiotic 2

95% of bacteria killed by antibiotic
5% survive – they have a mutation which makes them resistant to antibiotic 2 as well

Colony of bacteria resistant to antibiotic 1 and 2…

Antibiotic 3

Figure 1 Bacteria can develop resistance to many different antibiotics in a process of natural selection as this simple model shows

To prevent more resistant strains of bacteria appearing it is important not to overuse antibiotics. It's best to only use them when you really need them. Antibiotics don't affect viruses so people should not demand antibiotics to treat an illness which the doctor thinks is viral.

Some antibiotics treat very specific bacteria. Others treat many different types of bacteria. The right type of antibiotic must be used to treat each bacterial infection to prevent further antibiotic resistance developing. It is also important that people finish their course of medicine every time.

a Why is it important not to use antibiotics too frequently?

AQA Examiner's tip

Washing hands removes the pathogens on them, but it may not kill the pathogens.

The MRSA story

Hospitals use a lot of antibiotics to treat infections. As a result of natural selection, some of the bacteria in hospitals are resistant to many antibiotics. This is what has happened with **MRSA** (the bacterium methicillin-resistant *Staphylococcus aureus*).

As doctors and nurses move from patient to patient, these antibiotic-resistant bacteria are spread easily. MRSA alone now contributes to around 1000 deaths every year in UK hospitals.

There are a number of simple steps which can reduce the spread of microorganisms such as MRSA. We have known some of them since the time of Semmelweis, but they sometimes get forgotten!

- Antibiotics should only be used when they are really needed.
- Specific bacteria should be treated with specific antibiotics.
- Medical staff should wash their hands with soap and water or alcohol gel between patients. They should wear disposable clothing or clothing that is regularly sterilised.
- Visitors should wash their hands as they enter and leave the hospital.
- Patients infected with antibiotic-resistant bacteria should be looked after in isolation from other patients.
- Hospitals should be kept clean – there should be high standards of hygiene.

b Is MRSA a bacterium or a virus?

Mutation and pandemics

Another problem caused by the mutation of pathogens is that new forms of diseases can appear. These new strains can spread quickly and cause widespread illness because no one is immune to them and there is no effective treatment. For example the flu virus mutates easily. Every year there are new strains of the virus that your immune system doesn't recognise. There is no effective treatment against viruses at all. The existing flu vaccine is not effective against new strains of the virus, and it takes time to develop a new vaccine.

There may be a flu **epidemic** (in one country) or even a **pandemic** (across several countries). In 1918–19, a new strain of flu virus killed over 40 million people around the world.

With modern international travel, a new strain of pathogen can spread very quickly. In 2009 there was a pandemic of a new strain of flu, known as swine flu, which spread very fast. Internationally, countries worked to stop it spreading and the death toll was kept relatively low.

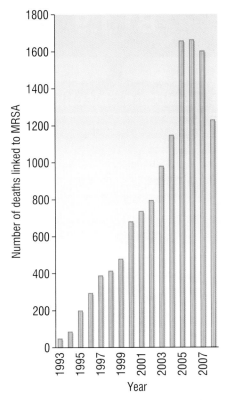

Figure 2 Data that show how the number of deaths in which MRSA played a part from 1993 (Source: National Statistics Office)

⊂⊃ links

For more information on the work of Semmelweis, look back at B1 1.4 Pathogens and disease.

Key points

- Many types of bacterium have developed antibiotic resistance as a result of natural selection. To prevent the problem getting worse we must not overuse antibiotics.

- If bacteria or viruses mutate, new strains of the pathogen can appear causing disease.

- New strains of disease which spread rapidly can cause epidemics and pandemics. Antibiotics and vaccinations may not be effective against the new strain.

Summary questions

1 Copy and complete using the words below.

antibiotics bacterium (virus) better disease mutation mutate resistant virus (bacterium)

If bacteria change or .... they may become .... to .... This means the medicine no longer makes you .... A .... in a .... or .... can also lead to a new form of ....

2 Make a flow chart to show how bacteria develop resistance to antibiotics.

3 Use Figure 2 to help you answer these questions.
   a How could you explain the increase in deaths linked to MRSA?
   b How could you explain the fall in deaths linked to MRSA, which still continues?

B1 1.9 Immunity

- How does your immune system work?
- How does vaccination protect you against disease?

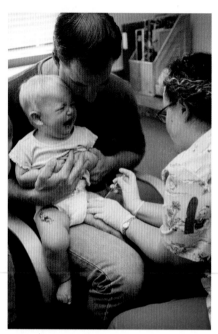

Figure 1 No one likes having a vaccination very much – but they save millions of lives!

Every cell has unique proteins on its surface called **antigens**. The antigens on the microorganisms that get into your body are different to the ones on your own cells. Your immune system recognises they are different.

Your white blood cells then make antibodies which join up with the antigens. This destroys the pathogens.

Your white blood cells 'remember' the right antibody needed to tackle a particular pathogen. If you meet that pathogen again, they can make the same antibody very quickly. So you become immune to that disease.

The first time you meet a new pathogen you get ill. That's because there is a delay while your body sorts out the right antibody needed. The next time, you completely destroy the invaders before they have time to make you feel unwell.

  a What is an antigen?

Vaccination

Some pathogens can make you seriously ill very quickly. In fact you can die before your body manages to make the right antibodies. Fortunately, you can be protected against many of these serious diseases by **immunisation** (also known as **vaccination**).

Immunisation involves giving you a **vaccine**. A vaccine is usually made of a dead or weakened form of the disease-causing microorganism. It works by triggering your body's natural immune response to invading pathogens.

A small amount of dead or inactive pathogen is introduced into your body. This gives your white blood cells the chance to develop the right antibodies against the pathogen without you getting ill.

Then, if you meet the live pathogens, your white blood cells can respond rapidly. They can make the right antibodies just as if you had already had the disease, so you are protected against it.

  b What is an antibody?

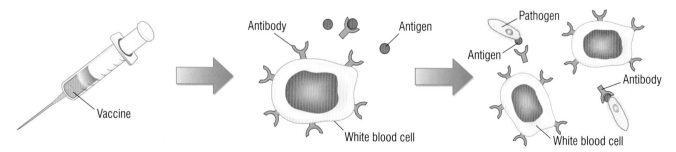

Small amounts of dead or inactive pathogen are put into your body, often by injection.

The antigens in the vaccine stimulate your white blood cells into making antibodies. The antibodies destroy the antigens without any risk of you getting the disease.

You are immune to future infections by the pathogen. That's because your body can respond rapidly and make the correct antibody as if you had already had the disease.

Figure 2 This is how vaccines protect you against dangerous infectious diseases

We use vaccines to protect us against both bacterial diseases (e.g. tetanus and diphtheria) and viral diseases (e.g. polio, measles and mumps). For example, the MMR vaccine protects against measles, mumps and rubella. Vaccines have saved millions of lives around the world. If a large proportion of the population is immune to a disease, the spread of the pathogen is very much reduced. One disease – smallpox – has been completely wiped out by vaccinations. Doctors hope polio will also disappear in the next few years.

c Give an example of one bacterial and one viral disease which you can be immunised against.

How Science Works

The vaccine debate

No medicine is completely risk free. Very rarely, a child will react badly to a vaccine with tragic results. Making the decision to have your baby immunised can be difficult.

Society needs as many people as possible to be immunised against as many diseases as possible. This keeps the pool of infection in the population very low. On the other hand, you know there is a remote chance that something may go wrong with a vaccination.

Because vaccines are so successful, we rarely see the terrible diseases they protect us against. A hundred years ago nearly 50% of all deaths of children and young people were caused by infectious diseases. The development of antibiotics and vaccines means that now only 0.5% of all deaths in the same age group are due to infectious disease. Many children were also left permanently damaged by serious infections. Parents today are often aware of the very small risks from vaccination – but sometimes forget about the terrible dangers of the diseases we vaccinate against.

If you are a parent it can be difficult to find unbiased advice to help you make a decision. The media highlight scare stories which make good headlines. The pharmaceutical companies want to sell vaccines. Doctors and health visitors can weigh up all the information, but they have vaccination targets set by the government.

links

For more information on antibiotics, look back at B1 1.8 Changing pathogens.

Summary questions

1 Copy and complete using the words below:

antibodies   pathogen   immunised   dead   immune inactive   white

People can be .... against a disease by introducing small quantities of .... or .... forms of a .... into your body. They stimulate the .... blood cells to produce .... to destroy the pathogen. This makes you .... to the disease in future.

2 Explain carefully, using diagrams if they help you:
a how the immune system of your body works
b how vaccines use your natural immune system to protect you against serious diseases.

3 Explain why vaccines can be used against both bacterial and viral diseases but antibiotics only work against bacteria.

Key points

- Your white blood cells produce antibodies to destroy the pathogens. Then your body will respond rapidly to future infections by the same pathogen, by making the correct antibody. You become immune to the disease.

- You can be immunised against a disease by introducing small amounts of dead or inactive pathogens into your body.

- We can use vaccinations to protect against both bacterial and viral pathogens.

How do we deal with disease?

The whooping cough story

In the 1970s, Dr John Wilson, a UK specialist in treating children, published a report suggesting that the pertussis (whooping cough) vaccine might cause brain damage in some children. The report was based on his study of a small group of 36 patients.

The media publicised the story and parents began to panic. The number of children being vaccinated against whooping cough fell from over 80% to around 30%. This was too low to protect the population from the disease.

People were so worried about the vaccine that they forgot that whooping cough itself can cause brain damage and death. In Scotland about 100 000 children suffered from whooping cough between 1977 and 1991. About 75 of them died. A similar pattern was seen across the whole of the UK.

An investigation into the original research discovered that it had serious flaws. Identical twin girls who were included in the study, and later died of a rare genetic disorder, had never actually had the whooping cough vaccine. It was a small study and only 12 of the children investigated had shown any symptoms close to the time of their whooping cough vaccination. Their parents were involved in claims for compensation from the vaccine manufacturers.

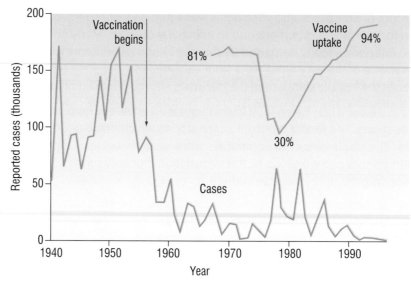

Figure 1 Graph showing the effect of the whooping cough scare on both uptake of the vaccine and the number of cases of the disease (Source: Open University)

No medical treatment (including vaccinations) is completely safe, but when the claims for compensation came to court, the whole study was questioned. After hearing all the evidence, the judge decided that the risks of whooping cough were far worse than any possible damage caused by the vaccine itself.

However, this judgement on the study got much less media coverage than the original scare story. Parents still felt there was 'no smoke without fire'. It was 20 years before vaccination levels, and the levels of whooping cough, returned to the levels before the scare. The number of people having vaccinations now is over 90%, and deaths from whooping cough are almost unknown in the UK.

Medicines for the future

Overuse of antibiotics has lead to spreading antibiotic resistance in many different bacteria. In recent years doctors have found strains of bacteria that are resistant to even the strongest antibiotics. When that happens, there is nothing more that antibiotics can do for a patient and he or she may well die.

The development of antibiotic-resistant strains of bacteria means scientitsts are constantly looking for new antibiotics. It isn't easy to find chemicals which kill bacteria without damaging human cells.

Penicillin and several other antibiotics are made by moulds. Scientists are collecting soil samples from all over the world to try and find another mould to produce a new antibiotic that will kill antibiotic-resistant bacteria such as MRSA.

Crocodiles have teeth full of rotting meat. They live in dirty water and fight a lot. But scientists noticed that although crocodiles often give each other terrible bites, the bites do not become infected. They have extracted a chemical known as 'crocodillin' from crocodile blood and it seems to be a powerful antibiotic. Now the race is on to try and turn these amazing chemicals into antibiotics we can use.

Fish such as this plaice are covered with a slime which helps to protect them from damage and infection. Scientists have analysed this slime and found it contains proteins which have antibiotic properties. The proteins have been isolated from the slime and they still kill bacteria. So maybe fish will provide us with an antibiotic for the future.

Honey has been used since the time of the Ancient Egyptians to help heal wounds. Scientists in Germany and Australia have found that certain types of honey have antibiotic properties. They kill many bacteria, including MRSA. Doctors are using manuka honey dressings more and more to treat infected wounds.

Figure 2 Where will the next antibiotic be found?

Activity

Produce a poster on antibiotic resistance in bacteria and the search for new antibiotics. Make sure you explain how antibiotic resistance has developed and why we need more antibiotics. Use the ideas given here and, if possible, look for more examples of possible sources of new antibiotics.

Summary questions

1 Give one advantage and one disadvantage of being vaccinated.
2 List three examples of bad science from the story of the whooping cough vaccine and explain why the story should never have been published.

Key points

- Vaccination protects individuals and society from the effects of a disease.
- The treatment of disease has changed as our understanding of how antibiotics and immunity has increased.

B1 2.1

Responding to change

- Why do you need a nervous system?
- What is a receptor?
- How do you respond to changes in your surroundings?

You need to know what is going on in the world around you. Your **nervous system** makes this possible. It enables you to react to your surroundings and coordinate your behaviour.

Your nervous system carries electrical signals (**impulses**) that travel fast – from 1 to 120 metres per second. This means you can react to changes in your surroundings very quickly.

a What is the main job of the nervous system?

The nervous system

Like all living things, you need to avoid danger, find food and, eventually, find a mate! This is where your nervous system comes into its own. Your body is particularly sensitive to changes in the world around you. Any changes (known as **stimuli**) are picked up by cells called **receptors**.

Receptor cells (e.g. the light receptor cells in your eyes) are like most animal cells. They have a nucleus, cytoplasm and a cell membrane. These receptors are usually found clustered together in special **sense organs**, such as your eyes and your skin. You have many different types of sensory receptor (see Figure 2).

b Where would you find receptors that respond to:
  i a loud noise
  ii touching a hot oven
  iii a strong perfume?

Figure 1 Your body is made up of millions of cells which have to work together. Whatever you do with your body – whether it's walking to school or playing on the computer – your movements need to be coordinated.

Ears – receptors sensitive to sound

Ears – receptors sensitive to changes in position for balance

Eyes – receptors sensitive to light

Nose and tongue – receptors sensitive to chemicals for taste and smell

Skin – receptors sensitive to touch, pressure, pain and temperature changes

Figure 2 This cat relies on its sensory receptors to detect changes in the environment

??? Did you know ...?

Some male moths have receptors so sensitive they can detect the scent of a female several kilometres away and follow the scent trail to find her!

How your nervous system works

Once a sensory receptor detects a stimulus, the information (sent as an electrical impulse) passes along special cells called **neurons**. These are usually found in bundles of hundreds or even thousands of neurons known as **nerves**.

The impulse travels along the neuron until it reaches the **central nervous system** or **CNS**. The CNS is made up of the brain and the spinal cord. The cells which carry impulses from your sense organs to your central nervous system are called **sensory neurons**.

c What is the difference between a neuron and a nerve?

Your brain gets huge amounts of information from all the sensory receptors in your body. It coordinates the information and sends impulses out along special cells. These cells carry information from the CNS to the rest of your body. The cells are called **motor neurons**. They carry impulses to make the right bits of your body – the **effector organs** – respond.

Effector organs are muscles or glands. Your muscles respond to the arrival of impulses by contracting. Your glands respond by releasing (**secreting**) chemical substances.

The way your nervous system works can be summed up as:

receptor → sensory neuron → coordinator (CNS) → motor neuron → effector

d What is the difference between a sensory neuron and a motor neuron?

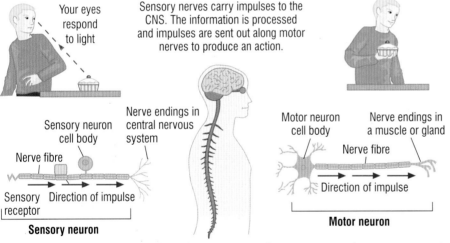

Figure 3 The rapid responses of our nervous system allow us to respond to our surroundings quickly and in the right way!

Summary questions

1 Copy and complete using the words below:

neurons receptors electrical CNS environment nervous

Your .... system carries fast .... impulses. Changes in the .... are picked up by your .... and impulses travel along your .... to your ....

2 Make a table to show the different types of sense receptor. For each one, give an example of the sort of things it responds to, e.g. touch receptors respond to an insect crawling on your skin.

3 Explain what happens in your nervous system when you see a piece of chocolate, pick it up and eat it.

Key points

- The nervous system uses electrical impulses to enable you to react quickly to your surroundings and coordinate what you do.

- Cells called receptors detect stimuli (changes in the environment).

- Like all animal cells, light receptor cells and other receptors have a nucleus, cytoplasm and cell membrane.

- Impulses from receptors pass along sensory neurons to the brain or spinal cord (CNS). Impulses are sent along motor neurons from the brain (CNS) to the effector organs.

Reflex actions

Learning objectives

- What is a reflex?
- Why are reflexes so important?

Your nervous system lets you take in information from your surroundings and respond in the right way. However, some of your responses are so fast that they happen without giving you time to think.

When you touch something hot, or sharp, you pull your hand back before you feel the pain. If something comes near your face, you blink. Automatic responses like these are known as **reflexes**.

What are reflexes for?

Reflexes are very important both for human beings and for other animals. They help you to avoid danger or harm because they happen so fast. There are also lots of reflexes that take care of your basic body functions. These functions include breathing and moving food through your gut.

It would make life very difficult if you had to think consciously about those things all the time – and would be fatal if you forgot to breathe!

a Why are reflexes important?

How do reflexes work?

Reflex actions involve just three types of neuron. These are:

- sensory neurons
- motor neurons
- relay neurons – these connect a sensory neuron and a motor neuron. Your relay neurons are in the CNS.

An electrical impulse passes from the sensory receptor along the sensory neuron to the CNS. It then passes along a relay neuron (usually in the spinal cord) and straight back along a motor neuron. From there the impulse arrives at the effector organ. The effector organ will be a muscle or a gland. We call this a **reflex arc**.

The key point in a reflex arc is that the impulse bypasses the conscious areas of your brain. The result is that the time between the stimulus and the reflex action is as short as possible.

b Why is it important that the impulses in a reflex arc do not go to the conscious brain?

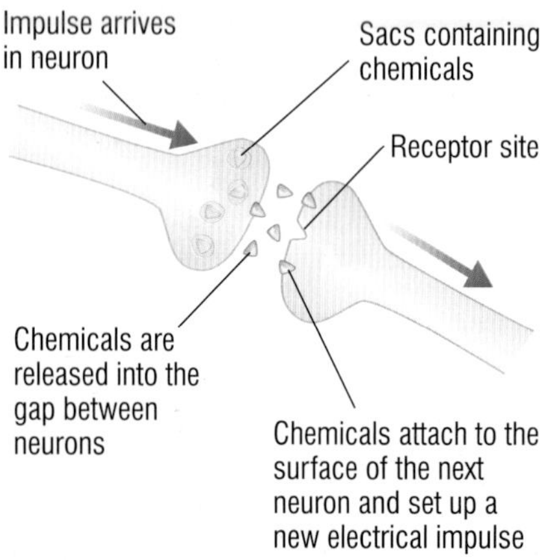

How synapses work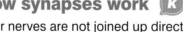

Your nerves are not joined up directly to each other. There are junctions between them called **synapses**. The electrical impulses travelling along your neurons have to cross these synapses. They cannot leap the gap. Look at Figure 1 to see what happens next.

The reflex arc in detail

Look at Figure 2. It shows what would happen if you touched a hot object.

When you touch it, a receptor in your skin is stimulated. An electrical impulse passes along a sensory neuron to the central nervous system – in this case the spinal cord.

Practical

The stick-drop test

You can investigate how quickly nerve impulses travel in your body using metre rules, and either stop clocks or ICT to measure how quickly you catch the ruler OR by standing in a circle holding hands with your eyes closed and measuring how long it takes a hand squeeze to pass around the circle.

Impulse arrives in neuron

Sacs containing chemicals

Receptor site

Chemicals are released into the gap between neurons

Chemicals attach to the surface of the next neuron and set up a new electrical impulse

Figure 1 When an impulse arrives at the junction between two neurons, chemicals are released which cross the synapse and arrive at receptor sites on the next neuron. This starts up an electrical impulse in the next neuron.

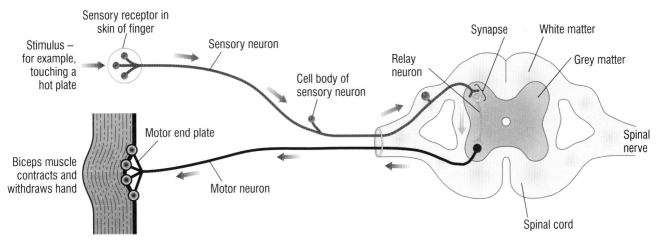

Sensory receptor in skin of finger

Stimulus – for example, touching a hot plate

Sensory neuron

Cell body of sensory neuron

Relay neuron

Synapse

White matter

Grey matter

Spinal nerve

Spinal cord

Motor end plate

Biceps muscle contracts and withdraws hand

Motor neuron

Figure 2 The reflex action which moves your hand away from something hot can save you from being burned. Reflex actions are quick and automatic; you do not think about them.

When an impulse from the sensory neuron arrives in the synapse with a relay neuron, a chemical messenger is released. This chemical crosses the synapse to the relay neuron. There it sets off an electrical impulse that travels along the relay neuron.

When the impulse reaches the synapse between the relay neuron and a motor neuron returning to the arm, another chemical is released.

This chemical crosses the synapse and starts an electrical impulse travelling down the motor neuron. When the impulse reaches the effector organ, it is stimulated to respond.

In this example the impulses arrive in the muscles of the arm, causing them to contract. This action moves the hand rapidly away from the source of pain. If the effector organ is a gland, it will respond by releasing (secreting) chemicals.

Most reflex actions can be shown as follows:

stimulus → receptor → coordinator → effector → response

This is not very different from a normal conscious action. However, in a reflex action the coordinator is a relay neuron either in the spinal cord or in the unconscious areas of the brain. The whole reflex is very fast indeed.

An impulse also travels up the spinal cord to the conscious areas of your brain. You know about the reflex action, but only after it has happened.

Summary questions

1 Copy and complete using the words below:

conscious motor reflex relay response sensory stimulus

In a .... arc the electrical impulse bypasses the .... areas of your brain. The time between the .... and the .... is as short as possible. Only .... neurons, ... neurons and .... neurons are involved.

2 Explain why some actions, such as breathing and swallowing, are reflex actions, while others such as speaking and eating are under your conscious control.

3 Draw a flow chart to explain what happens when you step on a pin. Make sure you include an explanation of how a synapse works.

Figure 3 Newborn babies have a number of special reflexes which disappear as they grow. This gripping reflex is one of them.

Key points

- Some responses to stimuli are automatic and rapid and are called 'reflex actions'.
- Reflex actions run everyday bodily functions and help you to avoid danger.

B1 2.3

Hormones and the menstrual cycle

Hormones are chemical substances that coordinate many processes within your body. Special **glands** make and release (secrete) these hormones into your body. Then the hormones are carried around your body to their target organs in the bloodstream. Hormones regulate the functions of many organs and cells. They can act very quickly, but often their effects are quite slow and long lasting.

A woman's **menstrual cycle** is a good example of control by hormones. Hormones are made in a woman's pituitary gland and her ovaries control her menstrual cycle. The levels of the different hormones rise and fall in a regular pattern. This affects the way her body works.

What is the menstrual cycle?

The average length of the menstrual cycle is about 28 days. Each month the lining of the womb thickens ready to support a developing baby. At the same time an egg starts maturing in the ovary.

About 14 days after the egg starts maturing it is released from the ovary. This is known as **ovulation**. The lining of the womb stays thick for several days after the egg has been released.

If the egg is fertilised by a sperm, then pregnancy may take place. The lining of the womb provides protection and food for the developing embryo. If the egg is not fertilised, the lining of the womb and the dead egg are shed from the body. This is the monthly bleed or **period**.

All of these changes are brought about by hormones. These are made and released by the **pituitary gland** (a pea-sized gland in the brain) and the **ovaries**.

a What controls the menstrual cycle?
b Why does the lining of the womb build up each month?

How the menstrual cycle works

Once a month, a surge of hormones from the pituitary gland in the brain starts eggs maturing in the ovaries. The hormones also stimulate the ovaries to produce the female sex hormone **oestrogen**.

- Follicle stimulating hormone (**FSH**) is secreted by the pituitary gland. It makes eggs mature in the ovaries. FSH also stimulates the ovaries to produce oestrogen.

- Oestrogen is made and secreted by the ovaries. It stimulates the lining of the womb to build up ready for pregnancy. It inhibits (slows down) the production of more FSH.

- Other hormones involved in the menstrual cycle are luteinising hormone (LH) and **progesterone**.

The hormones produced by the pituitary gland and the ovary act together to control what happens in the menstrual cycle. As the oestrogen levels rise they inhibit the production of FSH and encourage the production of LH by the pituitary gland. When LH levels reach a peak in the middle of the cycle, they stimulate the release of a mature egg.

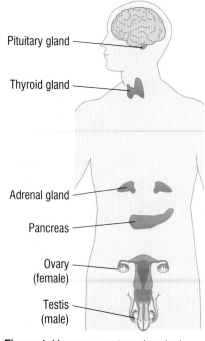

Pituitary gland

Thyroid gland

Adrenal gland

Pancreas

Ovary (female)

Testis (male)

Figure 1 Hormones act as chemical messages. They are made in glands in one part of the body but have an effect somewhere else.

Did you know ...?

A baby girl is born with ovaries full of immature eggs, but they do nothing until she has gone through the changes of **puberty**.

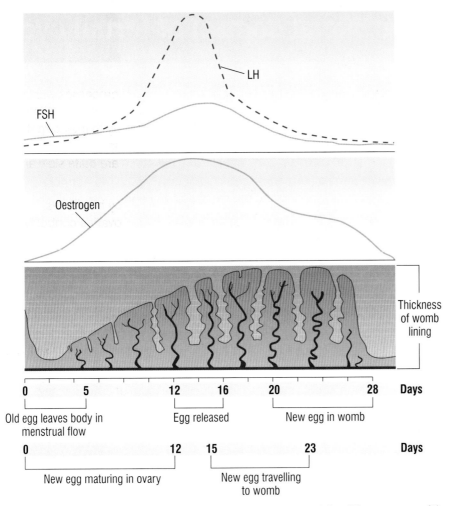

Figure 2 The changing levels of the female sex hormones control the different stages of the menstrual cycle

Summary questions

1 Copy and complete using the words below:

28 hormones FSH menstrual oestrogen ovary

During the .... cycle a mature egg is released from the .... about every .... days. The cycle is controlled by several .... including .... and ....

2 Look at Figure 2 above:
   a Explain what happens to FSH.
   b On which days is the female having a menstrual period?
   c Which hormone controls the build-up of the lining of the womb?

3 Produce a poster to explain the events of the menstrual cycle to women who are hoping to start a family. You will need to explain the graphs at the top of this page and show when a woman is most likely to get pregnant. Remember sperm can live for up to three days inside the woman's body.

Key points

● Hormones control the release of an egg from the ovary and the build-up of the lining of the womb in the menstrual cycle.

● Some of the hormones involved are FSH from the pituitary gland and oestrogen from the ovary.

B1 2.4 The artificial control of fertility

Learning objectives

- How can hormones be used to stop pregnancy?
- How can hormones help to solve the problems of infertility?

Contraceptive chemicals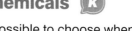

In the 21st century it is possible to choose when to have children – and when not to have them. One of the most important and widely used ways of controlling fertility is to use **oral contraceptives** (the **contraceptive pill**).

The pill contains female hormones, particularly oestrogen. The hormones affect women's ovaries, preventing the release of any eggs. The pill inhibits the production of FSH so no eggs mature in the ovaries. Without mature eggs, women can't get pregnant.

Anyone who uses the pill as a contraceptive has to take it very regularly. If they forget to take it, the artificial hormone levels drop. Then their body's own hormones can take over very quickly. This can lead to the unexpected release of an egg – and an unexpected baby.

a What is a contraceptive?

The first birth control pills contained very large amounts of oestrogen. They caused serious side effects such as high blood pressure and headaches in some women. Modern contraceptive pills contain much lower doses of oestrogen along with some progesterone. They cause fewer side effects. Some contraceptive pills only contain progesterone. These cause even fewer side effects. However, they are not quite so good at preventing pregnancy because they don't stop the eggs from maturing.

b What is the difference between the mixed pill and the progesterone-only pill?

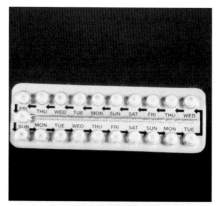

Figure 1 The contraceptive pill contains a mixture of hormones which effectively trick the body into thinking it is already pregnant, so no more eggs are released

Fertility treatments

In the UK as many as one couple in six have problems having a family when they want one. There are many possible reasons for this infertility. It may be linked to a lack of female hormones. Some women want children but do not make enough FSH to stimulate the eggs in their ovaries. Fortunately, artificial FSH can be used as a fertility drug. It stimulates the eggs in the ovary to mature and also triggers oestrogen production.

AQA Examiner's tip

FSH and LH are used in IVF to stimulate the eggs to mature.

??? Did you know ...?

In the early days of using fertility drugs there were big problems with the doses used. In 1971 an Italian doctor removed 15 four-month-old fetuses (ten girls and five boys) from the womb of a 35-year-old woman after treatment with fertility drugs. Not one of them survived.

Figure 2 Most people who take fertility drugs end up with one or two babies. But in 1983 the Walton family from Liverpool had six baby girls who all survived.

Fertility drugs are also used in **IVF** (*in vitro* fertilisation). Conception usually takes place in the fallopian tube. This is the tube between the ovary and the womb that the egg travels along. If the fallopian tubes are damaged, the eggs cannot reach the womb so women cannot get pregnant naturally.

Fortunately doctors can now help. They collect eggs from the ovary of the mother and fertilise them with sperm from the father outside the body. The fertilised eggs develop into tiny embryos. The embryos are inserted into the womb of the mother. In this way they bypass the faulty tubes.

During IVF the woman is given FSH to make sure as many eggs as possible mature in her ovaries. LH is also given at the end of the cycle to make sure all the mature eggs are released. IVF is expensive and not always successful.

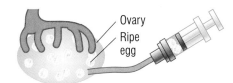

1 Fertility drugs are used to make lots of eggs mature at the same time for collection.

2 The eggs are collected and placed in a special solution in a Petri dish.

3 A sample of semen is collected and the sperm and eggs are mixed in the Petri dish.

4 The eggs are checked to make sure they have been fertilised and the early embryos are developing properly.

5 When the fertilised eggs have formed tiny balls of cells, 1 or 2 of the tiny embryos are placed in the womb of the mother. Then, if all goes well, at least one baby will grow and develop successfully.

Figure 3 New reproductive technology using hormones and IVF has helped thousands of infertile couples to have babies

How Science Works

The advantages and disadvantages of fertility treatment

The use of hormones to control fertility has been a major scientific breakthrough. But like most things, there are advantages and disadvantages! Here are some points to think about:

In the developed world, using the pill has helped make families much smaller than they used to be. There is less poverty because with fewer children being born there are fewer mouths to feed and more money to go round.

The pill has also helped to control population growth in countries such as China, where they find it difficult to feed all their people. In many other countries of the developing world the pill is not available because of a lack of money, education and doctors.

The pill can cause health problems so a doctor always oversees its use.

The use of fertility drugs can also have some health risks for the mother and it can be expensive for society and parents. A large multiple birth can be tragic for the parents if some or all of the babies die. It also costs hospitals a lot of money to keep very small premature babies alive.

Controlling fertility artificially also raises many ethical issues for society and individuals. For example, some religious groups think that preventing conception is denying life and ban the use of the pill.

The mature eggs produced by a woman using fertility drugs may be collected and stored, or fertilised and stored, until she wants to get pregnant later. But what happens if the woman dies, or does not want the eggs or embryos any more?

- What, in your opinion, are the main advantages and disadvantages of using artificial hormones to control female fertility?

Summary questions

1 Explain the meaning of the following terms: oral contraceptive, fallopian tube, fertility drug, *in vitro* fertilisation.

2 Explain how artificial female hormones can be used to:
   a prevent unwanted pregnancies
   b help people overcome infertility.

Key points

- Hormones can be used to control fertility.

- Oral contraceptives contain hormones, which stop FSH production so no eggs mature.

- FSH can be used as a fertility drug for women, to stimulate eggs to mature in their ovaries. These eggs may be used in IVF treatments.

B1 2.5

Controlling conditions

Learning objectives

- How are conditions inside your body controlled?

- Why is it so important to control your internal environment?

Figure 1 Everything you do affects your internal environment

AQA *Examiner's tip*

Sweating causes the body to cool. Energy from the body is used to evaporate the water in sweat.

Figure 2 You can change your behaviour to help control your temperature, for example by adding extra clothing or turning up the heating when it's really cold

The conditions inside your body are known as its **internal environment**. Your organs cannot work properly if this keeps changing. Many of the processes which go on inside your body aim to keep everything as constant as possible. This balancing act is called **homeostasis**.

It involves your nervous system, your hormone systems and many of your body organs.

a Why is homeostasis important?

Controlling water and ions

Water can move in and out of your body cells. How much it moves depends on the concentration of mineral ions (such as salt) and the amount of water in your body. If too much water moves into or out of your cells, they can be damaged or destroyed.

You take water and minerals into your body as you eat and drink. You lose water as you breathe out, and also in your sweat. You lose salt in your sweat as well. You also lose water and salt in your **urine**, which is made in your **kidneys**.

Your kidneys can change the amount of salt and water lost in your urine, depending on your body conditions. They help to control the balance of water and mineral ions in your body. The concentration of the urine produced by your kidneys is controlled by both nerves and hormones.

So, for example, imagine drinking a lot of water all in one go. Your kidneys will remove the extra water from your blood and you will produce lots of very pale urine.

b What do your kidneys control?

Controlling temperature

It is vital that your deep core body **temperature** is kept at 37 °C. At this temperature your **enzymes** work best. At only a few degrees above or below normal body temperature the reactions in your cells stop and you will die.

Your body controls your temperature in several ways. For example, you can sweat to cool down and shiver to warm up. Your nervous system is very important in coordinating the way your body responds to changes in temperature.

Once your body temperature drops below 35 °C you are at risk of dying from hypothermia. Several hundred old people die from the effects of cold each year. So do a number of young people who get lost on mountains or try to walk home in the snow after a night out.

If your body temperature goes above about 40–42 °C your enzymes and cells don't work properly. This means that you may die of heat stroke or heat exhaustion.

c What is the ideal body temperature?

Controlling blood sugar

When you digest a meal, lots of sugar (glucose) passes into your blood. Left alone, your blood glucose levels would keep changing. The levels would be very high straight after a meal, but very low again a few hours later. This would cause chaos in your body.

However, the concentration of glucose in your blood is kept constant by hormones made in your **pancreas**. This means your body cells are provided with the constant supply of energy that they need.

> **d** What would happen to your blood sugar level if you ate a packet of sweets?

⊂⊃ **links**

For more information about the control of blood sugar, see B3 3.7 Controlling blood glucose.

Figure 3 Sweets like this are almost all sugar. When you eat them your body has to deal with the effect on your blood.

Summary questions

1 Copy and complete using the words below:

body   constant   homeostasis   hormones   internal   nervous

Conditions in the .... environment of your .... must be kept .... This is called .... The control is given by both your .... and your .... system.

2 Why is it important to control:
   a water levels in the body
   b the body temperature
   c sugar (glucose) levels in the blood?

3 **a** Look at the marathon runners in Figure 1. List the ways in which the running is affecting their:
   i water balance
   ii ion balance
   iii temperature.
   b It is much harder to run a marathon in a costume than in running clothes. Explain why this is.

Key points

- Humans need to maintain a constant internal environment, controlling levels of water, ions and blood sugar, as well as temperature.

- Homeostasis is the result of the coordination of your nervous system, your hormones and your body organs.

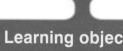

Hormones and the control of plant growth

Learning objectives

- What stimuli do plants respond to?
- How do plants respond to their environment?
- Why do farmers and gardeners use plant hormones?

Figure 1 Seedlings like this radish show you clearly how plant shoots respond to light – they grow towards it

??? Did you know ...?

The first scientists to show the way the shoot of a plant responds to light from one direction were Charles Darwin and his son Francis.

Practical

The effect of light on the growth of seedlings

You can investigate the effect of one-sided light on the growth of seedlings using a simple box with a hole cut in it and cress seedling growing in a Petri dish.

It is easy to see how animals, such as ourselves, take in information about the surroundings and then react to it. But plants also need to be coordinated. They are sensitive to light, water and gravity.

Plants are sensitive

When seeds are spread they may fall any way up in the soil. It is very important that when the seed starts to grow (germinate) the roots grow downwards into the soil. Then they can anchor the seedling and keep it stable. They can also take up the water and minerals needed for healthy growth.

At the same time the shoots need to grow upwards towards the light so they can **photosynthesise** as much as possible.

Plant roots are sensitive to gravity and water. The roots grow towards moisture and in the direction of the force of gravity. **Plant shoots** are sensitive to gravity and light. The shoots grow towards light and against the force of gravity. This means that whichever way up the seed lands, the plant always grows the right way up!

Plant responses

Plant responses happen as a result of plant hormones which coordinate and control growth. These responses are easy to see in young seedlings, but they also happen in adult plants. For example, the stems of a houseplant left on a windowsill will soon bend towards the light. The response of a plant to light is known as **phototropism**. The response of a plant to gravity is called **gravitropism** (also known as geotropism).

The responses of plant roots and shoots to light, gravity and moisture are controlled by a hormone called **auxin**. The response happens because of an uneven distribution of this hormone in the growing shoot or root. This causes an unequal growth rate. As a result the root or shoot bends in the right direction.

Phototropism can clearly be seen when a young shoot responds to light from one side only. The shoot will bend so it is growing towards the light. Auxin moves from the side of the shoot where the light is falling to the unlit side of the shoot. The cells on that side respond to the hormone by growing more – and so the shoot bends towards the light. Once light falls evenly on the shoot, the levels of auxin will be equal on all sides and so the shoot grows straight again.

Gravitropisms can be seen in roots and shoots. Auxin has different effects on root and shoot cells. High levels of auxin make shoot cells grow more but inhibit growth of root cells. This is why roots and shoots respond differently to gravity.

a What is the name of the plant hormone which controls phototropism and gravitropism?

1 A normal young bean plant is laid on its side in the dark. Auxin is equally spread through the tissues.

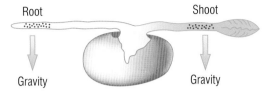

Root

Shoot

Gravity

Gravity

3 The root grows *more* on the side with *least* auxin, making it bend and grow down towards the force of gravity. When it has grown down, the auxin becomes evenly spread again.

The shoot grows *more* on the side with *most* auxin, making it bend and grow up away from the force of gravity. When it has grown up, the auxin becomes evenly spread again.

2 In the root, more auxin gathers on the lower side.

In the shoot, more auxin gathers on the lower side.

Figure 2 Gravitropism (or geotropism) in shoots and roots. The uneven distribution of the hormone auxin causes unequal growth rates so the roots grow down and the shoots grow up.

Using plant hormones **k**

Plant hormones can be used to manage plants grown in the garden or home. Farmers also use them to grow better crops.

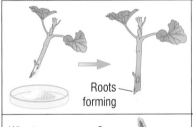

Roots forming

Gardeners and horticulturists rely on taking cuttings to produce lots of identical plants. Plant growth hormones are used as rooting powder. A little placed on the end of a cutting stimulates the growth of new roots and helps the cutting to grow into a new plant.

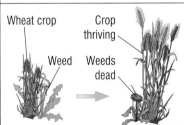

Wheat crop

Crop thriving

Weed

Weeds dead

You can use high doses of plant hormones as weed killers. Most weeds are broad-leaved plants which absorb a lot of hormone weed killer. This makes them go into rapid, uncontrolled growth which kills them. Narrow-leaved plants such as grasses and cereal are not affected, so the crop or lawn keeps growing well.

Figure 3 Some human uses of plant hormones

Summary questions

1 Copy and complete using the words below:

hormone auxin gravitropism light sensitive moisture

Plants are .... to ...., which is called phototropism. They respond to gravity which is .... Plants are also sensitive to .... These responses are coordinated by the plant .... called ....

2 Why are the responses of shoots and roots so important in the life of plants?

3 Explain carefully, using diagrams, how a plant shoot responds to light shining at it from one side only.

Key points

- Plants are sensitive to light, moisture and gravity.

- Plant responses are brought about by plant hormones (auxin).

- The responses of roots and shoots to stimuli such as light and gravity are the result of the unequal distribution of plant hormones.

- We can use plant growth hormones as weed killers and as rooting hormones on cuttings.

B1 2.7   Using hormones

Learning objectives

● What are some of the issues associated with the use of hormones to control human fertility?

● How much should we use plant hormones to produce our food?

Figure 1 Using hormones to control fertility has made it possible for women in their 50s and 60s to become pregnant and have a baby – but not everyone thinks this is a good idea

People can control human fertility. Infertile women can have treatment and have babies, while fertile women can choose not to have children. We can make thousands of identical plants and we can kill weeds as they grow. We do these things using hormones. But not everyone agrees with what is being done.

Woman 1

'I married late – I was 40 – and we wanted a family but my periods stopped when I was 41. Now we have a chance again. I haven't got any eggs so doctors will use FSH as a fertility drug to help them take lots of eggs from my donor, a younger woman. We want this child SO much!'

Woman 2

'We've got three lovely children. I decided to donate some of my eggs to help couples who aren't as lucky as we are. I don't mind the age of the woman who gets my eggs as long as she manages to have a baby and loves it!'

Man 1

'I think it is disgraceful and unnatural for women to have babies when they are older. We are interfering with nature and with God's will and no good will come of it. The mother might die before the child is an adult.'

Doctor

'All our evidence shows that infertility treatment can be just as successful in older women as it is in younger ones. We have to use artificial hormones to get the womb ready and use donor eggs, but once the women are pregnant their own hormones take over.'

Man 2

'I can't see anything wrong with older women having babies as long as they are fit and well. I know some people object to it, but some women have babies in their fifties naturally – and lots of men father children in their 60s and even their 70s and no one objects to that, do they?'

a Which hormone would doctors use to stimulate the ovaries of an egg donor?

⊂⊃ links
For information on plant growth hormones, look back at B1 2.6 Hormones and the control of plant growth.

Activity

Make your mind up!

There is a lot of debate about older mothers. Use what you have learned in this spread to help you write a 2–3-minute report for your school radio. Use the title: 'Older mothers – should science help?'

It will go out in a regular slot called 'Science issues', so students will be expecting some science as well as opinions.

Plant hormones, plant killers

Scientists have discovered that plant hormones such as auxin make effective weed killers. The hormones used in commercial weed killers are not natural hormones extracted from plants. They are made in chemical factories. These weed killers seem effective and safe. People use them on their lawns because the grass is not affected, but the weeds like dandelions and daisies are killed. Golf courses are kept weed-free in the same way.

Farmers around the world use hormone weed killers to kill off the weeds in cereal crops. They are one of the reasons why the yield of cereal crops is now so much bigger all across Europe. That means more food is available at cheaper prices.

But chemicals based on plant hormones (synthetic plant hormones) can cause serious problems. In the Vietnam War, one of these chemicals (Agent Orange) was sprayed on the forests. It works in the same way as natural plant hormones and in high doses it strips all the leaves off the trees. This made it easier for the US soldiers to find enemy fighters. It caused terrible damage to the forests. Not only that, hundreds of thousands of people were badly affected by the powerful chemicals.

b What is Agent Orange?

Practical

The effect of rooting compounds and weed killers on the growth of plants

You can investigate the effect of rooting hormone by taking some cuttings and growing half of them with rooting powder and half without.

Did you know ... ?

Agent Orange has been used to destroy areas of the Amazon rainforest, particularly for the building of the Tucurui dam in Brazil.

Activity

Is it worth it?

Synthetic plant hormones, like many scientific discoveries, can be used both to benefit people and to cause great harm. Some people have suggested that synthetic plant hormones should all be banned. Plan a short speech EITHER supporting this idea OR disagreeing with it.

Use evidence and persuasive writing in your speech.

Key points

- There are benefits and problems associated with the use of hormones to control fertility and these must be evaluated carefully.

- Plant hormones are very useful as weed killers but their use can damage the environment.

Summary questions

1 Make a table to summarise the main points for and against allowing older women to use hormones such as FSH to help them have a baby.

2 How can plant hormones be used to kill plants?

B1 3.1 Developing new medicines

Learning objectives

- What are the stages in testing and trialling a new drug?
- Why is testing new drugs so important?

Figure 1 The development of a new medicine takes millions of pounds, involves many people and lots of equipment

AQA **Examiner's tip**

Make sure you are clear that a medical drug is tested to establish:
- its effectiveness
- its toxicity
- the most appropriate dose.

AQA **Examiner's tip**

Remember, the cells, tissues and animals act as models to predict how the drug may behave in humans.

We are developing new medicines all the time, as scientists and doctors try to find ways of curing more diseases. We test new medicines in the laboratory. Every new medical treatment has to be extensively tested and trialled before it is used. This process makes sure that it works well and is as safe as possible.

A good medicine is:
- **Effective** – it must prevent or cure a disease or at least make you feel better.
- **Safe** – the drug must not be too toxic (poisonous) or have unacceptable side effects for the patient.
- **Stable** – you must be able to use the medicine under normal conditions and store it for some time.
- **Successfully taken into and removed from your body** – it must reach its target and be cleared from your system once it has done its work.

Developing and testing a new drug

When scientists research a new medicine they have to make sure all these conditions are met. It can take up to 12 years to bring a new medicine into your doctor's surgery. It can also cost a lot of money; up to about £350 million!

Researchers target a disease and make lots of possible new drugs. These are tested in the laboratory to find out if they are toxic and if they seem to do their job. They are tested on cells, tissues and even whole organs. Many chemicals fail at this stage.

The small numbers of chemicals which pass the earlier tests are now tested on animals. This is done to find out how they work in a whole living organism. It also gives information about possible doses and side effects. The tissues and animals are used as models to predict how the drugs may behave in humans.

Drugs that pass animal testing will be tested on human volunteers in clinical trials. First very low doses are given to healthy people to check for side effects. Then it is tried on a small number of patients to see if it treats the disease. If it seems to be safe and effective, bigger clinical trials take place to find the optimum dose for the drug.

If the medicine passes all the legal tests it is licensed so your doctor can prescribe it. Its safety will be monitored for as long as it is used.

a What are the important properties of a good new medicine?

Double-blind trials

In human trials, scientists use a **double-blind trial** to see just how effective the new medicine is. Some patients with the target disease agree to take part in the trials. They are either given a **placebo** that does not contain the drug or the new medicine. Neither the doctor nor the patients know who has received the real drug and who has received the placebo until the trial is complete. The patients' health is monitored carefully.

Often the placebo will contain a different drug that is already used to treat the disease. That is so the patient is not deprived of treatment by taking part in the trial.

Why do we test new medicines so thoroughly?

Thalidomide is a medicine which was developed in the 1950s as a sleeping pill. This was before there were agreed standards for testing new medicines. In particular, tests on pregnant animals, which we now know to be essential, were not carried out.

Then it was discovered that thalidomide stopped morning sickness during pregnancy. Because thalidomide seemed very safe for adults, it was assumed to be safe for unborn children. Doctors gave it to pregnant women to relieve their sickness.

Tragically, thalidomide was **not** safe for developing fetuses. It affected the fetuses of many women who took the drug in the early stages of pregnancy. They went on to give birth to babies with severe limb deformities.

The thalidomide tragedy led to a new law being passed. It set standards for the testing of all new medicines. Since the Medicines Act 1968, new medicines must be tested on animals to see if they have an effect on developing fetuses.

There is another twist in the thalidomide story. Doctors discovered it can treat leprosy. They started to use the drug against leprosy in the developing world but again children were born with abnormalities. Its use for leprosy has now been banned by the World Health Organisation (WHO).

However doctors are finding more uses for the drug. It can treat some autoimmune diseases (where the body attacks its own cells) and even some cancers. It is now used very carefully and never given to anyone who is or might become pregnant.

b Why was thalidomide prescribed to pregnant women?

Figure 2 This woman has limb deformities because her mother took thalidomide during her pregnancy. She was just one of thousands of people affected by the thalidomide tragedy, many of whom have gone on to live full and active lives.

Summary questions

1 Copy and complete using the words below:

effective trialled safe medicine stable tested

Every new .... has to be extensively .... and .... before you can use it to make sure that it works well. A good medicine can be taken into and removed from your body, and it is ...., ... and ....

2 **a** Testing a new medicine costs a lot of money and can take up to 12 years. Make a flow chart to show the main stages in testing new drugs.

   b Why is an active drug often used as the control in a clinical trial instead of a sugar pill placebo which does nothing?

3 **a** What were the flaws in the original development of thalidomide?

   b Why do you think that the World Health Organisation has stopped the use of thalidomide to treat leprosy but the drug is still being used in the developed world to treat certain rare conditions?

Key points

- When we develop new medicines they have to be tested and trialled extensively before we can use them.

- Drugs are tested to see if they work well. We also make sure they are not too toxic and have no unacceptable side effects.

- Thalidomide was developed as a sleeping pill and was found to prevent morning sickness in early pregnancy. It had not been fully tested and it caused birth defects.

B1 3.2 How effective are medicines?

Learning objectives

- What are statins?

- How good are statins at preventing cardiovascular disease?

- Can drugs you buy over the counter be as good as the drugs that your doctor prescribes?

The statin revolution

As you have seen, high blood cholesterol levels are linked to a higher than average risk of cardiovascular disease. In other words, you are more likely to have a heart attack or a stroke if your blood cholesterol is high.

Doctors now have an amazing weapon against high cholesterol levels and the problems they can cause. They can use a group of drugs called **statins**. Statins are drugs that lower the amount of cholesterol in your blood. They stop your liver producing too much cholesterol. Patients need to keep to a relatively low fat diet as well for the best effects.

a What are statins?

Here are some different opinions about these exciting new drugs:

A GP

'Some people just can't get their cholesterol level right by changing their diet. It doesn't matter how hard they try. I've been very pleased with the results using statins. Almost all my patients have now got healthy cholesterol levels. What's more, we have lost far fewer people to strokes and heart attacks since we started using the drugs.'

A Member of NICE (National Institute for Health and Clinical Excellence)

'We have looked at data from lots of really large, powerful research trials involving over 30 000 patients. The trials all show similar results. Using a statin drug can lower your chances of having a heart attack or stroke by 25 to 40%, and we didn't find too many side effects.'

Patient 1

'I'm so pleased with my new medicine, the pills have brought my cholesterol levels right down and I'm feeling really well.'

Patient 2

'The great thing about these new statins that the doctor has given me is that they control my cholesterol for me. It's back to the cream cakes and chips for me, and I won't have to worry about my heart!'

Patient 3

'I'm very worried about possible side effects with these new tablets – the leaflet said they can cause liver damage. I know my cholesterol levels were very high without the tablets, but I'm not sure about taking these tablets. I don't want my liver to be damaged!'

AQA **Examiner's tip**

Statins are medical drugs which are used to reduce cholesterol levels in the blood. This reduces the risk of heart disease.

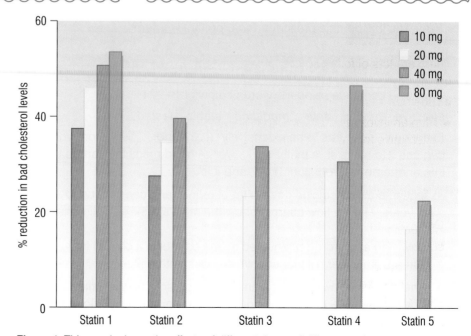

Figure 1 This graph shows the effects of different doses of different statins on the 'bad' cholesterol in the blood

Prescribed drugs *v.* non-prescribed

The medicines your doctor prescribes for you have been thoroughly tested and trialled. However some people choose to use non-prescribed medicines they buy for themselves. Some of these medicines are little more than sugar, flavouring and water. They will not hurt you – but they won't make you better either.

Some non-prescribed medicines can be dangerous. They are made from herbs and 'natural products' but can contain potentially dangerous chemicals. Remember that many of our effective prescribed medicines come from living organisms.

You can only tell if a non-prescribed medicine is as effective as a prescribed medicine if it undergoes double-blind clinical trials. Very few of them are ever evaluated in this way because of the expense.

One example of a non-prescribed medicine which seems to work well is the herb St John's Wort. If you suffer from **depression** your doctor may prescribe Prozac (fluoxetine). Some people prefer to use non-prescribed St John's Wort (*hypericum*). It is a herbal remedy which has been used as an antidepressant for around 2000 years.

There have now been some scientific studies carried out. They compare the effectiveness of St John's Wort to the most commonly used antidepressant medicines. The evidence so far suggests that the herbal treatment is as effective as the most common medicines used to treat depression. It also seems more effective than placebos and it has fewer side effects than the prescribed medicines.

> **b** Look at Figure 2. How much improvement in depression scores was seen over 12 weeks of using Prozac and St John's Wort?

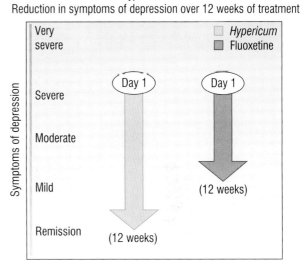

St. John's Wort *hypericum v.* Prozac fluoxetine
Reduction in symptoms of depression over 12 weeks of treatment

Figure 2 Data from one of a number of studies which show that *hypericum* (St John's Wort) is at least as effective as commonly prescribed drugs in treating depression

Activity

There are lots of food products which claim to lower blood cholesterol. Investigate one of these claims.

- See how much evidence you can discover.
- Plan an investigation to help show whether this dietary supplement or alternative food can really lower blood cholesterol levels.

Summary questions

1. Copy and complete using the words below:

   statins   cholesterol   lower   cardiovascular   risk

   If your blood .... levels are high you have an increased .... of .... disease. Drugs called .... can .... your risk and help to keep you healthy.

2. Explain why is it unwise to think that non-prescribed drugs cannot cause harmful side effects.

links

For more information on cholesterol levels, see B1 1.3 Inheritance, exercise and health.

Key points

- Statins lower the amount of cholesterol in the blood and can reduce the risk of cardiovascular disease by up to 40%.

- The effectiveness of both prescribed and non-prescribed drugs can only be measured in proper double-blind trials.

B1 3.3 Drugs

Learning objectives

- What is a drug?
- What is addiction?
- Why are drugs such as cannabis, cocaine and heroin such a problem?

A **drug** is a substance that alters the way in which your body works. It can affect your mind, your body or both. In every society there are certain drugs which people use for medicine, and other drugs which they use for pleasure.

Many of the drugs that are used both for medicine and for recreation come originally from natural substances, often plants. Many of them have been known to and used by indigenous (long-term inhabitants of an area) peoples for many years. Usually some of the drugs that are used for pleasure are socially acceptable and legal, while others are illegal.

Figure 1 Millions of pounds worth of illegal drugs are brought into the UK every year. It is a constant battle for the police to find and destroy drugs like these.

a What do we mean by 'indigenous peoples'?

Drugs are everywhere in our society. People drink coffee and tea, smoke cigarettes and have a beer, an alcopop or a glass of wine. They think nothing of it. Yet all of these things contain drugs – caffeine, nicotine and alcohol (the chemical ethanol). These drugs are all legal.

Other drugs, such as cocaine, ecstasy and heroin are illegal. Which drugs are legal and which are not varies from country to country. Alcohol is legal in the UK as long as you are over 18, but it is illegal in many Arab states. Heroin is illegal almost everywhere.

b Give an example of one drug which is legal and one which is illegal in the UK.

Because drugs affect the chemistry of your body, they can cause great harm. This is even true of drugs we use as medicines. However, because medical drugs make you better, it is usually worth taking the risk.

But legal recreational drugs, such as alcohol and tobacco, and illegal substances, such as solvents, cannabis and cocaine, can cause terrible damage to your body. Yet they offer no long-term benefits to you at all.

⚬⚬ links

For more information on the mental health problems that can be caused by cannabis, see B1 3.5 Does cannabis lead to hard drugs?

What is addiction?

Some drugs change the chemical processes in your body so that you may become addicted to them. You can become dependent on them. If you are addicted to a drug, you cannot manage properly without it. Some drugs, for example heroin and cocaine, are very addictive.

Once addicted, you generally need more and more of the drug to keep you feeling normal. When addicts try to stop using drugs they usually feel very unwell. They often have aches and pains, sweating, shaking, headaches and cravings for their drug. We call these **withdrawal symptoms**.

c What do we mean by 'addiction'?

The problems of drug abuse

People take drugs for a reason. Drugs can make you feel very good about yourself. They can make you feel happy and they can make you feel as if your problems no longer matter. Unfortunately, because most recreational drugs are addictive, they can soon become a problem themselves.

No drugs are without a risk. Cannabis is often thought of as a relatively 'soft' – and therefore safe – drug. But evidence is growing which shows that cannabis smoke contains chemicals which can cause mental illness to develop in some people.

Hard drugs, such as cocaine and heroin, are extremely addictive. Using them often leads to very severe health problems. Some of these come from the drugs themselves. Others come from the lifestyle that often goes with drugs.

Because these drugs are illegal, they are expensive. Young people often end up turning to crime to pay for their drug habit. They don't eat properly or look after themselves. They can also contract serious illnesses, such as hepatitis, STDs (sexually transmitted diseases) and HIV/Aids especially if drugs are taken intravenously (via a needle).

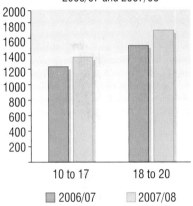

Figure 2 Illegal drugs are often linked with crime. In the UK more and more young people are being arrested for drug offences – using or selling illegal drugs.

Summary questions

1 Copy and complete using the words below:

mind cocaine ecstasy legal alcohol drug body

A .... alters the way in which your body works. It can affect the ...., the .... or both. Some drugs are .... e.g. caffeine and .... Other drugs, such as ...., ... and heroin are illegal.

2 **a** Why do people often need more and more of a drug?
 b What happens if you stop taking a drug when you are addicted to it?

3 **a** Why do people take drugs?
 b Explain some of the problems linked with using cannabis, cocaine and heroin.
 c Look at Figure 2. What does this tell you about the difference in drug use between boys and girls?
 d What does Figure 2 tell you about the trend in drug use in young people?
 e Why do you think young people continue to take these drugs when they are well aware of the dangers?

Key points

- Drugs change the chemical processes in your body, so you may become addicted to them.
- Addiction is when you become physically or mentally dependent on a drug.
- Smoking cannabis may cause mental health problems.
- Hard drugs, such as cocaine and heroin, are very addictive and can cause serious health problems.

B1 3.5

Does cannabis lead to hard drugs?

Learning objectives

- How do people move from using recreational drugs to hard drugs?

- Is cannabis harmful?

Figure 2 In the minds of many people – parents, teachers and politicians – cannabis is a 'gateway' drug. It opens the door to the use of other much harder drugs such as cocaine and heroin. Your health – and indeed your life itself – is at risk. How accurate is this picture?

Cannabis – the facts?

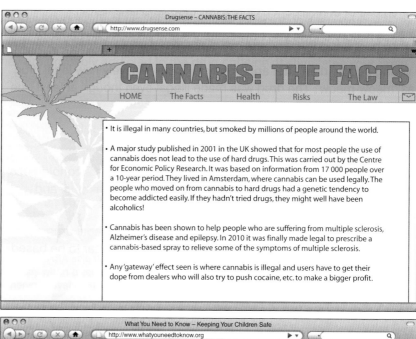

Drugsense – CANNABIS: THE FACTS

http://www.drugsense.com

CANNABIS: THE FACTS

| HOME | The Facts | Health | Risks | The Law |

- It is illegal in many countries, but smoked by millions of people around the world.

- A major study published in 2001 in the UK showed that for most people the use of cannabis does not lead to the use of hard drugs. This was carried out by the Centre for Economic Policy Research. It was based on information from 17 000 people over a 10-year period. They lived in Amsterdam, where cannabis can be used legally. The people who moved on from cannabis to hard drugs had a genetic tendency to become addicted easily. If they hadn't tried drugs, they might well have been alcoholics!

- Cannabis has been shown to help people who are suffering from multiple sclerosis, Alzheimer's disease and epilepsy. In 2010 it was finally made legal to prescribe a cannabis-based spray to relieve some of the symptoms of multiple sclerosis.

- Any 'gateway' effect seen is where cannabis is illegal and users have to get their dope from dealers who will also try to push cocaine, etc. to make a bigger profit.

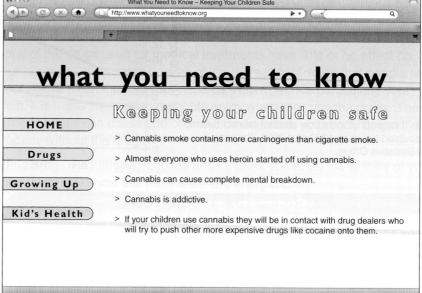

What You Need to Know – Keeping Your Children Safe

http://www.whatyouneedtoknow.org

what you need to know

Keeping your children safe

HOME

Drugs

Growing Up

Kid's Health

- Cannabis smoke contains more carcinogens than cigarette smoke.

- Almost everyone who uses heroin started off using cannabis.

- Cannabis can cause complete mental breakdown.

- Cannabis is addictive.

- If your children use cannabis they will be in contact with drug dealers who will try to push other more expensive drugs like cocaine onto them.

Figure 1 How can you find out the truth about cannabis and the effect it might have on you, your friend or – if you are a parent – your child?

a What diseases are helped by the chemicals in cannabis?

Cannabis – where do you stand?

A lot of scientific research has been done into the effects of cannabis on our health. The links between cannabis use and addiction to hard drugs has also been investigated.

Unfortunately many of the studies have been quite small. They have not used large sample sizes, so the evidence is not strong.

The UK Government downgraded cannabis to a Class C drug in 2004. Then stronger negative evidence emerged. It found that cannabis use can trigger mental health problems in people who are vulnerable to such problems. In 2009 the decision to downgrade was reversed and cannabis is now a Class B drug again.

What the doctors say

● The evidence is clear that for some people cannabis use can trigger mental illness. This may be serious and permanent. It is particularly the case for people who have a genetic tendency to mental health problems.

● A study has been carried out on 1600 14- to 15-year-old students in Australia. It showed that the youngsters who use cannabis regularly have a significantly higher risk of depression. However it doesn't work the other way round. Children who are already suffering depression are no more likely than anyone else to use cannabis.

Figure 3 The doctors at the Royal College of Psychiatrists are the people who deal with mental health problems of all kinds. They have some real concerns about cannabis-use.

● All the evidence suggests that teenagers are particularly vulnerable to mental health problems triggered by cannabis. Consider a teenager who starts smoking cannabis before they are 15. They are four times more likely to develop schizophrenia or another psychotic illness by the time they are 26 than a non-user.

Untangling the evidence

The evidence shows that almost all heroin users were originally cannabis users. This is not necessarily a case of cannabis use causing heroin addiction. Almost all cannabis users are originally smokers – but we don't claim that smoking cigarettes leads to cannabis use! In fact the vast majority of smokers do not go on to use cannabis. Just as the vast majority of cannabis users do not move on to hard drugs like heroin. Most studies suggest that cannabis can act as a 'gateway' to other drugs. However, that is **not** because it makes people want a stronger drug but because it puts them in touch with illegal drug dealers.

b How much does using cannabis before you are 15 appear to increase your risk of developing serious mental illness?

Summary questions

1 **a** What is meant by a 'gateway' drug?
  b Why is cannabis considered a gateway drug?

2 Cannabis is linked to some mental health problems, but tobacco is known to cause hundreds of thousands of deaths each year through heart disease and lung cancer. Why do you think cannabis is illegal and tobacco is legal?

Activity

You are going to set up a classroom debate. The subject is:

'We believe that cannabis should be made a legal drug.'

You are going to prepare **two** short speeches – one **for** the idea of legalising cannabis and one **against**.

You can use the information on these pages and also look elsewhere for information. Try books and leaflets and on the internet.

In both of your speeches you must base your arguments on scientific evidence as well as considering the social, moral and ethical implications of any change in the law. You have to be prepared to argue your case (both for and against) and answer any questions – so do your research well!

Key points

● People can progress from using recreational drugs such as cannabis to addiction to hard drugs because cannabis is illegal and has to be obtained from a drug dealer.

● Cannabis smoke contains chemicals which may cause mental illness in some people. Teenagers are particularly vulnerable to this effect.

B1 3.6 Drugs in sport

Learning objectives

- Can drugs make you better at sport?
- Is it ethical to use drugs to win?

The world of sport has a big problem with the illegal use of drugs. In theory, the only difference between competitors should be their natural ability and the amount they train. However, there are many performance-enhancing drugs that allow athletes to improve on their natural ability. The people who do this get labelled as cheats if they are caught.

Figure 1 Weightlifters need a lot of muscle so it can be tempting to cheat. Eleven Bulgarian weightlifters tested positive for anabolic steroids and were disqualified from the 2008 Olympics.

Performance-enhancing drugs

Different sports need different things from the competitors.

Anabolic **steroids** are drugs that help build up muscle mass. They are used by athletes who need to be very strong, such as weightlifters. Athletes who need lots of muscle to be very fast, such as sprinters, also sometimes use anabolic steroids. Taking anabolic steroids and careful training means you can make much more muscle and build it where you want it.

Strong painkilling drugs can allow an athlete to train and compete with an injury, causing further and perhaps permanent damage. These drugs are illegal for use by people involved in sport.

Different sports need great stamina – marathons and long distance cycling races are two examples. Some cyclists (and other athletes) use a drug to stimulate their body to make more red blood cells. This means they can carry more oxygen to their muscles. The drug is a compound found naturally in the body so drug-testers are looking for abnormally high levels of it.

Fast reactions are vital in many sports, and there are drugs that will make you very alert and on edge. On the other hand, in sports such as darts and shooting, you need very steady hands. Some athletes take drugs to slow down their heart and reduce any shaking in their hands to try and win medals.

a What are anabolic steroids and why do athletes use them?

Figure 2 The Tour de France has had many drug problems. Cyclists have died after using illegal drugs to help them go faster. Floyd Landis, the winner in 2006, was disqualified for using steroids.

Catching the cheats

Athletes found using illegal drugs are banned from competing. The sports authorities keep producing new tests for drugs and run random drugs tests to try and identify the cheats. But some competitors are always looking for new ways to cheat without being found out. So the illegal use of drugs in sport continues. Some medicines contain banned drugs which can enhance performance, so athletes need to be very careful so they don't end up 'cheating' by accident.

The ethics of using drugs in sport

There are lots of ways an athlete can improve their performance. Where does wanting to win end and cheating begin? Is the use of performance-enhancing substances ever acceptable in sport? These are questions scientists cannot answer – society has to decide.

For example, if an athlete lives and trains at high altitude for several weeks, their body makes a hormone which increases their red blood cell count. This is legal. But it is illegal to buy the hormone and inject it to make more red blood cells.

Here are some of the arguments that athletes use to justify the use of substances that are banned and could do them harm:

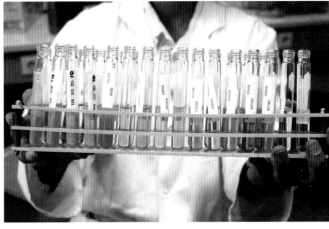

Figure 3 Athletes can be asked to produce a urine sample for a drug test at any time, whether they are competing, training or resting

- They want to win.
- They feel that other athletes are using these substances, and unless they take them they will be left behind.
- They think the health risks are just scare stories.
- Some athletes claim that they did not know they were taking drugs – their coaches supply them hidden in 'supplements'.

There are a number of ethical points that society needs to consider. Top athletes compete for the satisfaction of winning and millions of people enjoy watching them. Most performance-enhancing drugs risk the health of the athlete at the high doses used in training. They can even cause death. Even if the individual is prepared to take the risk, is this ethically acceptable? At the moment most people say 'no'.

Often the substances used by cheats are so expensive, or new, that most competitors can't afford them. This gives the richest competitors an unfair advantage. For example, most athletes could afford anabolic steroids if they wanted to use them, but not the most recent versions that are not detected by the drug-testing process.

There are some people who think that athletes should be able to do what they like with their bodies. At the moment most of society does not agree with this view – what do you think?

b Why do athletes use drugs which could cause them harm?

> ## AQA Examiner's tip
>
> Make sure you understand why athletes are banned from using some medical drugs.

Summary questions

1 Copy and complete using the words below:

   compete   performance-enhancing   muscles   steroids   athletes

   Some .... use .... drugs to help them .... more successfully. Many use anabolic .... which help them to develop bigger ....

2 Suggest the advantages and disadvantages to an athlete of using banned performance-enhancing drugs to help win a competition.

3 It has been suggested that athletes be allowed to use any drugs to improve their performance. Suggest arguments for and against this proposal.

> ### Key points
>
> - Anabolic steroids and other banned performance-enhancing drugs are used by some athletes.
> - The use of performance-enhancing drugs is considered unethical by most people.

Summary questions

1 a Why do new medicines need to be tested and trialled before doctors can use them to treat their patients?

b Why is the development of a new medicine so expensive?

c Do you think it would ever be acceptable to use a new medicine before all the trials had been completed?

2 a What is a statin?

b How do statins help reduce the number of people who suffer from cardiovascular disease?

c Which of the statins in Figure 1, B1 3.2 is most effective?

d The most effective drug is not always the one used. Why do you think other statins might be prescribed?

3 Some students decided to test whether drinking coffee could affect heart rate. They asked the class to help them with their investigation. They divided the class into two groups. Both groups had their pulses taken. They gave one group a drink of coffee. They waited for 10 minutes and then took their pulses again. They then followed the same procedure with the second group.

a What do you think the second group were asked to drink?

b State a control variable that should have been used.

c Explain why it would have been a good idea not to tell the two groups exactly what they were drinking.

d Study this table of results that they produced.

Group	Increase in pulse rate (beats per minute)
With caffeine	12, 15, 13, 10, 15, 16, 10, 15, 16, 21, 14, 13, 16
Without caffeine	4, 3, 4, 5, 7, 5, 7, 4, 2, 6, 5, 4, 7

Can you detect any evidence for systematic error in these results? If so, describe this evidence.

e Is there any evidence for a random error in these results? If so, describe this evidence.

f What is the range for the increase in pulse rates without caffeine?

g What is the mean (or average) increase in pulse rate:
   i with caffeine?
   ii without caffeine?

4 Look at Figure 3, B1 3.4. Compare the data in that graph to Figure 2, B1 3.3. Both show impact of drug taking on individuals in society.

a What are the similarities between the two data sets?

b Explain the relative impact of legal and illegal drugs on individuals and on society.

5 a Why do some athletes use illegal drugs, such as anabolic steroids, when they are training or competing?

b What are the arguments for and against the use of these performance-enhancing drugs?

c People sometimes use illegal performance-enhancing drugs on horses. They use pain killers, stimulants and substances which make the skin on their legs very sensitive. Sometimes they are given sedatives so they run slowly. Discuss the ethical aspects of giving performance-changing drugs to animals.

AQA Examination-style questions

1 People take drugs for many different reasons.

alcohol   heroin   penicillin   statin   steroid thalidomide

Choose a word from above to match the following sentences.

a an illegal drug which is highly addictive (1)

b a drug used by athletes to make them perform better (1)

c a medical drug which is used to reduce cholesterol levels (1)

2 A drug company wants to test a new painkiller called PainGo2. The company hope that the new drug will cure headaches quicker than PainGo1.

PainGo2 has to be tested in clinical trials. PainGo2 is twice as strong as PainGo1.

Phase 1 trial – a few healthy people will be given one or two tablets of PainGo2.

Phase 2 trial – a small group (200–300) of patients with headaches will be given PainGo2.

Phase 3 trial – 3 large groups (2000 in each group) of patients with headaches will be given either PainGo2 or PainGo1 or a placebo.

a What is the purpose of the Phase 1 trial? (1)

b Suggest why in Phase 2 the patients were asked to record how they felt after taking the PainGo2.

Suggest why. (1)

c What is a placebo? (1)

d Phase 3 was done as a double-blind trial by doctors who had patients with headaches.

In a double-blind trial who will know who is given the new drug?

Choose your answer from the choices below.

A *the patient only*

B *the doctor only*

C *both the doctor and the patient*

D *neither the doctor nor the patient* (1)

e Why is it important to use the placebo in the Phase 3 trial? (1)

f Why are some patients given PainGo1 in Phase 3? (1)

3 a Give **one** example of:
  i a legal recreational drug (1)
  ii an illegal recreational drug. (1)

b Some recreational drugs are addictive.
  i Give **one** example of a recreational drug that is very addictive. (1)
  ii Explain how the action of a drug makes a person become addicted to it. (1)

c Some doctors think that smoking cannabis causes depression. Doctors investigated the cannabis smoking habits of 1500 young adults.

The table shows the percentage of cannabis smokers in the investigation who became depressed.

How many times the men or women had smoked cannabis in the last 12 months	Percentage of men who became depressed	Percentage of women who became depressed
Less than 5 times	9	16
More than 5 times, but less than once per week	10	17
1–4 times per week	12	31
Every day	15	68

From the data, give **two** conclusions that can be drawn about the relationship between cannabis and depression. (2)

AQA, 2007

4 *In this question you will be assessed on using good English, organising information clearly and using specialist terms where appropriate.*

Read the description of an investigation into the link between smoking cannabis and heroin addiction.

> Six 'teenage' rats were given a small dose of THC – the active chemical in cannabis – every three days between the ages of 28 and 49 days. This is the equivalent of human ages 12 to 18.
>
> The amount of THC given was roughly equivalent to a human smoking one cannabis 'joint' every three days.
>
> A control group of six 'teenage' rats did not receive THC.
>
> After 56 days catheters (narrow tubes) were inserted in all twelve of the now adult rats and they were able to self-administer heroin by pushing a lever.
>
> All the rats began to self-administer heroin frequently. After a while, they stabilised their daily intake at a certain level.
>
> The ones that had been on THC as 'teenagers' stabilised their heroin intake at a much higher level than the others. They appeared to be less sensitive to the effects of heroin. This pattern continued throughout their lives.
>
> Reduced sensitivity to the heroin means that the rats take larger doses. This has been shown to increase the risk of addiction.

Evaluate this investigation with respect to establishing a link between cannabis smoking and heroin addiction in humans. Remember to include a conclusion to your evaluation. (6)

AQA, 2007

B1 4.2 | Adaptation in animals

Learning objectives

- How can hair help animals survive in very cold climates?
- What are the advantages – and disadvantages – of lots of body fat?
- How do animals adapt to hot, dry climates?

Animals have adaptations that help them to get the food and mates they need to survive and reproduce. They also have adaptations for survival in the conditions where they normally live.

Animals in cold climates

To survive in a cold environment you must be able to keep yourself warm. Animals which live in very cold places, such as the Arctic, are adapted to reduce the energy they lose from their bodies. You lose body heat through your body surface (mainly your skin). The amount of energy you lose is closely linked to your surface area : volume (SA : V) ratio.

AQA Examiner's tip

Remember, the *larger* the animal, the *smaller* the surface area : volume (SA : V) ratio.

Animals often have *increased* surface areas in *hot* climates, and *decreased* surface areas in *cold* climates.

∞ links

For more information about other implications of surface area : volume ratios, see B3 1.4 Exchanging materials – the lungs.

Maths skills

Surface area : volume ratio

The surface area : volume ratio is very important when you look at the adaptations of animals that live in cold climates. It explains why so many Arctic mammals, such as seals, walruses, whales and polar bears, are relatively large.

The ratio of surface area to volume falls as objects get bigger. You can see this clearly in the diagram. The larger the surface area : volume ratio, the larger the rate of energy loss. So mammals in a cold climate grow to a large size. This keeps their surface area : volume ratio as small as possible and so helps them hold on to their body heat.

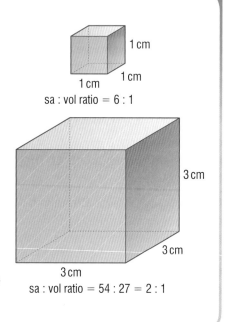

1 cm
1 cm
1 cm
sa : vol ratio = 6 : 1

3 cm
3 cm
3 cm
sa : vol ratio = 54 : 27 = 2 : 1

a Why are so many Arctic animals large?

Animals in very cold climates often have other adaptations too. The surface area of the thinly skinned areas of their bodies, like their ears, is usually very small. This reduces their energy loss.

Many Arctic mammals have plenty of insulation, both inside and out. Inside they have blubber (a thick layer of fat that builds up under the skin). On the outside a thick fur coat will insulate an animal very effectively. These adaptations really reduce the amount of energy lost through their skin.

The fat layer also provides a food supply. Animals often build up their fat in the summer. Then they can live off their body fat through the winter when there is almost no food.

b List three ways in which Arctic animals keep warm in winter.

Figure 1 The Arctic is a cold and bleak environment. However, the animals that live there are well adapted for survival. Notice the large size, small ears, thick coat and white camouflage of this polar bear.

Camouflage

Camouflage is important both to predators (so their prey doesn't see them coming) and to prey (so they can't be seen). The colours that would camouflage an Arctic animal in summer against plants would stand out against the snow in winter. Many Arctic animals, including the Arctic fox, the Arctic hare and the stoat, have grey or brown summer coats that change to pure white in the winter. Polar bears don't change colour. They have no natural predators on the land. They hunt seals all year round in the sea, where their white colour makes them less visible among the ice.

The colour of the coat of a lioness is another example of effective camouflage. The sandy brown colour matches perfectly with the dried grasses of the African savannah. Her colour hides the lioness from the grazing animals which are her prey.

Surviving in dry climates

Dry climates are often also hot climates – like deserts. Deserts are very difficult places for animals to live. There is scorching heat during the day, followed by bitter cold at night. Water is also in short supply.

The biggest challenges if you live in a desert are:
● coping with the lack of water
● stopping body temperature from getting too high.

Many desert animals are adapted to need little or nothing to drink. They get the water they need from the food they eat.

Mammals keep their body temperature the same all the time. So as the environment gets hotter, they have to find ways of keeping cool. Sweating means they lose water, which is not easy to replace in the desert.

c Why do mammals try to cool down without sweating in hot, dry conditions?

Animals that live in hot conditions adapt their behaviour to keep cool. They are often most active in the early morning and late evening, when it is not so hot. During the cold nights and the heat of the day they rest in burrows where the temperature doesn't change much.

Many desert animals are quite small, so their surface area is large compared to their volume. This helps them to lose heat through their skin. They often have large, thin ears to increase their surface area for losing energy.

Another adaptation of many desert animals is to have thin fur. Any fur they do have is fine and silky. They also have relatively little body fat stored under the skin. These features make it easier for them to lose energy through the surface of the skin.

Figure 2 Jerboas are very small and elephants are very big. They both show clear adaptations that help them survive in the hot, dry places where they live.

Summary questions

1 **a** List the main problems that face animals living in cold conditions like the Arctic.
   b List the main problems that face animals living in the desert.

2 Animals that live in the Arctic are adapted to keep warm through the winter. Describe three of these adaptations and explain how they work.

3 **a** Using Figure 2, describe the visible adaptations of a jerboa and an elephant to keeping cool in hot conditions.
   b Suggest other ways in which animals might be adapted to survive in hot, dry conditions.

Key points

● All living things have adaptations that help them to survive in the conditions where they live.

● Animals that are adapted for cold environments are often large, with a small **surface area : volume** (SA : V) ratio. They have thick insulating layers of fat and fur.

● Changing coat colour in the different seasons gives animals year-round camouflage.

● Adaptations for hot, dry environments include a large SA : V ratio, thin fur, little body fat and behaviour patterns that avoid the heat of the day.

B1 4.3

Adaptation in plants

Learning objectives

- How do plants lose water?

- How are plants adapted to live in dry conditions?

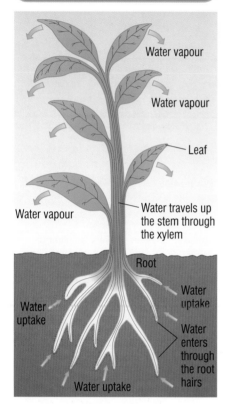

Figure 1 Plants lose water vapour from the surface of their leaves. When the conditions are hot and dry, they may lose water very quickly.

∞ links

For information on surface area:volume ratio, look back at B1 4.2 Adaptation in animals.

Figure 2 Marram grass grows on sand dunes. It has tightly curled leaves to reduce the surface area for water loss so it can survive the dry conditions.

Plants need light, water, space and nutrients to survive. There are some places where plants cannot grow. In deep oceans no light penetrates and so plants cannot photosynthesise. In the icy wastes of the Antarctic it is simply too cold for plants to grow.

Almost everywhere else, including the hot, dry areas of the world, you find plants growing. Without them there would be no food for the animals. But plants need water for photosynthesis and to keep their tissues supported. If a plant does not get the water it needs, it wilts and eventually dies.

a Why do plants need water?

Plants take in water from the soil through their roots. It moves up through the plant and into the leaves. There are small openings called **stomata** in the leaves of a plant. These open to allow gases in and out for photosynthesis and **respiration**. At the same time water vapour is lost through the stomata by evaporation.

The rate at which a plant loses water is linked to the conditions it is growing in. When it is hot and dry, photosynthesis and respiration take place quickly. As a result, plants also lose water vapour very quickly. Plants that live in very hot, dry conditions need special adaptations to survive. Most of them either reduce their surface area so they lose less water or store water in their tissues. Some do both!

b How do plants lose water from their leaves?

Changing surface area

When it comes to stopping water loss through the leaves, the surface area:volume ratio is very important to plants. A few desert plants have broad leaves with a large surface area. These leaves collect the dew that forms in the cold evenings. They then funnel the water towards their shallow roots.

Some plants in dry environments have curled leaves. This reduces the surface area of the leaf. It also traps a layer of moist air around the leaf. This reduces the amount of water the plant loses by evaporation.

Most plants that live in dry conditions have leaves with a very small surface area. This adaptation cuts down the area from which water can be lost. Some desert plants have small fleshy leaves with a thick cuticle to keep water loss down. The cuticle is a waxy covering on the leaf that stops water evaporating.

The best-known desert plants are the cacti. Their leaves have been reduced to spines with a very small surface area indeed. This means the cactus only loses a tiny amount of water. Not only that, its sharp spines also put animals off eating the cactus.

c Why do plants often reduce the surface area of their leaves?

Collecting water

Many plants that live in very dry conditions have specially adapted and very big root systems. They may have extensive root systems that spread over a very wide area, roots that go down a very long way, or both. These adaptations allow the plant to take up as much water as possible from the soil. The mesquite tree has roots that grow as far as 50 m down into the soil.

Storing water

Some plants cope with dry conditions by storing water in their tissues. When there is plenty of water after a period of rain, the plant stores it. Some plants use their fleshy leaves to store water. Others use their stems or roots.

For example, cacti don't just rely on their spiny leaves to help them survive in dry conditions. The fat green body of a cactus is its stem, which is full of water-storing tissue. These adaptations make cacti the most successful plants in a hot, dry climate.

Figure 3 A large saguaro cactus in the desert loses less than one glass of water a day. A UK apple tree can lose a whole bath of water in the same amount of time!

d In which parts can a plant store its water?

CO links
For more information about water loss in plants, see B3 1.9 Transpiration.

AQA **Examiner's tip**

Remember that plants need their stomata open for photosynthesis and respiration. This is why they lose water by evaporation from their leaves.

Summary questions

1 Copy and complete using the words below:

adaptations desert plants spines stems water

Cacti are .... that live in the .... They have two main .... to help them survive. Their leaves have become .... and they store .... in their ....

2 **a** Explain why plants lose water through their leaves all the time.
   b Why does this make living in a dry place such a problem?

3 Plants living in dry conditions have adaptations to reduce water loss from their leaves. Give three of these and explain how they work.

Key points

- Plants lose water vapour from the surface of their leaves.

- Plant adaptations for surviving in dry conditions include reducing the surface area of the leaves, having water-storage tissues and having extensive root systems.

B1 4.4 Competition in animals

Figure 1 Some herbivores only feed on one particular plant. Pandas only eat bamboo, so they are open to competition from other animals or to diseases that damage bamboo.

Figure 2 The coral snake (top) is poisonous but the milk snake (bottom) is not. The milk snake is a mimic – it looks like the coral snake. As long as the two species live in the same area the milk snake is protected. Other animals and people leave it alone thinking it is a poisonous coral snake!

Animals and plants grow alongside lots of other living things. Some will be from the same species and others will be completely different. In any area there is only a limited amount of food, water and space, and a limited number of mates. As a result, living organisms have to compete for the things they need.

The best adapted organisms are most likely to win the **competition** for resources. They will be most likely to survive and produce healthy offspring.

> **a** Why do living organisms compete?

What do animals compete for?

Animals compete for many things, including:

- food
- **territory**
- mates.

Competition for food

Competition for food is very common. Herbivores sometimes feed on many types of plant, and sometimes on only one or two different sorts. Many different species of herbivores will all eat the same plants. Just think how many types of animals eat grass!

The animals that eat a wide range of plants are most likely to be successful. If you are a picky eater, you risk dying out if anything happens to your only food source. An animal with wider tastes will just eat something else for a while!

Competition is common among carnivores. They compete for prey. Small mammals like mice are eaten by animals like foxes, owls, hawks and domestic cats. The different types of animals all hunt the same mice. So the animals which are best adapted to the area will be most successful.

Carnivores have to compete with their own species for their prey as well as with different species. Some successful predators are adapted to have long legs for running fast and sharp eyes to spot prey. These features will be passed on to their offspring.

Animals often avoid direct competition with members of other species when they can. It is the competition between members of the same species which is most intense.

Prey animals compete with each other too – to be the one that *isn't* caught! Their adaptations help prevent them becoming a meal for a predator. Some animals contain poisons which make anything that eats them sick or even kills them. Very often these animals also have bright warning colours so that predators quickly learn which animals to avoid. Poison arrow frogs are a good example.

> **b** Give one useful adaptation for a herbivore and one for a carnivore.

Competition for territory

For many animals, setting up and defending a territory is vital. A territory may simply be a place to build a nest. It could be all the space needed for an animal to find food and reproduce. Most animals cannot reproduce successfully if they have no territory. So they will compete for the best spaces. This helps to make sure they will be able to find enough food for themselves and for their young.

Competition for a mate

Competition for mates can be fierce. In many species the male animals put a lot of effort into impressing the females. The males compete in different ways to win the privilege of mating with a female.

In some species – like deer and lions – the males fight between themselves. Then the winner gets the females.

Many male animals display to the females to get their attention. Some birds have spectacular adaptations to help them stand out. Male peacocks have the most amazing tail feathers. They use them for displaying to other males (to warn them off) and to females (to attract them).

What makes a successful competitor?

A successful competitor is an animal that is adapted to be better at finding food or a mate than the other members of its own species. It also needs to be better at finding food than the members of other local species. It must be able to breed successfully.

Many animals are successful because they avoid competition with other species as much as possible. They feed in a way that no other local animals do, or they eat a type of food that other animals avoid. For example, one plant can feed many animals without direct competition. While caterpillars eat the leaves, greenfly drink the sap, butterflies suck nectar from the flowers and beetles feed on pollen.

Figure 3 The territory of a gannet pair may be small but without a space they cannot build a nest and reproduce

Figure 4 The spectacular display of a male peacock attracts females. Unlike deer and lions he doesn't need to fight and risk injury.

AQA Examiner's tip

Learn to look at an animal and spot the adaptations that make it a successful competitor.

Summary questions

1 a Give an example of animals competing with members of the same species for food.
   b Give an example of animals competing with members of other species for food.
   c Animals that rely on a single type of food can easily become extinct. Explain why.

2 a Give two ways in which animals compete for mates.
   b Suggest the advantages and disadvantages of the methods chosen in part **a**.

3 Explain the adaptations you would expect to find in:
   a an animal that hunts mice
   b an animal that eats grass
   c an animal that hunts and eats other animals
   d an animal that feeds on the tender leaves at the top of trees.

Key points

● Animals often compete with each other for food, territories and mates.

● Animals have adaptations that make them good competitors.

B1 4.5

Competition in plants

Plants compete fiercely with each other. They compete for:

- light for photosynthesis, to make food using energy from sunlight
- water for photosynthesis and to keep their tissues rigid and supported
- nutrients (minerals) so they can make all the chemicals they need in their cells
- space to grow, allowing their roots to take in water and nutrients, and their leaves to capture light.

a What do plants compete with each other for?

Why do plants compete?

Just like animals, plants are in competition both with other species of plants and with their own species. Big, tall plants such as trees take up a lot of water and nutrients from the soil. They also prevent light from reaching the plants beneath them. So the plants around them need adaptations to help them to survive.

When a plant sheds its seeds they might land nearby. Then the parent plant will be in direct competition with its own seedlings. Because the parent plant is large and settled, it will take most of the water, nutrients and light. So the plant will deprive its own offspring of everything they need to grow successfully. The roots of some desert plants even produce a chemical that stops seeds from germinating, killing the competition even before it begins to grow!

Sometimes the seeds from a plant will all land close together, a long way from their parent. They will then compete with each other as they grow.

b Why is it important that seeds are spread as far as possible from the parent plant?

Coping with competition

Plants that grow close to other species often have adaptations which help them to avoid competition.

Small plants found in woodlands often grow and flower very early in the year. This is when plenty of light gets through the bare branches of the trees. The dormant trees take very little water out of the soil. The leaves shed the previous autumn have rotted down to provide nutrients in the soil. Plants like snowdrops, anemones and bluebells are all adapted to take advantage of these things. They flower, set seeds and die back again before the trees are in full leaf.

Another way plants compete successfully is by having different types of roots. Some plants have shallow roots taking water and nutrients from near the surface of the soil. Others have long, deep roots, which go far underground. Both compete successfully for what they need without affecting the other.

If one plant is growing in the shade of another, it may grow taller to reach the light. It may also grow leaves with a bigger surface area to take advantage of all the light it does get.

Practical

Investigating competition in plants

Carry out an investigation to look at the effect of competition on plants. Set up two trays of seeds – one crowded and one spread out. Then monitor the plants' height and wet mass (mass after watering). Keep all of the conditions – light level, the amount of water and nutrients available and the temperature – exactly the same for both sets of plants. The differences in their growth will be the result of overcrowding and competition for resources in one of the groups. The data show growth of tree seedlings. You can get results in days rather than months by using cress seeds.

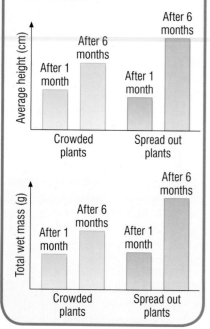

Some plants are adapted to prevent animals from eating them. They may have thorns, like the African acacia or the blackberry. They may make poisons that mean they taste very bitter or make the animals that eat them ill. Either way they compete successfully because they are less likely to be eaten than other plants.

c How can short roots help a plant to compete successfully?

Spreading the seeds

To reproduce successfully, a plant has to avoid competition with its own seedlings. Many plants use the wind to help them spread their seeds as far as possible. They produce fruits or seeds with special adaptations for flight to carry their seeds away. Examples of this are the parachutes of the dandelion 'clock' and the winged seeds of the sycamore tree.

d How do the fluffy parachutes of dandelion seeds help the seeds to spread out?

Some plants use mini-explosions to spread their seeds. The pods dry out, twist and pop, flinging the seeds out and away.

Juicy berries, fruits and nuts are adaptations to tempt animals to eat them. The fruit is digested and the tough seeds are deposited well away from the parent plant in their own little pile of fertiliser!

Fruits that are sticky or covered in hooks get caught up in the fur or feathers of a passing animal. They are carried around until they fall off hours or even days later.

Sometimes the seeds of several different plants land on the soil and start to grow together. The plants that grow fastest will compete successfully against the slower-growing plants. For example:

● The plants that get their roots into the soil first will get most of the available water and nutrients.
● The plants that open their leaves fastest will be able to photosynthesise and grow faster still, depriving the competition of light.

Figure 1 Plants have different types of roots to compete for water and nutrients in the soil

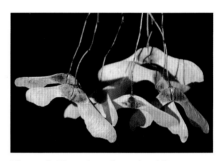
Figure 2 The winged seeds of the sycamore tree

Figure 3 Coconuts will float for weeks or even months on ocean currents, which can carry them hundreds of miles from their parents – and any other coconuts!

Summary questions

1 **a** How can plants overcome the problems of growing in the shade of another plant?
   b How do bluebell plants grow and flower successfully in spite of living under large trees in a wood?

2 **a** Why is it so important that plants spread their seeds successfully?
   b Give three examples of successful adaptations for spreading seeds.

3 The dandelion is a successful weed. Carry out some research and evaluate the adaptations that make it a better competitor than other plants on a school field.

Key points

● Plants often compete with each other for light, for water and for nutrients (minerals) from the soil.
● Plants have many adaptations that make them good competitors.

B1 4.6   How do you survive?

Learning objectives

- How do organisms survive in very unusual conditions?
- What factors are organisms competing for in a habitat?

So far in this chapter we have looked at lots of different ways in which living organisms are adapted. This helps them to survive and reproduce wherever they live. We have looked at why they need to compete successfully against their own species and others. Now we are going to consider three case studies of adaption in living organisms.

Figs and fig wasps

There are about 700 different species of fig trees. Each one has its own species of pollinating wasps, without which the trees will die. The fig flowers of the trees are specially adapted so that they attract the right species of wasp.

Female fig wasps have specially shaped heads for getting into fig flowers. They also have **ovipositors** that allow them to place their eggs deep in the flowers of the fig tree.

Male fig wasps vary. Some species can fly but others are adapted to live in a fig fruit all their life. If they are lucky, a female wasp will arrive in the flower and the male will fertilise her. After this he digs an escape tunnel for the female through the fruit and dies himself! The male wasp has special adaptations (such as the loss of his wings and very small eyes) which help him move around inside the fig fruit to find a female.

Figure 1 A fig tree

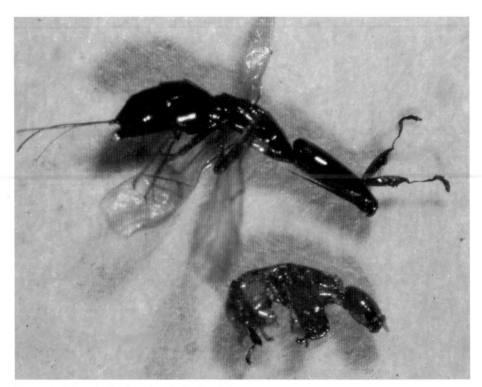

Figure 2 A female (top) and male (bottom) fig wasp

If a fig tree cannot attract the right species of wasp, it will never be able to reproduce. In fact in some areas the trees are in danger of extinction because the wasp populations are being wiped out.

The fastest predator in the world?

It takes you about 650 milliseconds to react to a crisis. But the star-nosed mole takes only 230 milliseconds from the moment it first touches its prey to gulping it down. That's faster than the human eye can see!

What makes this even more amazing is that star-nosed moles live underground and are almost totally blind. Their main sense organ is a crown of fleshy tendrils around the nose – incredibly sensitive to touch and smell but very odd to look at. The ultra-sensitive tendrils can try out 13 possible targets every second.

It seems likely that they have adapted to react so quickly because they can't see what is going on. They need to grab their prey as soon as possible after they touch it. If they don't it might move away or try to avoid them, and they wouldn't know where it had gone.

Figure 3 The star-nosed mole

A carnivorous plant

Venus flytraps are plants that grow on bogs. Bogs are wet and their peaty soil has very few nutrients in it. This makes it a difficult place for plants to live.

The Venus flytrap has special 'traps' that contain sweet smelling nectar. They sit wide open showing their red insides. Insects are attracted to the colour and the smell. Inside the trap are many small, sensitive hairs. As the insect moves about to find the nectar, it will brush against these hairs. Once the hairs have been touched, the trap is triggered. It snaps shut and traps the insect inside.

Special enzymes then digest the insect inside the trap. The Venus flytrap uses the nutrients from the digested bodies of its victims. This is in place of the nutrients that it cannot get from the poor bog soil. After the insect has been digested, the trap reopens ready to try again.

Figure 4 The Venus flytrap – an insect-eating plant

Activity

Case studies

- For each of these three case studies, list how the organisms are adapted for their habitat and how these adaptations help them to compete successfully against both their own species and other species.

- Choose three organisms that you know something about – or find out about three organisms which interest you. Make your own fact file on their adaptations and how these adaptations help them to compete successfully. Include at least one plant.

Summary questions

1 Explain how both of the animals featured compete successfully for food.

2 Why could any species of fig tree or fig wasp easily die out? Give a reason for each.

3 Carry out research to explain the adaptations of a giraffe and why they help it to compete successfully with other animals living in the same area.

Key points

- Organisms have adaptations which enable them to survive in the conditions in which they normally live.

- Plants often compete with each other for light, water and nutrients from the soil.

- Animals often compete with each other for food, mates and territory.

B1 4.7 Measuring environmental change

Learning objectives

- What affects the distribution of living things?
- What causes environmental changes?
- How can we measure environmental changes?

Figure 1 The distribution of bullhorn acacia ants depends on where the swollen-thorn acacia trees grow

⬭⬭ links

For more information about how environmental changes affect organisms, see B3 chapter 4 How humans can affect the environment.

Have you noticed different types of animals and plants when you travel to different places? The distribution of living organisms depends on the environmental conditions and varies around the world.

Factors affecting the distribution of organisms

Non-living factors have a big effect on where organisms live. The average temperature or average rainfall will have a big impact on what can survive. You don't find polar bears in countries where the average temperature is over 20°C, for example! The amount of rainfall affects the distribution of both plants and animals. Light, pH and the local climate all influence where living organisms are found.

The distribution of different species of animals in water is closely linked to the oxygen levels. Salmon can only live in water with lots of dissolved oxygen, but bloodworms can survive in very low oxygen levels.

Living organisms also affect the distribution of other living organisms. So, for example, koala bears are only found where eucalyptus trees grow. Parasites only live where they can find a host.

One species of ant eats nectar produced by the flowers of the swollen-thorn acacia tree. The ants hollow out the vicious thorns and live in them. So any animal biting the tree not only gets the sharp thorns, they get a mouth full of angry ants as well. The distribution of the ants depends on the trees.

a Which non-living environmental factor affects the distribution of polar bears?

Environmental changes

When the environment changes, it can cause a change in the distribution of living organisms in the area. Non-living factors often cause these changes in an environment.

The average temperature may rise or fall. The oxygen concentration in water may change. A change in the amount of sunlight, the strength of the wind or the average rainfall may affect an environment. Any of these factors can affect the distribution of living organisms.

Living factors can also cause a change in the environment where an organism lives, affecting distribution. A new type of predator may move into an area. A new disease-causing pathogen may appear and wipe out a species of animal or plant. Different plants may appear and provide food or a home for a whole range of different species.

b Give an example of a living and a non-living factor that can change an environment.

Measuring environmental change

When an environment changes, the living organisms in it are affected. If the change is big enough, the distribution of animals or plants in an area may change.

You can measure environmental change using non-living indicators. You can measure factors such as average rainfall, temperature, oxygen levels, pH and pollutant levels in water or the air, and much more. All sorts of different instruments are available to do these measurements. These range from simple rain gauges and thermometers to oxygen meters and dataloggers used in schools.

You can also use the changing distribution of living organisms as an **indicator** of environmental change. Living organisms are particularly good as indicators of pollution.

Lichens grow on places like rocks, roofs and the bark of trees. They are very sensitive to air pollution, particularly levels of sulfur dioxide in the atmosphere. When the air is clean, many different types of lichen grow. The more polluted the air, the fewer lichen species there will be. So a field survey on the numbers and types of lichen can be used to give an indication of air pollution. The data can be used to study local sites or to compare different areas of the country.

In the same way you can use invertebrate animals as water pollution indicators. The cleaner the water, the more species you will find. Some species of invertebrates are only found in the cleanest waters. Others can be found even in very polluted waters. Counting the different types of species gives a good indication of pollution levels, and can be used to monitor any changes.

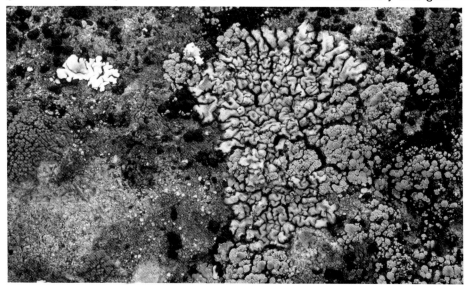

Practical

Indicators of pollution levels

Investigate both the variety of lichens in your local area and the number of invertebrate species in your local pond or stream. This will give you an idea of pollution levels in your area if you compare them to national figures.

Figure 2 Lichens grow well where the air is clean. In an area polluted with sulfur dioxide there would be fewer species. Lichens are good indicators of pollution.

Summary questions

1 Copy and complete these sentences using the words below:

   indicators   distribution   pollution   organisms

   Changes in the environment affect the .... of living .... This means living organisms can be used as .... of ....

2 Give three different methods you could use to collect environmental data. For each method, comment on its reliability and usefulness as a source of evidence of environmental change.

Key points

- Animals and plants may be adapted to cope with specific features of their environment, e.g. thorns, poisons and warning colours.

- Environmental changes may be caused by living or non-living factors.

- Environmental changes can be measured using non-living indicators.

- Living organisms can be used as indicators of pollution.

B1 4.8

The impact of change

Learning objectives

- How do changes in the environment affect the distribution of living organisms?

- How reproducible are the data about the effect of environmental change on living organisms?

Figure 1 The Dartford warbler

Changing birds of Britain

Temperatures in the UK seem to be rising. Many people like the idea – summer barbeques and low heating bills. But rising temperatures will have a big impact on many living organisms. We could see changes in the distribution of many species. Food plants and animals might become more common, or die out, in different conditions.

The Dartford warbler is small brown bird that breeds mainly in southern Europe. A small population lived in Dorset and Hampshire. By 1963, two very cold winters left just 11 breeding pairs in the UK. But temperatures have increased steadily since. Dartford warblers are now found in Wales, the Midlands and East Anglia. If climate change continues, Dartford warblers could spread through most of England and Ireland. However, in Spain the numbers are dropping rapidly – 25% in the last 10 years – as it becomes too warm. Scientists can simulate the distribution of birds as the climate changes. They predict that by the end of the century Spain could lose most of its millions of Dartford warblers.

Scientists predict that by the end of this century, if climate change continues at its present rate, the range of the average bird species will move nearly 550 km north-east. About 75% of all the birds that nest in Europe are likely to have smaller ranges as a result and many species will be lost for good.

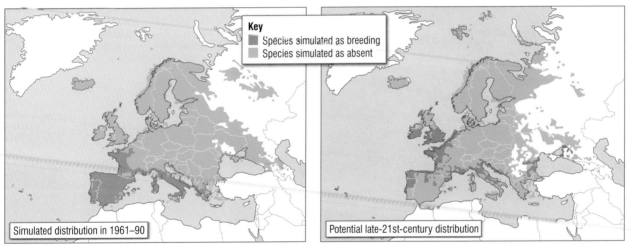

Key
- Species simulated as breeding
- Species simulated as absent

Simulated distribution in 1961–90

Potential late-21st-century distribution

Figure 2 The maps show how scientists think the distribution of these birds might change in the future

Table 1 Numbers of breeding pairs of Dartford warblers in the UK

Year	Number of breeding pairs
1961	450
1963	11
1974	560
1984	420
1994	1890
2010	3208

Activity

- Plot a bar graph to show the change in population of the Dartford warbler from 1961 to the present day. Draw an extra bar to show what you would expect the population to be in 2030 if climate change continues in the same way.

- Investigate the effect of climate change on the way birds migrate from one country to another and write a report for a wildlife programme or magazine.

Where are all the bees?

All around the world honey bees are disappearing. In the UK alone, around one in five bee hives has been lost in the last few years. In the United States, around 2 million colonies of bees were lost in 3 years. The bees had been struck down by a new, mystery disease called Colony Collapse Disorder or CCD. The bees either die, or simply fail to return to the hive. Without the mass of worker bees, those bees left in the hive quickly die.

Members of the British Beekeepers Association are alarmed. They say that if hives continue to be lost at the same rate there will be no honey bees left in Britain by 2018. You might think that having fewer bees doesn't really matter. It also means honey is more expensive to buy.

In fact, bees are vitally important in plant ecology. Honey bees pollinate flowers as they collect the nectar. Without them, flowers are not pollinated and fruit does not form. Without bees as pollinators we would have no apples, raspberries, cucumbers, strawberries, peaches … the list goes on and on. There would be cereal crops, because they are pollinated by the wind, but not much else.

No one yet fully understands what is happening to the bees and what is changing their distribution. Scientists think that viral diseases, possibly spread by a parasitic mite, are a major cause. So living factors – the agents of disease – are causing a major change in the environment of the honey bee. This in turn is affecting their distribution.

Other living and non-living factors affecting the environment have also been suggested. Flowering patterns are changing as temperatures vary with climate change. This may affect the food supply of the bees. Farmers spray chemicals that may build up in the bees. Some people have even suggested that mobile phones affect the navigation system of the bees.

Research is continuing all over the world. Disease-resistant strains of bees are being bred. Collecting the evidence to show exactly what environmental change is affecting the honey bee population is proving to be difficult. But until we can find out, the decline of the honey bee looks as if it will continue. There is a little good news – UK numbers have recovered slightly as more people have started keeping bees, probably as a result of all the publicity.

Figure 3 Honey bees are vital pollinators. Bee-pollinated fruits are worth about £50 billion of trade every year.

Activity

- List the main suggested causes for the decline of the honey bee. Use secondary sources to investigate the current state of the research findings for each cause.
- Produce a slide show to justify the investment of research funds into the loss of honey bees. Show what is happening to the bees, the main theories about what is causing the problem and how the problem is being tackled.

Summary questions

1 Using the information on this spread, what aspect of climate change seems to be linked to a change in the distribution of British birds?

2 a Why is the loss of honey bees so important?
   b Why is it important to find out whether the environmental cause of the problem is a living or non-living factor?

Key points

- Both living and non-living factors can cause changes in the environment that affect the distribution of living organisms.

- Reproducible data on the effect of environmental change are not always easy to collect or interpret.

Summary questions (k)

1 Match the following words to their definitions:

a	competition	A	an animal that eats plants
b	carnivore	B	an area where an animal lives and feeds
c	herbivore	C	an animal that eats meat
d	territory	D	the way animals compete with each other for food, water, space and mates

2 Cold-blooded animals like reptiles and snakes absorb heat from their surroundings and cannot move until they are warm.

a Why do you think that there are no reptiles and snakes in the Arctic?

b What problems do you think reptiles face in desert conditions and what adaptations could they have to cope with them?

c Most desert animals are quite small. How does this help them survive in the heat?

3 a What are the main problems for plants living in a hot, dry climate?

b Why does reducing the surface area of their leaves help plants to reduce water loss?

c Describe **two** ways in which the surface area of the leaves of some desert plants is reduced.

d How else are some plants adapted to cope with hot, dry conditions?

e Why are cacti such perfect desert plants?

4 a How does marking out and defending a territory help an animal to compete successfully?

b Bamboo plants all tend to flower and die at the same time. Why is this such bad news for pandas, but doesn't affect most other animals?

5 Why is competition between animals of the same species so much more intense than the competition between different species?

6 Use the bar charts from the practical activity on B1 4.5 to answer these questions.

a Describe what happens to the height of both sets of seedlings over the first six months and explain why the changes take place.

b The total wet mass of the seedlings after one month was the same whether or not they were crowded. After six months there was a big difference.

i Why do you think both types of seedling had the same mass after one month?

ii Explain why the seedlings that were more spread out each had more wet mass after six months.

c When scientists carry out experiments such as the one described, they try to use large sample sizes. Why?

d i Name a control variable mentioned in the practical.

ii Why were the other variables kept constant?

7 a Give **three** living factors that can change the environment and affect the distribution of living organisms.

b Give **three** non-living factors that can change the environment and affect the distribution of living organisms.

8 Maize is a very important crop plant. It has many uses – it is made into cornflakes and it is also grown for animal feed. The most important part of the plant is the cob, which fetches the most money. In an experiment to find the best growing conditions, three plots of land were used. The young maize plants were grown in different densities in the three plots.

The results were as follows:

	Planting density (plants/m²)		
	10	**15**	**20**
Dry mass of shoots (kg/m²)	9.7	11.6	13.5
Dry mass of cobs (kg/m²)	6.1	4.4	2.8

a What was the independent variable in this investigation?

b Draw a graph to show the effect of the planting density on the mass of the cobs grown.

c What is the pattern shown in your graph?

d This was a fieldwork investigation. What would the experimenter have taken into account when choosing the location of the three plots?

e Did the experimenter choose enough plots? Explain your answer.

f What is the relationship between the mass of cobs and the mass of shoots at different planting densities?

g The experimenter concluded that the best density for planting the maize is 10 plants per m². Do you agree with this as a conclusion? Explain your answer.

AQA Examination-style questions 🄺

1 The picture shows a solenodon.

Solenodons have lived on Earth since the Age of the Dinosaurs. They are only found in forests in Haiti and are the only mammals which have a poisonous bite. They are rarely seen because they feed at night. They mainly eat insects and spiders.

a The solenodon has adaptations which help it to survive.
   Match the adaptation to the correct letter (A, B, C, D or E) for the following:
   i This helps the solenodon to dig its burrow. (1)
   ii This helps the solenodon to detect its food. (1)

b The solenodon is at risk of dying out since new animals have been taken to the islands.
   Use the information and the picture to help answer the following questions.
   i The solenodon is not adapted to flee from predators. Suggest why. (1)
   ii If the solenodon is caught by a predator it can defend itself. Suggest how. (1)

2 Trees that live in the rainforests are very tall and often have broad leaves. This is a problem for young trees, which do not get much light.

a Choose the correct answer to complete the sentence.

   light   nutrients   space

   Rainforest trees have broad leaves so they can compete for .... (1)

b Choose the correct answer to complete the sentence.

   larger trees   large seeds with stored food

   Trees in the rainforest have adapted to lack of light near the ground by having .... (1)

3 The gemsbok is a large herbivore living in dry desert regions of South Africa. It feeds on grasses that are adapted to the dry conditions by obtaining moisture from the air as it cools at night. The table below shows the water content of these grasses and the feeding activity of the gemsbok over a 24-hour period.

Time of day	% water content of grasses	% of gemsboks feeding
03.00	18	40
06.00	23	60
09.00	25	20
12.00	08	17
15.00	06	16
18.00	05	19
21.00	07	30
24.00	14	50

a i Name the independent variable investigated. (1)
   ii Is this a categoric, ordered, discrete or continuous variable? (1)

b How does the water content of the grasses change throughout the 24-hour period? (1)

c Between which recorded times are more than 30% of the gemsboks feeding? (1)

d Suggest **three** reasons why the gemsboks benefit from feeding at this time. (3)

AQA, 2008

B1 5.1

Pyramids of biomass

Learning objectives

- Where does biomass come from?
- What is a pyramid of biomass?

Figure 1 Plants can produce a huge mass of biological material in just one growing season

Radiation from the Sun (**solar** or **light energy**) is the source of energy for all groups of living organisms on Earth.

Light (solar) energy pours out continually on to the surface of the Earth. Green plants and algae absorb some of this light energy using chlorophyll for photosynthesis. During photosynthesis some of the light energy is transferred to chemical energy. This energy is stored in the substances that make up the cells of the plants and algae. This new material adds to the **biomass**.

Biomass is the mass of material in living organisms. Ultimately all biomass is built up using energy from the Sun. Biomass is often measured as the dry mass of biological material in grams.

a What is the source of all the energy in the living things on Earth?

The biomass made by plants is passed on through food chains or food webs. It goes into the animals that eat the plants. It then passes into the animals that eat other animals. No matter how long the food chain or complex the food web, the original source of all the biomass involved is the Sun.

In a food chain, there are usually more producers (plants) than primary consumers (herbivores). There are also more primary consumers than secondary consumers (carnivores). If you count the number of organisms at each level you can compare them. However, the number of organisms often does not accurately reflect what is happening to the biomass.

Pyramids of biomass

The amount of biomass at each stage of a food chain is less than it was at the previous stage. We can draw the total amount of biomass in the living organisms at each stage of the food chain. When this biomass is drawn to scale, we can show it as a **pyramid of biomass**.

b What is a pyramid of biomass?

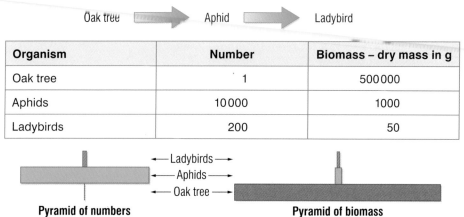

Organism	Number	Biomass – dry mass in g
Oak tree	1	500000
Aphids	10000	1000
Ladybirds	200	50

Pyramid of numbers   **Pyramid of biomass**

Figure 2 Using a pyramid of biomass shows us the amount of biological material involved at each level of this food chain much more effectively than a pyramid of numbers

Interpreting pyramids of biomass

The amount of material and energy contained in the biomass of organisms at each stage of a food chain is less than it was at the previous stage.

This is because:

- not all organisms at one stage are eaten by the stage above
- some material and energy taken in is passed out as waste by the organism
- when a herbivore eats a plant, lots of the plant biomass is used in respiration by the animal cells to release energy. Only a relatively small proportion of the plant material is used to build new herbivore biomass by making new cells, building muscle tissue etc. This means that very little of the plant biomass eaten by the herbivore in its lifetime is available to be passed on to any carnivore that eats it.

So, at each stage of a food chain the amount of energy in the biomass that is passed on gets less. A large amount of plant biomass supports a smaller amount of herbivore biomass. This in turn supports an even smaller amount of carnivore biomass.

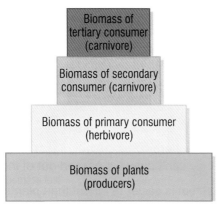

Figure 3 Any food chain can be turned into a pyramid of biomass like this

Summary questions

1 **a** What is biomass?
  b Why is a pyramid of biomass more useful for showing what is happening in a food chain than a pyramid of numbers?

2

Organism	Biomass, dry mass (g)
grass	100 000
sheep	5000
sheep ticks	30

Draw a pyramid of biomass for this grassland ecosystem.

3 Using the data in Figure 2, calculate the percentage biomass passed on from:
  a the producers to the primary consumers
  b the primary consumers to the secondary consumers.

Key points

- Radiation from the Sun (solar or light energy) is the main source of energy for all living things. The Sun's light energy is captured and used by green plants and algae during photosynthesis, to make new biomass.

- Biomass is the dry mass of living material in an animal or plant.

- The mass of living material at each stage of a food chain is less than at the previous stage. The biomass at each stage can be drawn to scale and shown as a pyramid of biomass.

B1 5.3 Decay processes

Figure 1 This tomato is slowly being broken down by the action of decomposers. You can see the fungi clearly but the bacteria are too small to be seen.

Plants take nutrients from the soil all the time. These nutrients are passed on into animals through food chains and food webs. If this was a one-way process the resources of the Earth would have been exhausted long ago.

Fortunately all these materials are recycled. Many trees shed their leaves each year, and most animals produce droppings at least once a day. Animals and plants eventually die as well. A group of organisms known as the **decomposers** then break down the waste and the dead animals and plants. In this process decomposers return the nutrients and other materials to the environment. The same material is recycled over and over again. This often leads to very stable communities of organisms.

a Which group of organisms take materials out of the soil?

The decay process

Decomposers are a group of microorganisms that include bacteria and fungi. They feed on waste droppings and dead organisms.

Detritus feeders, such as maggots and some types of worms, often start the process of decay. They eat dead animals and produce waste material. The bacteria and fungi then digest everything – dead animals, plants and detritus feeders plus their waste. They use some of the nutrients to grow and reproduce. They also release waste products.

The waste products of decomposers are carbon dioxide, water, and nutrients that plants can use. When we say that things decay, they are actually being broken down and digested by microorganisms.

The recycling of materials through the process of decay makes sure that the soil contains the mineral ions that plants need to grow. The decomposers also 'clean up' the environment, removing the bodies of all the dead organisms.

b What type of organisms are decomposers?

Conditions for decay

The speed at which things decay depends partly on the temperature. Chemical reactions in microorganisms, like those in most living things, work faster in **warm conditions**. They slow down and might even stop if conditions are too cold. Decay also stops if it gets too hot. The enzymes in the decomposers change shape and stop working.

Most microorganisms also grow better in **moist conditions**. The moisture makes it easier for them to dissolve their food and also prevents them from drying out. So the decay of dead plants and animals – as well as leaves and dung – takes place far more rapidly in warm, moist conditions than it does in cold, dry ones.

Although some microbes survive without oxygen, most decomposers respire like any other organism. This means they need oxygen to release energy, grow and reproduce. This is why decay takes place more rapidly when there is **plenty of oxygen** available.

c Why are water, warmth and oxygen needed for the process of decay?

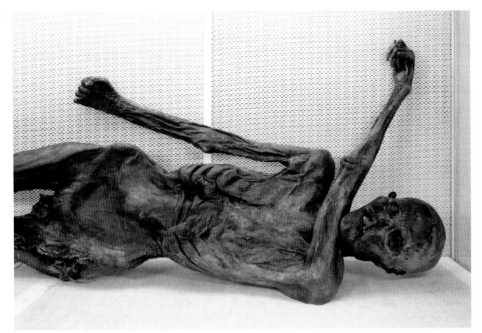

Figure 2 The decomposers cannot function at low temperatures so if an organism – such as this 4000-year-old man – is frozen as it dies, it will be preserved with very little decay

The importance of decay in recycling

Decomposers are vital for recycling resources in the natural world. What's more, we can take advantage of the process of decay to help us recycle our waste.

In **sewage treatment plants** we use microorganisms to break down the bodily waste we produce. This makes it safe to release into rivers or the sea. These sewage works have been designed to provide the bacteria and other microorganisms with the conditions they need. That includes a good supply of oxygen.

Another place where the decomposers are useful is in the garden. Many gardeners have a **compost heap**. Grass cuttings, vegetable peelings and weeds are put onto the compost heap. It is then left to allow decomposing microorganisms break all the plant material down. It forms a brown, crumbly substance known as compost which can be used as a fertiliser.

Key points

● Living things remove materials from the environment as they grow. They return them when they die through the action of the decomposers.

● Materials decay because they are broken down (digested) by microorganisms. Microorganisms digest materials faster in warm, moist conditions. Many of them also need oxygen.

● The decay process releases substances that plants need to grow.

● In a stable community the processes that remove materials (particularly plant growth) are balanced by the processes that return materials.

Summary questions

1 Copy and complete using the words below:

bacteria carbon dead decomposers digest microorganisms nutrients waste water

.... are a group of .... that includes fungi and .... They feed on .... droppings and .... organisms. They .... them and use some of the .... They also release waste products which include .... dioxide and ...., which plants can use.

2 Explain why the processes of decay are so important in keeping the soil fertile.

B1 5.4

The carbon cycle

Learning objectives

- What is the carbon cycle in nature?

- Which processes remove carbon dioxide from the atmosphere – and which processes return it?

Figure 1 Within the natural cycle of life and death in the living world, mineral nutrients are cycled between living organisms and the physical environment

??? Did you know ... ?

Every year about 166 gigatonnes of carbon are cycled through the living world. That's 166 000 000 000 tonnes – an awful lot of carbon!

Imagine a stable community of plants and animals. The processes that remove materials from the environment are balanced by processes that return materials. Materials are constantly cycled through the environment. One of the most important of these is carbon.

All of the main **molecules** that make up our bodies (carbohydrates, proteins, fats and DNA) are based on carbon atoms combined with other **elements**.

The amount of carbon on the Earth is fixed. Some of the carbon is 'locked up' in **fossil fuels** like coal, oil and gas. It is only released when we burn them.

Huge amounts of carbon are combined with other elements in carbonate rocks like limestone and chalk. There is a pool of carbon in the form of carbon dioxide in the air. It is also found dissolved in the water of rivers, lakes and oceans. All the time a relatively small amount of available carbon is cycled between living things and the environment. We call this the **carbon cycle**.

a What are the main sources of carbon on Earth?

Photosynthesis

Green plants and algae remove carbon dioxide from the atmosphere for photosynthesis. They use the carbon from carbon dioxide to make carbohydrates, proteins and fats. These make up biomass of the plants and algae. The carbon is passed on to animals that eat the plants. The carbon goes on to become part of the carbohydrates, proteins and fats in these animal bodies.

This is how carbon is taken out of the environment. But how is it returned?

b What effect does photosynthesis have on the distribution of carbon levels in the environment?

Respiration

Living organisms respire all the time. They use oxygen to break down glucose, providing energy for their cells. Carbon dioxide is produced as a waste product. This is how carbon is returned to the atmosphere.

When plants, algae and animals die their bodies are broken down by decomposers. These are animals and microorganisms such as blowflies, moulds and bacteria that feed on the dead bodies. The animals which feed on dead bodies and waste are called *detritus feeders*. They include animals such as worms, centipedes and many insects.

Carbon is released into the atmosphere as carbon dioxide when these organisms respire. All of the carbon (in the form of carbon dioxide) released by the various living organisms is then available again. It is ready to be taken up by plants and algae in photosynthesis.

Combustion

Fossil fuels contain carbon, which was locked away by photosynthesising organisms millions of years ago. When we burn fossil fuels, carbon dioxide is produced, so we release some of that carbon back into the atmosphere:

Photosynthesis: carbon dioxide + water (+ light energy) → glucose+ oxygen

Respiration: glucose + oxygen → carbon dioxide + water (+ energy)

Combustion: fossil fuel or wood + oxygen → carbon dioxide + water
(+ energy)

The constant cycling of carbon is summarised in Figure 2.

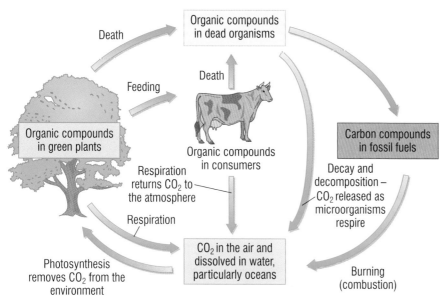

Figure 2 The carbon cycle in nature

Figure 3 Fossil fuels such as coal contain large amounts of carbon

Energy transfers

When plants and algae photosynthesise, they transfer light energy into chemical energy in the food they make. This chemical energy is transferred from one organism to another through the carbon cycle. Some of the energy can be used for movement or transferred as energy to the organisms and their surroundings at each stage. The decomposers break down all the waste and dead organisms and cycle the materials as plant nutrients. By this time all of the energy originally absorbed by green plants and algae during photosynthesis has been transferred elsewhere.

For millions of years the carbon cycle has regulated itself. However, as we burn more fossil fuels we are pouring increasing amounts of carbon dioxide into the atmosphere. Scientists fear that the carbon cycle may not cope. If the levels of carbon dioxide in our atmosphere increase it may lead to global warming.

Summary questions

1 a What is the carbon cycle?
   b What are the main processes involved in the carbon cycle?
   c Why is the carbon cycle so important for life on Earth?

2 a Where does the carbon come from that is used in photosynthesis?
   b Explain carefully how carbon is transferred through an ecosystem.

Key points

- The constant cycling of carbon in nature is known as the carbon cycle.

- Carbon dioxide is removed from the atmosphere by photosynthesis. It is returned to the atmosphere through respiration and combustion.

B1 5.5 | Recycling organic waste ⓚ

Learning objectives

● Why should we recycle organic kitchen and garden waste?

● How can we investigate the most effective way to recycle this organic waste?

Figure 1 Some landfill sites now collect the methane that is produced as organic material decays and use it to generate electricity. But if everyone recycled their own organic waste, we would need far fewer landfill sites and there would be no problem.

⁇? Did you know … ?

One tonne of organic kitchen and garden waste produces 200 to 400 m³ of gas. Around 27% of the methane produced in the UK each year comes from landfill sites.

Activity

Plan an assembly to be used with students in Years 7–9 suggesting that the school introduces a scheme to recycle all the organic waste from the kitchens and the school grounds to make compost. The compost could then be sold to the local community for charity. Remember, you need to explain why and how this should be done as well as recruit volunteers to help run the compost bins.

The problem of waste

People produce lots of waste – and getting rid of it is a big problem. Whenever we prepare food we produce **organic waste** to throw away, such as vegetable peelings. Gardening produces lots of organic waste too, including the grass cuttings when we mow the lawn. We put about 100 million tonnes of waste a year into landfill sites and about two thirds of that is organic matter. By recycling our organic waste we can reduce this mountain of waste material.

The kitchen and garden waste we put into landfill sites doesn't rot easily in the conditions there. It forms a smelly liquid which soaks into the ground and can pollute local rivers and streams. In these conditions the microorganisms that break down the plant and animal material produce mainly methane gas. This is a **greenhouse gas** that adds to the problem of global warming.

a Give two examples of the organic waste you might put into a compost bin.

The simplest way to recycle kitchen and garden waste is to make compost. Natural decomposing organisms break down all the plant material to make a brown, crumbly substance. This compost is full of the nutrients that have been released by the decomposers. The process takes from a few months to over a year. The compost forms a really good, natural fertiliser. It also greatly reduces the amount of rubbish you need to send to the landfill site.

b Which greenhouse gas, other than carbon dioxide, is given off as organic material decays in landfill sites?

Making compost

Composting can be done on a small scale or on a large scale. There are several different factors which are important in making successful compost:

● Compost can be made with or without oxygen – mixing your compost regularly helps air get in. If the microorganisms have oxygen they generate energy, which kills off weed seeds and speeds up the process. Without oxygen the process releases little energy and is slower.

● The warmer the compost mixture, the faster the compost will be made (up to about 70°C, at which point the microorganisms stop working properly).

● The decay process is faster in moist conditions than in dry ones. (In fact, decay does not take place at all in perfectly dry conditions.)

Practical

Investigating the decay of organic matter

We have seen that the presence of oxygen and moisture, as well as the temperature, affect the rate of decay. Choose one of these factors to investigate. Carry out any tests on the sort of materials that might go into a garden compost bin.

- Plan to find out what effect your chosen factor has on the rate at which the material decays.
- Pool the conclusions of each group to decide on the ideal conditions for composting organic waste.
- Comment on the limitations of the conclusions you can draw.

links

For more information about waste management and pollution, see B3 4.1 The effects of the population explosion and B3 4.2 Land and water pollution.

A Compost heap: The simplest and cheapest method. Kitchen and garden waste is put in a pile, with new material added to the top, and left to rot down.

B Compost bin: Bins are often made of plastic and may be sold cheaply by local councils to encourage people to recycle their organic waste. Instructions include watering the bin in dry weather and mixing the contents from time to time.

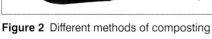

D Black bag composting: A black plastic bag is filled with kitchen and garden waste and sealed. The microorganisms work slowly as they have little or no oxygen, but in about a year the contents will have decomposed and formed compost.

C Council composting: Local councils may collect garden or kitchen waste and use large-scale bins to recycle the material to make compost. They may shred the material before adding it to the bins to increase the surface area. You can buy the compost from the schemes to put on your garden.

Figure 2 Different methods of composting

Summary questions

1 Why is it important to recycle organic kitchen and garden waste?

2 Evaluate each of the four methods of making compost shown in Figure 2, giving advantages and disadvantages of each.

3 How do mixing the compost regularly, adding a variety of different types of organic waste and watering in dry weather improve the composting process?

Key points

- Recycling organic kitchen and garden waste is necessary to reduce landfill, reduce the production of methane and to recycle the minerals and nutrients in the organic material.

- Composting organic waste can be done in a variety of different ways.

Summary questions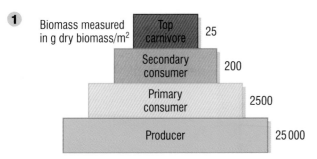

1

Biomass measured in g dry biomass/m²

Top carnivore	25
Secondary consumer	200
Primary consumer	2500
Producer	25 000

a From this diagram, calculate the percentage biomass passed on:

  i from producers to primary consumers

  ii from primary to secondary consumers

  iii from secondary consumers to top carnivores.

b In any food chain or food web the biomass of the producers is much larger than that of any other level of the pyramid. Why is this?

c In any food chain or food web there are only small numbers of top carnivores. Use your calculations to help you explain why.

d All of the animals in the pyramid of biomass shown here are cold blooded. What difference would it have made to the average percentage of biomass passed on between the levels if mammals and birds had been involved? Explain the difference.

2 The world population is increasing and there are food shortages in many parts of the world. Explain, using pyramids of biomass to help you, why it would make a better use of resources if people everywhere ate much less meat and more plant material.

3 Chickens for us to eat are often farmed intensively to provide meat as cheaply as possible. The birds arrive in the broiler house as 1 day-old chicks. They are slaughtered at 42 days of age when they weigh about 2 kg. The temperature, amount of food and water and light levels are carefully controlled. About 20 000 chickens are reared together in one house. The table below shows their weight gain.

Age (days)	1	7	14	21	28	35	42
Mass (g)	36	141	404	795	1180	1657	1998

a Plot a graph to show the growth rate of one of these chickens.

b Explain why the temperature is so carefully controlled in the broiler house.

c Explain why so many birds are reared together in a relatively small area.

d Why are birds for eating reared like this?

4 Microorganisms decompose organic waste and dead bodies. We preserve food to stop this decomposition taking place. Use your knowledge of decomposition to explain how each method stops the food going bad:

a Food may be frozen.

b Food may be cooked – cooked food keeps longer than fresh food.

c Food may be stored in a vacuum pack – with all the air sucked out.

d Food may be tinned – it is heated and sealed in an airtight container.

5

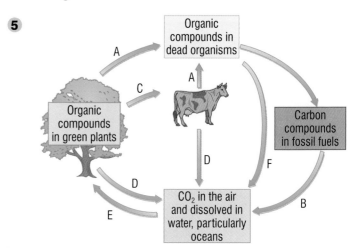

a How is carbon dioxide removed from the atmosphere in the carbon cycle?

b How does carbon dioxide get into the atmosphere?

c Where is most of the carbon stored?

d Why is the carbon cycle so important and what could happen if the balance of the reactions was disturbed?

6 a The temperature in the middle of a compost heap will be quite warm. Heat is produced as microbes respire. How does this help the compost to be broken down more quickly?

b In sewage works oxygen is bubbled through the tanks containing sewage and microorganisms. How does this help make sure the human waste is broken down completely?

AQA Examination-style questions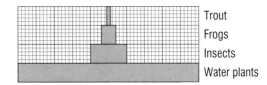

1 Rabbits eat very large amounts of grass. A single hawk eats a few rabbits.

   a Draw a pyramid of biomass for the rabbits, grass and the hawk. (2)

   b Much of the energy from the grass is not transferred to the hawk.
Suggest **two** reasons why. (2)

2 Choose words from below to complete each sentence.

   carbon dioxide cool dry insects microorganisms moist nitrogen oxygen rats warm

   a Plant waste in a compost heap is decayed by .... (1)

   b The plant waste decays faster in conditions which are .... and .... (2)

   c The plant waste will also decay faster when the air contains plenty of .... (1)

3 The diagram shows what happens to the energy in the food a calf eats.

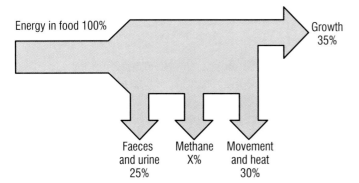

In the calculations show clearly how you work out your answer.

   a Calculate the percentage of energy lost in methane (X). (2)

   b The energy in the food the calf eats in one day is 10 megajoules.
Calculate the amount of this energy that would be lost in faeces and urine. (2)

   c Name the process which transfers the energy from the food into movement. (1)

   d The farmer decides to move his calf indoors so that it will grow quicker.
Suggest **two** reasons why. (2)

4 *In this question you will be assessed on using good English, organising information clearly and using specialist terms where appropriate.*

The constant cycling of carbon in nature is called 'The carbon cycle'.

Each autumn, trees lose their leaves.

Describe how the carbon in the leaves is recycled so that the trees can use it again. (6)

5 The diagram shows a pyramid of biomass drawn to scale.

Trout
Frogs
Insects
Water plants

   a What is the source of energy for the water plants? (1)

   b The ratio of the biomass of water plants to the biomass of insects is 5 : 1.
Calculate the ratio of the biomass of insects to the biomass of frogs.
Show clearly how you work out your answer. (2)

   c Give **two** reasons why the biomass of the frog population is smaller than the biomass of the insect population. (2)

   d Some insects die.
Describe how the carbon in the dead insect bodies may be recycled. (4)

AQA, 2006

B1 6.1

Inheritance

Learning objectives

- How do parents pass on genetic information to their offspring?

- In which part of a cell is the genetic information found?

Young animals and plants resemble their parents. Horses have foals and people have babies. Chestnut trees produce conkers that grow into little chestnut trees. Many of the smallest organisms that live in the world around us are actually identical to their parents. So what makes us the way we are?

Figure 1 This mother cat and her kittens are not identical, but they are obviously related

Why do we resemble our parents?

Most families have characteristics that we can see clearly from generation to generation. People like to comment when one member of a family looks very much like another. Characteristics like nose shape, eye colour and dimples are inherited. They are passed on to you from your parents.

Your resemblance to your parents is the result of information carried by **genes**. These are passed on to you in the sex cells (**gametes**) from which you developed. This genetic information determines what you will be like.

a Why do you look like your parents?

Chromosomes and genes

The genetic information is carried in the nucleus of your cells. It is passed from generation to generation during reproduction. The nucleus contains all the plans for making and organising a new cell. What's more, the nucleus contains the plans for a whole new you!

b In which part of a cell is the genetic information found?

Inside the nucleus of all your cells there are thread-like structures called **chromosomes**. The chromosomes are made up of a special chemical called **DNA** (deoxyribonucleic acid). This is where the genetic information is actually stored.

DNA is a long molecule made up of two strands that are twisted together to make a spiral. This is known as a double helix – imagine a ladder that has been twisted round.

Examiner's tip

Make sure you know the difference between chromosomes, genes and DNA.

Figure 2 The nucleus of each of your cells contains your chromosomes. The chromosomes carry the genes, which control the characteristics of your whole body.

Each different type of organism has a different number of chromosomes in its body cells. Humans have 46 chromosomes while turkeys have 82. You inherit half your chromosomes from your mother and half from your father, so chromosomes come in pairs. You have 23 pairs of chromosomes in all your normal body cells.

Each of your chromosomes contains thousands of genes joined together. These are the units of inheritance.

Each gene is a small section of the long DNA molecule. Genes control what an organism is like. They determine its size, its shape and its colour. Genes work at the level of the molecules in your body to control the development of all the different characteristics you can see. They do this by controlling all the different enzymes and other proteins made in your body.

Your chromosomes are organised so that both of the chromosomes in a pair carry genes controlling the same things. This means your genes also come in pairs – one from your father and one from your mother.

   c Where would you find your genes?

Some of your characteristics are decided by a single pair of genes. For example, there is one pair of genes which decides whether or not you will have dimples when you smile. However, most of your characteristics are the result of several different genes working together. For example, your hair and eye colour are both the result of several different genes.

Did you know that scientists are still not sure exactly how many genes we have? At the moment they think it is between 20 000 to 25 000.

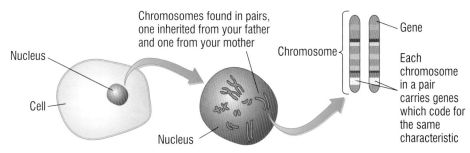

Figure 3 The nucleus of your cell contains the chromosomes that carry the genes which control the characteristics of your whole body

Summary questions

1 Copy and complete using the words below:

   chromosomes   genes   genetic   gametes   nucleus

   Offspring look like their parents because of .... information passed on to them in the .... (sex cells) from which they developed. The information is contained in the ...., which are found in the .... of the cell. The information is carried by the ....

2 **a** What is the basic unit of inheritance?
   b Offspring inherit information from their parents, but do not look exactly like them. Why not?

3 **a** Why do chromosomes come in pairs?
   b Why do genes come in pairs?
   c How many genes do scientists think humans have?

Key points

- Parents pass on genetic information to their offspring in the sex cells (gametes).

- The genetic information is found in the nucleus of your cells. The nucleus contains chromosomes, and chromosomes carry the genes that control the characteristics of your body.

- Different genes control the development of different characteristics.

B1 6.3

Genetic and environmental differences

Learning objectives

- What makes you different from the rest of your family?

- Why aren't identical twins exactly the same in every way?

Figure 1 However much this Falabella eats, it will never be as tall as the Shire. It just isn't in the genes.

Have a look at the ends of your fingers and notice the pattern of your fingerprints. No one else in the world will have exactly the same fingerprints as you. Even identical twins have different fingerprints. What factors make you so different from other people?

Nature – genetic variety

The genes you inherit determine a lot about you. An apple tree seed will never grow into an oak tree. Environmental factors, such as the weather or soil conditions do not matter. The basic characteristics of every species are determined by the genes they inherit.

Certain human characteristics are clearly inherited. Features such as eye colour, the shape of your nose and earlobes, your sex and dimples are the result of genetic information inherited from your parents. But your genes are only part of the story.

a Where do the genes you inherit come from?

Nurture – environmental variety

Some differences between you and other people are completely due to the environment you live in. For example, if a woman drinks heavily when she is pregnant, her baby may be very small when it is born and have learning difficulties. These characteristics are a direct result of the alcohol the fetus has to deal with as it develops. You may have a scar as a result of an accident or an operation. These characteristics are all environmental, not genetic.

Genes certainly play a major part in deciding how an organism will look. However, the conditions in which it develops are important too. Genetically identical plants can be grown under different conditions of light or soil nutrients. The resulting plants do not look identical. Plants deprived of light, carbon dioxide or nutrients do not make as much food as plants with plenty of everything. The deprived plants will be smaller and weaker. They have not been able to fulfil their 'genetic potential'.

b Why are genetically identical plants so useful for showing the effect of the environment on appearance?

Combined causes of variety

Many of the differences between individuals of the same species are the result of both their genes and the environment. For example, you inherit your hair colour and skin colour from your parents. However, whatever your inherited skin colour, it will be darker if you live in a sunny environment. If your hair is brown or blonde, it will be lighter if you live in a sunny country.

Your height and weight are also affected by both your genes and the conditions in which you grow up. You may have a genetic tendency to be overweight. However, if you never have enough to eat you will be underweight.

Figure 2 The differences in these cows are partly genetic and partly down to their environment, from the milk they drank as calves to the quality of the grass they eat each day

Investigating variety

It is quite easy to produce genetically identical plants to investigate variety. You can then put them in different situations to see how the environment affects their appearance. Scientists also use groups of animals that are genetically very similar to investigate variety. You cannot easily do this in a school laboratory.

The only genetically identical humans are identical twins who come from the same fertilised egg. Scientists are very interested in identical twins, to find out how similar they are as adults.

It would be unethical to take identical twins away from their parents and have them brought up differently just to investigate environmental effect. But there are cases of identical twins who have been adopted by different families. Some scientists have researched these separated identical twins.

Often identical twins look and act in a remarkably similar way. Scientists measure features such as height, weight and IQ (a measure of intelligence). The evidence shows that human beings are just like other organisms. Some of the differences between us are mainly due to genetics and some are largely due to our environment.

In one study, scientists compared four groups of adults:
- separated identical twins
- identical twins brought up together
- non-identical, same sex twins brought up together
- same sex, non-twin siblings brought up together.

The differences between the pairs were measured. A small difference means the individuals in a pair are very alike. If there was a big difference between the identical twins the scientists could see that their environment had more effect than their genes.

links

For more information on producing genetically identical plants, see B1 6.4 Cloning.

Figure 3 Whether identical twins are brought up together or apart, they are often very similar as adults

Table 1 Differences in pairs of adults

Measured difference in:	Identical twins brought up together	Identical twins brought up apart	Non-identical twins	Non-twin siblings
height (cm)	1.7	1.8	4.4	4.5
mass (kg)	1.9	4.5	4.6	4.7
IQ	5.9	8.2	9.9	9.8

Summary questions

1 Copy and complete using the words below.

combination   identical   developed   genes

Everybody is different, even .... twins. Some of the differences are caused by our .... Some differences are caused by the conditions in which we have .... Many differences are caused by a .... of both.

2 **a** Using the data from Table 1, explain which human characteristic appears to be mostly controlled by genes and which appears to be most affected by the environment.

b Why do you think non-twin siblings reared together were included in the study as well as twins reared together and apart?

3 You are given 20 pots containing identical cloned seedlings, all the same height and colour. Explain how you would investigate the effect of temperature on the growth of these seedlings compared to the impact of their genes.

AQA **Examiner's tip**

- Genes control the development of characteristics.
- Characteristics may be changed by the environment.

Key points

- The different characteristics between individuals of a family or species may be due to genetic causes, environmental causes or a combination of both.

B1 6.4 Cloning

Learning objectives

- How do we clone plants?
- How do we clone animals?
- Why do we want to create clones?

A clone is an individual that has been produced asexually and is genetically identical to the parent. Many plants reproduce naturally by cloning and this has been used by farmers and gardeners for many years.

Cloning plants

Gardeners can produce new plants by taking cuttings from older plants. How do you take a cutting? First you remove a small piece of a plant. This is often part of the stem or sometimes just part of the leaf. If you keep it in the right conditions, new roots and shoots will form. It will grow to give you a small, complete new plant.

Using this method you can produce new plants quickly and cheaply from old plants. The cuttings will be genetically identical to the parent plants.

Many growers now use hormone rooting powders to encourage cuttings to grow. Cuttings are most likely to develop successfully if you keep them in a moist atmosphere until their roots develop. We produce plants such as orchids and many conifer trees commercially by cloning in this way.

∞ links

For information on taking plant cuttings, look back at B1 2.6 Hormones and the control of plant growth.

a Why does a cutting look the same as its parent plant?

Cloning tissue

Taking cuttings is a form of artificial asexual reproduction. It has been carried out for hundreds of years. In recent years scientists have come up with a more modern way of cloning plants called **tissue culture**. It is more expensive but it allows you to make thousands of new plants from one tiny piece of plant tissue.

The first step is to use a mixture of plant hormones to make a small group of cells from the plant you want to clone produce a big mass of identical plant cells.

Then, using a different mixture of hormones and conditions, you can stimulate each of these cells to form a tiny new plant. This type of cloning guarantees that you can produce thousands of offspring with the characteristics you want from one individual plant.

Figure 1 Simple cloning by taking cuttings is a technique used by gardeners and nurserymen all around the world

b What is the advantage of tissue culture over taking cuttings?

Cloning animals

In recent years cloning animals has become quite common in farming, particularly transplanting cloned cattle embryos. Cows normally produce only one or two calves at a time. If you use embryo cloning, your best cows can produce many more top-quality calves each year.

How does embryo cloning work? You give a top-quality cow fertility hormones so that it produces a lot of eggs. You fertilise these eggs using sperm from a really good bull. Often this is done inside the cow and the embryos that are produced are then gently washed out of her womb. Sometimes the eggs are collected and you add sperm in a laboratory to produce the embryos.

Figure 2 Tissue culture makes it possible to produce thousands of identical plants quickly and easily

At this very early stage of development every cell of the embryo can still form all of the cells needed for a new cow. They have not become specialised.

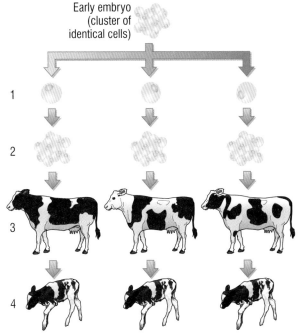

1 Divide each embryo into several individual cells.

2 Each cell grows into an identical embryo in the lab.

3 Transfer embryos into their host mothers, which have been given hormones to get them ready for pregnancy.

4 Identical cloned calves are born. They are not biologically related to their mothers.

Figure 3 Cloning cattle embryos

Cloning cattle embryos and transferring them to host cattle is skilled and expensive work. It is worth it because using normal reproduction, a top cow might produce 8–10 calves during her working life. Using embryo cloning she can produce more calves than that in a single year.

Cloning embryos means we can transport high-quality embryos all around the world. They can be carried to places where cattle with a high milk yield or lots of meat are badly needed for breeding with poor local stock. Embryo cloning is also used to make lots of identical copies of embryos that have been **genetically modified** to produce medically useful compounds.

AQA Examiner's tip

- Remember clones have identical genetic information.
- Make sure you are clear about the difference between a tissue and an embryo.

⃝⃝ links

For more information on cloning embryos, see B1 6.5 Adult cell cloning.

Key points

- New plant clones can be produced quickly and cheaply by taking cuttings from mature plants. The new plants are genetically identical to the older ones.

- A modern technique for cloning plants is tissue culture using cells from a small part of the original plant.

- Transplanting cloned embryos is one way in which animals are cloned.

Summary questions

1 Define the following words:
   a cuttings
   b tissue cloning
   c asexual reproduction
   d embryo cloning.

2 Make a table to compare the similarities and differences between tissue cloning and taking cuttings.

3 a Cloning cattle embryos is very useful. Why?
   b Draw a flow chart to show the stages in the embryo cloning of cattle.
   c Suggest some of the economic and ethical issues raised by embryo cloning in cattle.

B1 6.5 Adult cell cloning

Learning objectives

● How did scientists clone a sheep?

● What are the steps in the techniques of adult cell cloning?

True cloning of animals, without sexual reproduction involved at all, has been a major scientific breakthrough. It is the most complicated form of asexual reproduction you can find.

Adult cell cloning

To clone a cell from an adult animal is easy. The cells of your body reproduce asexually all the time to produce millions of identical cells. However, to take a cell from an adult animal and make an embryo or even a complete identical animal is a very different thing.

When a new whole animal is produced from the cell of another adult animal, it is known as **adult cell cloning**. This is still relatively rare. You place the nucleus of one cell into the empty egg cell of another animal of the same species. Then you place the resulting embryo into the womb of another adult female where it develops until it is born.

Here are the steps involved:

● The nucleus is removed from an unfertilised egg cell.

● At the same time the nucleus is taken from an adult body cell, e.g. a skin cell of another animal of the same species.

● The nucleus from the adult cell is inserted (placed) in the empty egg cell.

● The new cell is given a tiny electric shock that makes it start dividing to form embryo cells. These contain the same genetic information as the original adult cell and the original adult animal.

● When the embryo has developed into a ball of cells it is inserted into the womb of an adult female to continue its development.

Adult cell cloning has been used to produce a number of whole animal clones. The first large mammal ever to be cloned from the cell of another adult animal was Dolly the sheep, born in 1997.

Figure 1 Dolly the sheep was the first large mammal to be cloned from another adult mammal. She went on to have lambs of her own in the normal way.

a What is the name of the technique that produced Dolly the sheep?

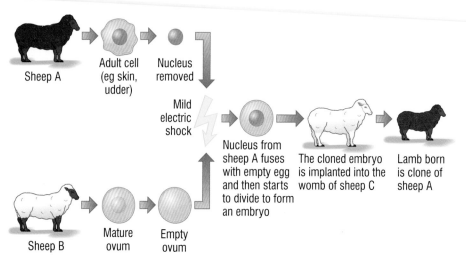

Figure 2 Adult cell cloning is still a very difficult technique – but scientists hope it may bring benefits in the future

AQA Examiner's tip

Animals can be cloned by using embryo transplants or by adult cell cloning.

When Dolly was produced she was the only success from hundreds of attempts. The technique is still difficult and unreliable, but scientists hope that it will become easier in future.

How Science Works

The benefits and disadvantages of adult cell cloning

One big hope for adult cell cloning is that animals that have been genetically engineered to produce useful proteins in their milk can be cloned. This would give us a good way of producing large numbers of cloned, medically useful animals.

This technique could also be used to help save animals from extinction, or even bring back species of animals that died out years ago. The technique could be used to clone pets or prized animals so that they continue even after the original has died. However, some people are not happy about this idea.

There are some disadvantages to this exciting science as well. Many people fear that the technique could lead to the cloning of human babies. This could be used to help infertile couples, but it could also be abused. At the moment this is not possible, but who knows what might be possible in the future?

Another problem is that modern cloning techniques produce lots of plants or animals with identical genes. In other words, cloning reduces variety in a population. This means the population is less able to survive any changes in the environment that might happen in the future. That's because if one of them does not contain a useful characteristic, none of them will.

In a more natural population, at least one or two individuals can usually survive change. They go on to reproduce and restock. This could be a problem in the future for cloned crop plants or for cloned farm animals.

b How might adult cell cloning be used to help people?

Summary questions

1 Copy and complete using the words below:

mammal   adult   technique   genetic   Dolly

In .... cell cloning an animal is produced that is an exact .... copy of another adult animal. .... the sheep was the first large .... to be produced using this modern cloning ....

2 Produce a flow chart to show how adult cell cloning works.

3 What are the main advantages and disadvantages of the development of adult cell cloning techniques?

links

For more information on adult cell cloning, see B1 6.7 Making choices about technology.

Did you know ...?

The only human clones alive at the moment are natural ones known as identical twins! But the ability to clone mammals such as Dolly the sheep has led to fears that some people may want to have a clone of themselves produced – whatever the cost.

Key points

- Scientists cloned Dolly the sheep using adult cell cloning.

- In adult cell cloning the nucleus of a cell from an adult animal is transferred to an empty egg cell from another animal. A small electric shock causes the egg cell to begin to divide and starts embryo development. The embryo is placed in the womb of a third animal to develop. The animal that is born is genetically identical to the animal that donated the original adult cell.

B1 6.6 Genetic engineering

Learning objectives

- What is genetic engineering?
- How are genes transferred from one organism to another?
- What are the issues involved in genetic engineering?

What is genetic engineering? **k**

Genetic engineering involves changing the genetic material of an organism. You take a gene from one organism and transfer it to the genetic material of a completely different organism. So, for example, genes from the chromosomes of a human cell can be 'cut out' using enzymes and transferred to the cell of a bacterium. The gene carries on making a human protein, even though it is now in a bacterium.

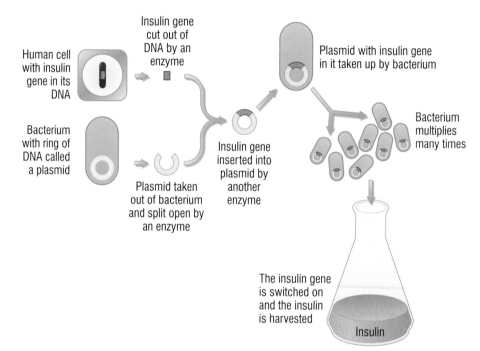

Human cell with insulin gene in its DNA

Insulin gene cut out of DNA by an enzyme

Plasmid with insulin gene in it taken up by bacterium

Bacterium with ring of DNA called a plasmid

Plasmid taken out of bacterium and split open by an enzyme

Insulin gene inserted into plasmid by another enzyme

Bacterium multiplies many times

The insulin gene is switched on and the insulin is harvested

Insulin

Figure 1 The principles of genetic engineering. A bacterial cell receives a gene from a human being so it makes the human hormone insulin.

a How is a gene taken out of one organism to be put into another?

If genetically engineered bacteria are cultured on a large scale they will make huge quantities of protein from other organisms. We now use them to make a number of drugs and hormones used as medicines.

Transferring genes to animal and plant cells

There is a limit to the types of proteins that bacteria are capable of making. As a result, genetic engineering has moved on. Scientists have found that genes from one organism can be transferred to the cells of another type of animal or plant at an early stage of their development. As the animal or plant grows it develops with the new desired characteristics from the other organism. For example, glowing genes from jellyfish have been used to produce crop plants which give off a blue light when they are attacked by insects. Then the farmer knows when they need spraying.

b Why are genes inserted into animals and plants as well as into bacteria?

The benefits of genetic engineering

Genetically engineered bacteria can make exactly the proteins we need, in exactly the amounts needed and in a very pure form. For example, people with diabetes need supplies of the hormone insulin. In the past people used animal insulin extracted from the pancreases of pigs and cattle. Now they can use pure human insulin produced by genetically engineered bacteria (see Figure 1).

We can use engineered genes to improve the growth rates of plants and animals. They can be used to improve the food value of crops as genetically modified (GM) crops usually have much bigger yields than ordinary crops. They can also be designed to grow well in dry, hot or cold parts of the world so could help to solve the problems of world hunger. Crops can be engineered to produce plants which make their own **pesticide** or are resistant to **herbicides** used to control weeds.

Human engineering

If there is a mistake in your genetic material, you may have a genetic disease. These can be very serious. Many people hope that genetic engineering can solve the problem.

It might become possible to put 'healthy' genes into the affected cells by genetic engineering, so they work properly. Perhaps the cells of an early embryo can be engineered so that the individual develops into a healthy person. If these treatments become possible, many people would have new hope of a normal life for themselves or their children.

   c What do we mean by a 'genetic disease'?

The disadvantages of genetic engineering

Genetic engineering is still a very new science. No one knows what all of the long-term effects might be. For example, insects may become pesticide-resistant if they eat a constant diet of pesticide-forming plants.

Some people are concerned about the effect of eating GM food on human health. Genes from genetically modified plants and animals might spread into the wildlife of the countryside. GM crops are often made infertile, which means farmers in poor countries have to buy new seed each year.

People might want to manipulate the genes of their future children. This may be to make sure they are born healthy, but there are concerns that people might want to use it to have 'designer' children with particular characteristics such as high intelligence. Genetic engineering raises issues for us all to think about.

Figure 2 You can't tell that food is genetically modified just by looking at it! In the UK, few GM foods are sold and they have to be clearly labelled. Many other countries, including the USA, are less worried and use GM food widely.

Key points

- Genes can be transferred to the cells of animals and plants at an early stage of their development so they develop desired characteristics. This is genetic engineering.

- In genetic engineering, genes from the chromosomes of humans and other organisms can be 'cut out' using enzymes and transferred to the cells of bacteria and other organisms.

- There are advantages and disadvantages associated with genetic engineering.

Summary questions

1 Copy and complete using the words below:

   cell   engineering   enzymes   gene   genetic   transfer

   Genetic .... involves changing the .... material of an organism. You cut a .... from one organism using .... and .... it to the .... of a completely different organism.

2 **a** Make a flow chart that explains the stages of genetic engineering.
   b Make two lists, one to show the possible advantages of genetic engineering and the other to show the possible disadvantages.

B1 6.7 | Making choices about technology

Cloning pets

Cc, or Copycat, was the first cloned cat to be produced. Most of the research into cloning had been focused on farm and research animals – but cats are thought of first and foremost as pets.

Much of the funding for cat cloning in the US comes from companies who are hoping to be able to clone people's dying or dead pets for them. It has already been shown that a successful clone can be produced from a dead animal. Cells from beef from a slaughter house were used to create a live cloned calf.

It took one hundred and eighty-eight attempts to make Cc, producing 87 cloned embryos, only one of which resulted in a kitten. Cloning your pet won't be easy or cheap. The issue is, should people be cloning their dead cats, or would it be better to give a home to one of the thousands of unwanted cats already in existence? Even if a favourite pet cat is cloned, it may look nothing like the original because the coat colour of many cats is the result of genes switching on and off at random in the skin cells. The clone will develop and grow in a different environment to the original cat as well. This means other characteristics that are affected by the environment will probably be different too.

Figure 1 The cat on the left is Rainbow. The cat on the right is Cc, Rainbow's clone. Rainbow and Cc share the same DNA – but they don't look the same.

To some people these are exciting events. To others they are a waste of time, money and the lives of all the embryos that don't make it. What do you think?

Did you know ...?

Dogs have also been cloned. In 2009, an American couple paid more than £100000 to have a clone of their much-loved pet Labrador. The new dog is called Lancelot encore (encore means 'again').

Figure 2 Lancelot encore, a clone of a much-loved pet, and a portrait of the original dog

Activity

In B1 6.4 and B1 6.5 there is information about cloning animals and plants for farming. Here you have two different stories about cloning animals for money (Cc and Lancelot encore).

There is talk of a local company setting up a laboratory to clone cats, dogs and horses for anyone in the country who wants to do this.

Write a letter or post a blog either *for* the application or *against* it. Make sure you use clear, sensible arguments and put the science of the situation across clearly.

The debate about GM foods

Ever since genetically modified foods were first introduced there has been controversy and discussion about them. For example, varieties of GM rice known as 'golden rice' and 'golden rice 2' have been developed. These varieties of rice produce large amounts of vitamin A. Up to 500 000 children go blind each year as a result of lack of vitamin A in their diets. In theory golden rice offers a solution to this problem. In fact, many people objected to the way trials of the rice were run and the cost of the product. No golden rice is yet being grown in countries affected by vitamin A blindness.

There is a lot of discussion about genetically modified crops. Here are some commonly expressed opinions.

Figure 3 The amount of beta carotene in golden rice and golden rice 2 is reflected in the depth of colour of the rice

John, 49, plumber, UK

'I'm very concerned about GM foods. Who knows what we're all eating nowadays. I don't want strange genes inside me, thank you very much. We've got plenty of fruit and vegetables as it is – why do we need more?'

Ali, 26, shop assistant, UK

'I think GM food is such a good idea. If the scientists can modify crops so they don't go off so quickly, food should get cheaper, and there will be more to go around. And what about these plants that produce pesticides? That'll stop a lot of crop spraying, so that should make our food cleaner and cheaper. It's typical of us in the UK that we moan and panic about it all.'

Tilahun, 35, farmer, Ethiopia

'I have some real worries about the GM crops that don't form fertile seeds. In the past, farmers in poorer countries just kept seeds from the previous year's crops, so it was cheap and easy. With the GM crops we have to buy new seeds every year – although I hear that won't be the case with golden rice. On the other hand, these GM crops don't need spraying very much. They grow well in our dry conditions, they give a much bigger crop yield and keep well too – so there are some advantages.'

Activity

You are going to produce a 5-minute slot for a daytime television show on '**Genetic engineering – a good thing or not?**' Using the information here and on B1 6.6 Genetic engineering (and extra research if you have time), plan out a script for your time on air, remembering that you have to inform the public about genetic engineering, entertain them and make them think about the issues involved.

Key points

- There are a number of economic, social and ethical issues concerning cloning and genetic engineering which need to be considered when making judgements about the use of this science.

Summary questions

1 People get very concerned about cloning. Do you think these fears are justified? Explain your answer.

2 Summarise the main advantages and disadvantages of genetic engineering expressed here.

B1 7.2

Accepting Darwin's ideas

Learning Objectives

- Why was Darwin's theory of evolution only gradually accepted?

Charles Darwin came back from his trip on *HMS Beagle* with new ideas about the variety of life on Earth. He read many books and thought about the ideas of many other people such as Lamarck, Lovell and Malthus. He gradually built up his theory of evolution by natural selection.

He knew his ideas would be controversial. He expected a lot of opposition both from fellow scientists and from religious leaders.

Building up the evidence

Darwin realised he would need lots of evidence to support his theories. This is one of the reasons why it took him so long to publish his ideas. He spent years trying to put his evidence together in order to convince other scientists.

He used the amazing animals and plants he had seen on his journeys as part of that evidence. They showed that organisms on different islands had adapted to their environments by natural selection. So they had evolved to be different from each other.

Darwin carried out breeding experiments with pigeons at his home. He wanted to show how features could be artificially selected. Darwin also studied different types of barnacles (small invertebrates found on seashore rocks) and where they lived. This gave him more evidence of organisms adapting and forming different species.

Darwin built up a network of friends, fellow scientists and pigeon breeders. He didn't travel far from home (he was often unwell) but he spent a lot of time discussing his ideas with this group of friends. They helped him get together the evidence he needed and he trusted them as he talked about his ideas.

Figure 1 The finches found on the different Galapagos islands look very different but all evolved from the same original type of finch by natural selection

Why did people object?

In 1859, Darwin published his famous book *On the Origin of Species by means of Natural Selection* (often known as *The Origin of Species*). The book caused a sensation. Many people were very excited by his ideas and defended them enthusiastically. Others were deeply offended, or simply did not accept them.

There were many different reasons why it took some scientists a long time to accept Darwin's theory of natural selection. They include:

● The theory of evolution by natural selection challenged the belief that God made all of the animals and plants that live on Earth. This religious view was the generally accepted belief among most people in early Victorian England.

● In spite of all Darwin's efforts, many scientists felt there was not enough evidence to convince them of his theory.

● There was no way to explain how variety and inheritance happened. The mechanism of how inheritance happens – by genes and genetics – was not known until 50 years *after* Darwin published his ideas. Because there was no mechanism to explain how characteristics could be inherited, it was much harder for people to accept and understand.

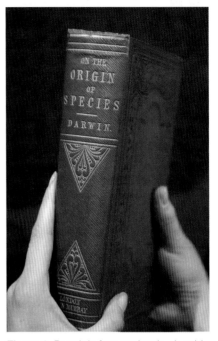

Figure 2 Darwin's famous book – it sold out on the first day of publication!

The arguments raged and it took some time before the majority of scientists accepted Darwin's ideas. However, by the time of his death in 1882 he was widely regarded as one of the world's great scientists. He is buried in Westminster Abbey along with other great people like Sir Isaac Newton.

Figure 3 It wasn't just scientists who were interested in Darwin's ideas. Cartoonists loved the idea of evolution too.

??? Did you know …?

Darwin let his children use the back of his original manuscript of *The Origin of Species* as drawing paper. Not many of these original pages exist. Darwin kept the ones that remain because of his children's drawings rather than his own writing!

Key points

● Darwin's theory of evolution by natural selection was only gradually accepted for a number of reasons. These include:

  – a conflict with the widely held belief that God made all the animals and plants on the Earth
  – insufficient evidence
  – no mechanism for explaining variety and inheritance – genetics were not understood for another 50 years.

Summary questions

1 **a** Darwin set out in *HMS Beagle* in 1831. How many years later did he publish *The Origin of Species*?
  b What was Darwin's big idea?

2 What type of evidence did Darwin put together to convince other scientists his ideas were right?

3 Why did it take some time before most people accepted Darwin's ideas?

B1 7.3

Natural selection

Learning objectives

- How does natural selection work?
- What is mutation?

Scientists explain the variety of life today as the result of a process called natural selection. The idea was first suggested about 150 years ago by Charles Darwin.

Animals and plants are always in competition with each other. Sometimes an animal or plant gains an advantage in the competition. This might be against other species or against other members of its own species. That individual is more likely to survive and breed. This is known as natural selection.

a Who first suggested the idea of natural selection?

Survival of the fittest 🄚

Charles Darwin was the first person to describe natural selection as the 'survival of the fittest'. Reproduction is a very wasteful process. Animals and plants always produce more offspring than the environment can support.

The individual organisms in any species show lots of variation. This is because of differences in the genes they inherit. Only the offspring with the genes best suited to their habitat manage to stay alive and breed successfully. This is natural selection at work.

Think about rabbits. The rabbits with the best all-round eyesight, the sharpest hearing and the longest legs will be the ones that are most likely to escape being eaten by a fox. They will be the ones most likely to live long enough to breed. What's more, they will pass those useful genes on to their babies. The slower, less alert rabbits will get eaten and their genes are less likely to be passed on.

b Why would a rabbit with good hearing be more likely to survive than one with less keen hearing?

The part played by mutation

New forms of genes result from changes in existing genes. These changes are known as mutations. They are tiny changes in the long strands of DNA.

Mutations occur quite naturally through mistakes made in copying DNA when the cells divide. Mutations introduce more variety into the genes of a species. In terms of survival, this is very important.

c What is a mutation?

Many mutations have no effect on the characteristics of an organism, and some mutations are harmful. However, just occasionally a mutation has a good effect. It produces an adaptation that makes an organism better suited to its environment. This makes it more likely to survive and breed.

Whatever the adaptation, if it helps an organism survive and reproduce it will get passed on to the next generation. The mutant gene will gradually become more common in the population. It will cause the species to evolve.

When new forms of a gene arise from mutation, there may be a relatively more rapid change in a species. This is particularly true if the environment changes. If the mutation gives the organism an advantage in the changed environment, it will soon become common.

🔗 **links**

For more information on the competition between plants and animals in the natural world, look back at B1 4.4 Competition in animals and B1 4.5 Competition in plants.

Figure 1 The natural world is often brutal. Only the best adapted predators capture prey – and only the best adapted prey animals escape.

?? Did you know ... ?

Fruit flies can produce 200 offspring every two weeks. The yellow star thistle, an American weed, produces around 150 000 seeds per plant per year. If all those offspring survived we'd be overrun with fruit flies and yellow star thistles!

🔗 **links**

For information on genes, see B1 6.1 Inheritance.

Natural selection in action

Malpeque Bay in Canada has some very large oyster beds. In 1915, the oyster fishermen noticed a few small, flabby oysters with pus-filled blisters among their healthy catch.

By 1922 the oyster beds were almost empty. The oysters had been wiped out by a destructive new disease (soon known as Malpeque disease).

Fortunately a few of the oysters had a mutation which made them resistant to the disease. These were the only ones to survive and breed. The oyster beds filled up again and by 1940 they were producing more oysters than ever.

A new population of oysters had evolved. As a result of natural selection, almost every oyster in Malpeque Bay now carries a gene that makes them resistant to Malpeque disease. So the disease is no longer a problem.

Figure 2 The tiny number of dandelion seeds that survive and grow into plants have a combination of genes that gives them an edge over all the others

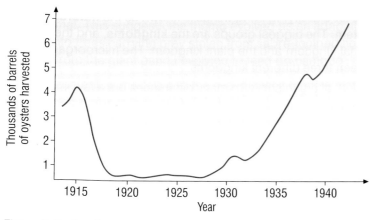

Figure 3 Oyster yields from Malpeque Bay 1915–40. As you can see, disease devastated the oyster beds. However, thanks to the process of natural selection, a healthy population of oysters managed to survive and reproduce again.

d What is Malpeque disease?

Summary questions

1 Copy and complete using the words below:

adaptation breed environment generation mutation selection organism survive

When a .... has a good effect it produces an .... that makes an .... better suited to its .... This makes it more likely to .... and .... The mutation then gets passed on to the next .... This is natural ....

2 Many features that help animals and plants survive are the result of natural selection. Give three examples, e.g. all-round eyesight in rabbits.

3 Explain how the following characteristics of animals and plants have come about in terms of natural selection.
  a Male red deer have large sets of antlers.
  b Cacti have spines instead of leaves.
  c Camels can tolerate their body temperature rising far higher than most other mammals.

Key points

● Natural selection works by selecting the organisms best adapted to a particular habitat.

● Different organisms in a species show a wide range of variation because of differences in their genes.

● The individuals with the characteristics most suited to their environment are most likely to survive and breed successfully.

● The genes that have produced these successful characteristics are then passed on to the next generation.

● Mutation is a change in the genetic material (DNA) which results in a new form of a gene.

B2 1.4

Diffusion

Learning objectives

- What is diffusion?
- What affects the rate of diffusion?

⚮ links

For more information about a specialised form of diffusion known as osmosis, see B3 1.1 Osmosis.

Your cells need to take in substances such as glucose and oxygen for respiration. Dissolved substances and gases can move into and out of your cells across the cell membrane. One of the main ways in which they move is by **diffusion.** Cells also need to get rid of waste products and chemicals that are needed elsewhere in your body.

Diffusion

Diffusion is the spreading out of the particles of a gas, or of any substance in solution (a solute). This results in the **net movement** (overall movement) of particles. The net movement is from an area of high concentration to an area of lower concentration. It takes place because of the random movement of the particles. All the particles are moving and bumping into each other and this moves them all around.

a What is diffusion?

Imagine a room containing a group of boys and a group of girls. If everyone closes their eyes and moves around briskly but randomly, children will bump into each other. They will scatter until the room contains a mixture of boys and girls. This gives you a good model of diffusion.

  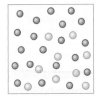

At the moment, when the blue particles are added to the red particles they are not mixed at all

As the particles move randomly, the blue ones begin to mix with the red ones

As the particles move and spread out, they bump into each other. This helps them to keep spreading randomly

Eventually, the particles are completely mixed and diffusion is complete

Figure 1 The random movement of particles results in substances spreading out or diffusing from an area of higher concentration to an area of lower concentration

Rates of diffusion

If there is a big difference in concentration between two areas, diffusion will take place quickly. Many particles will move randomly towards the area of low concentration. Only a few will move randomly in the other direction. However, if there is only a small difference in concentration between two areas, the net movement by diffusion will be quite slow. The number of particles moving into the area of lower concentration by random movement will only be slightly bigger than the number of particles that are leaving the area.

The net movement = particles moving in – particles moving out.

In general, the greater the difference in concentration, the faster the rate of diffusion. This difference between two areas of concentration is called the **concentration gradient**. The bigger the difference, the steeper the concentration gradient. The steeper the concentration gradient, the faster diffusion will take place. Diffusion occurs *down* a concentration gradient.

b What is meant by the net movement of particles?

Both types of particles can pass through this membrane – it is freely permeable

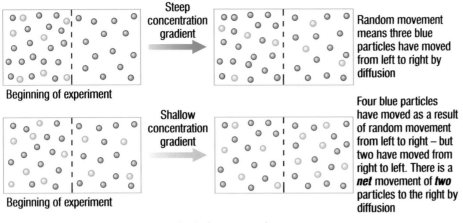

Steep concentration gradient

Random movement means three blue particles have moved from left to right by diffusion

Beginning of experiment

Shallow concentration gradient

Four blue particles have moved as a result of random movement from left to right – but two have moved from right to left. There is a **net** movement of **two** particles to the right by diffusion

Beginning of experiment

Figure 2 This diagram shows the effect of concentration on the rate of diffusion. This is why so many body systems are adapted to maintain steep concentration gradients.

Temperature also affects the rate of diffusion. An increase in temperature means the particles in a gas or a solution move more quickly. Diffusion takes place more rapidly as the random movement of the particles speeds up.

Diffusion in living organisms

Many important substances can move across your cell membranes by diffusion. Water is one, as well as simple sugars, such as glucose. The **amino acids** from the breakdown of proteins in your gut can also pass through cell membranes by diffusion.

The oxygen you need for respiration passes from the air into your lungs. From there it gets into your red blood cells through the cell membranes by diffusion. The oxygen moves along a concentration gradient from a region of high to low oxygen concentration.

Individual cells may be adapted to make diffusion easier and more rapid. The most common adaptation is to increase the surface area of the cell membrane. Increasing the surface area means there is more room for diffusion to take place. By folding up the membrane of a cell, or the tissue lining an organ, the area over which diffusion can take place is greatly increased. Therefore the rate of diffusion is also greatly increased. This means much more of a substance moves in a given time.

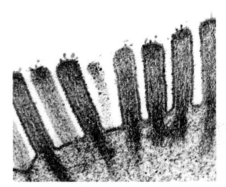

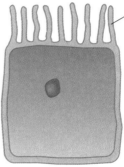

Infoldings of the cell membrane form microvilli, which increase the surface area of the cell

Figure 3 An increase in the surface area of a cell membrane means diffusion can take place more quickly. This is an intestinal cell.

Key points

- Dissolved substances and gases such as oxygen move in and out of cells by diffusion.

- Diffusion is the net movement of particles from an area where they are at a high concentration to an area where they are at a lower concentration.

- The greater the difference in concentration, the faster the rate of diffusion.

Summary questions

1 Copy and complete using the words below:

diffusion gas high lower random solute

_____ is the net movement of particles of a _____ or a _____ from an area of _____ concentration to an area of _____ concentration as a result of the _____ movement of the particles.

2 a Explain why diffusion takes place faster when there is an increase in temperature.

  b Explain in terms of diffusion why so many cells have folded membranes along at least one surface.

B2 1.5

Tissues and organs

Learning objectives

● What is a tissue?

● What is an organ?

∞ links

For more information on specialised cells, look back at B2 1.3 Specialised cells.

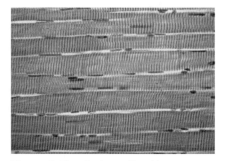

Figure 1 Muscle tissue like this contracts to move your skeleton around

Large **multicellular organisms** have to overcome the problems linked to their size. They develop different ways of exchanging materials. During the development of a multicellular organism, cells **differentiate**. They become specialised to carry out particular jobs. For example, in animals, muscle cells have a different structure to blood and nerve cells. In plants the cells where photosynthesis takes place are very different to root hair cells.

However, the adaptations of multicellular organisms go beyond specialised cells. Similar specialised cells are often found grouped together to form a tissue.

Tissues

A **tissue** is a group of cells with similar structure and function working together. **Muscular tissue** can contract to bring about movement. **Glandular tissue** contains secretory cells that can produce substances such as enzymes and hormones. **Epithelial tissue** covers the outside of your body as well as your internal organs.

Plants have tissues too. **Epidermal tissues** cover the surfaces and protect them. **Mesophyll tissues** contain lots of chloroplasts and can carry out photosynthesis. **Xylem** and **phloem** are the transport tissues in plants. They carry water and dissolved mineral ions from the roots up to the leaves and dissolved food from the leaves around the plant.

a What is a tissue?

Organs

Organs are made up of tissues. One organ can contain several tissues, all working together. For example, the stomach is an organ involved in the digestion of your food. It contains:

● muscular tissue to churn the food and **digestive juices** of the stomach together

● glandular tissue, to produce the digestive juices that break down food

● epithelial tissue, which covers the inside and the outside of the organ.

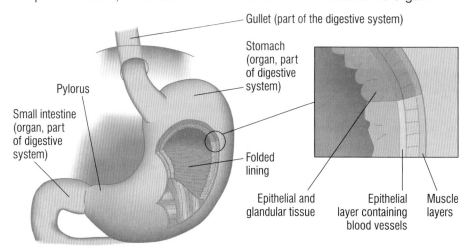

Figure 2 The stomach contains several different tissues, each with a different function in the organ

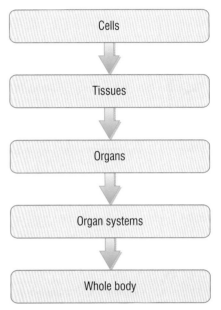

The pancreas is an organ that has two important functions. It makes hormones to control our blood sugar. It also makes some of the enzymes that digest our food. It contains two very different types of tissue to produce these different secretions.

To summarise, an organ is a collection of different tissues working together to carry out important functions in your body.

b What is an organ?

Different organs are combined in **organ systems** to carry out major functions in the body. These functions include transporting the blood or digesting food. The organ systems together make up your body.

Adaptations for exchange

Many of the organs of the body have developed to enable exchange to take place. For example:

● there is an exchange of gases in the lungs

● digested food moves from the **small intestine** into the blood

● many different dissolved substances are filtered out of the blood into the **kidney tubules**. Some of them then move back from the tubules into the blood.

These organs have adaptations that make the exchange of materials easier and more efficient.

Many of these adaptations increase the surface area over which materials are exchanged. The bigger the surface area, the more quickly diffusion can take place.

Other adaptations increase the concentration gradient across the membranes. The steeper the concentration gradient, the faster diffusion takes place. Many organs have a good blood supply, bringing substances in and taking them out. This helps to maintain the steep concentration gradient needed for diffusion to take place more rapidly.

? ? ? Did you know ... ?

A human liver cell is about $10\,\mu m$ $(1 \times 10^{-5}\,m)$ in diameter. A human liver is about $22.5\,cm$ $(2.5 \times 10^{-1}\,m)$ across. It contains a lot of liver cells!

Figure 3 Larger living organisms have many levels of organisation

---

Summary questions

1 Copy and complete using the words below:

specialised tissue differentiated function multicellular

A .... organism is made up of many different cells. Some of these cells have .... and become .... to carry out a particular .... in the body. A group of these specialised cells working together forms a ....

2 For each of the following, state whether they are a specialised cell, a tissue or an organ. Explain your answer.

a sperm

b kidney

c stomach

3 Find out and explain how the small intestine and the lungs are adapted to provide the biggest possible surface area for the exchange of materials within the organs.

Key points

● A tissue is a group of cells with similar structure and function.

● Organs are made of tissues. One organ may contain several types of tissue.

Organ systems

Learning objectives

- What are organ systems?
- What organs form the digestive system?
- What are plant organs?

?? ? Did you know ... ?

The digestive system is 6–9 m long. That is about 9×10^6 times longer than an average human cell!

Organ systems are groups of organs that all work together to perform a particular function. The way one organ functions often depends on others in the system. The human digestive system is a good example of an organ system.

The digestive system

The digestive system of humans and other mammals exchanges substances with the environment. The food you take in and eat is made up of large **insoluble molecules**. Your body cannot absorb and use these molecules. They need to be broken down or digested to form smaller, soluble molecules. These can then be absorbed and used by your cells. This process of digestion takes place in your **digestive system**.

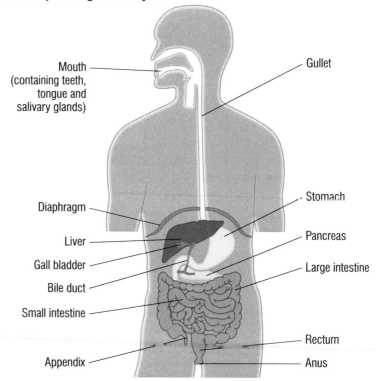

Mouth (containing teeth, tongue and salivary glands)
Gullet
Diaphragm
Stomach
Liver
Pancreas
Gall bladder
Large intestine
Bile duct
Small intestine
Appendix
Rectum
Anus

Figure 1 The main organs of the human digestive system

The digestive system is a **muscular tube** that squeezes your food through it. It starts at one end with your mouth, and finishes at the other with your anus. The digestive system contains many different organs. There are glands such as the pancreas and **salivary glands**. These glands make and release digestive juices containing enzymes to break down your food.

The stomach and the small intestine are the main organs where food is digested. Enzymes break down the large insoluble food molecules into smaller, soluble ones.

Your small intestine is also where the soluble food molecules are absorbed into your blood. Once there they get transported in the bloodstream around your body. The small intestine is adapted to have a very large surface area. This increases diffusion from the gut to the blood.

The muscular walls of the gut squeeze the undigested food onwards into your large intestine. This is where water is absorbed from the undigested food into your blood. The material left forms the faeces. Faeces are stored and then pass out of your body through the rectum and anus back into the environment.

a What is the digestive system and what does it do?

Plant organs

Animals are not the only organisms to have organs and organ systems – plants do too.

Plants have differentiated cells that form specialised tissues. These include mesophyll, xylem and phloem. Within the body of a plant, tissues such as these are arranged to form organs. Each organ carries out its own particular functions.

Plant organs include the leaves, stems and roots, each of which has a very specific job to do.

b What are the main organs in a plant?

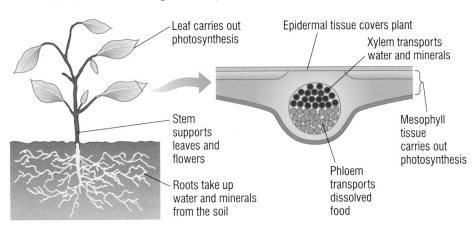

Figure 2 Plant organs and tissues

AQA Examiner's tip

Learn the sequence for multicellular organisms:

organism
↓
organ systems
↓
organs
↓
tissues
↓
cells

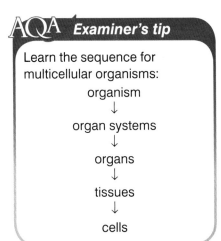

Summary questions

1 Match each of the following organs to its correct function.

A stem	**i** breaking down large insoluble molecules into smaller soluble molecules
B root	**ii** photosynthesising in plants
C small intestine for absorption	**iii** providing support in plants
D leaf	**iv** anchoring plants and obtaining water and minerals from soil

2 Explain the difference between organs and organ systems, giving two examples.

3 Using the human digestive system as an example, explain how the organs in an organ system rely on each other to function properly.

Key points

- Organ systems are groups of organs that perform a particular function.

- The digestive system in a mammal is an example of a system where substances are exchanged with the environment.

- Plant organs include stems, roots and leaves.

Summary questions 🅚

1 *Chlamydomonas* is a single-celled organism that lives under water. It can move itself to the light to photosynthesise, and stores excess food as starch.

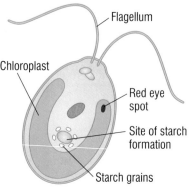

Flagellum

Chloroplast

Red eye spot

Site of starch formation

Starch grains

a What features does it have in common with most plant cells?

b What features are not like plant cells and what are they used for?

c Would you class *Chlamydomonas* as a plant cell or an animal cell? Explain why.

2

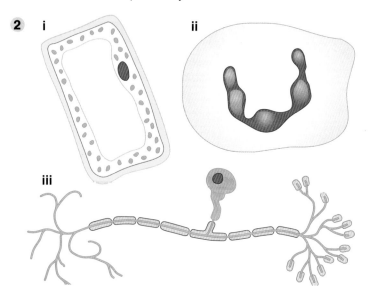

i

ii

iii

Each of these cells is specialised for a particular function in your body.

a Copy each of these diagrams and label the cells carefully. Carry out some research if necessary.

b Describe what you think is the function of each of these cells.

c Explain how the structure of the cell is related to its function.

3 a Draw and label a bacterial cell and a yeast cell.

b What are the common structures in all plant, algal and animal cells? Describe their functions.

4 a What is diffusion?

b If you cut your hand and then put it in a bowl of water, it looks as if there is a lot of blood. Explain why this happens.

c The scent of flowers in a garden is much more noticeable on a warm, still day than it is on a cold, still day. Explain this in terms of diffusion.

5 a What effect does surface area have on diffusion?

b Describe one way in which the following can be adapted to increase the surface area available for diffusion:
  i individual cells
  ii body organs.

6 Plants have specialised cells, tissues and organs just as animals do.

a Give three examples of plant tissues.

b What are the main plant organs and what do they do?

c Which plant tissues are found in all of the main plant organs and why?

7 It is possible to separate the different parts of a cell using a centrifuge which spins around rather like a very fast spin dryer. They are used to separate structures that might be mixed together in a liquid. One of their uses is to separate the different parts of a cell.

The cells are first broken open so that the contents spill out into the liquid. The mixture is then put into the centrifuge. The centrifuge starts to spin slowly and a pellet forms at the bottom of the tube. This is removed. The rest is put back into the centrifuge at a higher speed and the next pellet removed and so on.

Here are some results:

Centrifuge speed (rpm*)	Part of cell in pellet
3000	nuclei
10000	mitochondria
12000	ribosomes

*rpm = revolutions per minute

a From these observations can you suggest a link between the speed of the centrifuge and the size of the part of the cell found in the pellet?

b What apparatus would you need to test your suggestion?

c If your suggestion is correct, what results would you expect?

d What would be the easiest measurement to make to show the size of the mitochondria?

e Suggest how many mitochondria you might measure.

f How would you calculate the mean for the measurements you have taken?

AQA Examination-style questions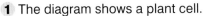

1 The diagram shows a plant cell.

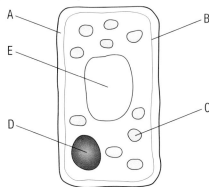

a Identify the structures listed. Choose the correct letter A, B, C, D or E for each structure.

  i nucleus (1)
  ii chloroplast (1)
  iii cell wall (1)

b Animal cells are different from plant cells. Give the letters of the two parts that are also found in animal cells. (2)

c What is a tissue? (2)

2 The parts of plant cells have important functions. **List A** contains names of cell parts. **List B** lists some functions of cell parts.

Match each cell part to its correct function.

List A	List B
nucleus	controls entry of materials into cell
mitochondria	produce protein
chloroplasts	release energy
ribosomes	controls cell activities
	absorb light for photosynthesis

(4)

3 Plant and animal organs contain tissues.

a Name one example of a plant tissue and describe its function. (2)

b i Name one example of an animal tissue. (1)
  ii Give an example of an organ where this tissue would be found. (1)
  iii What is the function of the tissue you have named? (1)

4 The diagram shows four ways in which molecules may move into and out of a cell. The dots show the concentration of molecules.

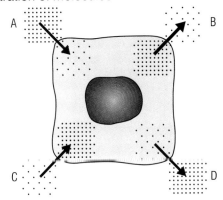

a Name the cell structure that controls the movement of materials into or out of cells. (1)

b i Name the process illustrated by A and B. (1)
  ii Explain the direction of the arrows in A and B. (2)

5 The diagram shows a yeast cell.

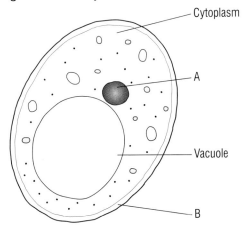

a Identify the parts labelled A and B. (2)

b The cytoplasm also contains mitochondria and ribosomes.
What is the function of these structures? (2)

c Suggest what is found in the vacuole. (1)

6 *In this question you will be assessed on using good English, organising information clearly and using specialist terms where appropriate.*

The digestive system is a group of organs which changes food from insoluble into soluble molecules. Soluble molecules can be absorbed into the blood stream. Some food cannot be digested.

Describe the functions (jobs) of the organs in the digestive system. (6)

B2 2.1

Photosynthesis

Learning objectives

- What is photosynthesis?
- What are the raw materials for photosynthesis?
- Where does the energy for photosynthesis come from and how do plants absorb it?

Like all living organisms, plants and algae need food. It provides them with the energy for respiration, growth and reproduction. But plants don't need to eat – they can make their own food. They do it by photosynthesis. This takes place in the green parts of plants (especially the leaves) when it is light. Algae can also carry out photosynthesis.

The process of photosynthesis

Photosynthesis can be summed up in the following equation:

$$\text{carbon dioxide} + \text{water} \xrightarrow{\text{(+ light energy)}} \text{glucose} + \text{oxygen}$$

The cells in algae and the leaves of a plant are full of small green parts called chloroplasts. They contain a green substance called chlorophyll.

During photosynthesis, light energy is absorbed by the chlorophyll in the chloroplasts. This energy is then used to convert carbon dioxide from the air plus water from the soil into a simple sugar called **glucose**. The chemical reaction also produces oxygen gas as a by-product. The gas is released into the air, which we can then use when we breathe it in.

a Write the word equation for photosynthesis.

Some of the glucose produced during photosynthesis is used immediately by the cells of the plant. However, a lot of the glucose made is converted into insoluble starch and stored.

Iodine solution is a yellowy-brown liquid. It turns dark blue when it reacts with starch. You can use this iodine test for starch to show that photosynthesis has taken place in a plant.

Practical

Producing oxygen

You can show that a plant is photosynthesising by the oxygen given off as a by-product. Oxygen is a colourless gas, but if you use water plants you can see and collect the bubbles of gas they give off when they are photosynthesising. The gas will relight a glowing splint, showing that it is oxygen.

Practical

Testing for starch

To show that light is vital for photosynthesis to take place:

Take a leaf from a plant kept in the light and a plant kept in the dark for at least 24 hours. Leaves have to be specially prepared so the iodine solution can reach the cells. Just adding iodine to a leaf is not enough, because the waterproof cuticle keeps the iodine out so it can't react with the starch. The green chlorophyll would mask any colour changes if the iodine did react with the starch. You need to treat the leaves by boiling them in ethanol first to destroy the waxy cuticle and remove the colour. The leaves are then rinsed in hot water to soften them. After treating the leaves, use iodine solution to show how important light is (see Figure 1).

- What happens in the test? Explain your observations.

Safety: Take care when using ethanol. It is volatile, flammable, and harmful. Always wear eye protection.

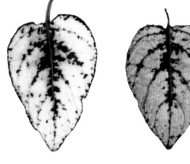

Figure 1 These **variegated** leaves came from a plant which has been kept in the light for several hours. The one on the right has been tested for starch, using iodine solution.

b What is chlorophyll?

Leaf adaptations

The leaves of plants are perfectly adapted because:

- most leaves are broad, giving them a big surface area for light to fall on
- they contain chlorophyll in the chloroplasts to absorb the light energy
- they have air spaces that allow carbon dioxide to get to the cells, and oxygen to leave them by diffusion
- they have veins, which bring plenty of water to the cells of the leaves.

These adaptations mean the plant can photosynthesise as much as possible whenever there is light available.

Algae are aquatic so they are adapted to photosynthesising in water. They absorb carbon dioxide dissolved in the water around them.

c How does the broad shape of leaves help photosynthesis to take place?

Practical

Observing leaves

Look at a whole plant leaf and then a section of a leaf under a microscope. You can see how well adapted it is. Compare what you can see with Figure 2.

- What magnification did you use?

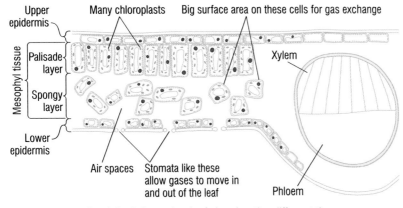

Figure 2 A section (slice) through a leaf showing the different tissues

---

Summary questions

1 Copy and complete using the words below:

carbon dioxide   chlorophyll   energy   gas   glucose   light   oxygen   water

During photosynthesis .... energy is absorbed by ...., a substance found in the chloroplasts. This .... is then used to convert .... from the air and .... from the soil into a simple sugar called .... is also produced and released as a ....

2 **a** Where does a plant get the carbon dioxide and water that it needs for photosynthesis, and how does it get the light it needs?

  b Where do algae get the same things from?

  c Work out the path taken by a carbon atom as it moves from being part of the carbon dioxide in the air to being part of a starch molecule in a plant.

B2 2.2   Limiting factors (k)

Learning objectives

● What factors limit the rate of photosynthesis in plants?

● How can we use what we know about limiting factors to grow more food?

You may have noticed that plants grow quickly in the summer, yet they hardly grow at all in the winter. Plants need certain things to grow quickly. They need light, warmth and carbon dioxide if they are going to photosynthesise as fast as they can.

Sometimes any one or more of these things can be in short supply. Then they may limit the amount of photosynthesis a plant can manage. This is why they are known as **limiting factors**.

a Why do you think plants grow faster in the summer than in the winter?

Light (k)

The most obvious factor affecting the rate of photosynthesis is light. If there is plenty of light, lots of photosynthesis can take place. If there is very little or no light, photosynthesis will stop. It doesn't matter what other conditions are like around the plant. For most plants, the brighter the light, the faster the rate of photosynthesis.

Practical

How does the intensity of light affect the rate of photosynthesis?

We can look at this experimentally (see Figure 1). At the start, the rate of photosynthesis goes up as the light intensity increases. This tells us that light intensity is a limiting factor.

When the light is moved away from this water plant, the rate of photosynthesis falls – shown by a slowing in the stream of oxygen bubbles being produced. If the light is moved closer (keeping the water temperature constant) the stream of bubbles becomes faster, showing an increased rate of photosynthesis.

However, we reach a point when no matter how bright the light, the rate of photosynthesis stays the same. At this point, light is no longer limiting the rate of photosynthesis. Something else has become the limiting factor.

The results can be plotted on a graph, which shows the effect of light intensity on the rate of photosynthesis.

● Why is light a limiting factor for photosynthesis?

● Name the **independent** and the **dependent variables** in this investigation.

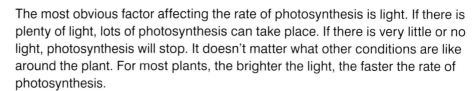

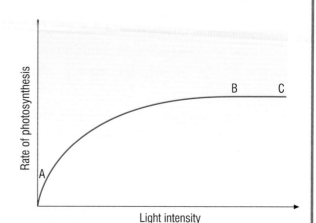

Bubbles of oxygen-rich gas

Figure 1 Investigating the effect of light intensity on the rate of photosynthesis

Temperature

Temperature affects all chemical reactions, including photosynthesis. As the temperature rises, the rate of photosynthesis increases as the reaction speeds up. However, photosynthesis is controlled by enzymes. Most enzymes are destroyed (denatured) once the temperature rises to around 40–50 °C. So if the temperature gets too high, the enzymes controlling photosynthesis are denatured. Therefore the rate of photosynthesis will fall (see Figure 2).

b Why does temperature affect photosynthesis?

Carbon dioxide levels

Plants need carbon dioxide to make glucose. The atmosphere only contains about 0.04% carbon dioxide. This means that carbon dioxide levels often limit the rate of photosynthesis. Increasing the carbon dioxide levels will increase the rate of photosynthesis.

On a sunny day, carbon dioxide levels are the most common limiting factor for plants. The carbon dioxide levels around a plant tend to rise at night. That's because in the dark a plant respires but doesn't photosynthesise. Then, as the light and temperature levels increase in the morning, the carbon dioxide all gets used up.

However, in a science lab or greenhouse the levels of carbon dioxide can be increased artificially. This means they are no longer limiting. Then the rate of photosynthesis increases with the rise in carbon dioxide.

In a garden, woodland or field rather than a lab, light, temperature and carbon dioxide levels interact and any one of them might be the factor that limits photosynthesis.

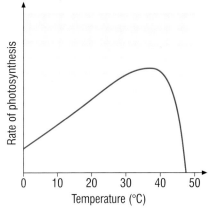

Figure 2 The effect of increasing temperature on the rate of photosynthesis

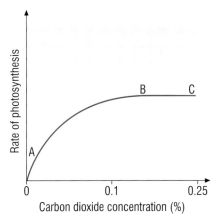

Figure 3 This graph shows the effect of increasing carbon dioxide levels on the rate of photosynthesis at a given light level and temperature

Summary questions

1 **a** What is photosynthesis?
  b What are the three main limiting factors that affect the rate of photosynthesis in a plant?

2 **a** In each of these situations *one* factor in particular is most likely to be limiting photosynthesis. In *each* case listed below, suggest which factor this is and explain why the rate of photosynthesis is limited.
   i a wheat field first thing in the morning
   ii the same field later on in the day
   iii plants growing on a woodland floor in winter
   iv plants growing on a woodland floor in summer.
  b Why is it impossible to be certain which factor is involved in each of these cases?

3 Look at the graph in Figure 1.
  a Explain what is happening between points A and B on the graph.
  b Explain what is happening between points B and C on the graph.
  c Look at Figure 2. Explain why it is a different shape to the other two graphs shown in Figures 1 and 3.

Key points

● The rate of photosynthesis may be limited by shortage of light, low temperature and shortage of carbon dioxide.

● We can manipulate the levels of light, temperature and carbon dioxide artificially to increase the rate of photosynthesis in food crops.

B2 2.3 How plants use glucose

Learning objectives

- What do plants do with the glucose they make?
- How do plants store food?
- What other materials do plant and algal cells need to produce proteins?

AQA Examiner's tip

Two important points to remember:

- Plants respire 24 hours a day to release energy.
- Glucose is soluble in water, but starch is insoluble.

Figure 2 Algal cells contain a nucleus and chloroplasts so they can photosynthesise

links

For more information about the transport of sugars in plants, see B3 2.5 Transport systems in plants.

Plants and algae make glucose when they photosynthesise. This glucose is vital for their survival. Some of the glucose produced during photosynthesis is used immediately by the cells. They use it for respiration to provide energy for cell functions such as growth and reproduction.

Using glucose

Plants cells and algal cells, like any other living cells, respire all the time. They use some of the glucose produced during photosynthesis as they respire. The glucose is broken down using oxygen to provide energy for the cells. Carbon dioxide and water are the waste products of the reaction.

Figure 1 Worldwide, algae produce more oxygen and biomass by photosynthesis than plants do – but we often forget all about them

The energy released in respiration is used to build up smaller molecules into bigger molecules. Some of the glucose is changed into starch for storage. Plants and algae also build up glucose into more complex carbohydrates like cellulose. They use this to strengthen the cell walls.

Plants use some of the glucose from photosynthesis to make amino acids. They do this by combining sugars with **nitrate ions** and other **mineral ions** from the soil. These amino acids are then built up into proteins to be used in the cells. This uses energy from respiration.

Algae also make amino acids. They do this by taking the nitrate ions and other materials they need from the water they live in.

Plants and algae also use glucose from photosynthesis and energy from respiration to build up fats and oils. These may be used in the cells as an energy store. They are sometimes used in the cell walls to make them stronger. In addition, plants often use fats or oils as an energy store in their seeds. They provide lots of energy for the new plant as it germinates.

Some algal cells are very rich in oils. They are even being considered as a possible source of biofuels for the future.

a Why do plants respire?

Starch for storage

Plants make food by photosynthesis in their leaves and other green parts. However, the food is needed all over the plant. It is moved around the plant in the phloem.

Plants convert some of the glucose produced in photosynthesis into starch to be stored. Glucose is soluble in water. If it were stored in plant cells it could affect the way water moves into and out of the cells. Lots of glucose stored in plant cells could affect the water balance of the whole plant.

Figure 3 Oilseed rape plants use energy from respiration and glucose from photosynthesis to produce oil to store in their seeds. We use this to make oil for cooking and as a source of biofuels.

Starch is insoluble in water. It will have no effect on the water balance of the plant. This means that plants can store large amounts of starch in their cells.

So, the main energy store in plants is starch and it is found all over a plant. It is stored in the cells of the leaves. The starch provides an energy store for when it is dark or when light levels are low.

Insoluble starch is also kept in special storage areas of a plant. Many plants produce **tubers** and bulbs. These help them to survive through the winter. They are full of stored starch. We often take advantage of these starch stores and eat them ourselves. Potatoes and onions are all full of starch to keep a plant going until spring comes again.

b What is the main storage substance in plants?

Summary questions

1 Copy and complete using the words below:

energy glucose growth photosynthesise respiration reproduction starch storage 24

Plants make .... when they .... Some of the glucose produced is used by the cells of the plant for ...., which goes on .... hours a day. It provides .... for cell functions, ... and .... Some glucose is converted to .... for ....

2 List as many ways as possible in which a plant uses the glucose produced by photosynthesis.

3 **a** Why is some of the glucose made by photosynthesis converted to starch to be stored in the plant?
  b Where might you find starch in a plant?
  c How could you show that a potato is a store of starch?

Practical

Making starch

The presence of starch in a leaf is evidence that photosynthesis has taken place. You can test for starch using the iodine test. See B2 2.1 Photosynthesis for details of how to treat the leaves so they will absorb the iodine. After this treatment, adding iodine will show you clearly if the leaf has been photosynthesising or not.

Figure 4 The leaf on the right has been kept in the dark. Its starch stores have been used for respiration or moved to other parts of the plant. The leaf on the left has been in the light and been able to photosynthesise. The glucose has been converted to starch, which is clearly visible when it reacts with iodine and turns blue-black.

Key points

● Plant and algal cells use the soluble glucose they produce during photosynthesis in several different ways:
  – for respiration
  – to convert into insoluble starch for storage
  – to produce fats or oils for storage
  – to produce fats, proteins or cellulose for use in the cells and cell walls.

● Plants and algal cells need other materials including nitrate ions to make the amino acids which make up proteins.

B2 2.4   Making the most of photosynthesis ⓚ

Learning objectives

- How can we control the environment in which plants are grown?

- What are the advantages and disadvantages of growing plants in an artificial environment?

?? ? Did you know ...?

The first recorded greenhouse was built in about 30 AD for Tiberius Caesar, a Roman emperor who wanted to eat cucumbers out of season.

The more a plant photosynthesises, the more biomass it makes and the faster it grows. It's not surprising that farmers want their plants to grow as fast and as big as possible. It helps them to make a profit.

In theory, if you give plants a warm environment with plenty of light, carbon dioxide and water, they should grow as fast as possible. Out in the fields it is almost impossible to influence any of these factors. However, people have found ways in which they can artificially control the environment of their plants.

The garden greenhouse

Lots of people have glass or perspex greenhouses in their gardens. Farmers use the same idea in huge plastic '**polytunnels**'. They are used for growing crops ranging from tomatoes to strawberries and potatoes.

So how does a greenhouse affect the rate of photosynthesis? Within the glass or plastic structure the environment is much more controllable than outside. Most importantly, the atmosphere is warmer inside than out. This affects the rate of photosynthesis, speeding it up so plants grow faster. They will flower and fruit earlier and produce higher yields. We can also use greenhouses to grow fruit like peaches, lemons and oranges, which don't normally grow well outside in the UK.

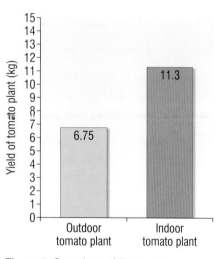

Figure 1 One piece of American research showed that the crop yield inside a greenhouse was almost double that of crops grown outdoors

Figure 2 Tomatoes certainly grow better in a greenhouse

a Why do plants grow faster in a greenhouse than outside?

Controlling a crop's environment

In a science lab you can change one factor at a time while keeping the others constant. Then you can judge how each one limits the rate of photosynthesis.

Outside, most plants are affected by a mixture of these factors. Early in the morning, light levels and temperature may limit the rate of photosynthesis. As light levels and temperature rise, carbon dioxide levels become limiting. On a bright, cold day, temperature might be the limiting factor. So there is a continuous interaction between the different factors.

Control through technology

Companies using big commercial greenhouses take advantage of what we know about limiting factors. They control the temperature and the levels of light and carbon dioxide. The levels are varied to get the fastest possible rates of photosynthesis. As a result the plants grow increasingly quickly.

The plants can even be grown in water with a perfect balance of mineral ions instead of soil, so nothing slows down their growth. This type of system is known as **hydroponics**.

The greenhouses are huge and conditions are controlled using computer software. It costs a lot of money but controlling the environment has many benefits. Turnover is fast, which means profits can be high. The crops are clean and unspoilt. There is no ploughing or preparing the land and in these systems crops can be grown where the land is poor.

b What are hydroponics?

It takes a lot of energy to keep conditions in the greenhouses just right – but fewer staff are needed. Monitoring systems and alarms are vital in case things go wrong, but for plants grown hydroponically, limiting factors are a thing of the past!

Figure 3 By controlling the temperature, light and carbon dioxide levels in a greenhouse like this you can produce the biggest possible crops – fast!

Summary questions

1 What are the main differences between a garden greenhouse and a hydroponics growing system?

2 What are the main benefits of artificially controlling the environment in which we grow our food plants?

B2 2.5 Organisms in their environment ⓚ

Learning objectives

- What factors affect the distribution of organisms in their natural environment?
- Are animals as well as plants affected by physical factors?

??? Did you know ... ?

Reindeer live in cold environments where most of the plants are small because temperature limits growth. They eat grass, moss and lichen. Reindeer travel thousands of miles as they feed. They cannot get enough food to survive in just one area.

In any habitat you will find different distributions of living organisms. These organisms form communities, with the different animals and plants often dependent on each other.

Factors affecting living organisms

A number of factors affect how living organisms are distributed in the environment. They include the following.

Temperature

You have seen that temperature is a limiting factor on photosynthesis and therefore growth in plants. In cold climates temperature is always a limiting factor. For example, Arctic plants are all small. This in turn affects the numbers of herbivores that can survive in the area.

Figure 1 Reindeer distribution depends on temperature, which affects the rate of photosynthesis and growth of their food

Nutrients

The level of mineral ions (e.g. nitrate ions) available has a big impact on the distribution of plants. Carnivorous plants such as Venus flytraps thrive where nitrate levels are very low because they can trap and digest animal prey. The nitrates they need are provided when they break down the animal protein. Most other plants struggle to grow in these areas with low levels of mineral ions.

Figure 2 The distribution of plants like these Venus flytraps depends heavily on nutrient levels

a How do nutrient levels affect the distribution of plants like the Venus fly trap?

Amount of light

Light limits photosynthesis, so it also affects the distribution of plants and animals. Some plants are adapted to living in low light levels. They may have more chlorophyll or bigger leaves. However, most plants need plenty of light to grow well.

The breeding cycles of many animal and plant species are linked to the day length. They only live and breed in regions where day length and light intensity are right for them.

Availability of water

The availability of water is important in the distribution of plants and animals in a desert. As a rule plants and animals are relatively rare in a desert. However, the distribution changes after it rains. A large number of plants grow, flower and set seeds very quickly while the water is available. These plants are eaten by many animals that move into the area to take advantage of them. If there is no water, there will be little or no life.

Availability of oxygen and carbon dioxide

The availability of oxygen has a big impact on water-living organisms. Some invertebrates can survive in water with very low oxygen levels. However, most fish need a high level of dissolved oxygen. The distribution of land organisms is not affected by oxygen levels as there is plenty of oxygen in the air and levels vary very little.

Carbon dioxide levels act as a limiting factor on photosynthesis and plant growth. They can also affect the distribution of organisms. For example, mosquitoes are attracted to the animals on whose blood they feed by high carbon dioxide levels. Plants are also more vulnerable to insect attacks in an area with high carbon dioxide levels.

b How do carbon dioxide levels affect the distribution of plants?

The physical factors that affect the distribution of living organisms do not work in isolation. They interact to create unique environments where different animals and plants can live.

??? Did you know ...?

Scientists thought that all organisms, apart from specialised microorganisms, needed oxygen to live. Then in 2010, multicellular organisms that do not need oxygen were discovered living deep under the Mediterranean seas. If more of these amazing organisms are found, our ideas of how oxygen affects the distribution of organisms will have to change.

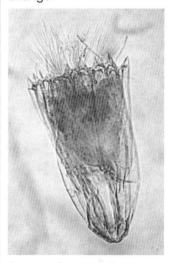

Figure 3 One of the first known multicellular organisms that do not need oxygen to respire

Figure 4 Mosquitoes are attracted to us by the carbon dioxide we breathe out

Key points

● Physical factors that may affect the distribution of living organisms include:
  – temperature
  – nutrients
  – the amount of light
  – the availability of water
  – the availability oxygen and carbon dioxide.

Summary questions

1 What are the physical factors most likely to affect living organisms?

2 How do carnivorous plants survive in areas with very low levels of nitrate ions whilst other plants cannot grow there?

3 Explain how the limiting factors for photosynthesis – light, temperature and carbon dioxide levels – also affect the distribution of animals directly and indirectly.

B2 2.6

Measuring the distribution of organisms ⓚ

Learning objectives

- How can you measure the distribution of living things in their natural environment?

- What are mean, median and mode? How do they help you understand your data?

It is often important to show how a physical factor (or changes in a physical factor) affects the distribution of living organisms. To do this you must be able to measure how those organisms are distributed in the first place.

Quadrats

The simplest way to sample an area (to count the number of organisms there) is to use a **quadrat.** A quadrat is usually a square frame made of wood or metal that you lay on the ground. This outlines your sample area.

A quadrat with sides 0.5 m long gives you a 0.25 m² sample area. Quadrats are used to investigate the size of a population of plants. They can also be used for animals that move very slowly, e.g. snails, sea anemones.

a What is a quadrat?

You use the same size quadrat every time and sample as many areas as you can. This makes your results as valid as possible. **Sample size** is very important. You must choose your sample areas *at random*. This ensures that your results reflect the true distribution of the organisms. So any findings you make will be valid. There are a number of ways to make sure that the samples you take are random. For example, the person with the quadrat closes their eyes, spins round, opens their eyes and walks 10 paces before dropping the quadrat. A random number generator is a more scientific way of deciding where to drop your quadrat.

You need to take a number of random readings and then find the **mean** number of organisms per m². This technique is known as **quantitative sampling**. You can use quantitative sampling to compare the distribution of the same organism in different habitats. You can use it to compare the variety of organisms in a number of different habitats.

Figure 1 Using a quadrat to measure barnacles on a rocky shore

← 0.5 m length →

Figure 2 It doesn't matter if organisms partly covered by a quadrat are counted as in or out as long as you decide and stick to it. In this diagram of a quadrat, you have six or seven plants per 0.25 m² (that's 24 or 28 plants per square metre), depending on the way you count.

🖩 *Maths skills*

Finding the range, the mean, the median and the mode

A student takes 10 random 1 m² quadrat readings looking at the number of snails in a garden. The results are:

4	4	3	4	5	2	6	5	4	3

The **range** of the data is the range between the minimum and maximum values – in this case from **2–6 snails per m².**

To find the **mean** distribution of snails in the garden, add all the readings together and divide by 10:

4 + 4 + 3 + 4 + 5 + 2 + 6 + 5 + 4 + 3/10 = 40/10 = **4 snails per m²**

The **median** is the middle value when the numbers are put in order – in this case, the range is 2–6 snails per m² so the median is **4 snails per m².**

The **mode** is the most frequently occurring value – in this case , **4 snails per m².**

Sampling is also used to measure changes in the distribution of organisms over time. You do this by repeating your measurements at regular time intervals. Finding the **range** of distribution and the **median** and **mode** of your data can also give you useful information (see Examiner's tip).

Counting along a transect

Sampling along a **transect** is another useful way of measuring the distribution of organisms. There are different types of transect. A line transect is most commonly used.

Transects are not random. You stretch a tape between two points. You sample the organisms along that line at regular intervals using a quadrat. This shows you how the distribution of organisms changes along that line. You can also measure some of the physical factors, such as, light levels and soil pH, that might affect the growth of the plants along the transect.

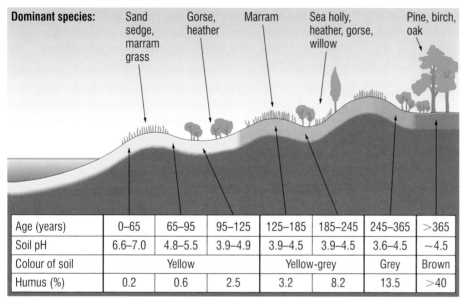

Dominant species:	Sand sedge, marram grass	Gorse, heather	Marram	Sea holly, heather, gorse, willow		Pine, birch, oak

Age (years)	0–65	65–95	95–125	125–185	185–245	245–365	>365
Soil pH	6.6–7.0	4.8–5.5	3.9–4.9	3.9–4.5	3.9–4.5	3.6–4.5	~4.5
Colour of soil	Yellow			Yellow-grey		Grey	Brown
Humus (%)	0.2	0.6	2.5	3.2	8.2	13.5	>40

Figure 3 In this transect of some sand dunes at Gibraltar Point you can clearly see the effect of changes in the physical factors on the distribution of the plants

Figure 4 Carrying out a transect of a rocky shore

Summary questions

1 Copy and complete using the words below:

transects habitat organisms environment quadrats distribution

Physical factors in the .... affect the .... of living .... Ways to measure the numbers of animals and plants in a .... include .... and ....

2 **a** How can you make sure your sampling with a quadrat is random?

b Why is it so important for samples to be random?

c In a series of 10 random 1 m² quadrats, a class found the following numbers of dandelions: 6, 3, 7, 8, 4, 6, 5, 7, 9, 8. What is the mean density of dandelions per m² on the school field?

3 Explain the ways in which the information you get from quadrats and transects is similar and how it differs.

B2 2.7

How valid is the data?

Learning objectives

- Will the method used answer the question that has been asked?
- Have all the variables been controlled?
- Does the size of your sample matter?

Environments are changing naturally all the time. But people also have an effect on the environment. This can be locally, e.g. dropping litter or building a new road, or on a worldwide scale with possible global warming and climate change. A change in the distribution of living organisms can be evidence of a change in the environment. However, if you want to use this type of data as evidence for environmental change it is important to use **reproducible** and **valid** methods to collect your results.

Reproducible, valid data

When you measure the distribution of living organisms you want your investigation to be reproducible and valid. In a reproducible investigation, other people can do the same investigation and get results that are very similar or the same as yours. And for the investigation to be valid it must answer the question you are asking. For example: What is the population density of snails in this garden?

One important factor is the size of your sample. If you do 10 quadrats, your data will not be as reproducible or as valid as if you carry out 100 quadrats.

Your method of sampling must be appropriate. If you want to measure the distribution of plants in an area, random quadrats work well. If you want to measure change in distribution over a range of habitats, a transect is a better technique to use.

If you are trying to measure change over time, you must be able to replicate your method every time you repeat your readings.

Changes in the distribution of a species are often used as evidence of environmental change. You must use a method of measuring that works regardless of who is collecting the data.

Controlling variables

When you are working in a lab you can control as many of the **variables** as possible. Then other scientists can carry out the investigation under the same conditions. This increases the likelihood that your results will be reproducible.

In fieldwork, it is not possible to control all the variables of the natural environment, but you can control some. For example, you can always measure at the same time of day. However, you cannot control the weather or the arrival of different organisms.

You must be clear about the problems of collecting data if you want to use them as evidence of environmental change.

A penguin case study

In the early 1980s Dee Boersma noticed that the numbers of penguins in a breeding colony in Argentina were falling. In 1987 she set up a research project making a transect of the colony with 47 permanent stakes, 100 metres apart.

Figure 1 If you are trying to find evidence of environmental change in an area as big as this, it is important to use a method that is as valid as possible

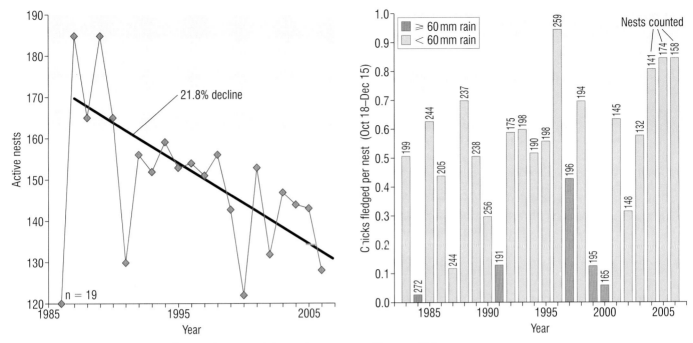

Figure 2 Patagonian penguins reflect environmental change in a very sensitive way. This graph shows clearly the effect of heavy rain on chick survival.

Every year Dee counted the active nests within a 100 m² circle around 19 of the stakes. She surveyed the remaining sites less regularly. However, Dee found the same pattern everywhere – numbers were falling.

What is causing these changes? Climate change seems to be significant:

- There have been several breeding seasons where unusually heavy rainfall has occurred. This has destroyed many nests and killed many chicks (see Figure 2).
- There have been changes in the numbers of small fish that the penguins eat. This is in response to changes in the water temperature. So there has been less food available in some years.

However, in biology things are rarely simple. The penguins are also affected by oil and waste from nearby shipping lanes. Around 20 000 penguins were killed by one major oil spill in 1991 alone. People catch the same small fish that the penguins feed on. Thousands of tourists visit the colony every year. They trample the area and cause stress to the birds.

Many factors, probably including climate change, are involved in the distribution changes of the penguins.

Figure 3 The penguin population at Punta Tombo fell by almost 22% between 1987 and 2006

Summary questions

1 What is meant by the terms: **a** reproducible and **b** valid, when you are talking about scientific data?

2 Look at Figure 2 and Figure 3 and the text above to help you answer this question.
   a When was the penguin population at Punta Tombo at its peak?
   b When was the population at its lowest? Suggest a reason for this.
   c How could Professor Boersma's data be used as evidence for environmental change?

3 Professor Boersma is widely respected in the scientific community. In what ways can you see that her data are both reproducible and valid?

Key points

- Different methods can be used to collect environmental data.

- Validity and reproducibility must be considered carefully as it is difficult to control variables in fieldwork.

- Sample size is an important factor in both reproducibility and validity of data.

Summary questions ⓚ

1 a Write the word equation for photosynthesis.

b Much of the glucose made in photosynthesis is turned into an insoluble storage compound. What is this compound?

2 The figures in the table show the mean growth of two sets of oak seedlings. One set was grown in 85% full sunlight, the other set in only 35% full sunlight.

Year	Mean height of seedlings grown in 85% full sunlight (cm)	Mean height of seedlings grown in 35% full sunlight (cm)
2005	12	10
2006	16	12.5
2007	18	14
2008	21	17
2009	28	20
2010	35	21
2011	36	23

The figures in the table show the mean growth of two sets of oak seedlings. One set was grown in 85% full sunlight, the other set in only 35% full sunlight.

a Plot a graph to show the growth of both sets of oak seedlings.

b Using what you know about photosynthesis and limiting factors, explain the difference in the growth of the two sets of seedlings.

3 More of the biomass and oxygen produced by photosynthesis comes from algae than from plants.

a Where do you find most algae?

b How do algal cells use the products of photosynthesis?

4 Palm oil is made from the fruit of oil palms. Large areas of tropical rainforests have been destroyed to make space to plant these oil palms, which grow rapidly.

a Why do you think that oil palms grow rapidly in the conditions that support a tropical rainforest?

b Where does the oil in the oil palm fruit come from?

c What is it used for in the plant?

d How else is glucose used in the plant?

5 Here are the yields of some different plants grown in Bengal, India. The yields per acre when grown normally in the field and when grown hydroponically are compared.

Name of crop	Hydroponic crop per acre (kg)	Ordinary soil crop per acre (kg)
wheat	3629	2540
rice	5443	408
potatoes	70760	8164
cabbage	8164	5896
peas	63503	11340
tomatoes	181437	9072
lettuce	9525	4080
cucumber	12700	3175

a Why are yields always higher when the crops are grown hydroponically?

b Which crops would it be most economically sensible to grow hydroponically? Explain your choice.

c Which crops would it be least sensible to grow hydroponically? Explain your choice.

d What are the benefits and problems of growing crops:

i in their natural environment

ii in an artificially manipulated environment?

AQA Examination-style questions

1 The picture shows a snail. Snails feed on plants.

Some students wanted to investigate the distribution of snails in the hedges on two sides of their school field. All the hedges were trimmed to a height of 1.5 metres. One side of the field was very open but the opposite side was shaded by trees. The students thought there would be more snails in the hedges on the open side because birds living in the trees would eat the snails. In the investigation they:

● measured a transect of 50 metres along the hedge on the open side of the field
● leaned a 1 m² quadrat against the hedge every 5 metres
● counted all the snails they could see in the quadrat
● recorded the data in a table
● repeated the investigation with the hedge that was shaded by trees.

a Choose the correct answer to complete each sentence.

  i The idea that birds in the trees eat the snails is a
  .... (1)

  conclusion   hypothesis   test

  ii A transect is a .... (1)

  line   square   triangle

  iii One thing that was controlled in this investigation was the .... (1)

  light intensity   number of trees   size of quadrat

b The data recorded by the students can be seen in the table.

	Number of snails									
Quadrat number	1	2	3	4	5	6	7	8	9	10
Open hedge	3	3	5	3	2	3	6	3	6	2
Hedge shaded by trees	2	3	4	3	5	2	1	4	1	5

Use the data to answer the questions. Choose the correct answer.

  i The mean for the number of snails in the open hedge is [3 / 3.6 / 5]. (1)

  ii The median for the number of snails in the shaded hedge is [2 / 3 / 4]. (1)

c One student said he didn't think the results would be valid. Suggest **one** reason why. (1)

2 A farmer has decided to grow strawberry plants in polytunnels, similar to the one shown in the diagram.

The tunnels are enclosed spaces with walls made of plastic sheeting. The farmer decides to set up several small polytunnels, as models, so he can work out the best conditions for the strawberry plants to grow. He needs help from a plant biologist who provides some data.

The data is shown in the graph.

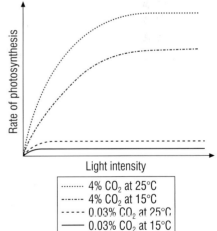

Rate of photosynthesis / Light intensity

```
·········· 4% CO₂ at 25°C
------ 4% CO₂ at 15°C
- - - - 0.03% CO₂ at 25°C
———— 0.03% CO₂ at 15°C
```

a *In this question you will be assessed on using good English, organising information clearly and using specialist terms where appropriate.*

You are advising the farmer.

Using all the information given, describe the factors the farmer should consider when building his model tunnels so he can calculate the optimal conditions for growing strawberry plants. (6)

b Biologists often use models in their research. Suggest **one** reason why. (1)

AQA, 2007

B2 3.1 | Proteins, catalysts and enzymes

Learning objectives

- What is a protein?
- What do proteins do?
- What is an enzyme and how do they work?

Did you know ...?

15–16% of your body mass is protein – second only to water, unless you are overweight. Protein is found in tissues ranging from your hair and nails to the muscles that move you around and the enzymes that control your body chemistry.

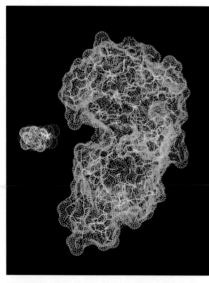

Figure 1 Enzymes are made up of chains of amino acids folded together, as you can see in this computer-generated image

AQA Examiner's tip

Remember that the way an enzyme works depends on the shape of the active site that allows it to bind with the substrate.

Protein molecules are very important in your body. A protein molecule is made up of long chains of small units called amino acids. Different arrangements of amino acids give you different proteins.

Proteins carry out many different functions in your body. They act as:

- structural components such as muscles and tendons
- hormones such as insulin
- antibodies, which destroy pathogens
- catalysts in the form of enzymes.

a What is an amino acid?

Controlling the rate of reactions

In everyday life we control the rates of chemical reactions all the time. You increase the temperature of your oven to speed up chemical reactions when you cook. You lower the temperature in your fridge to slow down reactions in stored food. Sometimes we use special chemicals known as **catalysts** to speed up reactions for us. A catalyst speeds up a chemical reaction, but it is not used up in the reaction. You can use a catalyst over and over again.

b What is a catalyst?

Enzymes – biological catalysts

In your body, chemical reaction rates are controlled by **enzymes**. These are special **biological catalysts** that speed up reactions.

Enzymes are large protein molecules. The long chains of amino acids are folded to produce a molecule with a specific shape. This special shape allows other molecules (substrates) to fit into the enzyme protein. We call this the **active site**. The shape of an enzyme is vital for the way it works.

Enzymes are involved in:

- building large molecules from lots of smaller ones
- changing one molecule into another
- breaking down large molecules into smaller ones.

Enzymes do not change a reaction in any way – they just make it happen faster. Different enzymes catalyse (speed up) specific types of reaction. In your body you need to build large molecules from smaller ones, e.g. making glycogen from glucose or proteins from amino acids. You need to change certain molecules into different ones, e.g. one sugar into another, such as glucose to fructose, and to break down large molecules into smaller ones, e.g. breaking down insoluble food molecules into small soluble molecules, such as glucose. All these reactions are speeded up using enzymes.

Practical

Breaking down hydrogen peroxide

Investigate the effect of:

a manganese(IV) oxide, and **b** raw liver,

on the breakdown of hydrogen peroxide solution.

● Describe your observations and interpret the graph (see Figure 2).

Safety: Wear eye protection.

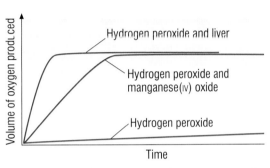

Figure 2 The decomposition of hydrogen peroxide to oxygen and water goes much faster using a catalyst like manganese(IV) oxide. Raw liver contains the enzyme catalase, which speeds up the same reaction.

How do enzymes work?

The **substrate** (reactant) of the reaction fits into the active site of the enzyme. You can think of it like a lock and key. Once it is in place the enzyme and the substrate bind together.

The reaction then takes place rapidly and the products are released from the surface of the enzyme (see Figure 3). Remember that enzymes can join small molecules together as well as break up large ones.

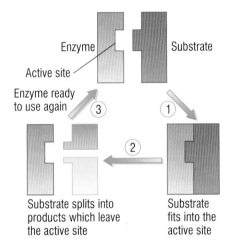

Figure 3 Enzymes act as catalysts using the 'lock-and-key' mechanism shown here

Summary questions

1 Match each word with its correct definition:

A catalyst	i the special part in the structure of an enzyme where the substrate binds
B enzyme	ii a substance that speeds up a chemical reaction without being changed itself
C active site	iii a biological catalyst made of protein

2 a What is a protein?
  b How are proteins used in the body?

3 a What is an enzyme?
  b What are enzymes made of?
  c How do enzymes act to speed up reactions in your body?

Key points

● Protein molecules are made up of long chains of amino acids.

● Proteins act as structural components of tissues, as hormones, as antibodies and as catalysts.

● Catalysts increase the rate of chemical reactions without changing themselves. Enzymes are biological catalysts.

● Enzymes are proteins. The amino acid chains are folded to form the active site.

B2 3.2 Factors affecting enzyme action

Learning objectives

- How does increasing the temperature affect your enzymes?

- Why does a change in pH affect your enzymes?

A container of milk left at the back of your fridge for a week or two will be disgusting. The milk will go off as enzymes in bacteria break down the protein structure.

Leave your milk in the sun for a day and the same thing happens – but much faster. Temperature affects the rate at which chemical reactions take place even when they are controlled by biological catalysts.

Biological reactions are affected by the same factors as any other chemical reactions. Factors such as concentration, temperature and surface area all affect them. However, in living organisms an increase in temperature only works up to a certain point.

a Why does milk left in the sun go off quickly?

links

For more information about how body temperature is maintained at a constant level for optimum enzyme activity, see B3 3.5 Controlling body temperature.

The effect of temperature on enzyme action

The reactions that take place in cells happen at relatively low temperatures. Like other reactions, the rate of enzyme-controlled reactions increases as the temperature increases.

However, this is only true up to temperatures of about 40 °C. After this the protein structure of the enzyme is affected by the high temperature. The long amino acid chains begin to unravel. As a result, the shape of the active site changes. We say the enzyme has been **denatured**. It can no longer act as a catalyst, so the rate of the reaction drops dramatically. Most human enzymes work best at 37 °C.

b What does it mean if an enzyme is denatured?

Practical

Investigating the effect of temperature on enzymes

You can show the effect of temperature on the rate of enzyme action using simple practical procedures.

The enzyme amylase (found in your saliva) breaks down starch into simple sugars. You can mix starch solution and amylase together and keep them at different temperatures. Then you test samples from each temperature with iodine solution at regular intervals.

- How does iodine solution show you if starch is present?

- Why do we test starch solution without any amylase added?

- What conclusion can you draw from the results?

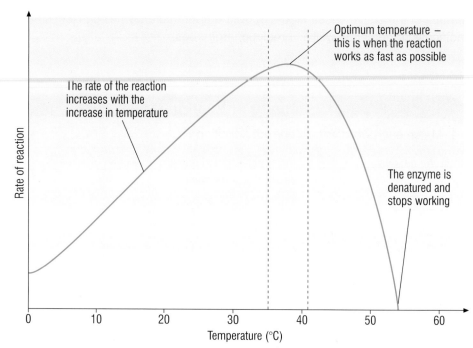

Figure 1 The rate of an enzyme-controlled reaction increases as the temperature rises – but only until the protein structure of the enzyme breaks down

Effect of pH on enzyme action

The shape of the active site of an enzyme comes from forces between the different parts of the protein molecule. These forces hold the folded chains in place. A change in the pH affects these forces. That's why it changes the shape of the molecule. As a result, the active site is lost, so the enzyme no longer acts as a catalyst.

Different enzymes have different pH levels at which they work best. A change in the pH can stop them working completely.

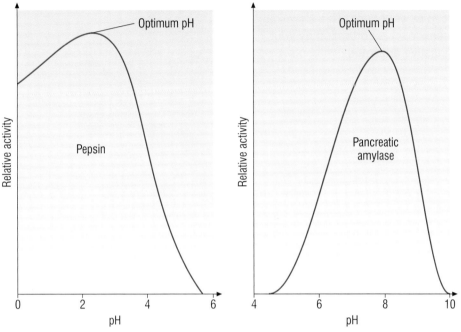

Figure 2 These two digestive enzymes need very different pH levels to work at their maximum rate. Pepsin is found in the stomach, along with hydrochloric acid, while pancreatic amylase is in the small intestine along with alkaline bile.

Without enzymes, none of the reactions in your body would happen fast enough to keep you alive. This is why it is so dangerous if your temperature goes too high when you are ill. Once your body temperature reaches about 41 °C, your enzymes start to be denatured and you will soon die.

Summary questions

1 Copy and complete using the words below:

active site cells denatured enzyme increase protein reactions shape temperatures 40 °C

The chemical .... that take place in living .... happen at relatively low .... The rate of these ....-controlled reactions .... with an increase in temperature. However, this is only true up to temperatures of about .... After this the .... structure of the enzyme is affected and the .... of the .... is changed. The enzyme has been ....

2 Look at Figure 2.
   a At which pH does pepsin work best?
   b At which pH does amylase work best?
   c What happens to the activity of the enzymes as the pH increases?
   d Explain why this change in activity happens.

 Did you know ...?

Not all enzymes work best at around 40 °C. Bacteria living in hot springs survive at temperatures up to 80 °C and higher. On the other hand, some bacteria that live in the very cold, deep seas have enzymes that work effectively at 0 °C and below.

Figure 3. The magical light display of a firefly is caused by the action of an enzyme called luciferase

AQA *Examiner's tip*

Enzymes aren't killed (they are molecules, not living things themselves) – use the term 'denatured'.

Key points

● Enzyme activity is affected by temperature and pH.

● High temperatures and the wrong pH can affect the shape of the active site of an enzyme and stop it working.

B2 3.3 Enzymes in digestion

Learning objectives

- Where are your digestive enzymes made?
- How are enzymes involved in the digestion of your food?

Your food is made up of large, insoluble molecules that your body cannot absorb. They need to be broken down or **digested** to form smaller, soluble molecules. These can then be absorbed and used by your cells. This chemical breakdown is controlled by your digestive enzymes.

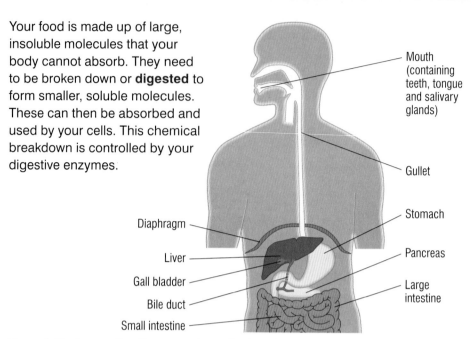

Mouth (containing teeth, tongue and salivary glands)

Gullet

Diaphragm

Liver

Gall bladder

Bile duct

Small intestine

Stomach

Pancreas

Large intestine

Figure 1 The human digestive system is a collection of organs all working together to digest your food

Learn the different types of digestive enzyme and the end products of the breakdown of your food.

Make sure you know where the different digestive enzymes are made.

Most of your enzymes work *inside* the cells of your body, controlling the rate of the chemical reactions. Your digestive enzymes are different. They work *outside* your cells. They are produced by specialised cells in glands (like your salivary glands and your pancreas), and in the lining of your gut.

The enzymes then pass out of these cells into the gut itself. Your gut is a hollow, muscular tube that squeezes your food. It helps to break up your food into small pieces with a large surface area for your enzymes to work on. It mixes your food with your digestive juices so that the enzymes come into contact with as much of the food as possible. The muscles of the gut move your food along from one area to the next.

a How do your digestive enzymes differ from most of your other enzymes?

Digesting carbohydrates

Enzymes that break down carbohydrates are called **carbohydrases**. Starch is one of the most common carbohydrates that you eat. It is broken down into sugars in your mouth and small intestine. This reaction is catalysed by an enzyme called **amylase**.

Amylase is produced in your salivary glands. So the digestion of starch starts in your mouth. Amylase is also made in your pancreas and your small intestine. No digestion takes place inside the pancreas. All the enzymes made there flow into your small intestine, where most of the starch you eat is digested.

b What is the name of the enzyme that breaks down starch in your gut?

Digesting proteins

The breakdown of protein food like meat, fish and cheese into amino acids is catalysed by **protease** enzymes. Proteases are produced by your stomach, your pancreas and your small intestine. The breakdown of proteins into **amino acids** takes place in your stomach and small intestine.

c Which enzymes break down protein in your gut?

Digesting fats

The **lipids** (fats and oils) that you eat are broken down into **fatty acids** and **glycerol** in your small intestine. The reaction is catalysed by **lipase** enzymes. These are made in your pancreas and your small intestine. Again, the enzymes made in the pancreas are passed into the small intestine.

Once your food molecules have been completely digested into soluble glucose, amino acids, fatty acids and glycerol, they leave your small intestine. They pass into your bloodstream to be carried around the body to the cells that need them.

d Which enzymes break down fats in your gut?

Did you know ...?

When Alexis St Martin suffered a terrible gunshot wound in 1822, Dr William Beaumont managed to save his life. However, Alexis was left with a hole (or fistula) from his stomach to the outside world. Dr Beaumont then used this hole to find out what happened in Alexis' stomach as he digested food!

Practical

Investigating digestion

You can make a model gut using a special bag containing starch and amylase enzymes. When the enzyme has catalysed the breakdown of the starch, you can no longer detect the presence of starch inside the 'gut'.

● How can you test for starch?

Smaller molecules of sugar diffuse out of the gut. Test the water in the beaker for (reducing) sugar.

● How can you test for this?

Figure 2 This apparatus provides you with a model of the gut. You can use it to investigate the effects of factors like temperature and pH on how the gut enzymes work.

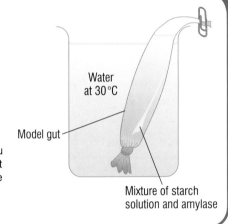

Water at 30 °C

Model gut

Mixture of starch solution and amylase

Summary questions

1 Copy and complete using the words below:

*absorbed broken down cells digestive food
insoluble soluble*

The .... you eat is made up of large .... molecules that need to be .... to form smaller, ... molecules. These can be .... by your body and used by your .... This chemical breakdown is controlled by your .... enzymes.

2 Make a table that describes amylase, protease and lipase. For each enzyme show where it is made, which reaction it catalyses and where it works in the gut.

3 Why is digestion of your food so important? Explain your answer in terms of the molecules involved.

Key points

● Digestive enzymes are produced by specialised cells in glands and in the lining of the gut. They work outside of the body cells in the gut itself.

● Different enzymes catalyse the breakdown of carbohydrates, proteins and fats into smaller, soluble molecules during digestion.

B2 3.4

Speeding up digestion

Learning objectives

- Why does your stomach contain hydrochloric acid?
- What is bile and why is it so important in digestion?

∞ **links**

For information on the sensitivity of enzymes to temperature and pH, look back at B2 3.2 Factors affecting enzyme action.

Your digestive system produces many enzymes that speed up the breakdown of the food you eat. As your body is kept at a fairly steady 37 °C, your enzymes have an ideal temperature that allows them to work as fast as possible.

Keeping the pH in your gut at ideal levels isn't that easy because different enzymes work best at different pH levels. For example, the protease enzyme found in your stomach works best in acidic conditions.

On the other hand, the proteases made in your pancreas need alkaline conditions to work at their best.

So, your body makes a variety of different chemicals that help to keep conditions ideal for your enzymes all the way through your gut.

a Why do your enzymes almost always have the right temperature to work at their best?

Changing pH in the gut

You have around 35 million glands in the lining of your stomach. These secrete protease enzymes to digest the protein you eat. The enzymes work best in an acid pH. So your stomach also produces a concentrated solution of hydrochloric acid from the same glands. In fact, your stomach produces around 3 litres of acid a day! This acid allows your stomach protease enzymes to work very effectively. It also kills most of the bacteria that you take in with your food.

Finally, your stomach also produces a thick layer of mucus. This coats your stomach walls and protects them from being digested by the acid and the enzymes.

b How does your stomach avoid digesting itself?

Practical

Breaking down protein

You can see the effect of acid on pepsin, the protease found in the stomach, quite simply. Set up three test tubes: one containing pepsin, one containing hydrochloric acid and one containing a mixture of the two. Keep them at body temperature in a water bath. Add a similar-sized chunk of meat to all three of them. Set up a webcam and watch for a few hours to see what happens.

- What conclusions can you make?

Figure 1 These test tubes show clearly the importance of protein-digesting enzymes and hydrochloric acid in your stomach. Meat was added to each tube at the same time.

After a few hours – depending on the size and type of the meal you have eaten – your food leaves your stomach. It moves on into your small intestine. Some of the enzymes that catalyse digestion in your small intestine are made in your pancreas. Some are also made in the small intestine itself. They all work best in an alkaline environment.

The acidic liquid coming from your stomach needs to become an alkaline mix in your small intestine. So how does it happen?

Your liver makes a greenish-yellow alkaline liquid called **bile**. Bile is stored in your gall bladder until it is needed.

As food comes into the small intestine from the stomach, bile is squirted onto it. The bile neutralises the acid from the stomach and then makes the semi-digested food alkaline. This provides the ideal conditions needed for the enzymes in the small intestine.

c Why does the food coming into your small intestine need neutralising?

Altering the surface area

It is very important for the enzymes of the gut to have the largest possible surface area of food to work on. This is not a problem with carbohydrates and proteins. However, the fats that you eat do not mix with all the watery liquids in your gut. They stay as large globules (like oil in water) that make it difficult for the lipase enzymes to act.

This is the second important function of the bile. It **emulsifies** the fats in your food. This means bile physically breaks up large drops of fat into smaller droplets. This provides a much bigger surface area for the lipase enzymes to act on. The larger surface area helps the lipase chemically break down the fats more quickly into fatty acids and glycerol.

Did you know ...?

Sometimes gall stones block the gall bladder and bile duct. The stones can range from a few millimetres to several centimetres long and can cause terrible pain.

Figure 2 Gall stones

AQA Examiner's tip

Remember, food is not digested in the liver or the pancreas.
Bile is *not* an enzyme and it does *not* break down fat molecules.
Bile emulsifies fat droplets to increase the surface area, which in turn increases the rate of fat digestion by lipase.

Summary questions

1 Copy and complete using the words below:

alkaline emulsifies gall bladder liver neutralises small intestine

Bile is an .... liquid produced by your .... It is stored in the .... and released onto food as it enters the .... It .... the acidic food from the stomach and makes it alkaline. It also .... fats.

2 Look at Figure 1.
   a In what conditions does the protease from the stomach work best?
   b How does your body create the right pH in the stomach for this enzyme?
   c In what conditions does the proteases in the small intestine work best?
   d How does your body create the right pH in the small intestine for this enzyme?

3 Draw a diagram to explain how bile produces a big surface area for lipase to work on and explain why this is important.

Key points

● The enzymes of the stomach work best in acid conditions.

● The enzymes made in the pancreas and the small intestine work best in alkaline conditions.

● Bile produced by the liver neutralises acid and emulsifies fats.

B2 3.6

High-tech enzymes

- What are the advantages and disadvantages of using enzymes in detergents?
- Can doctors use enzymes to help keep you healthy?

The pros and cons of biological detergents 🄚

For many people, biological washing powders have lots of benefits. Children can be messy eaters and their clothes get lots of mud and grass stains as well. Many of the stains that adults get on their clothes – sweat, food and drink – are biological too. So these enzyme-based washing powders are effective and therefore widely used.

Biological powders have another advantage. They are very effective at cleaning at low temperatures. Therefore they use a lot less electricity than non-biological detergents. That's good for the environment and cheaper for the consumer.

Figure 1 Biological detergents come in many different forms

Figure 2 The enzymes in biological detergents are held in tiny capsules – these are seen under an electron microscope

However, when biological detergent was first manufactured many factory staff developed allergies. They were reacting to enzyme dust in the air – proteins often trigger allergies. Some people using the powders were affected in the same way. But there was a solution – the enzymes were put in tiny capsules and then most of the allergy problems stopped.

Unfortunately, it got bad publicity, which some people still remember. However, research (based on 44 different studies) was published by the British Journal of Dermatology in 2008. This showed that biological detergents do not seem to be a major cause of skin problems.

Some people worry about all the enzymes going into our rivers and seas from biological detergents. The waste water from washing machines goes into the sewage system. Also, the low temperatures used to wash with biological detergents may not be as good at killing pathogens on the clothes.

Practical

Plan and carry out an investigation to compare the effectiveness of a biological detergent with a non-biological detergent at 40°C.

Enzymes and medicine

Some of the ways in which enzymes are used in medicine

TO DIAGNOSE DISEASE

If your liver is damaged or diseased, some of your liver enzymes may leak out into your bloodstream. If your symptoms suggest your liver isn't working properly, doctors can test your blood for these enzymes. This will tell them if your liver really is damaged.

TO DIAGNOSE AND CONTROL DISEASE

People who have diabetes have too much glucose in their blood. As a result, they also get glucose in their urine. One commonly used test for sugar in the urine relies on a colour change on a test strip. The test strip contains a chemical indicator and an enzyme. It is placed in a urine sample. The enzyme catalyses the breakdown of any glucose found in the urine. The strip changes colour if the products of this reaction are present. This shows that glucose was present in the original sample.

TO CURE DISEASE

- If your pancreas is damaged or diseased it cannot make enzymes. So, you have to take extra enzymes – particularly lipase – to allow you to digest your food. The enzymes are in special capsules to stop them being digested in your stomach.
- If you have a heart attack, an enzyme called streptokinase will be injected into your blood as soon as possible. It dissolves clots in the arteries of the heart wall and reduces the amount of damage done to your heart muscle.
- An enzyme is being used to treat a type of blood cancer in children. The cancer cells cannot make one particular amino acid. They need to take it from your body fluids. The enzyme speeds up the breakdown of this amino acid. The cancer cells cannot get any and they die. Your normal cells can make the amino acid so they are not affected.

Figure 3 Enzymes are vital in the human body, so it is not surprising that they are widely used in the world of medicine as well

Activity

Make a poster with the title 'Enzymes in medicine' which could be displayed on the walls of the science department to inform and interest students in KS3 and/or KS4. Use this material as a starting point and do some more research about the way enzymes are used, to help you make your poster as interesting as possible.

Key points

- Enzymes in detergents break down biological stains such as sweat. They work at low temperatures so use less electricity, which is cheaper and environmentally friendly. They originally caused problems with allergies, but this has been solved now. The lower-temperature washes are less good at killing pathogens; but higher temperatures can denature the enzymes.

- Enzymes can be produced industrially, both to diagnose and to treat disease.

Summary questions

1 Some people think that biological detergents are better for the environment than non-biological detergents. Why is this?

2 Write a short report in the use of one enzyme in industry or medicine. Explain things such as where the enzyme comes from, what it does, why it is an advantage to use it and what disadvantages there might be.

Summary questions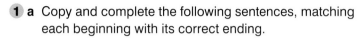

1 a Copy and complete the following sentences, matching each beginning with its correct ending.

A	A catalyst will speed up a reaction	i	.... could not occur without enzymes.
B	Living organisms make very efficient catalysts	ii	.... made of protein.
C	All enzymes are	iii	.... binds to the active site.
D	The reactions that keep you alive	iv	.... known as enzymes.
E	The substrate of an enzyme	v	.... a specific type of molecule.
F	Each type of enzyme affects	vi	.... but is not changed itself.

b Explain how an enzyme catalyses a reaction. Use diagrams if they make your explanation clearer.

2 The table gives some data about the relative activity levels of an enzyme at different pH levels.

pH	Relative activity
4	0
6	3
8	10
10	1

a Plot a graph of this data.

b Does this enzyme work best in an acid or an alkaline environment?

c This is a protein-digesting enzyme. Where in the gut do you think it might be found? Explain your answer.

3 The results in these tables come from a student who was investigating the breakdown of hydrogen peroxide using manganese(IV) oxide and mashed raw potato.

Table 1 Manganese(IV) oxide

Temperature (°C)	Time taken (s)
20	106
30	51
40	26
50	12

Table 2 Raw mashed potato

Temperature (°C)	Time taken (s)
20	114
30	96
40	80
50	120
60	no reaction

a Draw a graph of the results using manganese(IV) oxide.

b What do these results tell you about the effect of temperature on a catalysed reaction? Explain your observation.

c Draw a graph of the results when raw mashed potato was added to the hydrogen peroxide.

d What is the name of the enzyme found in living cells that catalyses the breakdown of hydrogen peroxide?

e What does this graph tell you about the effect of temperature on an enzyme-catalysed reaction?

f Why does temperature have this effect on the enzyme-catalysed reaction but not on the reaction catalysed by manganese(IV) oxide?

g How could you change the second investigation to find the temperature at which the enzyme works best?

AQA Examination-style questions ⓚ

1 Enzymes are chemicals produced in living cells.

a Copy and complete the following sentences, using some of the words below.

amylase bile catalysts fats lipase protease protein sugars

i Enzymes are described as biological .... (1)
ii Enzyme molecules are made of .... (1)
iii The enzyme that digests starch is called .... (1)
iv The substance that neutralises stomach acid is called .... (1)
v Glycerol is one of the products of the digestion of .... (1)

b An enzyme works well in pH 7.

i What happens to this enzyme when it is placed in an acid solution? (1)
ii Give **one** other factor that will affect the activity of the enzyme. (1)

c Explain what happens to starch when it is digested. (2)

AQA, 2002

2 Enzymes have many uses in the home and in industry.

a Which type of organisms are used to produce these enzymes?

Choose the correct answer from the following options:

mammals microorganisms plants (1)

b Babies may have difficulty digesting proteins in their food. Baby-food manufacturers use enzymes to 'predigest' the protein in baby food to overcome this difficulty.

Copy and complete the following sentences, using some of the words below.

amino acids amylases proteases sugars

i Proteins are 'predigested' using enzymes called .... (1)
ii This predigestion produces .... (1)

c A baby-food manufacturer uses enzyme **V** to predigest protein.
He tries four new enzymes, **W**, **X**, **Y** and **Z**, to see if he can reduce the time taken to predigest the protein. The graph shows the time taken for the enzymes to completely predigest the protein.
The manufacturer uses the same concentration of enzyme and the same mass of protein in each experiment.

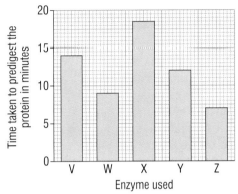

i How long did it take enzyme **V** to predigest the protein? (1)
ii Which enzyme would you advise the baby food manufacturer to use?
Choose the correct answer from the following options:

enzyme V enzyme W enzyme X enzyme Y enzyme Z

Give a reason for your answer. (2)
iii Give **two** factors which should be controlled in the baby-food manufacturer's investigations.
Choose the correct answer from the following options:

oxygen concentration temperature light intensity pH (2)

3 *In this question you will be assessed on using good English, organising information clearly and using specialist terms where appropriate.*

Describe the roles of the liver and pancreas in the digestion of fats. (6)

B2 4.1

Aerobic respiration ⓚ

Learning objectives

- What is aerobic respiration?
- Where in your cells does respiration take place?

Did you know … ?

The average energy needs of a teenage boy are 11 510 kJ of energy every day – but teenage girls only need 8830 kJ a day. This is partly because on average girls are smaller than boys, but also because boys have more muscle cells, which means more mitochondria demanding fuel for aerobic respiration.

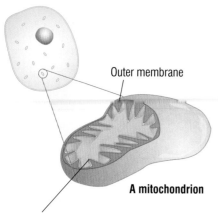

Outer membrane

A mitochondrion

Folded inner membrane gives a large surface area where the enzymes which release cellular respiration are found

Figure 1 Mitochrondria are the powerhouses that provide energy for all the functions of your cells

One of the most important enzyme-controlled processes in living things is aerobic respiration. It takes place all the time in plant and animal cells.

Your digestive system, lungs and circulation all work to provide your cells with the glucose and oxygen they need for respiration.

During aerobic respiration, glucose reacts with oxygen. This reaction releases energy that your cells can use. This energy is vital for everything that goes on in your body.

Carbon dioxide and water are produced as waste products of the reaction. We call the process aerobic respiration because it uses oxygen from the air.

Aerobic respiration can be summed up by the equation:

glucose + oxygen → carbon dioxide + water (+ energy)

a Why is aerobic respiration so important?

Practical

Investigating respiration

Animals, plants and microorganisms all respire. It is possible to show that cellular respiration is taking place. You can either deprive a living organism of the things it needs to respire, or show that waste products are produced from the reaction.

Depriving a living thing of food and/or oxygen would kill it. This would be unethical. So we concentrate on the products of respiration. Carbon dioxide is the easiest to identify. We can also measure the energy released to the surroundings.

Limewater goes cloudy when carbon dioxide bubbles through it. The higher the concentration of carbon dioxide, the quicker the limewater goes cloudy. This gives us an easy way of showing that carbon dioxide has been produced. We can also look for a rise in temperature to show that energy is being released during respiration.

- Plan an ethical investigation into aerobic respiration in living organisms.

Mitochondria – the site of respiration

Aerobic respiration involves lots of chemical reactions. Each reaction is controlled by a different enzyme. Most of these reactions take place in the mitochondria of your cells.

Mitochondria are tiny rod-shaped parts (organelles) that are found in almost all plant and animal cells. They have a folded inner membrane. This provides a large surface area for the enzymes involved in aerobic respiration.

The number of mitochondria in a cell shows you how active the cell is.

b Why do mitochondria have folded inner membranes?

Reasons for respiration

Respiration releases energy from the food we eat so that our cells can use it.

- Living cells need energy to carry out the basic functions of life. They build up large molecules from smaller ones to make new cell material. Much of the energy released in respiration is used for these 'building' activities (synthesis reactions). For example, in plants the sugars, nitrates and other nutrients are built up into amino acids. The amino acids are then built up into proteins.

- In animals, energy from respiration is used to make muscles contract. Muscles are working all the time in your body. Even when you sleep your heart beats, you breathe and your gut churns. All muscular activities use energy.

- Finally, mammals and birds keep their bodies at a constant temperature inside almost regardless of the temperature of their surroundings. So on cold days you will use energy to keep warm, while on hot days you use energy to sweat and keep your body cool.

Figure 2 When the weather is cold, birds like this robin use up a lot of energy from respiration just to keep warm. Giving them extra food supplies can mean the difference between life and death.

Summary questions

1 Copy and complete using the words below:

aerobic respiration   mitochondria   glucose   waste products   energy   water

.... is released from .... in a reaction with oxygen by a process known as .... This takes place in the .... of the cells. Carbon dioxide and .... are formed as ....

2 Why do muscle cells have many mitochondria but fat cells very few?

3 You need a regular supply of food to provide energy for your cells. If you don't get enough to eat you become thin and stop growing. You don't want to move around and you start to feel cold.

 a What are the three main uses of the energy released in your body during aerobic respiration?

 b How does this explain the symptoms of starvation described above?

4 Suggest an experiment to show that: a oxygen is taken up, and
 b carbon dioxide is released, during aerobic respiration.

Key points

- Aerobic respiration involves chemical reactions that use oxygen and sugar and release energy. The reaction is summed up as:

 glucose + oxygen → carbon dioxide + water (+ energy)

- Most of the reactions in aerobic respiration take place inside the mitochondria.

- The energy released during respiration is used to build large molecules from smaller ones and allows muscles to contract. In mammals and birds, it enables them to maintain a steady body temperature.

Summary questions 🄚

1 Edward and Jess wanted to investigate the process of cellular respiration. They set up three vacuum flasks. One contained live, soaked peas. One contained dry peas. One contained peas which had been soaked and then boiled. They took daily observations of the temperature in each flask for a week. The results are shown in the table.

Day	Room temperature (°C)	Temperature in flask A containing live, soaked peas (°C)	Temperature in flask B containing dry peas (°C)	Temperature in flask C containing soaked, boiled peas (°C)
1	20.0	20.0	20.0	20.0
2	20.0	20.5	20.0	20.0
3	20.0	21.0	20.0	20.0
4	20.0	21.5	20.0	20.0
5	20.0	22.0	20.0	20.0
6	20.0	22.2	20.0	20.5
7	20.0	22.5	20.0	21.0

a Plot a graph to show these results.

b Explain the results in flask A containing the live, soaked peas.

c Why were the results in flask B the same as the room temperature readings?

d Why did Edward and Jess record room temperature in the lab every day?

e How would you explain the results seen in flask C? Why is the temperature at 20°C for the first five days? Give two possible explanations why the temperature then increases.

2 It is often said that taking regular exercise and getting fit is good for your heart and your lungs.

	Before getting fit	After getting fit
Amount of blood pumped out of the heart during each beat (cm³)	64	80
Heart volume (cm³)	120	140
Breathing rate (breaths/ min)	14	12
Pulse rate (beats/min)	72	63

a The table shows the effect of getting fit on the heart and lungs of one person. Display this data in four bar charts.

b Use the information on your bar charts to explain exactly what effect increased fitness has on:
  i your heart
  ii your lungs.

3 Look at the graph that shows the difference between a fit and unfit person and the time taken to repay oxygen debt.

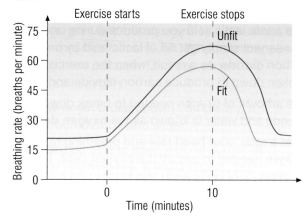

a Explain what is happening to both people.

b Why is the graph for the unfit person different from the graph for the fit person?

c What could the unfit person do to change their body responses to be more like those of the fit person? [H]

4 Athletes want to be able to use their muscles aerobically for as long as possible when they compete. They train to develop their heart and lungs. Many athletes also train at altitude. There is less oxygen in the air so your body makes more red blood cells, which helps to avoid oxygen debt. Sometimes athletes remove some of their own blood, store it and then just before a competition transfuse it back into their system. This is called blood doping and it is illegal. Other athletes use hormones to stimulate the growth of extra red blood cells. This is also illegal.

a What is aerobic respiration?

b Why do athletes want to be able to use their muscles aerobically for as long as possible?

c How does developing more red blood cells by training at altitude help athletic performance?

d How does blood doping help performance?

e Explain in detail what happens to the muscles if the body cannot supply enough glucose and oxygen when they are working hard. [H]

f It is legal to train at altitude but illegal to carry out blood doping or to take hormones that stimulate the development of red blood cells. What do you think about this situation?

AQA Examination-style questions

1 The diagram shows a group of muscle cells from the wall of the intestine.

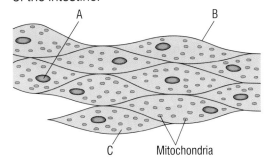

a Choose the correct words to name the structures labelled **A**, **B** and **C**.

cell membrane   cell wall   chloroplast   cytoplasm nucleus (3)

b Suggest **two** ways that these muscle cells are adapted to release a lot of energy? (2)

2 Respiration is a chemical process.

a Where does respiration take place? Choose the correct answer.

chloroplasts   mitochondria   nuclei   ribosomes (1)

b Which food material is used in respiration? (1)

c Name the **two** waste materials that are produced in respiration. (2)

d Respiration is important in muscle contraction. Explain why. (2)

3 a Copy and complete the word equation for aerobic respiration.

oxygen + ... → water + ... (+ energy) (2)

b i Which substance is missing in anaerobic respiration? (1)

ii What is made during anaerobic respiration? (1)

iii Muscles get tired during anaerobic respiration. Explain why. (1)

4 An athlete started a fitness programme. He was advised to eat a diet containing 18 000 kJ per day.

a The athlete was told that 80% of this energy was needed to keep his body temperature at normal levels. Calculate the remaining number of kilojoules available to the athlete. Show your working. (2)

b The athlete decided to double his amount of exercise and assumed he should increase the number of kilojoules in his diet.
Using only the information available to the athlete, calculate the extra energy is he likely to need. (1)

c The energy supplied in the diet must be transferred to the muscles.
Explain in detail this process of energy transfer to the muscles. (4)

5 *In this question you will be assessed on using good English, organising information clearly and using specialist terms where appropriate.*

The bar charts show what happens in an athlete's muscles when running in two races of different distances.

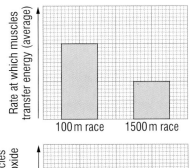

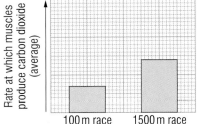

The equations show two processes that occur in muscle cells.

aerobic respiration	glucose + oxygen → carbon dioxide + water
anaerobic respiration	glucose → lactic acid

Use all the information to explain what happens in the athlete's muscles when running in the two races. (6)

B2 5.1 Cell division and growth 🄚

Learning objectives

- How are chromosomes arranged in body cells?
- What is mitosis?
- What is cell differentiation and how does it differ in animals and plants?

⚭ **links**

For more information on alleles, look at B2 5.5 Inheritance in action.

New cells are needed for an organism, or part of an organism, to grow. They are also needed to replace cells which become worn out and to repair damaged tissue. However, the new cells must have the same genetic information as the originals. Then they can do the same job.

Each of your cells has a nucleus containing the instructions for making both new cells and all the tissues and organs needed to make an entire new you. These instructions are carried in the form of genes.

A gene is a small packet of information that controls a characteristic or part of a characteristic, of your body. It is a section of DNA. Different forms of the same gene are known as **alleles**. The genes are grouped together on chromosomes. A chromosome may carry several hundred or even thousands of genes.

You have 46 chromosomes in the nucleus of your body cells. They are arranged in 23 pairs. One of each pair is inherited from your father and one from your mother. Your sex cells (gametes) have only one of each pair of chromosomes.

a Why are new cells needed?

Mitosis 🄚

The cell division in normal body cells produces two identical cells and is called **mitosis**. As a result of mitosis all your body cells have the same chromosomes. This means they have the same genetic information.

In asexual reproduction, the cells of the offspring are produced by mitosis from the cells of their parent. This is why they contain exactly the same alleles as their parent with no genetic variation.

How does mitosis work? Before a cell divides it produces new copies of the chromosomes in the nucleus. Then the cell divides once to form two genetically identical cells.

In some parts of an animal or plant, cell division like this carries on rapidly all the time. Your skin is a good example. You constantly lose cells from the skin's surface, and make new cells to replace them. In fact about 300 million body cells die every minute so mitosis is very important.

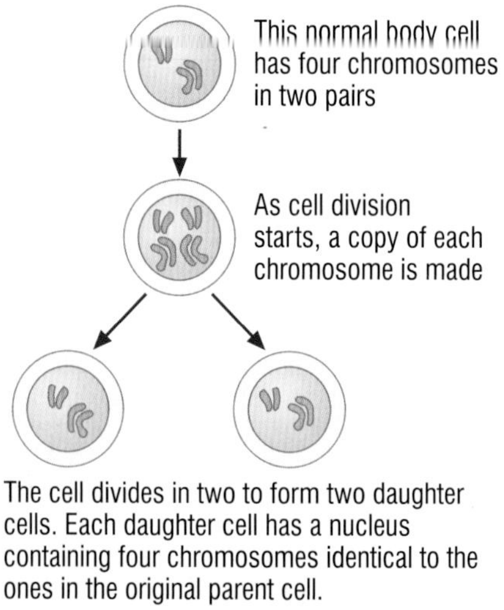

This normal body cell has four chromosomes in two pairs

As cell division starts, a copy of each chromosome is made

The cell divides in two to form two daughter cells. Each daughter cell has a nucleus containing four chromosomes identical to the ones in the original parent cell.

Figure 1 Two identical cells are formed by the simple division that takes place during mitosis. For simplicity this cell is shown with only two pairs (not 23).

Practical

Observing mitosis

View a special preparation of a growing root tip under a microscope. You should be able to see the different stages of mitosis as they are taking place. Use Figure 2 for reference.

- Describe your observations of mitosis.

b What is mitosis?

Differentiation

In the early development of animal and plant embryos the cells are unspecialised. Each one of them (known as a **stem cell**) can become any type of cell that is needed.

In many animals, the cells become specialised very early in life. By the time a human baby is born most of its cells are specialised. They will all do a particular job, such as liver cells, skin cells or muscle cells. They have differentiated. Some of their genes have been switched on and others have been switched off.

This means that when, for example, a muscle cell divides by mitosis it can only form more muscle cells. So in a mature (adult) animal, cell division is mainly restricted. It is needed for the repair of damaged tissue and to replace worn out cells. This is because in most adult cells differentiation has already occurred. Specialised cells can divide by mitosis, but they only form the same sort of cell. Therefore growth stops once the animal is mature.

In contrast, most plant cells are able to differentiate all through their life. Undifferentiated cells are formed at active regions of the stems and roots. In these areas mitosis takes place almost continuously.

Plants keep growing all through their lives at these 'growing points'. The plant cells produced don't differentiate until they are in their final position in the plant. Even then the differentiation isn't permanent. You can move a plant cell from one part of a plant to another. There it can redifferentiate and become a completely different type of cell. You can't do that with animal cells – once a muscle cell, always a muscle cell.

We can produce huge numbers of identical plant clones from a tiny piece of leaf tissue. This is because in the right conditions, a plant cell will become unspecialised and undergo mitosis many times. Each of these undifferentiated cells will produce more cells by mitosis. Given different conditions, these will then differentiate to form a tiny new plant. The new plant will be identical to the original parent.

It is difficult to clone animals because animal cells differentiate permanently, early in embryo development. The cells can't change back. Animal clones can only be made by cloning embryos in one way or another, although adult cells can be used to make an embryo.

⚬⚬ links

For information on cell differentiation, look back to B2 1.5 Tissues and organs.

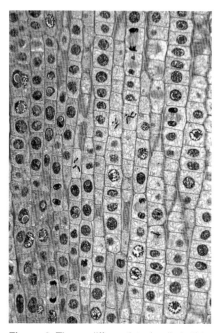

Figure 2 The undifferentiated cells in this onion root tip are dividing rapidly. You can see mitosis taking place, with the chromosomes in different positions as the cells divide.

AQA **Examiner's tip**

Cells produced by mitosis are genetically identical.

Summary questions

1 Copy and complete using the words below:

chromosomes   genetic information   genes   growth
mitosis   nucleus   replace

New cells are needed for .... and to .... worn out cells. The new cells must have the same .... in them as the originals. Each cell has a .... containing the .... grouped together on .... The type of cell division that produces identical cells is known as ....

2 a Explain why the chromosome number must stay the same when the cells divide to make other normal body cells.

   b Why is mitosis so important?

3 a What is differentiation?

   b How does differentiation differ in animal and plant cells?

   c How does this difference affect the cloning of plants and animals?

Key points

- In body cells, chromosomes are found in pairs.

- Body cells divide by mitosis to produce more identical cells for growth, repair and replacement, or in some cases asexual reproduction.

- Most types of animal cell differentiate at an early stage of development. Many plant cells can differentiate throughout their life.

B2 5.4 From Mendel to DNA

Learning objectives

- What did Mendel's experiments teach us about inheritance?
- What is DNA?
- How are specific proteins made in the body? [H]

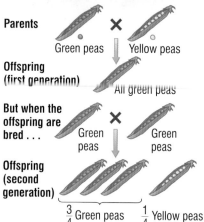

Parents — Green peas ✕ Yellow peas

Offspring (first generation) — All green peas

But when the offspring are bred . . . Green peas ✕ Green peas

Offspring (second generation) — $\frac{3}{4}$ Green peas $\frac{1}{4}$ Yellow peas

Figure 1 Gregor Mendel, the father of modern genetics. His work was not recognised in his lifetime but now we know just how right he was!

Until about 150 years ago people had no idea how information was passed from one generation to the next. Today we can identify people by the genetic information in their cells.

Mendel's discoveries

Gregor Mendel was born in 1822 in Austrian Silesia. He was clever but poor, so he became a monk to get an education.

He worked in the monastery gardens and became fascinated by the peas growing there. He carried out some breeding experiments using peas. He used smooth peas, wrinkled peas, green peas and yellow peas for his work. Mendel cross-bred the peas and counted the different offspring carefully. He found that characteristics were inherited in clear and predictable patterns.

Mendel explained his results by suggesting there were separate units of inherited material. He realised that some characteristics were dominant over others and that they never mixed together. This was an amazing idea for the time.

a Why did Gregor Mendel become a monk?

Mendel kept records of everything he did, and analysed his results. This was almost unheard of in those days. Eventually in 1866 Mendel published his findings.

He had never seen chromosomes nor heard of genes. Yet he explained some of the basic laws of genetics using mathematical models in ways that we still use today.

Mendel was ahead of his time. As no one knew about genes or chromosomes, people simply didn't understand his theories. He died 20 years later with his ideas still ignored – but convinced that he was right.

b What was unusual about Mendel's scientific technique at the time?

Sixteen years after Mendel's death, his work was finally recognised. By 1900, people had seen chromosomes through a microscope. Other scientists discovered Mendel's papers and repeated his experiments. When they published their results, they gave Mendel the credit for what they observed.

From then on ideas about genetics developed rapidly. It was suggested that Mendel's units of inheritance might be carried on the chromosomes seen under the microscope. And so the science of genetics as we know it today was born.

DNA – the molecule of inheritance

The work of Gregor Mendel was just the start of our understanding of inheritance. Today, we know that our features are inherited on genes carried on the chromosomes found in the nuclei of our cells.

These chromosomes are made up of long molecules of a chemical known as DNA (deoxyribonucleic acid). This has a double helix structure. Your genes are small sections of this DNA. The DNA carries the instructions to make the proteins that form most of your cell structures. These proteins also include the enzymes that control your cell chemistry. This is how the relationship between the genes and the whole organism builds up. The genes make up the chromosomes in the nucleus of the cell. They control the proteins, which make up the different specialised cells that form tissues. These tissues then form organs and organ systems that make up the whole body.

The genetic code

The long strands of your DNA are made up of combinations of four different chemical bases (see Figure 2). These are grouped into threes and each group of three codes for an amino acid.

Each gene is made up of hundreds or thousands of these bases. The order of the bases controls the order in which the amino acids are put together so that they make a particular protein for use in your body cells. Each gene codes for a particular combination of amino acids, which make a specific protein.

A change or mutation in a single group of bases can be enough to change or disrupt the whole protein structure and the way it works.

A section of three bases like this codes for one amino acid

Figure 2 DNA codes for the amino acids that make up the proteins that make up the enzymes that make each individual

DNA fingerprinting

Unless you have an identical twin, your DNA is unique to you. Other members of your family will have strong similarities in their DNA. However, each individual has their own unique pattern. Only identical twins have the same DNA. That's because they have both developed from the same original cell.

The unique patterns in your DNA can be used to identify you. A technique known as 'DNA fingerprinting' can be applied to make the patterns known as **DNA fingerprints**.

These patterns are more similar between people who are related than between total strangers. They can be produced from very tiny samples of DNA from body fluids such as blood, saliva and semen.

The likelihood of two identical samples coming from different people (apart from identical twins) is millions to one. As a result, DNA fingerprinting is very useful in solving crimes. It can also be used to find the biological father of a child when there is doubt.

?? Did you know ...?

The first time DNA fingerprinting was used to solve a crime, it identified Colin Pitchfork as the murderer of two teenage girls and cleared an innocent man of the same crimes.

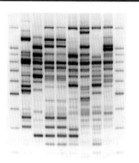

Figure 3 A DNA fingerprint

Summary questions

1 **a** How did Mendel's experiments with peas convince him that there were distinct 'units of inheritance' that were not blended together in offspring?
   b Why didn't people accept his ideas?
   c The development of the microscope played an important part in helping to convince people that Mendel was right. How?

2 Two men claim to be the father of the same child. Explain how DNA fingerprinting could be used to find out which one is the real father.

3 Explain the saying 'One gene, one protein'.   **[H]**

Key points

- Gregor Mendel was the first person to suggest separately inherited factors, which we now call genes.

- Chromosomes are made up of large molecules of DNA.

- A gene is a small section of DNA that codes for a particular combination of amino acids, which make a specific protein.   **[H]**

- Everyone (except identical twins) has unique DNA that can be used to identify them using DNA fingerprinting.

B2 5.7

Stem cells and embryos – science and ethics

- Does everyone agree with the use of embryonic stem cells?

- Are there any problems related to embryo screening?

The stem cell dilemma

Doctors have treated people with adult stem cells for many years by giving bone marrow transplants. Now scientists are moving ever closer to treating very ill people using embryonic stem cells. This area of medicine raises many issues. People have strong opinions about using embryonic stem cells – here are some of them:

In favour of using embryonic stem cells in medical research and possible treatments	Against using embryonic stem cells in medical research and possible treatments

- Embryonic stem cells offer one of the best chances of finding treatments for many different and often very serious conditions, including paralysis from spinal injury, Alzheimer's and diabetes.
- The embryos used are generally spare embryos from infertility treatment which would be destroyed anyway.
- Embryos are being created from adult cells for use in research and therapy – they would never become babies.
- It may be possible to use embryonic stem cells from the umbilical cord of newborn babies, so that no embryos need to be destroyed for the research and treatments to go ahead.
- Embryonic stem cells could be used to grow new tissues and organs for transplants.

- Embryonic stem cell treatments are very experimental and there is a risk that they may cause further problems such as the development of cancers.
- All embryos have the potential to become babies. It is therefore wrong to experiment on them or destroy them.
- Embryos cannot give permission to be used in experiments or treatments, so it is unethical.
- It is taking a long time to develop any therapy that works – the money and research time would be better spent on other possible treatments such as new drugs or using adult stem cells.

Activity 1

Your class is going to produce a large wall display covered with articles both for and against stem cell research. Your display is aimed at students in Years 10–11. Make sure the level of content is right for your target group.

Try and carry out a survey or a vote with your target group before the display is put up to assess attitudes to the use of embryonic stem cells. Record your findings.

Work on your own or in a small group to produce one piece of display material either in favour of stem cell research or against it. Use a variety of resources to help you – the material in this chapter is a good starting point. Make sure that your ideas are backed up with as much scientific evidence as possible.

Once the material has been displayed for a week or two, repeat your initial survey or vote. Analyse the data to see if easy access to information has changed people's views.

The ethics of screening

Today we not only understand the causes of many genetic disorders, we can also test for them. However, being able to test for a genetic disorder doesn't necessarily mean we should always do it.

- Huntington's disease is inherited through a dominant allele. It causes death in middle age. People in affected families can take a genetic test for the faulty allele. Some people in affected families take the test and use it to help them decide whether to marry or have a family. Others prefer not to know.

- Some couples with an inherited disorder in their family have any developing embryos tested during pregnancy. Cells from the embryo are checked. If it is affected, the parents have a choice. They may decide to keep the baby, knowing that it will have a genetic disorder when it is born. On the other hand, they may decide to have an abortion. This prevents the birth of a child with serious problems. Then they can try again to have a healthy baby.

- Some couples with an inherited disorder in the family have their embryos screened before they are implanted in the mother. Embryos are produced by IVF (*in vitro* fertilisation). Doctors remove a single cell from each embryo and screen it for inherited disorders. Only healthy embryos free from genetic disorders are implanted back into their mother, so only babies without that disorder are born.

	H	h
h	Hh	hh
h	Hh	hh

H = dominant, Huntington's disease
h = recessive, no Huntington's disease

Offspring genotype: 50% Hh, 50% hh

Phenotype: 50% Huntington's disease
50% healthy

Figure 1 A genetic diagram for Huntington's disease

Activity 2

Genetic counsellors help families affected by particular genetic disorders to understand the problems and the choices available. Plan a role play of an interview between a genetic counsellor and a couple who already have one child with cystic fibrosis, and would like to have another child.

Either: Plan the role of the counsellor. Make sure you have all the information you need to be able to explain the chances of another child being affected and the choices that are open to the parents.

Or: Plan the role of a parent or work in pairs to give the views of a couple. Think carefully about the factors that will affect your decision, e.g. can you cope with another sick child? Are you prepared to have an abortion? Do you have religious views on the matter? What is fairest to the unborn child, and the child you already have? Is it ethical to choose embryos to implant?

Summary questions

1 What are the main ethical issues associated with the use of embryonic stem cells?

2 It would cost a lot of money to screen all embryos for genetic conditions. Put forward two arguments for, and two against, this process.

Key points

- It is important that people make informed judgements about the use of embryonic stem cells in medical research and treatment.

- There are a number of economic, social and ethical issues surrounding the screening of embryos.

Summary questions *k*

1 a What is mitosis?

b Explain, using diagrams, what takes place when a cell divides by mitosis.

c Mitosis is very important during the development of a baby from a fertilised egg. It is also important all through life. Why?

2 What is meiosis and where does it take place?

3 a Why is meiosis so important?

b Explain, using labelled diagrams, what takes place when a cell divides by meiosis. **[H]**

4 a What are stem cells?

b It is hoped that many different medical problems may be cured using stem cells. Explain how this might work.

c There are some ethical issues associated with the use of embryonic stem cells. Explain the arguments both for and against their use.

5 Hugo de Vries is one of the scientists who made the same discoveries as Mendel several years after Mendel's death. Write a letter from Hugo to one of his friends after he has found Mendel's writings. Explain what Mendel did, why no one took any notice of him and how the situation has changed so that you (Hugo) can come up with a clear explanation for the results of your own experiments. Explain your attitude to Mendel.

6 Whether you have a straight thumb or a curved one is decided by a single gene with two alleles. The allele for a straight thumb, S, is dominant to the curved allele, s. Use this information to help you answer these questions.

Josh has straight thumbs but Sami has curved thumbs. They are expecting a baby.

a We know exactly what Sami's thumb alleles are. What are they and how do you know?

b If the baby has curved thumbs, what does this tell you about Josh's thumb alleles? Draw and complete a Punnett square to show the genetics of your explanation.

c If the baby has straight thumbs, what does this tell us about Josh's thumb alleles? Draw and complete a Punnett square to show the genetics of your explanation. **[H]**

7 Amjid grew some purple flowering pea plants from seeds he had bought at the garden centre. He planted them in his garden.

Here are his results.

Seeds planted	247
Purple-flowered plants	242
White-flowered plants	1
Seeds not growing	4

a Is the white-flowered plant an anomaly? Why?

b Are the seeds that did not grow anomalies? Why?

c Suggest other investigations Amjid could carry out into the cause of the colour of the white-flowered plant.

Amjid was interested in these plants, so he collected the seed from some of the purple-flowered plants and used them in the garden the following year. He made a careful note of what happened.

Here are his results:

Seeds planted	100
Purple-flowered plants	295
White-flowered plants	102
Seeds not growing	6

Amjid was slightly surprised. He did not expect to find that a third of his flowers would be white.

d i The purple allele (P) is dominant and the allele for white flowers (p) is recessive. Draw a genetic diagram that explains Amjid's numbers of purple and white flowers.

ii How accurate were Amjid's results compared with the expected ratio?

e How could Amjid have improved his method of growing the peas to make his results more valid? **[H]**

AQA Examination-style questions 🄺

1 Copy and complete the following sentences using the words or symbols below:

characteristics cytoplasm fitness genes nucleus proteins tissue

2 23 46 X XX XY Y

In the body cells of a boy there are .... chromosomes that are found in the .... The boy's cells can be identified as male by the .... chromosome. On all the chromosomes there are sections called .... that determine the .... of the boy. (5)

2 The drawing shows some of the stages of reproduction in horses.

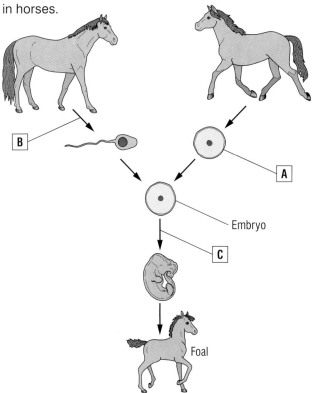

a i Name this type of reproduction (1)
ii Name the type of cell labelled **A**. (1)

b Name the type of cell division taking place at the stages labelled:
i B (1)
ii C. (1)

c How does the number of chromosomes in each cell of the embryo compare with the number of chromosomes in cell **A**? (1)

d When the foal grows up it will look similar to its parents but it will **not** be identical to either parent.
i Explain why it will look similar to its parents. (1)
ii Suggest **two** reasons why it will **not** be identical to either of its parents. (2)

AQA, 2001

3 When an embryo is formed, the cells divide and start to differentiate. Some adult cells are still able to differentiate.

a What is meant by the term *differentiation*? (1)

b What name do we give to cells which have not differentiated? (1)

c Give an example of adult cells that can differentiate. (1)

d Some of the embryo cells may be used in the future to treat conditions such as paralysis.
There are people who do not think we should use embryos in this way. What is an ethical reason for objecting to the use of embryos? (1)

4 *In this question you will be assessed on using good English, organising information clearly and using specialist terms where appropriate.*

Doctors all over the world are investigating the use of stem cells to treat a wide variety of disorders.

Many doctors use adult stem cells but some use embryonic stem cells. There is evidence that adult stem cells do not cause cancer tumours if they are transferred soon after being removed from the body. Embryonic stem cells multiply very quickly and there is a risk of cancer developing after treatment with them.

Bone marrow cells are stem cells which continually replace your blood cells every day of your life.

Adult stem cells from bone marrow have been used successfully to treat leukaemia for over 40 years. Many patients with damage to the nervous system have reported improvements in movement following treatment with adult stem cells, but more research is needed before widespread use of the treatment.

One doctor said, 'It is safer to use adult stem cells. Using embryonic stem cells is not ethical.'

Using the information and your own knowledge explain the statement made by the doctor. (6)

B2 6.1

The origins of life on Earth

Learning objectives

- What is the evidence for the origins of life on Earth?
- What are fossils?
- What can we learn from fossils?

There is no record of the origins of life on Earth. It is a puzzle that can never be completely solved. There is not much valid evidence for what happened – no one was there to see it! We don't even know exactly when life on Earth began. However, most scientists think it was somewhere between 3 to 4 billion years ago.

There are some interesting ideas and well-respected theories that explain most of what you can see around you. The biggest problem we have is finding the evidence to support the ideas.

a When do scientists think life on Earth began?

What can we learn from fossils?

Some of the best evidence we have about the history of life on Earth comes from **fossils**. Fossils are the remains of organisms from many thousands or millions of years ago that are found preserved in rocks, ice and other places. For example, fossils have revealed the world of the dinosaurs. These lizards dominated the Earth at one stage and died out millions of years before humans came to dominate the Earth.

 Maths skills

Time scales for the evolution of life are big:

- A thousand years is 10^3 years.
- A million years is 10^6 years.
- A billion years is 10^9 years.

You have probably seen a fossil in a museum or on TV, or maybe even found one yourself. Fossils can be formed in a number of ways:

- They may be formed from the hard parts of an animal. These are the bits that do not decay easily, such as the bones, teeth, claws or shells.
- Another type of fossil is formed when an animal or plant does not decay after it has died. This happens when one or more of the conditions needed for decay are not there. This may be because there is little or no oxygen present. It could be because poisonous gases kill off the bacteria that cause decay. Sometimes the temperature is too low for decay to take place. Then the animals and plants are preserved in ice. These ice fossils are rare, but they give a clear insight into what an animal looked like. They can also tell us what an animal had been eating or the colour of a long-extinct flower. We can even extract the DNA and compare it to modern organisms.
- Many fossils are formed when harder parts of the animal or plant are replaced by other minerals. This takes place over long periods of time. These are the most common fossils (see Figure 3).
- Some of the fossils we find are not of actual animals or plants, but of traces they have left behind. Fossil footprints, burrows, rootlet traces and droppings are all formed. These help us to build up a picture of life on Earth long ago.

b Which is the most common type of fossil?

An incomplete record

The fossil record is not complete for several reasons. Many of the very earliest forms of life were soft-bodied organisms. This means they have left little fossil trace. It is partly why there is so little valid evidence of how life began. There is no fossil record of the earliest life forms on Earth.

Most organisms that died did not become fossilised – the right conditions for fossil formation were rare. Also, many of the fossils that were formed in the rocks have been destroyed by geological activity. Huge amounts of rock have been broken down, worn away, buried or melted over the years. As this happens the fossil record is lost too. Finally, there are many fossils that are still to be found.

In spite of all these limitations, the fossils we have found can still give us a 'snapshot' of life millions of years ago.

Figure 2 This baby mammoth was preserved in ice for at least 10 000 years. Examining this kind of evidence helps scientists check the accuracy of ideas based on fossil skeletons alone.

1 The reptile dies and falls to the ground

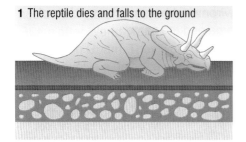

2 The flesh rots, leaving the skeleton to be covered in sand or soil and clay before it is damaged

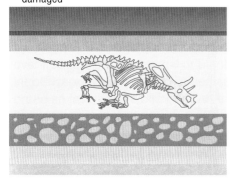

3 Protected, over millions of years, the skeleton becomes mineralised and turns to rock. The rocks shift in the earth with the fossil trapped inside.

4 Eventually, the fossil emerges as the rocks move and erosion takes place

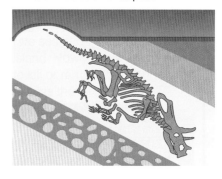

Figure 3 It takes a very long time for fossils to form, but they provide us with invaluable evidence of how life on Earth has developed

Summary questions

1 Copy and complete using the words below:

animal   decay   evidence   fossils   Ice fossils   minerals   plant

One important piece of .... for how life has developed on Earth are .... The most common type are formed when parts of the .... or .... are replaced by .... as it decays. Some fossils are formed when an organism does not .... after it dies. An example is ...., which are very rare.

2 There are several theories about how life on Earth began.
   a Why is it impossible to know for sure?
   b Why are fossils such important evidence for the way life has developed?

3 How do ice fossils help scientists check the evidence provided by the main fossil record?

Key points

- Fossils are the remains of organisms from many years ago that are found in rocks.

- Fossils may be formed in different ways.

- Fossils give us information about organisms that lived millions of years ago.

- It is very difficult for scientists to know exactly how life on Earth began because there is little evidence that is valid.

B2 6.3 More about extinction

- How does environmental change over long time scales affect living organisms?
- What caused the mass extinctions of the past?

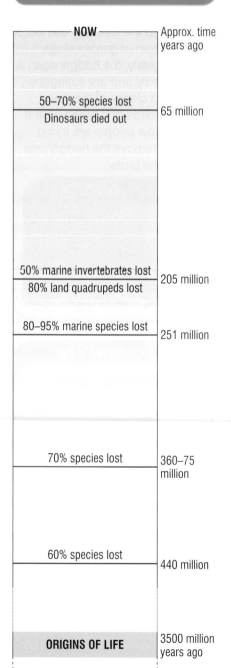

Figure 2 The five main extinction events so far in the evolutionary history of the Earth

It isn't just changes in living organisms that bring about extinctions. The biggest influences on survival are changes in the environment.

Environmental changes

Throughout history, the climate and environment of the Earth has been changing. At times the Earth has been very hot. At other times, temperatures have fallen and the Earth has been in the grip of an Ice Age. These changes take place over millions and even billions of years.

Organisms that do well in the heat of a tropical climate won't do well in the icy conditions of an Ice Age. Many of them will become extinct through lack of food or being too cold to breed. However, species that cope well in cold climates will evolve and thrive by natural selection.

Changes to the climate or the environment have been the main cause of extinction throughout history. There have been five occasions during the history of the Earth when big climate changes have led to extinction on an enormous scale (see Figure 2).

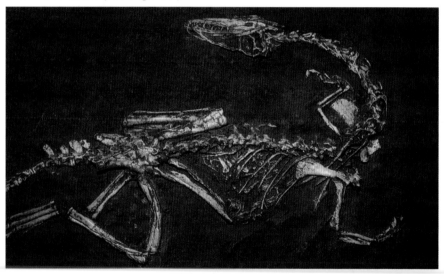

Figure 1 The dinosaurs ruled the Earth for millions of years, but when the whole environment changed, they could not adapt and most of them died out. Mammals, which could control their own body temperature, had an advantage and became dominant.

a Why are Ice Ages often linked to extinctions?

Extinction on a large scale

Fossil evidence shows that at times there have been mass extinctions on a global scale. During these events many (or even most) of the species on Earth die out. This usually happens over a relatively short time period of several million years. Huge numbers of species disappear from the fossil record.

The evidence suggests that a single catastrophic event is often the cause of these mass extinctions. This could be a massive volcanic eruption or the collision of giant asteroids with the surface of the Earth.

b What is a mass extinction?

What destroyed the dinosaurs?

The most recent mass extinction was when the dinosaurs became extinct around 65 million years ago. In 2010 an international team of scientists published a review of all the evidence put together over the last 20 years. They agreed that around 65 million years ago a giant asteroid collided with the Earth in Chicxulub in Mexico.

We can see a huge crater (180 km in diameter) there. Scientists have identified a layer of rock formed from crater debris in countries across the world. The further you move away from the crater, the thinner the layer of crater debris in the rock. Also, deep below the crater, scientists found lots of a mineral only formed when a rock is hit with a massive force such as an asteroid strike.

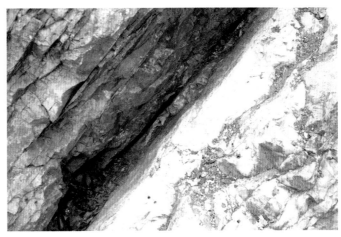

Figure 3 This layer of debris from the asteroid crater appears in rocks that are 65 million years old – the time the dinosaurs died out

The asteroid impact would have caused huge fires, earthquakes, landslides and tsunamis. Enormous amounts of material would have been blasted into the atmosphere. The accepted theory is that the dust in the atmosphere made everywhere almost dark. Plants struggled to survive and the drop in temperatures caused a global winter. Between 50–70% of all living species, including the dinosaurs, became extinct.

No sooner had this work been published than a group of UK scientists published different ideas and evidence. They suggest that the extinction of the dinosaurs started sooner (137 million years ago) and was much slower than previously thought.

Their idea is that the melting of the sea ice (caused by global warming) flooded the seas and oceans with very cold water. A drop in the sea temperature of about 9 °C triggered the mass extinction. Their evidence is based on an unexpected change in fossils and minerals that they found in areas of Norway.

As you can see, building up a valid, evidence-based history of events so long ago is not easy to do. Events can always be interpreted in different ways.

⚬⚬ links

For more information about the way people are changing the environment and bringing about extinction, see B3 chapter 4 How humans can affect the environment.

AQA Examiner's tip

Remember that the time scales in forming new species and mass extinctions are huge.

Try to develop an understanding of time in millions and billions of years.

Summary questions

1 a Give four causes of extinction in species of living organisms.
  b Give two possible causes of mass extinction events.

2 Why do you think extinction is an important part of evolution?

3 a Summarise the evidence for a giant asteroid impact as the cause of the mass extinction event that resulted in the death of the dinosaurs.
  b Explain why scientists think that low light levels and low temperatures would have followed a massive asteroid strike. Why would these have caused mass extinctions?

Key points

● Extinction can be caused by environmental change over geological time.

● Mass extinctions may be caused by single catastrophic events such as volcanoes or asteroid strikes.

B2 6.4

Isolation and the evolution of new species

Learning objectives

- How do new species arise?
- How do populations become isolated?
- Do new species always form at the same rate?
- How does speciation take place in an isolated population? [H]

??? Did you know ... ?

Sometimes the organisms are separated by **environmental isolation**. This is when the climate changes in one area where an organism lives but not in others. For example, if the climate becomes warmer in one area plants will flower at a different time of year. The breeding times of the plants and the animals linked with them will change and new species emerge.

Figure 1 Both the marsupial koala and the eucalyptus tree have evolved in geographical isolation in Australia

After a mass extinction, scientists have noticed that huge numbers of new species appear in the fossil record. This is evolution in action. Natural selection takes place and new organisms adapted to the different conditions evolve. But evolution is happening all the time. There is a natural cycle of new species appearing and others becoming extinct.

Isolation and evolution

You have already learnt about the role of genetic variation and natural selection in evolution. Any population of living organisms contains genetic variety. If one population becomes isolated from another, the conditions they are living in are likely to be different. This means that different characteristics will be selected for. The two populations might change so much over time that they cannot interbreed successfully. Then a new species evolves.

How do populations become isolated?

The most common way is by **geographical isolation**. This is when two populations become physically isolated by a geographical feature. This might be a new mountain range, a new river or an area of land becoming an island.

There are some well-known examples of this. Australia separated from the other continents over 5 million years ago. That's when the Australian populations of marsupial mammals that carry their babies in pouches became geographically isolated.

As a result of natural selection, many different species of marsupials evolved. Organisms as varied as kangaroos and koala bears appeared. Across the rest of the world, competition resulted in the evolution of other mammals with more efficient reproductive systems. In Australia, marsupials remain dominant.

a What is geographical isolation?

Organisms in isolation

Organisms on islands are geographically isolated from the rest of the world. The closely related but very different species on the Galapagos Islands helped Darwin form his ideas about evolution.

When a species evolves in isolation and is found in only one place in the world, it is said to be **endemic** to that area. An area where scientists are finding many new endemic species is Borneo. It is one of the largest islands in the world. Borneo still contains huge areas of tropical rainforest.

Between 1994 and 2006 scientists discovered over 400 new species in the Borneo rainforest. There are more than 25 species of mammals found only on the island. All of these organisms have evolved through geographical isolation.

Higher

Speciation **k**

Any population will contain natural genetic variety. This means it will contain a wide range of alleles controlling its characteristics, that result from sexual reproduction and mutation. In each population, the alleles which are selected will control characteristics which help the organism to survive and breed successfully. This is natural selection. Sometimes part of a population becomes isolated with new environmental conditions. Alleles for characteristics that enable organisms to survive and breed successfully in the new conditions will be selected. These are likely to be different from the alleles that gave success in the original environment. As a result of the selection of these different alleles, the characteristic features of the isolated organisms will change. Eventually they can no longer interbreed with the original organisms and a new species forms. This is known as **speciation.**

This is what has happened on the island of Borneo, in Australia and on the Galapagos Islands. If conditions in these isolated places are changed or the habitat is lost, the species that have evolved to survive within it could easily become extinct.

Figure 2 Orang-utans like these are just one example of the many endemic species that have evolved in isolation in Borneo

b What is an endemic organism?

Geographical isolation may involve very large areas like Borneo or very small regions. Mount Bosavi is the crater of an extinct volcano in Papua New Guinea. It is only 4 km wide and the walls of the crater are 1 km high. The animals and plants trapped within the crater have evolved in different ways to those outside.

Very few people have been inside the crater. During a 3-week expedition in 2009 scientists discovered around 40 new species. These included mammals, fish, birds, reptiles, amphibians, insects and plants. All of these species are the result of natural selection caused by the specialised environment of the isolated crater. They include an enormous 82 cm long rat that weighs 1.5 kg!

Figure 3 Mount Bosavi in Papua New Guinea – a small, geographically isolated environment where many new species have evolved

Key points

- New species arise when two populations become isolated.

- Populations become isolated when they are separated geographically, e.g. on islands.

- There are natural cycles linked to environmental change when species form and when species die out.

- In an isolated population alleles are selected that increase successful breeding in the new environment.   **[H]**

- Speciation takes place when an isolated population becomes so different from the original population that successful interbreeding can no long take place.   **[H]**

Summary questions

1 Copy and complete using the words below:

geographically interbreeding populations evolution species selection

When two .... become .... isolated .... may take place. Natural .... in each area means the populations become so different that successful .... can no longer take place. New .... have evolved.

2 **a** How might populations become isolated?
   b Why does this isolation lead to the evolution of new species?

3 Explain how genetic variation and natural selection result in the formation of new species in isolated populations.   **[H]**

Summary questions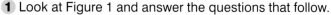

1 Look at Figure 1 and answer the questions that follow.

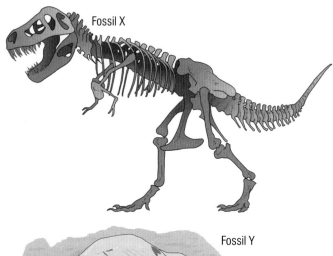

Fossil X

Fossil Y

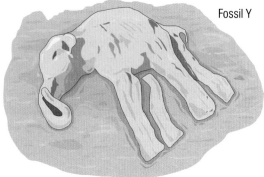

Figure 1

a What is a fossil?

b Explain fully how fossil X and fossil Y were formed.

c How can fossils like these be used as evidence for the development of life on Earth and what are their limitations?

d Why are fossils of little use in helping us understand how life on Earth began?

2 a What is extinction?

b How does mass extinction differ from species extinction?

c What is the evidence for the occurrence of mass extinctions throughout the history of life on Earth?

d Suggest at least two theories about the possible causes of mass extinctions and explain the sort of evidence that is used to support these ideas.

e What important part have mass extinctions played in the evolution of life on Earth and why?

3

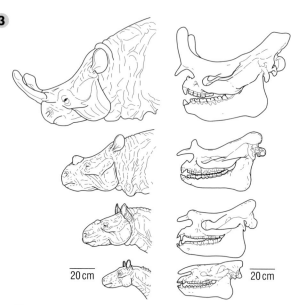

20 cm   20 cm

Figure 2

a This sequence of skulls comes from the fossil record of a group of animals known as perissodactyls. Suggest a possible living relative of these animals.

b How do you think these organisms changed as they evolved, based on the evidence of the diagram above?

c What are the limitations of this type of evidence?

d What other fossil remains would you want to see to understand more about the lives of these extinct organisms?

4 How does evolution take place?

5 Describe how evolution takes place in terms of speciation. Explain the roles of isolation and genetic variation in the process of speciation. Use as many examples and as much evidence as you can in your answer. **[H]**

AQA Examination-style questions 🄺

1 The diagram shows a timeline for the evolution of some groups of animals. The earliest forms of the animals shown below the line for **Present day** are extinct.

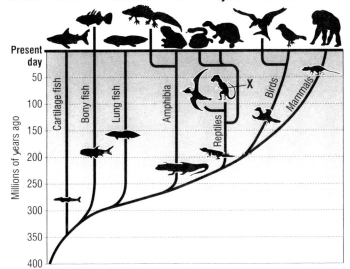

Use information from the diagram to answer these questions.

a Name the **four** groups of animals that developed legs. (1)

b Which group of animals shown in the diagram evolved first? (1)

c The animal labelled **X** has been extinct for over 50 million years.

How do scientists know that it once lived? (1)

d Copy and complete the sentence by choosing the correct words from below.

diseases enzymes hormones plants predators rocks

Animals may become extinct because of new .... and new .... (2)

AQA, 2003

2 a What is meant by the term 'extinction'? (2)

b The bar charts show the population of the world from the 17th to the 20th century and the number of animal extinctions that have taken place over the same period.

Use the information in the bar charts to answer the questions.

i What was the world population in the 19th century? (1)

ii How many animals became extinct in the 18th century? (1)

iii What is the relationship between the population of humans and the number of animal extinctions? (2)

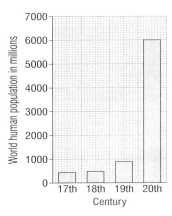
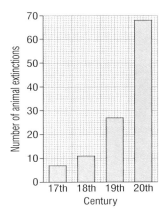

c Between 1900 and 1960 (20th century) 64 animals became extinct.

i How many animals became extinct from 1960–2000?
Show your working. (2)

ii Suggest a reason for the difference in numbers between the beginning and the end of the 20th century. (2)

3 The diagram shows how the number of groups of animals has changed during the history of life on Earth.

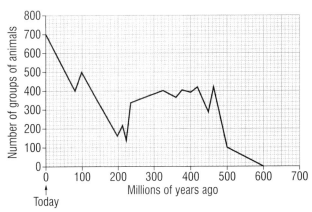

a i How long ago did the first living animals appear on Earth? Give your answer in millions of years. (1)

ii How long did it take for the number of groups to rise to 400? Give your answer in millions of years. (1)

b i Calculate the proportion of groups that disappeared between 100 million years and 80 million years ago. Show your working. (2)

ii Give **two** reasons why some groups of animals disappeared during the history of life on Earth (2)

AQA, 2008

4 *In this question you will be assessed on using good English, organising information clearly and using specialist terms where appropriate.*

Describe how new species may arise by isolation. **[H]** (6)

1 a i Put the following structures into the correct order from the smallest to the largest. (1)

cell   chromosome   gene   nucleus

smallest   largest

------------   ------------   ------------   ------------

    ii What is the function of the nucleus? (1)

b Plant cells contain chloroplasts.

    i What is the role of chloroplasts in photosynthesis? (1)

    ii Name the gas produced in photosynthesis. (1)

2 The diagrams show three processes.
Match the correct letter to the process.

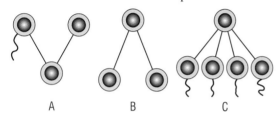

A   B   C

Process	Letter
Fertilisation	
Meiosis	
Mitosis	

(3)

3 The diagram shows two villi in the small intestine of a healthy person.

The small intestine is an organ in the digestive system.

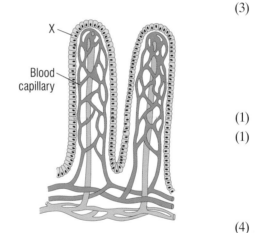

X

Blood capillary

a i Name another organ in the digestive system. (1)

    ii Name tissue X. (1)

b The villi are surrounded by digested food materials which must enter the blood capillaries.

Explain how these materials enter the blood. (4)

4 The graph shows the effect of temperature on photosynthesis.

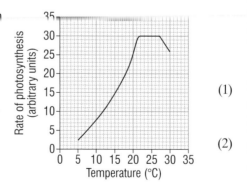

Rate of photosynthesis (arbitrary units)

Temperature (°C)

a i Between which temperatures is the rate of photosynthesis fastest?

.... and .... °C (1)

    ii Suggest why the rate of photosynthesis stays the same between these two temperatures. (2)

b A greenhouse owner wants to grow lettuces as quickly and cheaply as possible in winter.

At what temperature should he keep his greenhouse in order to grow the lettuces as quickly and cheaply as possible? .... °C

Explain your answer. (3)

AQA *Examiner's tip*

When reading graphs (see Q4)

Do not be put off by the term 'arbitrary units' just look at the numbers. Sometimes examiners use this term to avoid writing very complex numbers or unit names.

AQA *Examiner's tip*

Photosynthesis questions often ask about limiting factors.

If raising the temperature does not increase the rate of photosynthesis any further, some other factor must be preventing this. Ask yourself 'What do plants need for photosynthesis?'

5 The picture shows a model of a protein.

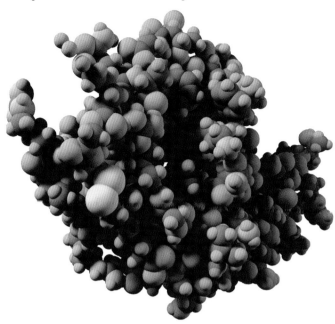

Some proteins are enzymes but proteins also have other functions.

a i Give two other functions of proteins.

1 ....

2 .... (2)

ii What is the function of an enzyme? (1)

b This protein is normally found in neutral conditions. What would happen to the protein if it was placed in acid conditions? (2)

c When the model protein is put together the scientists use smaller molecules to make the specific shape.

i Choose the correct answer to complete the sentence.

amino acids   fatty acids   lactic acid

The smaller molecules used to make the model protein are .... (1)

ii Cells are able to put the smaller molecules together in the correct order.

Explain how the cell does this. (1)

6 Some cattle are affected by an inherited condition called glycogen storage disease.

a i Where is glycogen stored? (1)

ii Cattle with this disease become tired easily.

Explain why. (2)

b Glycogen storage disease can be inherited by a calf whose parents do not have the disease.

i Use the symbols G and g and a genetic diagram to explain how this is possible. (4)

ii If the same parents have another calf, what is the probability that it will not have glycogen storage disease? (1)

7 *In this question you will be assessed on using good English, organising information clearly and using specialist terms where appropriate.*

Describe the changes which take place in the human body during exercise to ensure that the muscles receive enough oxygen and what happens if oxygen is in short supply.

(6)

AQA *Examiner's tip*

Q7 requires a description in a logical order. Think about your answer before writing. Make a brief list of the key words and number them in the correct sequence. Rehearse your answer in your head and change the numbers if necessary. Now write your answer using the numbered words as a guide.

Do not forget to cross out any notes which are not intended for marking.

B3 1.1

Osmosis ⓚ

Learning objectives

- What is osmosis?
- How is osmosis different from diffusion?
- Why is osmosis so important?

AQA *Examiner's tip*

Remember, diffusion refers to movement of any particles from a region of high concentration to a region of low concentration.
Osmosis only refers to movement of water molecules.

Diffusion takes place when particles can spread freely from one place to another. However, the solutions inside cells are separated from those outside by the cell membrane. This membrane does not let all types of particles through. Membranes which only let some types of particles through are called **partially permeable**.

Osmosis ⓚ

Partially permeable cell membranes let water move across them. Remember that a **dilute** solution of sugar contains a *high* concentration of water (the solvent). It has a *low* concentration of sugar (the solute). A **concentrated** sugar solution contains a relatively *low* concentration of water and a *high* concentration of sugar.

The cytoplasm of a cell is made up of chemicals dissolved in water inside a partially permeable bag of cell membrane. The cytoplasm contains a fairly concentrated solution of salts and sugars. Water moves from a high concentration of water molecules (in a dilute solution) to a less concentrated solution of water molecules (in a concentrated solution) across the membrane of the cell.

This special type of diffusion, where only water moves across a partially permeable membrane, is called **osmosis**.

a   What is the difference between diffusion and osmosis?

Practical

Investigating osmosis

You can make model cells using bags made of partially permeable membrane (see Figure 1). You can see what happens to them if the concentrations of the solutions inside or outside the 'cell' change.

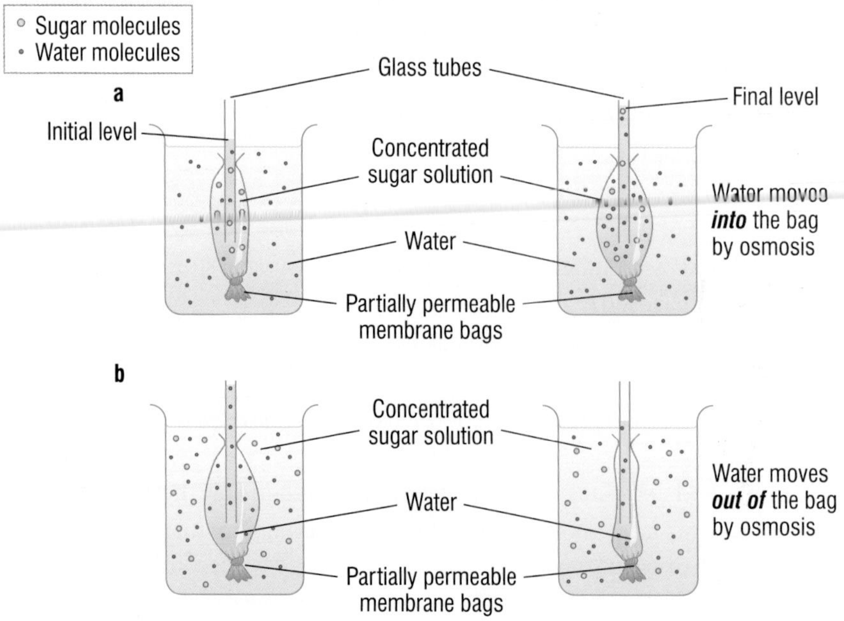

Figure 1 A model of osmosis in a cell. In **a** the 'cell' contents are more concentrated than the surrounding solution. In **b** the 'cell' contents are less concentrated than the surrounding solution.

The concentration inside your cells needs to stay the same for them to work properly. However, the concentration of the solutions outside your cells may be very different to the concentration inside them. This can cause water to move into or out of the cells by osmosis.

Osmosis in animals

If a cell uses up water in its chemical reactions, the cytoplasm becomes more concentrated. More water immediately moves in by osmosis. If the cytoplasm becomes too dilute because more water is made in chemical reactions, water leaves the cell by osmosis. So osmosis restores the balance in both cases.

However, osmosis can also cause big problems in animal cells. If the solution outside the cell is more dilute than the cell contents, water will move into the cell by osmosis. The cell will swell and may burst.

If the solution outside the cell is more concentrated than the cell contents, water will move out of the cell by osmosis. The cytoplasm will become too concentrated and the cell will shrivel up. Then it can no longer survive. Once you understand the effect osmosis can have on cells, the importance of maintaining constant internal conditions becomes clear.

> **b** How does osmosis help maintain body cells at a specific concentration?

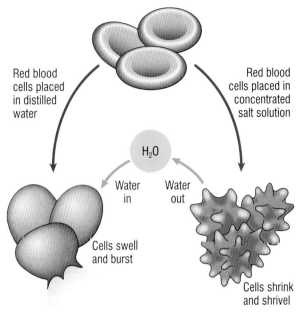

Red blood cells placed in distilled water

Red blood cells placed in concentrated salt solution

H_2O

Water in

Water out

Cells swell and burst

Cells shrink and shrivel

Figure 2 Osmosis can destroy your red blood cells, so it is important to keep your body fluids at the right concentration

Osmosis in plants 🄚

Plants rely on osmosis to support their stems and leaves. Water moves into plant cells by osmosis. This causes the vacuole to swell and press the cytoplasm against the plant cell walls. The pressure builds up until no more water can physically enter the cell. This makes the cell hard and rigid.

This swollen state keeps the leaves and stems of the plant rigid and firm. So plants need the fluid surrounding the cells to always have a higher concentration of water (to be a more dilute solution of chemicals) than the cytoplasm of the cells. This keeps water moving by osmosis in the right direction. If the solution surrounding the plant cells is more concentrated than the cell contents, water will leave the cells by osmosis. The cells will not support the plant tissues. Osmosis is important in all living organisms.

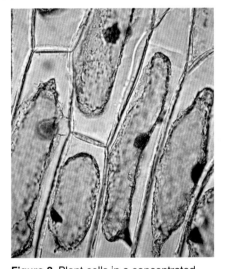

Figure 3 Plant cells in a concentrated sugar solution

Summary questions

1 Define the following words: diffusion, osmosis, partially permeable membrane.

2 **a** Explain, using a diagram, what has happened to the plant cells in Figure 3.
   b Explain, using a diagram, what would happen to these cells if you put them in distilled water.

3 Animals that live in fresh water have a constant problem with their water balance. The single-celled organism called *Amoeba* has a special vacuole in its cell. It fills with water and then moves to the outside of the cell and bursts. A new vacuole starts forming straight away. Explain in terms of osmosis why the *Amoeba* needs one of these vacuoles.

Key points

- Osmosis is a special case of diffusion.

- Osmosis is the diffusion/ movement of water from a dilute to a more concentrated solution through a partially permeable membrane that allows water to pass through.

- Differences in the concentrations of solutions inside and outside a cell cause water to move into or out of the cell by osmosis.

B3 1.2

Active transport

Learning objectives

- What is active transport?
- Why is active transport so important?

Cells need to move substances in and out. Water often moves across the cell boundaries by osmosis. Dissolved substances also need to move in and out of cells. There are two main ways in which this happens. Substances move by diffusion, along a concentration gradient. This must be in the right direction to be useful to the cells. However, sometimes the substances needed by a cell have to be moved against a concentration gradient, or across a partially permeable membrane. This needs a special process called **active transport**.

Moving substances by active transport

Active transport allows cells to move substances from an area of low concentration to an area of high concentration. This movement is *against* the concentration gradient. As a result, cells can absorb ions from very dilute solutions. It also enables them to move substances, such as sugars and ions, from one place to another through the cell membranes.

a How does active transport differ from diffusion and osmosis?

It takes energy for the active transport system to carry a molecule across the membrane and then return to its original position (see Figure 1). The energy for active transport comes from cellular respiration. Scientists have shown in a number of different cells that the rate of respiration and the rate of active transport are closely linked (see Figure 2).

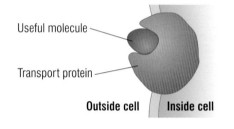

Useful molecule

Transport protein

Outside cell **Inside cell**

Transport protein rotates and releases molecule inside cell (using energy)

Transport protein rotates back again (often using energy)

Figure 1 Active transport uses energy to move substances against a concentration gradient

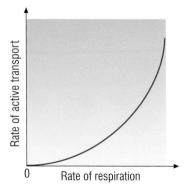

Rate of active transport

0 Rate of respiration

Figure 2 The rate of active transport depends on the rate of respiration

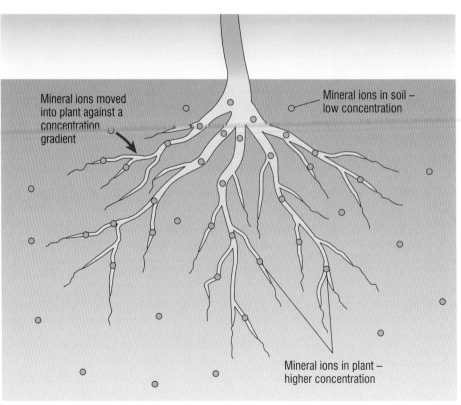

Mineral ions moved into plant against a concentration gradient

Mineral ions in soil – low concentration

Mineral ions in plant – higher concentration

Figure 3 Plants use energy from respiration in active transport to move mineral ions from the soil into the roots against a concentration gradient

In other words, if a cell is making lots of energy, it can carry out lots of active transport. Examples include root hair cells and the cells lining your gut. Cells involved in a lot of active transport usually have lots of mitochondria to provide the energy they need.

b Why do cells that carry out a lot of active transport have lots of mitochondria?

The importance of active transport

Active transport is widely used in cells. There are some situations where it is particularly important. For example, the mineral ions in the soil are usually found in very dilute solutions. These solutions are more dilute than the solution within the plant cells. By using active transport, plants can absorb these mineral ions, even though it is against a concentration gradient (see Figure 3).

Sugar such as glucose is always actively absorbed out of your gut and kidney tubules into your blood. This is often done against a large concentration gradient.

Figure 4 Crocodiles have special salt glands in their tongues. These remove excess salt from the body against the concentration gradient by active transport. That's why crocodiles can live in estuaries and even the sea.

??? Did you know ... ?

People with cystic fibrosis (see B2 5.6 Inherited conditions in humans) have thick, sticky mucus in their lungs, gut and reproductive systems. This is the result of a mutation affecting a protein involved in the active transport system of the mucus-producing cells.

Summary questions

1 Copy and complete using the words below:

concentration transport osmosis against mitochondria diffusion energy

.... and .... depend on a .... gradient in the right direction to work. Substances are moved .... a concentration gradient by active ...., which uses .... produced by ....

2 Explain how active transport works in a cell.

3 Diffusion and osmosis do not need energy. Why is energy needed for active transport and where does it come from?

4 Why is active transport so important to:
   a marine birds such as albatrosses, which have special salt glands producing very salty liquid?
   b plants?

Key points

- Substances are sometimes absorbed against a concentration gradient by active transport.

- Active transport uses energy from respiration.

- Cells can absorb ions from very dilute solutions, and actively absorb substances such as sugar and salt against a concentration gradient using active transport.

B3 1.3 The sports drink dilemma

Learning objectives

- How do sports drinks differ from ordinary soft drinks?
- Do sports drinks live up to their claims?

People love soft drinks. In the UK we spend £8–9 billion every year on them. Most of these soft drinks contain mainly water. Colouring, flavouring and some sugar or sweeteners are added, along with tiny amounts of mineral ions. Sometimes carbon dioxide gas is added for fizz.

Professional athletes and people who just enjoy sport often buy special sports drinks. They think these help their performance and recovery after exercise. Nearly £250 million worth of sports drinks were used last year.

What happens when you exercise?

When you exercise you release energy by respiration to make your muscles contract and move your body, using up sugar. You also sweat to keep your body temperature stable. Sweat contains water and mineral ions. The more you sweat, the more water and mineral ions you lose. This can affect the concentration of your body fluids. If the body fluids become concentrated, water will leave your cells by osmosis. The cells will become **dehydrated**.

If the water and mineral ions you lose in sweating are not replaced, the mineral ion/water balance of your body will be disturbed. Then your cells will not work as efficiently as usual. To keep exercising at your best, you need to replace the sugar used in respiration and the water and mineral ions lost through sweating. This also applies to recovering properly after exercise. Here is where manufacturers of sports drinks claim to help.

a How do you lose water and mineral ions when you exercise?

What is a sports drink?

A sports drink is mainly water. It also contains sugar (often glucose). It contains more mineral ions than most normal soft drinks. It also has colourings and flavourings added to make it pleasant to drink. Most sports drinks claim to aid hydration of the tissues, help replace lost energy and replace lost electrolytes (the mineral ions you lose when you sweat). But how good are they at doing this?

b What is a sports drink?

Figure 1 The runners in the London marathon certainly use plenty of sports drinks

How Science Works

Evaluating sports drinks

Sports drinks are usually more expensive than normal soft drinks. There is plenty of evidence to show that sports drinks do what they claim. They contain lots of water so they dilute the body fluids. This allows water to move back into the cells and **rehydrate** them by osmosis. They contain salt, which raises your ion levels, so ions move back into your cells by diffusion. They raise the blood sugar levels so sugar moves back into your cells by diffusion and active transport.

However, sports drinks are expensive. Are they worth the money? There is a lot of evidence which shows that using sports drinks, particularly for normal short-term exercise rather than endurance sports such as marathon running, is not needed. Jeanette Crosland is consultant nutritionist to the British Olympic team. She has examined a lot of evidence and says '**Isotonic** sports drinks are not really necessary in activities lasting less than 1 hour, when plain water will suffice'.

So, simply drinking tap water will keep your cells **hydrated**. Ordinary orange squash will replace the sugar. If you make dilute orange squash and add a pinch of salt it will replace the most important mineral ions. This gives you a 'sports' drink as effective as most commercial products. Evidence is also building that milk drinks are one of the most effective ways of rehydrating your cells and replacing the sugars and salts used during exercise. Milk provides your muscles with extra protein and gives you vitamins as well.

Figure 2 Sports drinks are a growing market as more and more people try to improve their performance

Table 1 Data on sports drinks compared to milky drinks from the *Journal of the International Society of Sports Nutrition*

Nutrient value	250 cm³ skimmed milk (0.1% fat)	250 cm³ semi-skimmed chocolate milk (2% fat)	250 cm³ sports drink 1	250 cm³ sports drink 2
Energy (kJ)	90	189	52	53
Protein (g)	9	8	0	0
Carbohydrate (g)	13	27	15	15
Sodium ions (mg)	133	159	115	211
Potassium ions (mg)	431	446	31	95

Summary questions

1 Copy and complete using the words below:

   salt   respiration   energy   water   ions   exercise

   When you .... you release energy from .... in your muscles. You lose .... and .... such as salt in your sweat as you cool down. You need to replace the .... as well as the .... and water you have lost through sweat.

2 **a** How do sports drinks differ from ordinary soft drinks?
   b Some people claim that drinking an ordinary soft drink during exercise is as effective as a sports drink. How could you investigate that claim?

3 **a** How would you display the data given in Table 1? Explain your answer.
   b What do you think are the advantages and disadvantages of using water, orange squash or milk drinks over special sports drinks, both from the data given here and your wider knowledge?

Key points

- Most soft drinks contain water, sugar and mineral ions.

- Sports drinks contain sugars to replace the sugar used in energy release during activity. They also contain water and ions to replace the water and mineral ions lost during sweating.

- Evidence suggests that for normal levels of exercise water is at least as effective as a sports drink.

B3 1.4 Exchanging materials – the lungs

Learning objectives

- What makes an organ efficient when it comes to exchanging gases or solutes?

- What are your alveoli?

- How are your lungs adapted to make gas exchange as efficient as possible?

🔗 links

For information on surface area : volume ratio, look back to B2 4.2 The effect of exercise on the body.

As living organisms get bigger and more complex, their surface area : volume ratio gets smaller. This makes it increasingly difficult to exchange materials quickly enough with the outside world. Gases and food molecules can no longer reach every cell inside the organism by simple diffusion. So in many larger organisms there are special surfaces where gas and **solute** exchange take place. They are adapted to be as effective as possible. You can find them in people, in other animals and in plants.

a Why do gas and solute exchange get more difficult as organisms get bigger and more complex?

Adaptations for exchanging materials

There are various adaptations to make the process of exchange more efficient. The effectiveness of an **exchange surface** can be increased by:

- having a large surface area
- being thin, which provides a short diffusion path
- having an efficient blood supply, in animals. This moves the diffusing substances away and maintains a concentration (diffusion) gradient
- being **ventilated**, in animals, to make gaseous exchange more efficient by maintaining steep concentration gradients.

Different organisms have very different adaptations for the exchange of materials, such as the leaves of a plant, the gills of a fish and the kidneys of a desert rat. For example, scientists have recently discovered that the common musk turtle has a specially adapted tongue. It is covered in tiny buds that greatly increase the surface area. The tongue also has a good blood supply. These turtles don't just use their tongue for eating – they use it for **gaseous exchange** too. The buds on the tongue absorb oxygen from the water that passes over them. Most turtles have to surface regularly for air. However, the musk turtle's tongue is so effective at gaseous exchange that it can stay underwater for months at a time.

b How is the tongue of a common musk turtle adapted for gaseous exchange?

Many of your own organ systems are specialised for exchanging materials. One of them is your breathing system, particularly your lungs.

Exchange of gases in the lungs

Your lungs are specially adapted to make gas exchange more efficient. They are made up of clusters of **alveoli**. These tiny air sacs give the lungs a very large surface area. This is important for the most effective diffusion of the oxygen and carbon dioxide.

The alveoli also have a rich blood supply. This maintains a concentration gradient in both directions. Oxygen is constantly moved from the air in the lungs into the blood and carbon dioxide is constantly delivered into the lungs from the blood.

Figure 1 The common musk turtle has a very unusual tongue, adapted for gaseous exchange

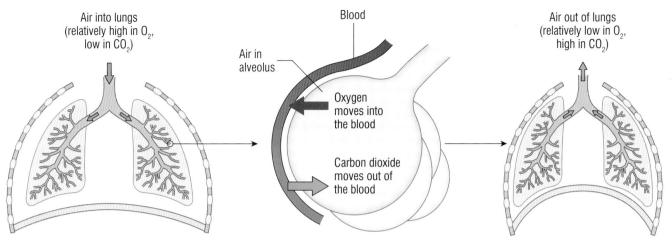

Figure 2 An exchange of gases between the air and the blood takes place in the alveoli of the lungs

As a result, gas exchange takes place along the steepest concentration gradients possible. This makes the exchange rapid and effective. The layer of cells between the air in the lungs and the blood in the **capillaries** is also very thin. This allows diffusion to take place over the shortest possible distance.

c What is the function of the alveoli?

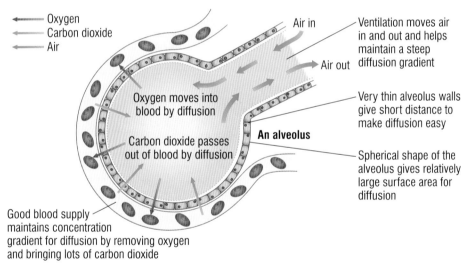

Figure 3 The alveoli are adapted so that gas exchange can take place as efficiently as possible in the lungs

Key points

- Certain features such as a large surface area, short diffusion paths and steep concentration gradients increase the effectiveness of an exchange surface.

- The alveoli are the air sacs in the lungs.

- The lungs are adapted to make gaseous exchange as efficient as possible. They have many alveoli, which provide a large surface area with a good blood supply and short diffusion distances. The lungs are ventilated to maintain steep diffusion gradients.

Summary questions

1 **a** Why are gas and solute exchange surfaces so important in larger organisms?
   b Give four common adaptations of exchange surfaces.

2 What is meant by the term 'gaseous exchange' and why is it so important in your body?

3 How are the lungs adapted to allow gas exchange to take place?

B3 1.5 Ventilating the lungs ⓚ

For a gas exchange system to work efficiently you need a steep concentration gradient. Humans, like many big, complex mammals, move air in and out of the lungs regularly. They maintain a steep concentration gradient of both oxygen in and carbon dioxide out. This is known as ventilating the lungs or **breathing**. It takes place in your specially adapted **breathing system.**

a What is meant by 'ventilating the lungs'?

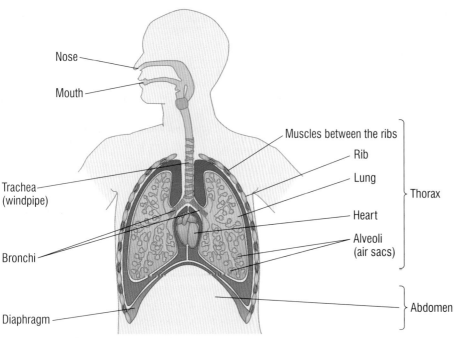

Figure 1 The breathing system supplies your body with vital oxygen and removes waste carbon dioxide

Nose
Mouth
Trachea (windpipe)
Bronchi
Diaphragm
Muscles between the ribs
Rib
Lung
Heart
Alveoli (air sacs)
Thorax
Abdomen

The breathing system

Your lungs are found in your chest or **thorax** and are protected by your bony ribcage. They are separated from the digestive organs beneath (in your **abdomen**) by the **diaphragm**. The diaphragm is a strong sheet of muscle. The job of your breathing system is to move air in and out of your lungs. The lungs provide an efficient surface for gas exchange (in the alveoli).

b What is the thorax?

Moving air in and out of the lungs

Ventilation of the lungs is brought about by movements of your ribcage and diaphragm. You can see and feel movements of the ribcage, but not of the diaphragm. When you breathe in, oxygen-rich air moves into your lungs. This maintains a steep concentration gradient with the blood. As a result oxygen continually diffuses into your bloodstream through the gas exchange surfaces of your alveoli. Breathing out removes carbon dioxide-rich air from the lungs. This maintains a diffusion gradient so carbon dioxide can continually diffuse out of the bloodstream into the air in the lungs.

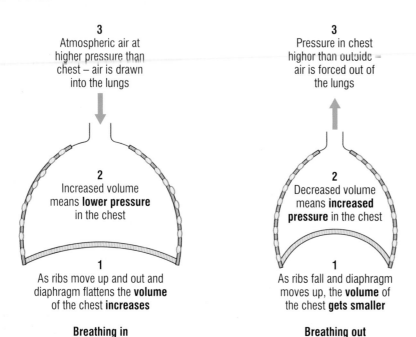

3 Atmospheric air at higher pressure than chest – air is drawn into the lungs

2 Increased volume means **lower pressure** in the chest

1 As ribs move up and out and diaphragm flattens the **volume** of the chest **increases**

Breathing in

3 Pressure in chest higher than outside – air is forced out of the lungs

2 Decreased volume means **increased pressure** in the chest

1 As ribs fall and diaphragm moves up, the **volume** of the chest **gets smaller**

Breathing out

Figure 2 Ventilation of the lungs

Practical

Comparing air breathed in and breathed out

This simple investigation (see Figure 3) allows you to demonstrate that the air you breathe in (tube A) is different from the air you breathe out (tube B). You can use limewater as an indicator of the presence of carbon dioxide. It is a colourless solution that turns cloudy when carbon dioxide is bubbled through it. The higher the concentration of carbon dioxide, the faster it turns cloudy.

Using sensors, scientists have measured the changes in the levels of oxygen and carbon dioxide in the air that goes into and comes out of your lungs (see Table 1).

Table 1 The composition of inhaled and exhaled air (~ means approximately)

Atmospheric gas	% of air breathed in	% of air breathed out
nitrogen	~80	~80
oxygen	20	~16
carbon dioxide	0.04	~4

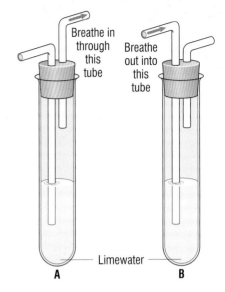

Breathe in through this tube

Breathe out into this tube

Limewater

A   B

Figure 3 Comparing the level of carbon dioxide in air you breathe in and breathe out

When you breathe in, your **intercostal muscles** contract, pulling your ribs upwards and outwards. At the same time your diaphragm muscles contract. This flattens your diaphragm from its normal, **domed** shape. These two movements *increase* the volume of your thorax. Because the same amount of gas is now inside a much bigger space, the pressure inside your thorax drops. Pressure inside the thorax is now lower than the pressure of air outside your body. As a result, air moves into your lungs.

When the intercostal muscles relax, your ribs drop down and in again. When the diaphragm relaxes it curves back up into your thorax. As a result the volume of your thorax gets smaller again. This increases the pressure inside the chest so the air is squeezed and forced out of the lungs. That's how you breathe out.

c Which muscles bring about ventilation of the lungs?

Summary questions

1 Copy and complete using the words below:

ventilated breathing movements ribcage lungs thorax diaphragm

The organs of your .... system include the ...., which are found in your ...., and your .... Your lungs are .... by the .... of your .... and your diaphragm.

2 Explain clearly how air is moved into and out of your lungs.

3 **a** Draw a bar chart to show the difference in composition between the air you breathe in and the air you breathe out (use Table 1 above).

   b People often say we breathe in oxygen and breathe out carbon dioxide. Use your bar chart to explain why this is wrong.

   c How is your breathing system adapted to make these gas exchanges as efficient as possible?

AQA Examiner's tip

Remember the sequence for breathing in:
- muscles contract
- volume of thorax increases
- pressure in thorax decreases
- air enters lungs.

Key points

- The lungs are in your thorax protected by your ribcage and separated from your abdomen by the diaphragm.

- The intercostal muscles contract to move your ribs up and out and flatten the diaphragm, increasing the volume of your thorax. The pressure decreases and air moves in.

- The intercostal muscles relax and the ribs move down and in, and the diaphragm domes up, decreasing the volume of your thorax. The pressure increases and air is forced out.

B3 1.6   Artificial breathing aids

Learning objectives

- What happens if the surface area of the gas exchange surface in the lungs is reduced, or you can't use your muscles to ventilate your lungs?

- Can a machine breathe for you?

- How good are artificial lungs?

There are many different reasons why people sometimes struggle to breathe and get enough oxygen into their lungs. For example:

- The tubes leading to the lungs may be very narrow so less air gets through them.

- The structure of the alveoli can break down. This results in a few big air sacs that have a smaller surface area for gas exchange than healthy alveoli.

- Some people are paralysed in an accident or by disease so they can't breathe.

There are a number of artificial aids for supporting or taking over breathing that have saved countless lives. They work in two main ways – **negative pressure** and **positive pressure**.

a Why might someone need an artificial breathing aid?

The 'iron lung' – negative pressure

Polio is a disease that can leave people paralysed and unable to breathe. To keep polio sufferers alive until their bodies recovered, an external negative-pressure ventilator was developed. This was commonly known as the iron lung. Nowadays we are all vaccinated against polio and it has almost been wiped out worldwide.

The patient lay in a metal cylinder with their head sticking out and a tight seal around the neck. Air was pumped out of the chamber, lowering the pressure inside to form a **vacuum**. As a result, the chest wall of the patient moved up. This increased the volume and decreased the pressure inside the chest. So air from the outside was drawn into the lungs, just like normal breathing.

The vacuum then switched off automatically and air moved back into the chamber, increasing the pressure. The ribs moved down, lowering the volume and increasing the pressure inside the thorax. This forced air out of the lungs.

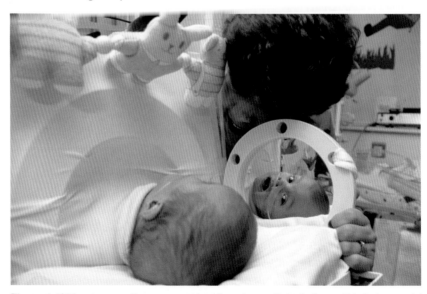

Figure 1 Without a negative pressure iron lung to ventilate its lungs this baby would have died

A more modern version, the 'shell', is a mini-cylinder that fits just around the chest so it is much easier for the patient to use. It was used mainly with paralysed patients. However, negative pressure ventilation is not used much anymore. It has been overtaken by positive pressure systems.

b What is an iron lung?

Positive pressure breathing

A positive pressure ventilator forces a carefully measured 'breath' of air into your lungs under a positive pressure. It's a bit like blowing up a balloon. Once the lungs have been inflated the air pressure stops. The lungs then deflate as the ribs move down again, forcing the air back out of the lungs.

Positive pressure ventilation can be used in patients with many different problems. It can be given using a simple face mask or by a tube going into the **trachea**. Positive pressure bag ventilators are held and squeezed by doctors or nurses in emergency treatments. They are very simple and temporary but can save lives. Full-scale positive pressure ventilating machines can keep patients alive through major surgery. They can help people who are paralysed to survive for years.

One of the big benefits of positive pressure ventilation is that patients do not have to be placed inside in an iron lung machine. The equipment can be used at home and the patient can even move about. Another benefit is that patients can have some control over the machine. Modern systems can link a ventilator with computer systems, which help patients manage their own breathing much more easily.

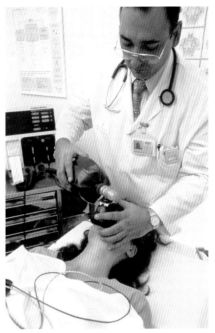

Figure 2 Using a positive pressure bag ventilator

Activity

Artificial aids to breathing

Use the content of this page and your own research to help you put together a presentation evaluating three different types of artificial aids to breathing. There are long-term machines and short-term solutions, systems used in surgery and systems that can be used at home. Decide which you are interested in and evaluate:

a how they work

b how effective they are at replacing the normal breathing system of the patient

c the advantages and disadvantages of each system.

Summary questions

1 Copy and complete using the words below:

negative   breathing   positive   body   aids   breathe

Artificial .... take over or help out a patient when their own .... is struggling or they cannot .... Older machines used external .... pressure but most modern machines use a .... pressure system.

2 **a** Explain the difference between the way an external negative pressure aid to breathing works and an internal positive pressure aid to breathing works.

b Which is most similar to the natural pattern of breathing of the body?

Key points

● Different types of artificial breathing aids have been developed over the years to help people when their lungs or breathing systems don't function properly.

● The different methods have advantages and disadvantages.

B3 1.7

Exchange in the gut

Learning objectives

- What are the adaptations in your small intestine that allow you to absorb food efficiently?

- Why are your villi so important?

∞ links

For information on glucose, amino acids, fatty acids and glycerol, look back to B2 3.3 Enzymes in digestion.

The food you eat is broken down in your gut. Food molecules get turned into simple sugars, such as glucose, amino acids, fatty acids and glycerol. Your body cells need these products of digestion to provide fuel for respiration and the building blocks for growth and repair. A successful exchange surface is very important.

Absorption in the small intestine

For the digested food molecules to reach your cells they must move from inside your small intestine into your bloodstream. They do this by a combination of diffusion and active transport.

a Why must the products of digestion get into your bloodstream?

The digested food molecules are small enough to pass freely through the walls of the small intestine into the blood vessels. They move in this direction because there is a very high concentration of food molecules in the gut and a much lower concentration in the blood. They move into the blood down a steep concentration gradient.

The lining of the small intestine is folded into thousands of tiny finger-like projections known as **villi** (singular: villus). These greatly increase the uptake of digested food by diffusion (see Figure 1). Only a certain number of digested food molecules can diffuse over a given surface area of gut lining at any one time. Increasing the surface area means there is more room for diffusion to take place (see Figure 2).

Each individual villus is itself covered in many microscopic microvilli. This increases the surface area available for diffusion even more.

b What is a villus?

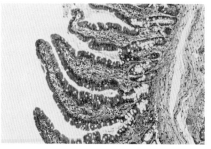

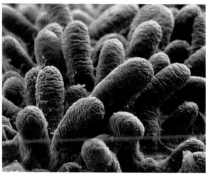

Like the alveoli of the lungs, the lining of the small intestine has an excellent blood supply. This carries away the digested food molecules as soon as they have diffused from one side to the other. So a steep concentration gradient is maintained all the time, from the inside of the intestine to the blood (see Figure 3). This in turn makes sure diffusion is as rapid and efficient as possible down the concentration gradient.

c Why is it so important that the villi have a rich blood supply?

Figure 1 The villi of the small intestine increase the surface area available for diffusion many times so we can absorb enough digested food to survive

Gut with villi — Length 5 cm

Gut without villi — Length 5 cm — Total stretched length = 5 cm

Total stretched length = 45 cm

Figure 2 The effect of folding on the available surface for exchange

Active transport in the small intestine

Diffusion isn't the only way in which dissolved products of digestion move from the gut into the blood. As the time since your last meal gets longer you can have more dissolved food molecules in your blood than in your digestive system. Glucose and other dissolved food molecules are then moved from the small intestine into the blood by active transport. The digested food molecules have to move against the concentration gradient. This makes sure that none of the digested food is wasted and lost in your faeces.

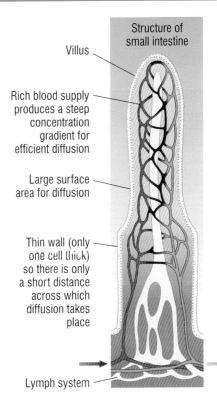

Structure of small intestine

Villus

Rich blood supply produces a steep concentration gradient for efficient diffusion

Large surface area for diffusion

Thin wall (only one cell thick) so there is only a short distance across which diffusion takes place

Lymph system

Figure 3 Thousands of finger-like projections in the wall of the small intestine – the villi – make it possible for all the digested food molecules to be transferred from your small intestine into your blood by diffusion and active transport

??? Did you know ...?

Although your gut is only around 7 metres long and a few centimetres wide, the way it is folded into your body along with the villi and microvilli give you a surface area for the absorption of digested products of 200–300 m²!

Summary questions

1 In the following sentences, match each beginning (A, B, C or D) to its correct ending (1 to 4).

A	Food needs to be broken down into small soluble molecules …	1	… by diffusion and active transport.
B	The villi are …	2	… carry away the digested food to the cells and maintain a steep concentration gradient.
C	Food molecules move from the small intestine into the bloodstream …	3	… so diffusion across the gut lining can take place.
D	The small intestine has a rich blood supply to …	4	… finger-like projections in the lining of the small intestine which increase the surface area for diffusion.

2 Explain why a folded gut wall can absorb more nutrients than a flat one.

3 Coeliac disease is caused by gluten, a protein found in wheat, oats and rye. The villi become flattened and the lining of the small intestine becomes damaged.
   a Why do you think people with untreated coeliac disease are often quite thin?
   b If someone with coeliac disease stops eating any food containing gluten, they will gradually gain weight and no longer suffer malnutrition. Suggest why this might be.

Key points

● The villi in the small intestine provide a large surface area with an extensive network of blood capillaries.

● This makes villi well adapted to absorb the products of digestion by diffusion and active transport.

B3 1.8

Exchange in plants

Learning objectives

- How are the leaves of plants adapted for gaseous exchange?

- How are roots adapted for the efficient uptake of water and mineral ions?

∞ **links**

For information on photosynthesis, look back to B2 2.1 Photosynthesis.

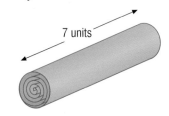

Surface area = 22 units^2

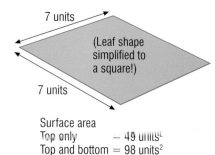

(Leaf shape simplified to a square!)

Surface area
Top only   = 49 units^2
Top and bottom = 98 units^2

Figure 1 The wide, flat shape of most leaves greatly increases the surface area for collecting light and exchanging gases, compared with more cylindrical leaves

Animals aren't the only living organisms that need to exchange materials. Plants rely heavily on diffusion to get the carbon dioxide they need for photosynthesis. They use osmosis to take water from the soil and active transport to obtain mineral ions from the soil. Plants have adaptations that make these exchanges as efficient as possible.

Gas exchange in plants

Plants need carbon dioxide and water for photosynthesis to take place. They get the carbon dioxide they need by diffusion through their leaves. The flattened shape of the leaves increases the surface area for diffusion. Most plants have thin leaves. This means the distance the carbon dioxide has to diffuse from the outside air to the photosynthesising cells is kept as short as possible.

What's more, leaves have many air spaces in their structure. These allow carbon dioxide to come into contact with lots of cells and give a large surface area for diffusion.

a How are leaves adapted for efficient diffusion of carbon dioxide?

However, there is a problem. Leaf cells constantly lose water by **evaporation**. If carbon dioxide could diffuse freely in and out of the leaves, water vapour would also be lost very quickly. Then the leaves – and the plant – would die.

The leaf cells do not need carbon dioxide all the time. When it is dark, they don't need carbon dioxide because they are not photosynthesising. Sometimes light is a limiting factor on the rate of photosynthesis. Then the carbon dioxide produced by respiration can be used for photosynthesis. But on bright, warm, sunny days a lot of carbon dioxide needs to come into the leaves by diffusion.

Leaves are adapted to allow carbon dioxide in only when it is needed. They are covered with a waxy **cuticle**. This is a waterproof and gasproof layer.

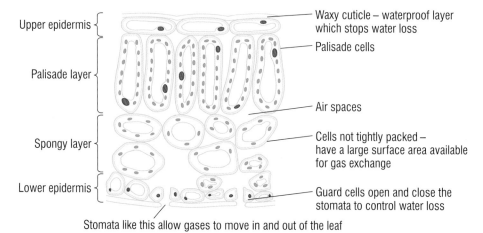

Figure 2 This cross-section of a leaf shows the arrangement of the cells inside, with plenty of air spaces and short diffusion distances. This means that the carbon dioxide needed for photosynthesis reaches the cells as efficiently as possible.

All over the leaf surface are small openings known as stomata. The stomata can be opened when the plant needs to allow air into the leaves. Carbon dioxide from the atmosphere diffuses into the air spaces and then into the cells along a concentration gradient. At the same time oxygen produced by photosynthesis is removed from the leaf by diffusion into the surrounding air. This maintains a concentration gradient for oxygen from the cells into the air spaces of the leaf. The stomata can be closed the rest of the time to limit the loss of water. The opening and closing of the stomata is controlled by the **guard cells**. Water is also lost from the leaves by diffusion when the stomata are open.

b Why don't leaves need carbon dioxide all the time?

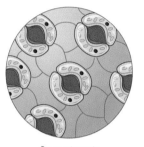
Open stomata

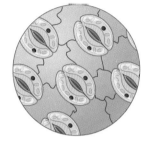
Closed stomata

Figure 3 Guards cells open and close the stomata to control the carbon dioxide going into the leaf and water vapour leaving it

Uptake of water and mineral ions in plants

Plant roots are adapted to take water and mineral ions from the soil as efficiently as possible. The roots themselves are thin, divided tubes with a large surface area. The cells on the outside of the roots near the growing tips have special adaptations that increase the surface area. These **root hair cells** have tiny projections from the cells which push out between the soil particles.

Water moves into the root hair cells by osmosis across the partially permeable root cell membrane. It then has only a short distance to move across the root to the xylem, where it is moved up and around the plant.

Plant roots are also adapted to take in mineral ions using active transport. They have plenty of mitochondria to supply the energy they need. They also have all the advantages of a large surface area and the short pathways needed for the movement of water.

links

For information on stomata, look back to B1 4.3 Adaptation in plants.

??? Did you know …?

Root hairs have an amazing effect – a 1 m^2 area of lawn grass has 350 m^2 of root surface area!

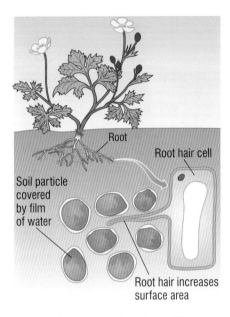

Root
Root hair cell
Soil particle covered by film of water
Root hair increases surface area

Figure 4 Many small roots, and the presence of microscopic root hairs on the individual root cells, increase diffusion of substances from the soil into the plant

links

For information on xylem, look back to B2 1.5 Tissues and organs.

Key points

- Plants have stomata that allow them to obtain carbon dioxide from the atmosphere.

- Carbon dioxide enters the leaf by diffusion. Leaves have a flat, thin shape and internal air spaces to increase the surface area available for diffusion.

- Most of the water and mineral ions needed by a plant are absorbed by the root hair cells, which increase the surface area of the roots.

Summary questions

1 **a** What are stomata?
  b Describe their role in the plant.
  c How are they controlled?

2 **a** How are plant roots adapted for the absorption of water and mineral ions?
  b How do the adaptations of plants for the exchange of materials compare with human adaptations in the lungs and the gut?

B3 1.9

Transipiration ⓚ

Learning objectives

- What is transpiration?
- When do plants transpire fastest?

Figure 1 The transpiration stream in trees like these redwoods can pull many litres of water metres above the ground

The top of a tree may be many metres from the ground. Yet the leaves at the top need water just as much as the lower branches. So how do they get the water they need?

Water loss from the leaves

The stomata on the surface of plant leaves can be opened and closed by the guard cells that surround them. Plants open their stomata to take in carbon dioxide for photosynthesis. However, when the stomata are open, plants lose water vapour through them as well. This loss of water vapour is called evaporation.

As water evaporates from the surface of the leaves, more water is pulled up through the xylem to take its place. This constant movement of water molecules through the xylem from the roots to the leaves is known as the **transpiration stream**. It is driven by the evaporation of water from the leaves. So anything that affects the rate of evaporation will affect **transpiration**.

a What is the transpiration stream?

The effect of the environment on transpiration

Anything that increases the rate of photosynthesis will increase the rate of transpiration. This happens because more stomata are opened up to let carbon dioxide in. In turn, more water is lost by evaporation through the open stomata. So warm, sunny conditions increase the rate of transpiration.

Conditions that increase the rate of evaporation of water when the stomata are open will also make transpiration happen more rapidly. Hot, dry, windy conditions increase the rate of transpiration.

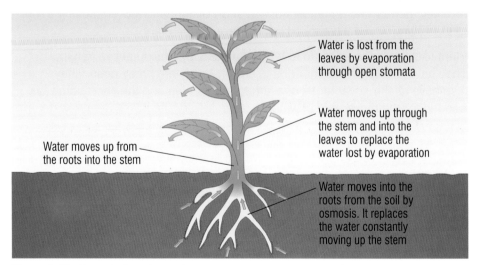

Water is lost from the leaves by evaporation through open stomata

Water moves up through the stem and into the leaves to replace the water lost by evaporation

Water moves up from the roots into the stem

Water moves into the roots from the soil by osmosis. It replaces the water constantly moving up the stem

Figure 2 The transpiration stream

b Give three conditions that will increase the rate of evaporation from a leaf.

Controlling water loss

Most plants have a variety of adaptations which help them to photosynthesise as much as possible, while losing as little water as possible.

Most leaves have a waxy, waterproof layer (the cuticle) to prevent uncontrolled water loss. In very hot environments the cuticle may be very thick and shiny. Most of the stomata are found on the underside of the leaves. This protects them from the direct light and energy from the Sun, and reduces the time they are open.

If a plant begins to lose water faster than it is replaced by the roots, it can take some drastic measures. The whole plant may wilt. **Wilting** is a protection mechanism against further water loss. The leaves all collapse and hang down. So the surface area available for water loss by evaporation is greatly reduced.

The stomata close, which stops photosynthesis and risks overheating. But this prevents most water loss and any further wilting. The plant will remain wilted until the temperature drops, the sun goes in or it rains.

Practical

Evidence for transpiration

There are a number of experiments which can be done to investigate the movement of water in plants by transpiration. Many of them use a piece of apparatus known as a potometer.

A potometer can be used to show how the uptake of water by the plant changes with different conditions. This gives you a good idea of the amount of water lost by the plant in transpiration.

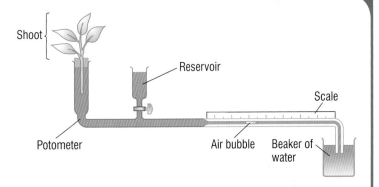

Figure 3 A potometer is used to show the water uptake of a plant under different conditions

Summary questions

1 a What is transpiration?
  b Describe how water moves up a plant in the transpiration stream.

2 a What part of the leaves helps the plant to reduce water loss under normal conditions?
  b How will transpiration in a plant be affected if the top leaf surfaces are coated in petroleum jelly?
  c How will transpiration in a plant be affected if the bottom leaf surfaces are coated in petroleum jelly?
  d Explain the effect on transpiration of turning a fan onto the leaves of the plant.
  e What does a potometer actually measure?

3 Water lilies have their stomata on the tops of their leaves.
  a How will this affect transpiration in water lilies?
  b How will the plants cope with this situation?

Key points

- The loss of water vapour from the surface of plant leaves is known as transpiration.

- Water is lost through the stomata, which are opened and closed to let in carbon dioxide for photosynthesis.

- Transpiration is more rapid in hot, dry, windy or bright conditions.

Summary questions 🅚

1 a Produce a table to compare diffusion, osmosis and active transport. Write a brief explanation of the advantages and disadvantages of all three processes in cells.

b Josh thinks that an increase in temperature would increase the rate of osmosis. Abi isn't so sure. Plan and describe an investigation that you could carry out to see if temperature has any effect on the rate of osmosis. Explain the results you would expect to get and why.

2 This graph was produced by someone who was involved in the development of a particular brand of sports drink. It shows the blood sodium ion concentrations of groups of marathon runners. Seven drank full-strength sports drink, eight drank half-strength sports drink and six drank plain water.

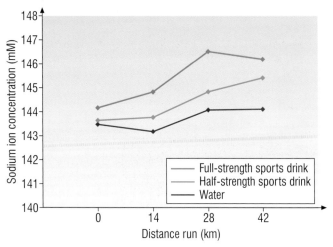

a Describe what has happened to the blood sodium levels of each group of runners.

b How could you use this evidence to support the idea that drinking a sports drink while exercising is a good idea?

c How could you use this evidence to support the idea that sports drinks are not really necessary and are a waste of money?

d What are the limitations of this research from the data you have been given and how could you improve the repeatability, reproducibility and validity of the results?

3 a How are the lungs adapted to allow the exchange of oxygen and carbon dioxide between the air and the blood?

b Explain what the experiment shown below tells us about inhaled and exhaled air.

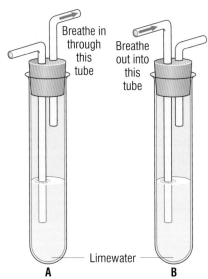

4 Some people stop breathing in their sleep, which disturbs them and can be dangerous. A nasal intermittent positive pressure ventilation system forces air into their lungs under pressure at regular intervals through a small facial mask they wear all night. The air enters the lungs, expanding the chest and is then squeezed out again as the chest falls.

a Explain how this differs from normal breathing.

b Explain the advantages of a system like this over an iron lung.

5 Compare the adaptations of plant leaves for the exchange of carbon dioxide, oxygen and water vapour with the adaptations of the roots for the absorption of water and mineral ions.

AQA Examination-style questions

1 During marathon races, athletes are advised to drink sports drinks.

Choose the correct words from the list below to complete the sentences.

alcohol fat ions protein starch sugar water

While running the athletes sweat.

The sports drink replaces the .... and .... lost in sweat.

The drinks are also a source of energy because they contain . (3)

2 The diagram shows an alveolus and a blood capillary.

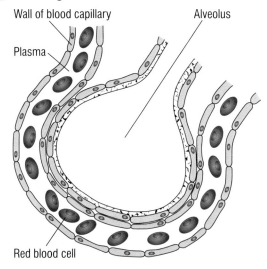

Wall of blood capillary   Alveolus

Plasma

Red blood cell

The alveolus and the blood capillary are gas exchange surfaces.

a i Where in the body would these structures be found? (1)

ii Give **two** features visible in the diagram that allow efficient gas exchange to take place. (2)

b i Name the gas that moves from the alveolus into the blood. (1)

ii Choose the correct word to complete the sentence.

diffusion osmosis ventilation

Gases are drawn into the alveolus by the process of .... (1)

iii Describe **two** changes that take place in the body to draw gases into the alveolus. (2)

3 Substances move in and out of plants.
List A shows some processes.
List B shows descriptions for these processes.
Match each process with its correct description. .

List A	List B
active transport	how water is lost through stomata
osmosis	enables root cells to absorb ions from very dilute soil water
evaporation	transport of sugar through the plant
	movement of water from cell to cell

(3)

4 *In this question you will be assessed on using good English, organising information clearly and using specialist terms where appropriate.*

The diagram shows a design for an artificial lung.

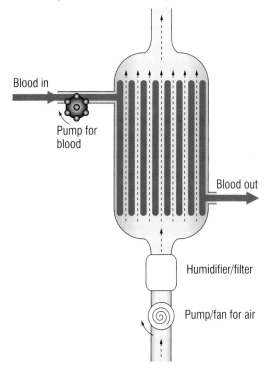

Blood in

Pump for blood

Blood out

Humidifier/filter

Pump/fan for air

Many people with lung disease are confined to a wheelchair or are unable to do much exercise. Scientists hope that a portable artificial lung, the size of a spectacle case, can be developed. This device might replace the need for lung transplants and allow patients to live a normal life.

When scientists design an artificial lung, what features of a normal lung must they copy? Suggest the advantages of the artificial lung compared with a lung transplant. (6)

B3 2.1

The circulatory system and the heart

Learning objectives

- What is your circulatory system?
- How does your heart work?

You are made up of billions of cells and most of them are far from a direct source of food or oxygen. A **transport system** is vital to supply the needs of your body cells and remove the waste material they produce. This is the function of your **blood circulation system**. It has three parts – the pipes (**blood vessels**), the pump (the **heart**) and the liquid (the **blood**).

a What are the main parts of your circulatory system?

A double circulation

You have two transport systems, called a **double circulation**. One carries blood from your heart to your lungs and back. This allows oxygen and carbon dioxide to be exchanged with the air in the lungs. The other carries blood around the rest of your body and back again to the heart.

A double circulation like this is vital in warm-blooded, active animals like humans. It makes our circulatory system very efficient. Fully **oxygenated** blood returns to the heart from the lungs. This blood can then be sent off to different parts of the body at high pressure. So more areas of your body can receive fully oxygenated blood quickly.

In your circulatory system **arteries** carry blood away from your heart to the organs of the body. Blood returns to your heart in the **veins**.

b Why do we need a blood circulation system?

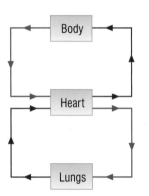

Figure 1 The two separate circulation systems supply the lungs and the rest of the body

The heart as a pump

Your heart is the organ that pumps blood around your body. It is made up of two pumps (for the double circulation) that beat together about 70 times each minute. The walls of your heart are almost entirely muscle. This muscle is supplied with oxygen by the **coronary arteries**.

c What do your coronary arteries do?

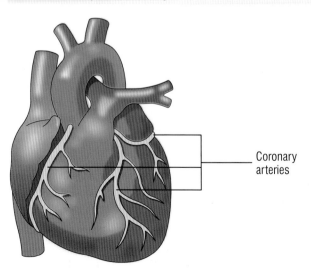

Coronary arteries

Figure 2 The muscles of the heart work hard so they need a good supply of oxygen and glucose. This is supplied by the blood in the coronary arteries.

The structure of the human heart is perfectly adapted for pumping blood to your lungs and your body. The two sides of the heart fill and empty at the same time. This gives a strong, coordinated heart beat.

Blood enters the top chambers of your heart (the **atria**). The blood coming into the right atrium from the **vena cava** is **deoxygenated** blood from your body. The blood coming into the left atrium in the **pulmonary vein** is oxygenated blood from your lungs. The atria contract together and force blood down into the **ventricles**. Valves close to stop the blood flowing backwards out of the heart.

- The ventricles contract and force blood out of the heart.
- The right ventricle forces deoxygenated blood to the lungs in the **pulmonary artery**.
- The left ventricle pumps oxygenated blood around the body in a big artery called the **aorta**.

As the blood is pumped into these two big vessels, valves close to make sure the blood flows in the right direction.

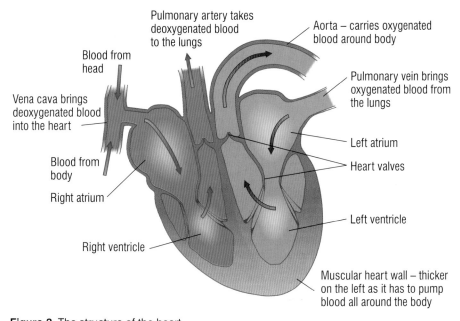

Figure 3 The structure of the heart

Labels on figure:
- Pulmonary artery takes deoxygenated blood to the lungs
- Aorta – carries oxygenated blood around body
- Blood from head
- Vena cava brings deoxygenated blood into the heart
- Pulmonary vein brings oxygenated blood from the lungs
- Blood from body
- Left atrium
- Heart valves
- Right atrium
- Left ventricle
- Right ventricle
- Muscular heart wall – thicker on the left as it has to pump blood all around the body

AQA *Examiner's tip*

Remember:
- The heart has *four* chambers.
- Ventricles pump blood *out* of the heart.

Summary questions

1 Copy and complete using the words below:

heart   oxygen   organ   circulatory   body   glucose   pumps

Your .... system transports substances such as ...., carbon dioxide and .... around the body.
Your .... is a muscular .... that .... blood around the ....

2 Make a flowchart showing the route of a unit of blood as it passes through the heart and the lungs.

3 Blood in the arteries is usually bright red because it is full of oxygen. This is not true of the arteries leading from the heart to the lungs. Why not?

Key points

- The circulation system consists of the blood vessels, the heart and the blood.
- Human beings have a double circulation.
- The heart is an organ that pumps blood around the body.
- The valves make sure blood flows in the right direction through the heart.

B3 2.2

Keeping the blood flowing

Learning objectives

- Where do substances enter and leave the blood?
- What happens if the veins close up or the valves fail?

??? Did you know ...?

No cell in your body is more than 0.05 mm away from a capillary!

Artery

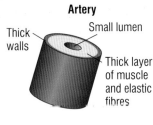

Thick walls — Small lumen
Thick layer of muscle and elastic fibres

Vein

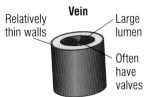

Relatively thin walls — Large lumen
Often have valves

Capillary

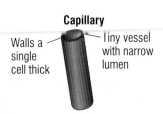

Walls a single cell thick
Tiny vessel with narrow lumen

Figure 1 The three main types of blood vessels

Practical

Blood flow

- You can practise finding your pulse and look for the valves in the veins in your hands and wrist.

Blood is carried around your body in three main types of blood vessels, each adapted for a different function.

The blood vessels

Your **arteries** carry blood away from your heart to the organs of your body. This blood is usually bright red oxygenated blood. The arteries stretch as the blood is forced through them and go back into shape afterwards. You can feel this as a pulse where the arteries run close to the surface (like your wrist). Because the blood in the arteries is under pressure, it is very dangerous if an artery is cut. That's because the blood spurts out rapidly every time the heart beats.

The **veins** carry blood towards your heart. It is usually low in oxygen and so is a deep purply-red colour. Veins do not have a pulse. They often have **valves** to prevent the backflow of blood as it moves back to the heart.

The **capillaries** form a huge network of tiny vessels linking the arteries and the veins. Capillaries are narrow with very thin walls. This enables substances, such as oxygen and glucose, to diffuse easily out of your blood and into your cells. Similarly the substances produced by your cells, such as carbon dioxide, pass into the blood through the walls of the capillaries.

a Substances can only enter and leave the blood in the capillaries. Why is this?

Problems with blood flow through the heart

If the supply of oxygen to your heart is interrupted it can cause pain, a heart attack and even death. The coronary arteries that supply blood to the heart muscle can become narrow as you age. They also get narrower when fatty deposits form on the lining of the vessel. Doctors often solve the problem with **stents**. A stent is a metal mesh that is placed in the artery. A tiny balloon is inflated to open up the blood vessel and the stent at the same time. As soon as this is done the blood flows freely. Doctors can put a stent in place without a general anaesthetic.

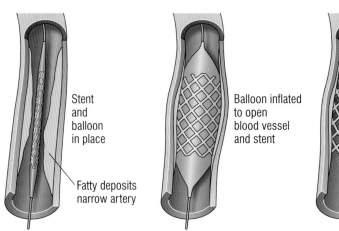

Stent and balloon in place
Fatty deposits narrow artery

Balloon inflated to open blood vessel and stent

Stent holds artery open

Figure 2 A stent being positioned in an artery

How Science Works

Using stents and artificial valves

It isn't only coronary arteries that can narrow and cause problems. Stents can be used to open up an artery almost anywhere in the body. Many stents now also release drugs to prevent the blood from clotting. However, there are some questions about the costs and benefits of this treatment.

Doctors can also carry out bypass surgery. In this operation they replace the narrow or blocked coronary arteries with bits of veins from other parts of the body. This works for badly blocked arteries where stents cannot help. However, the surgery is expensive and involves a general anaesthetic.

b What is a stent?

Leaky valves

The heart valves keep the blood flowing in the right direction. These valves have to withstand a lot of pressure. They may weaken and start to leak, so the heart does not work so well. The person affected can become very breathless. They will eventually die if the problem is not solved.

Doctors can operate on the heart and replace the faulty valve. Mechanical valves are made of materials such as titanium and polymers. They last for a very long time. However, with a mechanical valve you have to take medicine for the rest of your life. This medicine prevents your blood from clotting.

Biological valves are based on valves taken from animals such as pigs or cattle. These work extremely well and the patient does not need any medication. However, they only last for about 15 years.

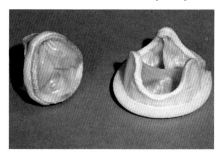 

Figure 3 Both biological and mechanical heart valves work very well. They both have advantages and disadvantages for the patient.

Summary questions

1 Describe the following blood vessels:
   a artery
   b vein
   c capillary.

2 **a** Draw a diagram that explains the way the arteries, veins and capillaries are linked to each other and to the heart.
   b Label the diagram and explain what is happening in the capillaries.

3 Make a table to show the advantages and disadvantages of:
   a using a stent to improve the blood flow through the coronary arteries and carrying out bypass surgery
   b mechanical and biological replacement heart valves.

AQA **Examiner's tip**

Don't be confused by the names:
- **a**rteries carry blood **a**way from the heart
- veins carry blood to the heart
- valves prevent backflow.

AQA **Examiner's tip**

Learn the sequence:
veins → atria → ventricles → arteries
V → A → V → A

Key points

- The main types of blood vessels are arteries, veins and capillaries.
- Substances diffuse in and out of the blood in the capillaries.
- Stents can be used to keep narrowed or blocked arteries open.
- Damaged heart valves can be replaced.

B3 2.5

Transport systems in plants ⓚ

Learning objectives

- What substances are transported in plants?
- How does transport in the xylem and the phloem differ?

∞ **links**

For information on phloem, look back to B2 1.5 Tissues and organs.

Plants make sugar by photosynthesis in the leaves and other green parts. This sugar is needed all over the plant. Similarly, water and mineral ions move into the plant from the soil through the roots, but they are needed by every cell of the plant. Plants have two separate transport systems to move substances around their bodies.

Phloem – moving food

The phloem transports the sugars made by photosynthesis from the leaves to the rest of the plant. This includes the growing areas of the stems and roots. Here the sugars are needed for making new plant cells. Food is also transported to the storage organs where it is needed to provide an energy store for the winter. Phloem is a living tissue.

Greenfly and other aphids are plant pests. They stick their sharp mouthparts right into the phloem and feed on the sugary fluid. If too many of them attack a plant they can kill it by taking all of the food.

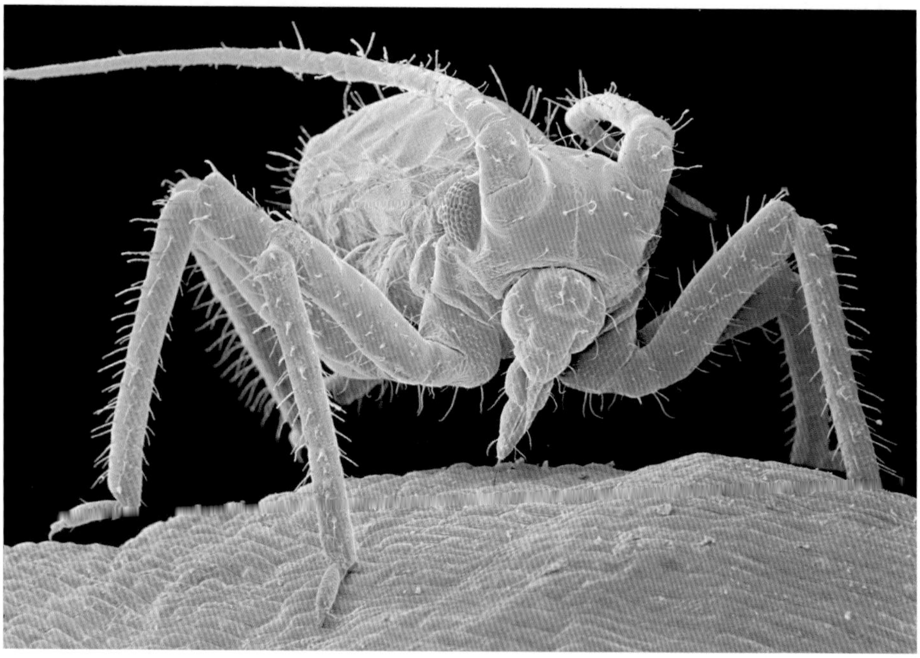

Figure 1 Aphids take the liquid full of dissolved sugars directly from the phloem

Xylem – moving water and mineral ions

The xylem is the other transport tissue in plants. It carries water and mineral ions from the soil around the plant. Mature xylem cells are dead. In woody plants like trees, the xylem makes up the bulk of the wood and the phloem is found in a ring just underneath the bark. This makes young trees in particular very vulnerable to damage by animals. That's because if a complete ring of bark is eaten, transport in the phloem stops. Then the tree will die.

∞ **links**

For information on xylem, look back to B2 1.5 Tissues and organs.

a Which plant transport tissue is living?
b What is transported in the xylem?

Why is transport so important?

It is very important to move the food made by photosynthesis around the plant. All the cells need sugars for respiration as well as to provide materials for growth. The movement of water and mineral ions from the roots is equally important. The mineral ions are needed for the production of proteins and other molecules within the cells.

The water is needed for several reasons. One is for photosynthesis, where carbon dioxide and water are combined to make sugar. Another is that water is needed to hold the plant upright. When a cell has plenty of water inside it the vacuole presses the cytoplasm against the cell walls. This pressure of the cytoplasm against the cell walls gives support for young plants and for the structure of the leaves. For young plants and soft-stemmed plants – although not trees – this is the main method of support.

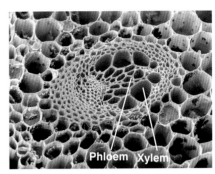

Figure 2 The phloem and xylem are arranged in vascular bundles in the stem

Figure 3 A simple way of demonstrating that water moves up the xylem

AQA Examiner's tip

Don't confuse xylem and phloem:

- For **ph**loem think '**f**ood' (sugar) transport.
- For xylem think 'transports water'.

Summary questions

1 Copy and complete using the words below:

   xylem   phloem   two   water   sugars   roots   leaves   plant

   Plants have .... transport systems. The .... transports .... and mineral ions from the .... to the stems and leaves. The .... transports dissolved .... from the .... to the rest of the ....

2 a Why does a plant need a transport system?
   b Explain why a constant supply of sugar and water are so important to the cells of a plant.

3 A local woodland trust has set up a scheme to put protective plastic covers around the trunks of young trees. Some local residents are objecting to this, saying it spoils the look of the woodland. Write a letter to your local paper explaining exactly why this protection is necessary.

Key points

- Flowering plants have separate transport systems.
- Xylem tissue transports water and mineral ions from the roots to the stems and leaves.
- Phloem tissue transports dissolved sugars from the leaves to the rest of the plant, including the growing regions and storage organs.

Summary questions ⓚ

1 Here are descriptions of two heart problems. In each case use what you know about the heart and the circulatory system to explain the problems caused by the condition.

   a Sometimes babies are born with a 'hole in the heart' – there is a gap in the central dividing wall of the heart. They may look blue in colour and have very little energy.

   b The coronary arteries supplying blood to the heart muscle itself may become clogged with fatty material. The person affected may get chest pain when they exercise or even have a heart attack.

2 In each of the following examples, explain the effect on the blood and what this will mean to the person involved:

   a an athlete running a race after acting as a blood donor and giving blood

   b someone who eats a diet low in iron.

3 a How are the red blood cells adapted for the carriage of oxygen?

   b The graph shows the effect of an increased carbon dioxide concentration on the way haemoglobin carries oxygen.

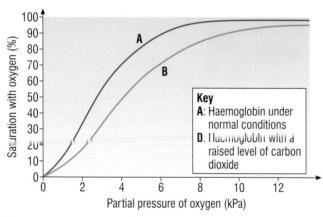

Figure 1 Graph to show the effect of carbon dioxide concentration on the reaction between haemoglobin and oxygen

   i What is the percentage saturation of haemoglobin under normal conditions when the partial pressure of oxygen is 2 and 6?

   ii What is the percentage saturation of haemoglobin when the partial pressure of oxygen is 2 and 6 and the concentration of carbon dioxide is raised?

   iii What does this tell you about events in the blood capillaries in the lungs?

   iv How does the concentration of carbon dioxide in the tissues affect gaseous exchange between the cells and the blood?

   v Why do these data suggest that haemoglobin-based oxygen-carrying artificial blood would be effective?

4 If a patient has a blocked blood vessel, doctors may be able to open up the blocked vessels with a stent or replace the clogged up blood vessels with bits of healthy blood vessels taken from other parts of the patient's body.

Figure 2 shows you the results of these procedures in one group of patients after one year.

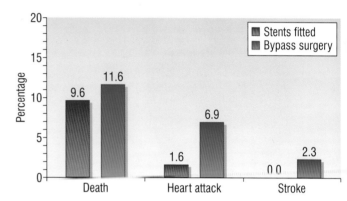

Figure 2 Results after 1 year

   a What is a stent and how does it work?

   b Which technique does the evidence suggest is the most successful for treating blocked coronary arteries? Explain your answer.

   c What additional information would you need to decide whether this evidence was repeatable, reproducible and valid?

5 Arteries, veins, xylem and phloem are all transport vessels in living organisms.

   a Make a table to compare arteries and veins.

   b Make a table to compare xylem and phloem tissue.

   c Comment on the two different systems.

AQA Examination-style questions

1 a Platelets are found in the blood plasma. Some sick people need platelets as part of their treatment.

What is the function of platelets? (1)

b Some people donate whole blood, but the National Blood Service also needs platelet donations.

Read the facts about blood donation and platelet donation in the table below.

Use information from the table and your own knowledge to answer the questions.

i The National Blood Service needs more platelet donors.
Why? (1)

ii Give **two** reasons why doctors prefer platelet donation for seriously ill patients who require platelets. (2)

iii Give **one** disadvantage of platelet donation for the National Blood Service. (1)

iv Blood platelet donors choose to donate because they know the benefits to patients but there *are* disadvantages to donating platelets instead of whole blood.
Give **two** disadvantages for the donor of platelets. (2)

v Give **one** advantage to the donor for platelet donation over whole blood donation. (1)

2 The photograph shows a red blood cell in part of a blood clot. The fibres labelled **X** are produced in the early stages of the clotting process.

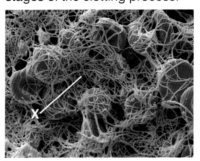

a Suggest how the fibres labelled **X** help in blood-clot formation. (1)

b The average diameter of a real red blood cell is 0.008 millimetres.

On the photograph, the diameter of the red blood cell is 100 millimetres.

Use the formula to calculate the magnification of the photograph.

diameter on photograph = real diameter × magnification

Magnification = (2)

c Some blood capillaries have an internal diameter of approximately 0.01 millimetres.

i Use information given in part **b** to explain why only one red blood cell at a time can pass through a capillary. (2)

ii Explain the advantages of red blood cells passing through a capillary one at a time. (2)

	Blood donation	Platelet donation
Age of donors	17+	17+
Number of possible donations per year	2–3	8–12
Diet before donating	normal diet	a few days of low fat food, no aspirin or other 'blood-thinning drugs'
Volume removed	470 cm³ blood	400–600 cm³ of straw coloured liquid
Time to test blood before donation	time for confidential questionnaire plus a few minutes for a finger-prick test to find out haemoglobin levels	often a previous blood donor; extra blood tests take about 8 weeks to check platelet levels
Usual time to donate	10 minutes to donate blood plus resting time; about 1 hour in total	90 minutes to donate platelets plus resting time; about 2 hours in total
Time for blood to get back to normal	about 16 weeks	a few days
Keeping time	depends on treatment – blood is separated into different parts such as red cells or plasma; some is frozen	5 days
Number of people to benefit from a single donation	blood is often split into components, including platelets; 3–7 people may benefit	three adults or up to 12 children
Benefit to person receiving platelets	may require platelets from several donors	platelets received from one donor

B3 3.1

Controlling internal conditions

Learning objectives

- What body conditions need to be controlled?

- How do you get rid of the waste products from your cells?

∞ **links**

For information on homeostasis, look back to B1 2.5 Controlling conditions.

For your body to work properly the conditions surrounding your millions of cells must stay as constant as possible. On the other hand, almost everything you do tends to change things. For example:

- as you move you produce energy that warms the body
- as you respire you produce waste
- when you digest food you take millions of molecules into your body.

Yet somehow you keep your internal conditions constant within a very narrow range. How do you manage this? The answer is through homeostasis. Many of the functions in your body help to keep your internal environment as constant as possible. Now you are going to find out more about some of them.

a What is homeostasis?

Figure 1 Whatever you choose to do in life, the conditions inside your body will stay more or less exactly the same

Removing waste products

No matter what you are doing, the cells of your body are constantly producing waste products. These are products of the chemical reactions that take place in the cells. The more extreme the conditions you put yourself in, the more waste products your cells make.

There are two main poisonous waste products – carbon dioxide and urea. They cause major problems for your body if their levels are allowed to build up.

Carbon dioxide

Carbon dioxide is produced during respiration. Every cell in your body respires, and so every cell produces carbon dioxide. It is vital that you remove this carbon dioxide because dissolved carbon dioxide produces an acidic solution. This would affect the working of all the enzymes in your cells.

The carbon dioxide moves out of the cells into your blood. Your bloodstream carries it back to your lungs. Almost all of the carbon dioxide is removed from your body via your lungs when you breathe out. The air you breathe in contains only 0.04% carbon dioxide. However, the air you breathe out contains about 4% carbon dioxide.

b How do you remove carbon dioxide from your body?

AQA Examiner's tip

Don't confuse *urea* and *urine*. Urea is made in the liver; urine is produced by the kidney. Urine contains urea.

Urea

The other main waste product of your body is urea.

When you eat more protein than you need, or when body tissues are worn out, the extra protein has to be broken down. Amino acids cannot be used as fuel for your body. Your **liver** removes the amino group and converts it into urea.

The rest of the amino acid molecule can then be used in respiration or to make other molecules. The urea passes from the liver cells into your blood.

Urea is poisonous and if the levels build up in your blood it will cause a lot of damage. Fortunately the urea is filtered out of your blood by your kidneys. It is then passed out of your body in your urine, along with any excess water and salt.

c Where is urea made?

Maintaining body balance

Water and ions enter your body when you eat or drink. The water and ion content of your body are carefully controlled, preventing damage to your cells. Water is lost through breathing, through sweating and in urine. The ions are lost in sweat and urine.

If the concentrations of your body fluids change, water will move into or out of your cells by osmosis. This could damage or destroy the cells. You saw this when you looked at the importance of keeping hydrated when you exercise. So water balance is vital.

It is also very important to control your body temperature. If it goes too high or too low it can be fatal. Finally, it is very important to control the levels of sugar in your blood. The amount of sugar coming into your body and the energy needed by your cells are always changing and a balance must always be maintained. So homeostasis plays a very important role in your body.

Figure 2 The average person produces up to 900 litres of urine a year!

⚭ links

For information on osmosis, look back to B3 1.1 Osmosis.

For information on keeping hydrated, look back to B3 1.3 The sports drink dilemma.

For information on body temperature, see B3 3.5 Controlling body temperature.

For information on controlling glucose levels, see B3 3.7 Controlling blood glucose.

Summary questions

1 Copy and complete using the words below:

*blood   carbon dioxide   constant   controlled   environment
enzymes   homeostasis   sugar   temperature   urea   water*

The internal .... of your body is kept relatively .... by a whole range of processes that together are known as .... Waste products such as .... and .... have to be removed from your .... all the time. The .... and ion concentration in your blood are constantly .... and so is your blood .... level. Your body .... is kept within a narrow range so your .... work effectively.

2 There are two main waste products that have to be removed from the human body – carbon dioxide and urea. For each waste product, describe:
a how it is formed
b why it has to be removed
c where it is removed from the body.

3 Draw a spider diagram with the word 'homeostasis' in the centre and make as many links in the diagram as you can. Label the links made.

Key points

- The internal conditions of your body have to be controlled to maintain a constant internal environment. These include your body temperature, your water and ion balance and your blood sugar levels.

- Carbon dioxide is produced during respiration and leaves the body via the lungs when you breathe out.

- Urea is produced by your liver as excess amino acids are broken down, and is removed by your kidneys in the urine.

B3 3.3

Dialysis – an artificial kidney ⓚ

Your kidneys can be damaged and destroyed by infections. Some people have a genetic problem that means their kidneys fail. In others, the kidneys are damaged during an accident. Whatever the cause, untreated failure of both your kidneys can lead to death. Toxins, such as urea, build up in the body, and the salt and water balance of your body is upset.

Dialysis

For centuries kidney failure meant certain death, but we now have two effective methods of treating this problem:

- We can carry out the function of the kidney artificially using **dialysis.**
- We can replace the failed kidneys with a healthy one in a **kidney transplant**.

a Why is kidney failure such a threat to life?

The machine that carries out the functions of the kidney is known as a **dialysis machine**. It relies on the process of dialysis to clean the blood. In a dialysis machine a person's blood leaves their body and flows between partially permeable membranes. On the other side of these membranes is the dialysis fluid. The dialysis fluid contains the same concentration of useful substances as the blood.

If your kidneys don't work, the concentrations of urea and mineral ions build up in the blood. Treatment by dialysis restores the concentrations of these dissolved substances to normal levels. Then as you carry on with normal life, urea and other substances build up again. So dialysis has to be repeated at regular intervals.

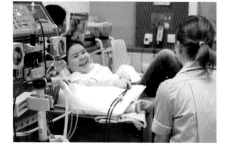

Figure 1 A dialysis machine. These 'artificial kidneys' not only save lots of lives, but allow sufferers from kidney failure to lead relatively full, active lives

It takes around eight hours for dialysis to be complete. So people with kidney failure have to remain attached to a dialysis machine for hours several times a week. They also have to manage their diets carefully. This helps keep their blood chemistry as stable as possible so that they can lead a normal life between sessions.

b What process does dialysis depend on?

How dialysis works

During dialysis, it is vital that patients lose the excess urea and mineral ions that have built up in the blood. It is equally important that they do not lose useful substances from their blood. These include glucose and useful mineral ions.

The loss of these substances is prevented by the careful control of the dialysis fluid. The dialysis fluid contains the same concentration of glucose and mineral ions as the blood. So there is *no net* movement of glucose and useful mineral ions out of the blood. This makes sure that glucose and useful mineral ions are not lost. Because the dialysis fluid contains normal plasma levels of mineral ions, any excess ions are removed from the blood. The excess ions move out by diffusion along a concentration gradient.

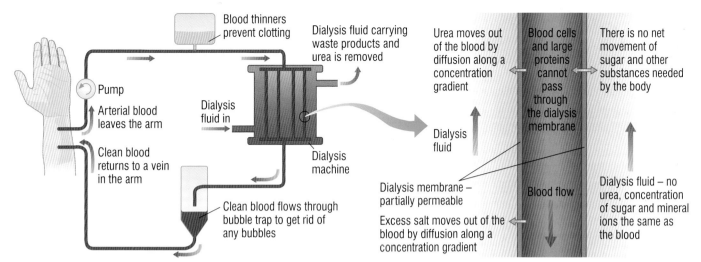

Figure 2 A dialysis machine relies on simple diffusion to clean the blood, removing the waste products which would damage the body as they build up

In contrast, the dialysis fluid contains no urea. This makes a steep concentration gradient from the blood to the fluid. So, much of the urea leaves the blood. The whole process of dialysis depends on diffusion along concentration gradients, which have to be maintained by the flow of fluid. There is no active transport.

Many people go to hospital to receive dialysis. However, in 1964 home dialysis machines were made available for the first time. They are big and expensive but at least some people can have dialysis at home. Even with all our modern technology, dialysis machines are still quite large. They are certainly much bigger than the kidneys they replace! There is even a form of dialysis which takes place inside the body cavity!

Dialysis has some disadvantages. You have to follow a very carefully controlled diet. You also have to spend regular, long sessions connected to a dialysis machine. Over many years, the balance of substances in the blood can become more difficult to control, no matter how careful the dialysis. Even so, for many people with kidney failure, dialysis keeps them alive. Fortunately, in dialysis we have successfully copied the action of the kidney in the body.

AQA Examiner's tip

Look at as many different examples of dialysis diagrams as you can. Identify the membrane. Be clear about what diffuses through the membrane. What is in the dialysis fluid?

Summary questions

1 Produce a flowchart to explain how a dialysis machine works.

2 a Why do people with kidney failure have to control their intake of protein and salt?
   b Why can patients with kidney failure eat and drink what they like during the first few hours of dialysis?

3 a Explain the importance of dialysis fluid containing no urea and normal plasma levels of salt, glucose and minerals.
   b Both blood and dialysis fluid are constantly circulated through the dialysis machine. Explain why the constant circulation of dialysis fluid is so important.

Key points

- People suffering from kidney failure may be treated by regular sessions on a kidney dialysis machine or by having a kidney transplant.

- In a dialysis machine, the concentration of dissolved substances in the blood is restored to normal levels.

- The levels of useful substances in the blood are maintained, while urea and excess mineral ions pass out from the blood into the dialysis fluid.

B3 3.4

Kidney transplants ⓚ

Diseased kidneys can be replaced in a kidney transplant using a single healthy kidney from a donor. The donor kidney is joined to the blood vessels in the groin of the patient (the **recipient**). If all goes well, it will function normally to clean and balance the blood. One kidney can balance your blood chemistry and remove your waste urea for a lifetime.

The rejection problem

The main problem with transplanting a kidney is that the new kidney comes from a different person. The antigens (proteins on the cell surface) of the donor organ will be different to those of the recipient (person who needs the new kidney). There is a risk that the antibodies of the immune system of the recipient will attack the antigens on the donor organ. This results in rejection and destruction of the donated kidney.

> **a** There is one situation where there is no risk of a new kidney being rejected. What do you think that might be?

There are a number of ways of reducing the risk of rejection. The match between the antigens of the donor and the recipient is made as close as possible. For example, we can use a donor kidney with a 'tissue type' very similar to the recipient (from people with the same blood group).

The recipient is given drugs to suppress their **immune response** (**immunosuppressant drugs**) for the rest of their lives. This helps to prevent the rejection of their new organ. Immunosuppressant drugs are improving all the time. Nowadays the need for a really close tissue match is getting less important.

The disadvantage of taking immunosuppressant drugs is that they prevent the patients from dealing effectively with infectious diseases. They have to take great care if they become ill in any way. However, most people feel this is a small price to pay for a new, working kidney.

Transplanted organs don't last forever. The average transplanted kidney works for around 9 years although some last much longer. Once the organ starts to fail the patient has to return to dialysis. Then they have to wait until another suitable kidney is found.

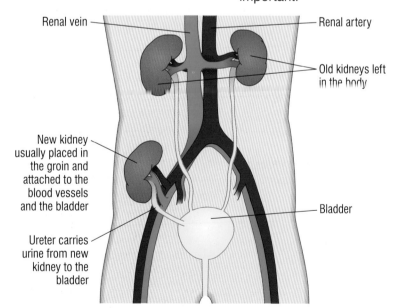

Renal vein

Renal artery

Old kidneys left in the body

New kidney usually placed in the groin and attached to the blood vessels and the bladder

Ureter carries urine from new kidney to the bladder

Bladder

Figure 1 A donor kidney takes over the functions of failed kidneys, which are usually left in place

How Science Works

Dialysis *v.* transplants

The great advantage of receiving a kidney transplant is that you are free from the restrictions which come with regular dialysis sessions. You can also eat what you want. An almost completely normal life is the dream of everyone waiting for a kidney transplant.

The disadvantages are mainly to do with the risk of rejection. You have to take medicine every day of your life in case the kidney is rejected. You also need regular check-ups to see if your body has started to reject the new organ. However, the biggest disadvantage is that you may never get the chance of a transplant at all.

Dialysis is much more readily available than donor organs, so it is there whenever kidneys fail. It enables you to lead a relatively normal life. However, you are tied to a special diet and regular sessions on the machine. Long term dialysis is much more expensive than a transplant.

Finding the donors

The main source of kidneys is from people who die suddenly. The deaths are often from road accidents or from strokes and heart attacks. In the UK, organs can be taken from people if they carry an organ donor card or are on the online donor register. Alternatively, a relative of someone who has died suddenly can give their consent.

There are never enough donor kidneys to go around. Many of us do not register as donors. What's more, as cars become safer, fewer people die in traffic accidents. This is very good news, but it means there are fewer potential donors. At any one time there are thousands of people having kidney dialysis. Most would love to have a kidney transplant but never get the opportunity. In 2008–9, 2497 people in the UK had kidney transplants. However, by the end of 2009 there were still almost 7000 people on dialysis waiting for a kidney.

Some scientists are working on **xenotransplantation**, producing genetically engineered pigs with organs that could be used for human transplants. Other scientists hope that stem cell research will produce a way of growing new kidneys on demand, so no one dies waiting for a suitable organ to become available.

Figure 2 This young woman has been given a new lease of life by a kidney transplant. A lack of donors means not everyone who suffers from kidney failure is so lucky. For more information on kidney treatment, see B3 3.6 Treatment and temperature issues.

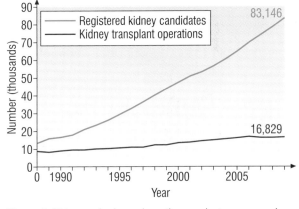

Figure 3 This graph shows how the gap between people needing a kidney and available organs is getting bigger in the US. The same pattern is seen in most other countries, including the UK.

∞ links

For information on stem cell research, look back to B2 5.3 Stem cells.

Summary questions

1 How does someone with a kidney transplant overcome the problems of kidney failure?

2 Sometimes a live donor – usually a close family member – will donate a kidney. These transplants have a higher rate of success than normal transplants from dead, unrelated donors.
   a Suggest two reasons why live transplants from a close family member have a higher success rate than normal transplants.
   b Why do you think that live donor transplants are relatively rare?

3 Produce a table to compare the advantages and disadvantages of treating kidney failure with dialysis or with a kidney transplant. Which treatment do you think is preferable and why?

Key points

- In a kidney transplant, diseased or damaged kidneys are replaced with a healthy kidney from a donor.

- To try and prevent rejection of the donor kidney, the tissue types of the donor and the recipient are matched as closely as possible. Immunosuppressant drugs are also used.

B3 3.5   Controlling body temperature ⓚ

Learning objectives

- How does your body monitor its temperature?

- How does your body stop you getting too hot?

- How does your body keep you warm?

Figure 1 People in different parts of the world live in conditions of extreme heat and extreme cold and still maintain a constant internal body temperature

AQA *Examiner's tip*

Remember that the thermoregulatory centre is in the brain and it monitors the temperature of the blood.

Wherever you go and whatever you do, your body temperature needs to stay around 37 °C. This is the temperature at which your enzymes work best. Your skin temperature can vary enormously without problems. It is the temperature deep inside your body, known as the **core body temperature**, which must be kept stable.

At only a few degrees above or below normal body temperature your enzymes don't function properly. All sorts of things can affect your internal body temperature, including:

- energy produced in your muscles during exercise
- fevers caused by disease
- the external temperature rising or falling.

Basic temperature control

You can change your clothing, light a fire, and turn on the heating or air-conditioning to help control your body temperature. However, it is your internal control mechanisms that are most important.

a Why is control of your body temperature so important?

Control of your core body temperature relies on the **thermoregulatory centre** in your brain. This centre contains receptors that are sensitive to temperature changes. They monitor the temperature of the blood flowing through the brain itself.

Extra information comes from the temperature receptors in the skin. These send impulses to the thermoregulatory centre, giving information about the skin temperature. The receptors are so sensitive they can detect a difference in temperature of as little as 0.5 °C!

If your temperature starts to go up, your sweat glands release more sweat, which cools the body down. Sweating also makes you lose water and mineral ions. Therefore you need to take in more drink to replace the water and ions you have lost.

Your skin also looks redder as more blood flows through it, cooling you down.

If your temperature starts to go down you will look pale as less blood flows through your skin. This means you lose less energy.

Cooling the body down

If you get too hot, your enzymes denature and can no longer catalyse the reactions in your cells. When your core body temperature begins to rise, impulses are sent from the thermoregulatory centre to the body so more energy is released:

- The blood vessels that supply your skin capillaries dilate (open wider). This lets more blood flow through the capillaries. Your skin flushes, so you lose more energy by radiation.

- Your rate of sweating goes up. This extra sweat cools your body down as it evaporates. In humid weather when the sweat does not evaporate it is much harder to keep cool.

Higher

Higher

Reducing energy loss

It is just as dangerous for your core temperature to drop as it is for it to rise. If you get very cold, the rate of the enzyme-controlled reactions in your cells falls too low. You don't release enough energy and your cells begin to die. If your core body temperature starts to fall, impulses are sent from your thermoregulatory centre to the body to conserve and even release more energy:

- The blood vessels that supply your skin capillaries constrict (close up) to reduce the flow of blood through the capillaries. This reduces the energy released by radiation through the surface of the skin.
- Sweat production is reduced. Less sweat evaporates so less energy is released.
- You may shiver – your muscles contract and relax rapidly. These muscle contractions need lots of respiration, which releases more energy. This raises your body temperature. As you warm up, the shivering stops.

b Why is a fall in your core body temperature so dangerous?

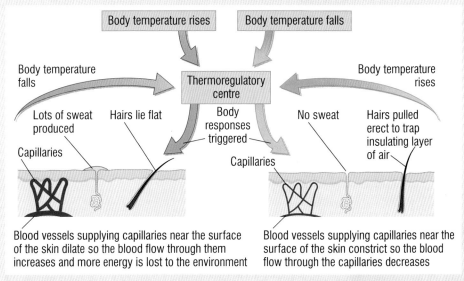

Figure 2 Changes in your core body temperature set off automatic responses to oppose the changes and maintain a steady internal environment

Key points

- Your body temperature is monitored and controlled by the thermoregulatory centre in your brain.
- Your body temperature must be kept at the level at which enzymes work best.
- Your body responds to cool you down or warm you up if your core body temperature changes.
- The blood vessels that supply the capillaries in the skin dilate and constrict to control the blood flow to the surface. **[H]**
- Energy is released through the evaporation of sweat from the surface of the skin to cool the body down. **[H]**
- Shivering involves contraction of the muscles that produces energy from respiration to warm the body. **[H]**

Summary questions

1 Copy and complete using the words below:

red sweating water rise skin temperature energy

If you exercise hard your body .... will start to .... Your skin goes .... and your rate of .... increases so you lose more .... through your .... Your temperature returns to normal and you need to drink .... to replace the water you have lost through sweating.

2 **a** Why is it so important to maintain a body temperature of about 37 °C?
   b Explain the role of:
      i the thermoregulatory centre in the brain, and
      ii the temperature sensors in the skin in maintaining a constant core body temperature.

3 Explain how the body responds to both an increase and a decrease in core temperature to return its temperature to normal levels. **[H]**

B3 3.7 Controlling blood glucose ⓚ

Learning objectives

- How is your blood glucose level controlled?
- What is type 1 diabetes and how is it treated?

AQA Examiner's tip

Make sure you understand the difference between:

- glucose – a sugar found in the blood
- glycogen – a storage carbohydrate found in the liver and muscles
- glucagon – a hormone. **[H]**

Take care with the different spellings – errors often lead to marks being lost in exams.

⚭ **links**

For information on glycogen, look back to B2 4.2 The effect of exercise on the body.

It is very important that your cells have a constant supply of the glucose they need for respiration. You have a system in your body that controls your blood sugar levels to within very narrow limits.

a Why are the levels of glucose in your blood so important?

Insulin and the control of blood glucose levels

When you digest a meal, large amounts of glucose pass into your blood. Without a control mechanism your blood glucose levels would vary significantly. They would range from very high after a meal to very low several hours later – so low that cells would not have enough glucose to respire.

This situation is prevented by your pancreas. The pancreas is a small pink organ found under your stomach. It constantly monitors and controls your blood glucose concentration using two hormones. The best known of these is **insulin**.

When your blood glucose concentration rises after you have eaten a meal, insulin is released. Insulin allows glucose to move from the blood into your cells where it is used. Soluble glucose is also converted to an insoluble carbohydrate called glycogen. Insulin controls the storage of glycogen in your liver. This glycogen can be converted back into glucose when it is needed. Your blood glucose stays stable within a narrow range of concentrations.

b Name one hormone involved in the control of your blood sugar levels.

What causes diabetes?

If your pancreas does not make enough (or any) insulin, your blood sugar concentration is not controlled. You have **type 1 diabetes**.

Without insulin your blood glucose levels get very high after you eat. Eventually your kidneys excrete glucose in your urine. You produce lots of urine and feel thirsty all the time. Without insulin, glucose cannot get into the cells of your body, so you lack energy and feel tired. You break down fat and protein to use as fuel instead, so you lose weight. Type 1 diabetes usually starts in young children and teenagers.

Before there was any treatment for diabetes, people would waste away. Eventually they would fall into a coma and die. Fortunately there are now some very effective ways of treating diabetes.

c Why do people with untreated diabetes feel very tired and lack energy?

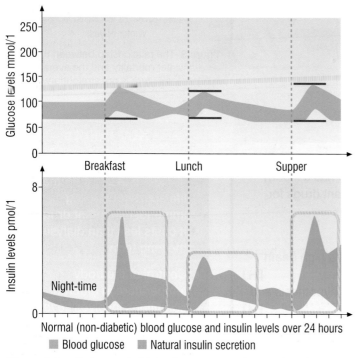

Normal (non-diabetic) blood glucose and insulin levels over 24 hours

■ Blood glucose   ■ Natural insulin secretion

Figure 1 Insulin is secreted from the pancreas after meals to keep your blood glucose stable within narrow limits

Treating diabetes

If you have type 1 diabetes you need replacement insulin before meals. Insulin is a protein, which would be digested in your stomach. So it is usually given as an injection to get it into your blood.

This injected insulin allows glucose to be taken into your body cells and converted into glycogen in the liver. This stops the concentration of glucose in your blood from getting too high. Then, as the blood glucose levels fall, the glycogen is converted back to glucose. As a result your blood glucose levels are kept as stable as possible.

If you have type 1 diabetes you also need to be careful about the levels of carbohydrate you eat. You need to have regular meals. Like everyone else, you need to exercise to keep your heart and blood vessels healthy. This needs careful planning to keep your blood sugar levels steady and your cells supplied with glucose.

Insulin injections treat diabetes successfully but they do not cure it. Until a cure is developed, someone with type 1 diabetes has to inject insulin every day of their life.

Figure 2 The treatment of type 1 diabetes involves regular blood sugar tests and insulin injections

Glucagon and control of blood glucose levels

Higher

The control of blood sugar doesn't just involve insulin. When your blood glucose concentration falls below the ideal range, the pancreas secretes **glucagon**. Glucagon makes your liver break down glycogen, converting it back into glucose. In this way the stored sugar is released back into the blood.

By using two hormones and the glycogen store in your liver, your pancreas keeps your blood glucose concentration fairly constant.

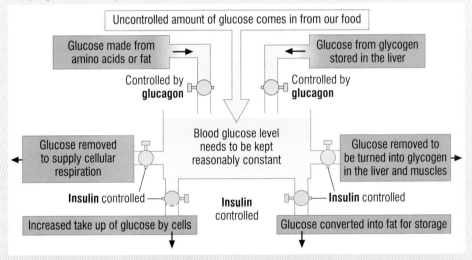

Figure 3 This model of your blood glucose control system shows the blood glucose as a tank. It has both controlled and uncontrolled inlets and outlets. In every case the control is given by the hormones insulin and glucagon.

AQA Examiner's tip

The pancreas produces two hormones:
- Insulin reduces blood glucose concentration.
- Glucagon increases blood glucose concentration. [H]

Key points

- Your blood glucose concentration is monitored and controlled by your pancreas.

- The pancreas produces the hormone insulin, which allows glucose to move from the blood into the cells.

- In type 1 diabetes, the blood glucose may rise to fatally high levels because the pancreas does not secrete enough insulin. It can be treated by injections of insulin before meals.

- Glucagon allows glycogen to be converted back into glucose and released into the blood. [H]

Summary questions

1 Define the following words: hormone, insulin, diabetes, glycogen.

2 a Explain how your pancreas keeps the blood glucose levels of your body constant.
  b Why is it so important to control the level of glucose in your blood?

3 What is type 1 diabetes and how can it be treated?

B3 3.8 Treating diabetes

Learning objectives

- How has the treatment of diabetes developed over the years?
- How is type 2 diabetes treated?

The treatment of diabetes has changed a great deal over the years.

Using insulin from other organisms

In the early 1920s Frederick Banting and Charles Best made some dogs diabetic by removing their pancreases. Then they gave them extracts of pancreas taken from other dogs. We now know these extracts contained insulin. Banting and Best realised that extracts of animal pancreas could keep people with diabetes alive. Many dogs died in the search for a successful treatment. However, the lives of millions of people have been saved over the years.

For years, insulin from pigs and cows was used to treat affected people although there were problems. Animal insulin is not identical to human insulin and the supply depended on how many animals were killed for meat. So sometimes there was not enough insulin to go round.

In recent years genetic engineering has been used to develop bacteria that can produce pure human insulin. This is genetically identical to natural human insulin and the supply is constant. This is now used by most people with type 1 diabetes. However, some people do not think this type of interference with genetic material is ethical.

Figure 1 Treatments like this human insulin allow a person to manage type 1 diabetes and live with it but they do not cure the condition

Curing type 1 diabetes

Scientists and doctors want to find a treatment that means people with diabetes never have to take insulin again. However, so far none of them is widely available.

- Doctors can transplant a pancreas successfully. However, the operations are quite difficult and rather risky. These transplants are still only carried out on a few hundred people each year in the UK. There are 250 000 people in the UK with type 1 diabetes and there are simply not enough donors available. What's more, the patient exchanges one sort of medicine (insulin) for another (immunosuppressants).
- Transplanting the pancreatic cells that make insulin from both dead and living donors has been tried, with very limited success so far.

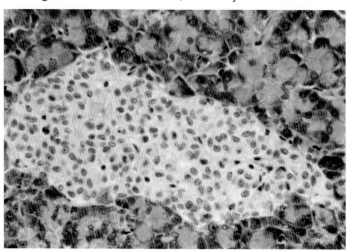

Figure 2 Part of the pancreas. The tissue stained red makes digestive enzymes while the central yellow area contains the cells that make insulin.

In 2005, scientists produced insulin-secreting cells from **embryonic stem cells** and used them to cure diabetes in mice. In 2008, UK scientists discovered a completely new technique. Using genetic engineering they turned mouse pancreas cells, which normally make enzymes, into insulin-producing cells. Other groups are using adult stem cells from diabetic patients.

Scientists hope that eventually they will be able to genetically engineer human pancreatic cells so they work properly. Then they will be able to return them to the patient with no rejection issues. It still seems likely that the easiest cure will be to use stem cells from human embryos that have been specially created for the process. But, for some people, this is not ethically acceptable.

Much more research is needed. However, scientists hope that before too long type 1 diabetes will be an illness we can cure rather than simply treat and manage.

Treating type 2 diabetes

Type 2 diabetes is another, more common type of diabetes that is often a result of obesity, lack of exercise or both. In this type of diabetes the pancreas still makes insulin, although it may make less. Most importantly, your cells stop responding to insulin properly.

If you develop type 2 diabetes you can often deal with it without needing to inject insulin. Many people can restore their normal blood glucose balance by taking three simple steps:

● eating a balanced diet with carefully controlled amounts of carbohydrates

● losing weight

● doing regular exercise.

If this doesn't work there are drugs that:

● help insulin work better on the body cells

● help your pancreas make more insulin

● reduce the amount of glucose you absorb from your gut.

Only if none of these treatment options work will you end up having insulin injections. This sort of diabetes usually affects older people. However, it is becoming more and more common in young people.

⊂⊃ **links**

For information on embryonic stem cells, look back to B2 5.3 Stem cells.

Figure 3 Losing weight and taking exercise, like these young people, seem simple ways to overcome type 2 diabetes. However, some people object to being given this advice and ignore it until they need medication to control the diabetes.

⊂⊃ **links**

For information on type 2 diabetes, look back to B1 1.2 Weight problems.

Activity

Much of the research into treatments for diabetes, both past and present, have involved ethical issues. Evaluate the main ethical issues associated with each of the treatment methods described in this spread.

Summary questions

1 Copy and complete using the words below:

insulin   obesity   cured   older people   exercise   diabetes

Type 1 .... is treated by injecting .... regularly and cannot be .... Type 2 diabetes usually starts in .... It is often linked to .... and lack of ....

2 **a** Compare modern insulin treatment with the original insulin used to treat diabetics and evaluate the two treatments.

   b Transplanting a pancreas to replace natural insulin production seems to be the ideal treatment for type 1 diabetes. Compare this treatment with insulin injections and explain why it is not more widely used.

Key points

● A variety of different methods are being used or developed to treat diabetes using genetic engineering and stem cell techniques.

● Type 2 diabetes is treated by careful attention to diet and taking more exercise alone. If this doesn't work, drugs may be needed.

Summary questions 🄚

1 a Draw and annotate a diagram explaining the basic principles of homeostasis.

b Write a paragraph explaining why control of the conditions inside your body is so important.

2 A patient with kidney failure has dialysis three times a week. Every month the blood is checked to ensure that the machine is working properly. The blood is tested for its urea content (URR test), which should be above 64%. Also the amount of blood being filtered compared with the amount of fluid in the body (Kt/V test) should be more than 1.1.

Look at this chart and answer the questions below.

Test	Target	Jan	Feb	Mar	April	May	June	July	Aug
Kt/V	≥1.2	1.1	1.15	1.2	1.23	1.24	1.2	1.2	1.2
URR	≥65	60	62	64	65	66	65	65	65

a What was the range for the Kt/V test?

b What was the pattern for the Kt/V test?

c How do the Kt/V test results compare to those for the URR test?

d Can you say that there is a causal link between the two sets of test results?

e For how many months were both tests satisfactory?

f Urologists say that the two tests really measure the same thing. Why then is it a good idea to do both tests?

g What are the economic issues related to kidney dialysis?

h What are the social issues related to kidney dialysis?

3

- ▓ Mean daily mortality 2003
- ▓ Mean daily mortality 1999–2002
- — Mean daily summer temperature 2003
- — Mean daily summer temperature 1999–2002

In August 2003 a heat wave hit Europe. The graph shows the effect it had on the number of deaths in Paris.

a What effect did the Paris heat wave have on deaths in the city?

b From the data, what temperature begins to have an effect on the death rate?

c Explain why more people die when conditions are very hot.

4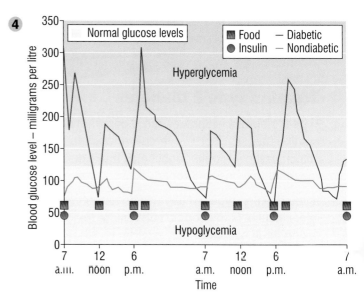

The graph shows the blood glucose levels of a non-diabetic person and someone with type 1 diabetes managed with regular insulin injections. They both eat at the same times. Use this graph to help you answer the questions below:

a What happens to the blood glucose levels in both individuals after eating?

b What is the range of blood glucose concentration of the normal subject?

c What is the range of blood glucose concentration of the person with diabetes?

d The graph shows the effect of regular insulin injections on the blood glucose level of someone with diabetes. Why are the insulin injections so important to their health and wellbeing? What does this data suggest are the limitations of insulin injections?

e People with diabetes have to monitor the amount of carbohydrate in their diet. Explain why.

AQA Examination-style questions

1 a The human body must keep internal conditions constant.

List A shows some conditions.

List B shows some monitoring or control centres.

Match each condition with its correct monitoring or control centre. (3)

List A	List B
blood glucose level	kidneys
body temperature	pancreas
blood water content	thermoregulatory centre
	skin

b Choose the correct words from the list below to complete the sentence.

amino   fatty   kidney   lactic   liver   lung   pancreas

Urea is produced in the .... by the breakdown of .... acids. (2)

2 a Which **two** of the following substances are found in the urine of a healthy person?

glucose   mineral ions   proteins   water (2)

b A person with kidney disease can be treated by dialysis.
The diagram shows how dialysis works.
The circles represent molecules of different substances.

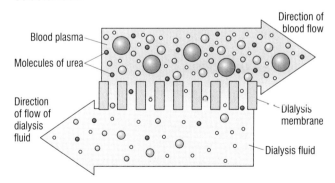

Choose the correct word or phrase to complete each sentence.

i During dialysis, urea moves out of the .... (1)

blood cells   blood plasma   dialysis fluid

ii During dialysis, urea moves into the .... (1)

blood cells   blood plasma   dialysis fluid

iii Urea moves by the process of .... (1)

diffusion   digestion   transpiration

iv To allow the movement of urea, the dialysis membrane is .... (1)

impermeable   partially permeable   thick

v The urea can pass through the membrane because the urea molecules are .... (1)

large   round   small

c For most patients, a kidney transplant is better than continued dialysis treatment.

Choose the correct phrase to complete the sentence.

One major problem with a kidney transplant is that .... (1)

drug treatment is needed to suppress the immune system

hospital visits are needed three times a week

yearly costs are higher than for dialysis

AQA, 2002

3 When a person has a kidney transplant, the donor kidney must be matched to their tissue type.

Choose the correct words from the list below to complete the sentences.

antibodies   antiseptics   aspirin   immunosuppressants protein   urea

On the surface of the kidney cells are antigens.

Antigens are made of ....

The antigens may be attacked by the person's ....

To prevent the attack on the donor kidney the person is given drugs called .... (3)

4 When a person gets too cold, the organs cannot function properly. Below 35 °C the person could die. Alcohol causes blood vessels to stay dilated.

A person found collapsed on a cold mountain should not be given an alcoholic drink. Explain why. **[H]** (4)

5 *In this question you will be assessed on using good English, organising information clearly and using specialist terms where appropriate.*

A person with type 1 diabetes cannot produce enough of the hormone insulin.

Some diabetics use an insulin pump that is attached to the body. They can increase or decrease the amount of insulin which is injected, depending on their lifestyle.

Describe how insulin controls blood glucose levels and explain why a diabetic may need to change their insulin levels at certain times. (6)

B3 4.1

The effects of the population explosion

Learning objective

- What effect is the growth in human population having on the Earth and its resources?

Figure 1 The Earth – as the human population grows, our impact on the planet gets bigger every day

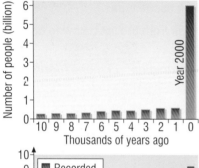

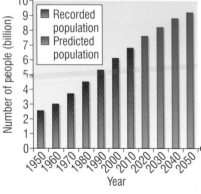

Figure 2 This record of human population growth shows the massive increase during the past 60 years – and predicts more to come

??? Did you know ...?

Current UN predictions suggest that the world population will soar to 244 billion by 2150 and 134 trillion by 2300!

Humans have been on Earth for less than a million years. Yet our activity has changed the balance of nature on the planet enormously. Several of the changes we have made seem to be driving many other species to extinction. Some people worry that we may even be threatening our own survival.

Human population growth

For many thousands of years people lived on the Earth in quite small numbers. There were only a few hundred million of us. We were scattered all over the world, and the effects of our activity were usually small and local. Any changes could easily be absorbed by the environment where we lived.

However, in the past 200 years or so the human population has grown very quickly. By 2010 the human population was almost 7 billion people, and it is still growing.

If the population of any other species of animal or plant suddenly increased like this, nature would tend to restore the balance. Predators, lack of food, build-up of waste products or diseases would reduce the population again. But we have discovered how to grow more food than we could ever gather from the wild. We can cure or prevent many killer diseases. We have no natural predators. This helps to explain why the human population has grown so fast.

In many parts of the world our standard of living has also improved enormously. In the UK, we use vast amounts of electricity and fuel to provide energy for our homes and places of work. We use fossil fuels like oil to produce this electricity. We also use oil and oil-based fuels to move about in cars, planes, trains and boats at high speed and to make materials like plastics. We have more than enough to eat and if we are ill we can often be made better.

a Approximately how many people were living on the Earth in 2010?

The effect on land and resources

The increase in the numbers of people has had a big effect on our environment. All these billions of people need land to live on. More and more land is used for the building of houses, shops, industrial sites and roads. Some of these building projects destroy the habitats of other living organisms.

We use billions of acres of land around the world for farming. Wherever people farm, the natural animal and plant populations are destroyed.

In quarrying, we dig up great areas of land for the resources it holds, such as rocks and metal ores. This also reduces the land available for other organisms.

b How do people reduce the amount of land available for other animals and plants?

The huge human population drains the resources of the Earth. Raw materials are rapidly being used up. This includes **non-renewable** energy resources such as oil and natural gas. Also, once metal ores are processed they cannot be replaced.

Managing waste

The growing human population also means vastly increased amounts of waste. This includes human bodily waste and the rubbish from packaging, uneaten food and disposable goods. The dumping of this waste is another way in which we reduce the amount of land available for any other life apart from scavengers.

There has also been an increase in manufacturing and industry to produce the goods we want. This in turn has led to **industrial waste**.

The waste we produce presents us with some very difficult problems. If it is not handled properly it can cause serious pollution. Our water may be polluted by **sewage**, by fertilisers from farms and by toxic chemicals from industry. The air we breathe may be polluted with smoke and poisonous gases such as sulfur dioxide.

The land itself can be polluted with toxic chemicals from farming such as pesticides and herbicides. It can also be contaminated with industrial waste, such as heavy metals. These chemicals in turn can be washed from the land into waterways.

Figure 3 In the UK alone hundreds of thousands of new houses and miles of new road systems are continuously being built. Every time we clear land like this, the homes of countless animals and plants are destroyed.

If our ever-growing population continues to affect the **ecology** of the Earth, everyone will pay the price.

c What substances commonly pollute:
i water
ii air
iii land?

Key points

- The human population is growing rapidly and the standard of living is increasing.

- More waste is being produced. If it is not handled properly it can pollute the water, the air and the land.

- The activities of humans reduce the amount of land available for other animals and plants.

- Raw materials, including non-renewable resources, are being used up rapidly.

Summary questions

1 Copy and complete these sentences using the words below:

diseases farming food increase population predators treat 200

The human .... has increased dramatically in the past .... years. Better .... methods mean we have more .... We can .... and prevent many .... We have no natural .... All this has allowed the numbers of humans to ....

2 a List examples of how the standard of living has increased over the past 100 years?
b Give three examples of resources that humans are using up.

3 Write a paragraph clearly explaining how the ever-increasing human population causes pollution in a number of different ways.

B3 4.2 Land and water pollution

Learning objectives

- How do people pollute the land?
- How do people pollute the water?

As the human population grows, more waste is produced. If it is not handled carefully, it may pollute the land, the water or the air.

Polluting the land

People pollute the land in many different ways. The more people there are, the more bodily waste and waste water from our homes (sewage) is produced. If the human waste is not treated properly, the soil becomes polluted with unpleasant chemicals and gut parasites. In the developed world people produce huge amounts of household waste and hazardous (dangerous) industrial waste. The household waste goes into landfill sites, which take up a lot of room and destroy natural habitats. Toxic chemicals also spread from the waste into the soil.

Toxic chemicals are also a problem in industrial waste. They can poison the soil for miles around. For example, after the Chernobyl nuclear accident in 1986 the soil was contaminated thousands of miles away from the original accident. Almost 30 years on, sheep from some farms in North Wales still cannot be sold for food because the radioactivity levels are too high.

a What is human bodily waste mixed with waste water known as?

Land can also be polluted as a side effect of farming. Weeds compete with crop plants for light, water and mineral ions. Animal and fungal pests attack crops and eat them. Farmers increasingly use chemicals to protect their crops. Weedkillers (or herbicides) kill weeds but leave the crop unharmed. Pesticides kill the insects that might otherwise attack and destroy the crop. The problem is that these chemicals are poisons. When they are sprayed onto crops they also get into the soil. From there they can be washed out into streams and rivers (see next page). They can also become part of food chains. The toxins get into organisms that feed on the plants or live in the soil. This can lead to dangerous levels of poisons building up in the top predators (see Figure 3).

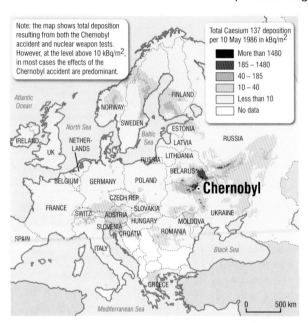

Note: the map shows total deposition resulting from both the Chernobyl accident and nuclear weapon tests. However, at the level above 10 kBq/m², in most cases the effects of the Chernobyl accident are predominant.

Total Caesium 137 deposition per 10 May 1986 in kBq/m²
- More than 1480
- 185 – 1480
- 40 – 185
- 10 – 40
- Less than 10
- No data

Figure 1 The accident at Chernobyl nuclear power plant polluted the land a long way away

Figure 2 Welsh sheep

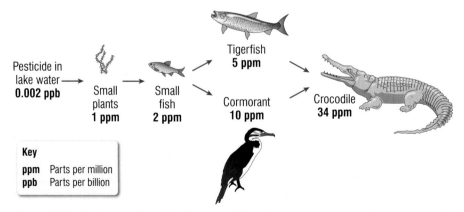

Pesticide in lake water 0.002 ppb → Small plants 1 ppm → Small fish 2 ppm → Tigerfish 5 ppm, Cormorant 10 ppm → Crocodile 34 ppm

Key
ppm Parts per million
ppb Parts per billion

Figure 3 The feeding relationships between different organisms can lead to dangerous levels of toxins building up in the top predators

Polluting the water

A growing human population means a growing need for food. Farmers add fertilisers to the soil to make sure it stays **fertile** year after year. The minerals in these fertilisers, particularly the nitrates, are easily washed from the soil into local streams, ponds and rivers. Untreated sewage that is washed into waterways or pumped out into the sea also causes high levels of nitrates in the water.

The nitrates and other minerals fertilise the water plants, which grow rapidly. Some plants die naturally. Others die because there is so much competition for light. There is a big increase in microorganisms feeding on the dead plants. These microorganisms use up a lot of oxygen. This increase in decomposers leads to a fall in oxygen levels dissolved in the water. This means there isn't enough oxygen to support some of the fish and other animals living in it. They die – and are decomposed by yet more microorganisms. This uses up even more oxygen.

Eventually, the oxygen levels in the water fall so low that all aquatic animals die, and the pond or stream becomes 'dead'. This is called **eutrophication**.

b Name a mineral in fertilisers and sewage that causes eutrophication.

Toxic chemicals such as pesticides and herbicides or poisonous chemicals from landfill sites can also be washed into waterways. These chemicals can have the same effect on aquatic food webs as they do to life on land. The largest carnivorous fish die or fail to breed because of the build up of toxic chemicals in their bodies.

In many countries, including the UK, there are now strict controls on the use of chemicals on farms. The same applies to the treatment of sewage and to landfill sites, to help avoid these problems arising.

Pollution levels in water can be measured in many different ways. Oxygen and pH levels are measured using instruments. The water can be analysed to show the levels of polluting chemicals such as pesticides or industrial waste. Bioindicators – species which can only be found in very clean or very polluted water – are also used to monitor pollution levels in our waterways.

AQA Examiner's tip

Don't get herbicides and pesticides mixed up! Remember: herbicides are used to kill weed plants while pesticides kill insect pests.

Figure 4 This stream may look green and healthy but all the animal life it once supported is dead as a result of eutrophication

Summary questions

1 Copy and complete these sentences using the words below:

water chemicals air waste pollute land population

As the human .... grows, more .... is produced. Unless this is properly handled it may .... the ...., the water or the .... Toxic .... are often washed from the land into the ....

2 Farming can cause pollution of both the land and the water. Explain how this pollution comes about, and how they are linked.

Key points

- Toxic chemicals such as pesticides and herbicides can pollute the land.

- If sewage is not properly handled and treated it can pollute the water.

- Fertilisers and toxic chemicals can be washed from the land into the water and pollute it.

B3 4.3 Air pollution

When the air you breathe is polluted, no one escapes the effects. A major source of air pollution is burning fossil fuels. As the human population grows and living standards increase we are using more oil, coal and natural gas. We also burn huge amounts of petrol, diesel and aviation (aeroplane) fuel made from oil. Fossil fuels are a non-renewable resource – eventually they will all be used up.

a Name three fossil fuels.

The formation of acid rain

When fossil fuels are burned, carbon dioxide is released into the atmosphere as a waste product. In addition, fossil fuels often contain sulfur impurities. These react with oxygen when they burn to form sulfur dioxide gas. At high temperatures, for example in car engines, nitrogen oxides are also released into the atmosphere.

Sulfur dioxide and nitrogen oxides can cause serious breathing problems for people if the concentrations get too high.

The sulfur dioxide and nitrogen oxides also dissolve in rainwater and react with oxygen in the air to form dilute sulfuric acid and nitric acid. This produces **acid rain**, which has been measured with a pH of 2.0 – more acidic than vinegar!

b What are the main gases involved in the formation of acid rain?

Figure 1 In some parts of Europe and America, huge areas of woodland are dying as a result of acid rain

The effects of acid rain

Acid rain directly damages the environment. If it falls onto trees it may kill the leaves and, as it soaks into the soil, it can destroy the roots as well. Whole ecosystems can be destroyed.

Acid rain also has an indirect effect on our environment. As acid rain falls into lakes, rivers and streams the water in them becomes slightly acidic. If the concentration of acid gets too high, plants and animals can no longer survive. Many lakes and streams have become 'dead' – no longer able to support life.

c How does acid rain kill trees?

Acid rain is difficult to control. It is formed by pollution from factories. It also comes from the cars and other vehicles we use every day. The worst effects of acid rain are often not felt by the country that produced the pollution (see Figure 2). The sulfur dioxide and nitrogen oxides are carried high in the air by the winds. As a result, it is often relatively 'clean' countries that get the acid rain from their dirtier neighbours. Their own clean air goes on to benefit someone else.

The UK and other countries have worked hard to stop their vehicles, factories and power stations producing the polluting gases. They have introduced measures to reduce the levels of sulfur dioxide and nitrogen oxides in the air. Low-sulfur petrol and diesel are now used in vehicles. More and more cars are fitted with catalytic converters. Once hot, these remove the acidic nitrogen oxides before they are released into the air. There are strict rules about the levels of sulfur dioxide and nitrogen oxides in the exhaust fumes of new cars.

In the UK we have introduced cleaner, low-sulfur fuels such as gas in power stations and started generating more electricity from nuclear power. We have also put systems in power station chimneys to clean the flue gases before they are released into the atmosphere.

As a result, the levels of sulfur dioxide in the air, and of acid rain, have fallen steadily over the past 40 years. Many European countries have done the same (see Figure 3). Unfortunately there are still many countries around the world that do not have controls in place.

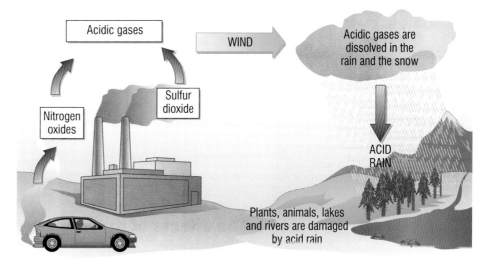

Figure 2 Air pollution in one place can cause acid rain – and serious pollution problems – somewhere else entirely, even in another country

Global dimming

One form of air pollution involves an increase in the number of tiny solid particles in the air. The sulfur products from the burning of fossil fuels are part of this problem. So is smoke from any type of burning. These particles reflect sunlight so less light hits the surface of the Earth. This causes a dimming effect. Global dimming could lead to a cooling of the temperatures at the surface of the Earth.

In Europe, where sulfur emissions and smoke are being controlled, dimming is being reversed. In many developing countries, dimming continues to get worse as air pollution grows.

Figure 3 Bar chart to show the reductions in sulfur emissions made by European countries in recent years

Summary questions

1 Copy and complete using the words below:

acid rain carbon dioxide fossil nitric nitrogen oxides sulfur sulfuric

When .... fuels are burned, the pollutant gases ...., ... dioxide and .... are released into the atmosphere. The sulfur dioxide and nitrogen oxides dissolve in rainwater and react with oxygen to form dilute .... acid and .... acid. This is known as ....

2 a Explain how pollution from cars and factories burning fossil fuels pollute:
  i the air
  ii the water
  iii the land.
 b In order to get rid of acid rain it is important that all countries in an area control their production of sulfur dioxide and nitrogen oxides. Explain why this is.

3 a What is global dimming?
 b From Figure 3, what was the percentage reduction in sulfur emissions in Europe between 1980 and 2002?
 c Dimming has been reversed over Europe between 1980 and the present day. Suggest an explanation for this.

Key points

- When we burn fossil fuels, carbon dioxide is released into the atmosphere.

- Sulfur dioxide and nitrogen oxides can be released when fossil fuels are burnt. These gases dissolve in rainwater and make it more acidic.

- Acid rain may damage trees directly. It can make lakes and rivers too acidic so plants and animals cannot live in them.

- Air pollution can cause global dimming as tiny solid particles in the air reflect away the sunlight.

B3 4.4 Deforestation and peat destruction

Learning objectives

- What is deforestation?
- Why does loss of biodiversity matter?
- What is the link between cows and methane?
- What is the effect of destroying peat bogs?

As the world population grows we need more land, more food and more fuel. One solution to this has been to cut down huge areas of forests. The loss of our forests may have many long-term effects on the environment and ecology of the Earth.

The effects of deforestation

All around the world, large-scale **deforestation** is taking place for timber and to clear the land for farming. When the land is to be used for farming, the tress are often felled and burned in what is known as 'slash-and-burn' clearance. The wood isn't used, it is just burned. The land produced is only fertile for a short time, after which more forest is destroyed. No trees are planted to replace those cut down.

Figure 1 Tropical rainforests are being destroyed by slash-and-burn clearance to provide cheap food for countries like ours

Deforestation increases the amount of carbon dioxide released into the atmosphere. Burning the trees leads to an increase in carbon dioxide levels from combustion. The dead vegetation left behind decays. It is attacked by decomposing microorganisms, which release more carbon dioxide.

Normally, trees and other plants use carbon dioxide in photosynthesis. They take it from the air and it gets locked up for years in plant material like wood. So when we destroy trees we lose a vital carbon dioxide 'sink'. Dead trees don't take carbon dioxide out of the atmosphere. In fact they add to the carbon dioxide levels as they are burned or decay.

a What is deforestation?

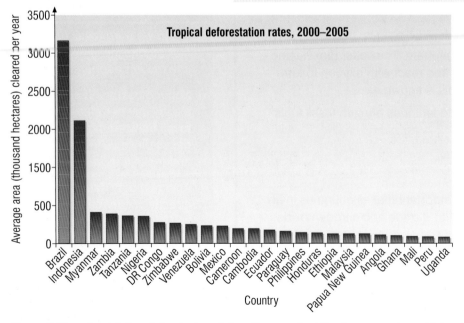

Figure 2 The rate of deforestation is devastating. For an animal like the orang-utan, which eats around 300 different plant species, losing the forest habitat is driving the species to extinction

Loss of biodiversity

Tropical rainforests contain more diversity of living organisms than any other land environment. When we lose these forests, we also lose **biodiversity** as many species of animals and plants die out. Many of these species have not yet been identified or studied. We could be destroying sources of new medicines or food for the future.

Deforestation is taking place at a tremendous rate. In Brazil alone an area about a quarter the size of England is lost each year. When the forests are cleared, they are often replaced by a monoculture (single species) such as oil palms. This process also greatly reduces biodiversity.

Cows, rice and methane

It isn't just carbon dioxide levels that are increasing in the atmosphere as a result of deforestation.

Much of the deforested land is used to produce food for the ever-increasing world population. One of these foods is rice. As rice grows in swampy conditions, known as paddy fields, **methane** is released. Methane is another gas that affects global warming.

Another food – and another source of methane – is from cattle. Cows produce methane during their digestive processes and release it at regular intervals. In recent years the number of cattle raised to produce cheap meat for fast food, such as burgers, has grown enormously. So the levels of methane are rising. Many of these cattle are raised on farms created by deforestation.

b Where does the methane that is building up in the atmosphere come from?

Peat bog destruction

Peat bogs are another resource that is being widely destroyed. Peat bogs form over thousands of years, usually in marshy areas. They are made of plant material that cannot decay completely because the conditions are very acidic and lack oxygen. Peat acts as a massive carbon store.

Peat can be burned as a fuel and is also widely used by gardeners because it helps to improve the properties of the soil. When peat is burned or used in gardens, carbon dioxide is released into the atmosphere and the carbon store is lost. Peat is formed very slowly so it is being destroyed faster than it is made. In the UK, the government is trying to persuade gardeners to use alternative 'peat-free' composts to reduce carbon dioxide emissions. Compost can be made from bark, from garden waste, from coconut husks and other sources – the problem is persuading gardeners to use them.

Summary questions

1 Define the following words:

   deforestation   slash-and-burn   biodiversity   peat

2 Give three reasons why deforestation increases the amount of carbon dioxide in the atmosphere.

3 **a** Why are the numbers of:
   i rice fields and cattle in the world increasing
   ii peat bogs in the world decreasing?
   b Why is this cause for concern?

AQA *Examiner's tip*

Remember that trees, plants in peat bogs and algae in the sea all use carbon dioxide for photosynthesis. Carbon compounds are then 'locked up' in these plants.

Figure 3 Peat-free compost effectively replaces peat-based compost – protecting peat bogs and reducing carbon dioxide emissions

Key points

- Deforestation is the destruction or removal of areas of forest or woodland.

- Large-scale deforestation has led to an increase in the amount of carbon dioxide released into the atmosphere (from burning and the actions of microorganisms). It has also reduced the rate at which carbon dioxide is removed from the air by plants.

- More rice fields and cattle have led to increased levels of methane in the atmosphere because rice and cattle both produce methane as they grow.

- The destruction of peat bogs releases carbon dioxide into the atmosphere.

B3 4.5

Global warming ⓚ

How humans can affect the environment

Learning objectives

- What is global warming?
- How will global warming affect life on Earth?

⚭ **links**

For information on photosynthesis, look back to B2 2.1 Photosynthesis.

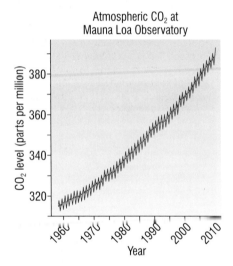

Figure 1 The atmospheric carbon dioxide readings for this graph are taken monthly on a mountain-top in Hawaii. There is a clear upward trend, which shows no sign of slowing down.

Many scientists are very worried that the climate of the Earth is getting warmer. This is often called **global warming**.

Changing conditions

For millions of years there has been a natural balance in the levels of carbon dioxide in the atmosphere. The carbon dioxide released by living things into the atmosphere from respiration has been matched by the amount removed. Carbon dioxide is removed by plants for photosynthesis and huge amounts are dissolved in the oceans, lakes and rivers. We say that the carbon dioxide is **sequestered** in plants and water, or that plants and water act as carbon dioxide sinks.

As a result, carbon dioxide levels in the air stayed about the same for a long period. However now, as a result of human activities, the levels of carbon dioxide are increasing. Unfortunately, the numbers of plants available to absorb it are decreasing. The speed of these changes means that the natural sinks cannot cope. So the levels of carbon dioxide in the atmosphere are building up. At the same time, the levels of methane are increasing too.

a Give two reasons for the observed increase in atmospheric carbon dioxide levels.

The greenhouse effect

Energy from the Sun reaches the Earth and much of it is radiated back out into space. However, gases such as carbon dioxide and methane absorb some of this energy so it can't escape. As a result, the Earth and its surrounding atmosphere are kept warm and ideal for life. Because carbon dioxide and methane act like a greenhouse around the Earth they are known as **greenhouse gases**. The way they keep the surface of the Earth warm is known as the **greenhouse effect** and it is vital for life on Earth.

b Name two greenhouse gases.

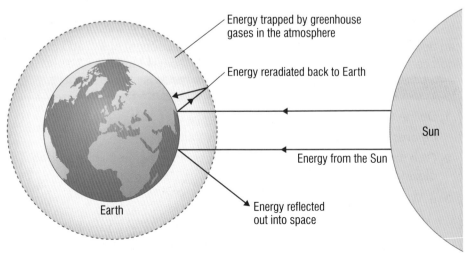

Figure 2 The greenhouse effect – vital for life on Earth

Global warming

However, as the levels of carbon dioxide and methane go up, the greenhouse effect is increasing. There are more greenhouse gases in the atmosphere to trap the energy of the Sun and the temperature at the Earth's surface is going up. The change is very small – only about 0.55 °C from the 1970s to the present day. This is not much – but an increase of only a few degrees Celsius may cause:

- **big changes in the Earth's climate:** As the climate changes due to global warming, many scientists think that we will see an increase in severe and unpredictable weather conditions. Some people think the very high winds and extensive flooding seen around the world in the 21st century are early examples of the effects of global warming.

- **a rise in sea levels:** If the Earth warms up, the ice caps at the north and south poles and many glaciers will melt. This will cause sea levels to rise. There is evidence that this is already happening. It will mean more flooding for low-lying shores and eventually parts of countries, or even whole countries, may disappear beneath the seas.

- **reduced biodiversity:** As the climate changes, many organisms will be unable to survive and will become extinct, e.g. the loss of polar bears as the ice melts.

- **changes in migration patterns:** As climates become colder or hotter, and the seasons change, the migration patterns of birds, insects and mammals may change.

- **changes in distribution:** Some animals may extend their range as climate change makes conditions more favourable. Others may find their range shrinks. Some will disappear completely from an area or a country.

What's more, as sea temperatures rise less carbon dioxide can be held in the water, which makes the problem worse. Global warming is a big problem for us all.

Figure 3 Puffin populations in Northern Scotland failed to rear their chicks because a rise in sea temperatures reduced the numbers of small fish that puffins feed on. They may need to move to new breeding sites if they are to survive.

Summary questions

1 Copy and complete these sentences using the words below:

   climate   carbon dioxide   temperature   atmosphere   biodiversity   methane   global warming

   .... and .... levels in the .... are increasing and contributing to .... An increase in .... of only a few degrees could cause .... change and affect ....

2 a Use the data in Figure 1 to produce a bar chart showing the maximum recorded level of carbon dioxide in the atmosphere every tenth year from 1970 to the year 2010.
   b Explain the trend you can see on your chart.
   c Describe and explain the greenhouse effect. How might it affect the conditions on Earth?

3 Research one possible result of global warming and write a report, giving examples of organisms that have been or might be affected.

Key points

- Increasing levels of carbon dioxide and methane in the atmosphere give an increased greenhouse effect, leading to global warming – an increase in the temperature of the surface of the Earth.

- Global warming may cause a number of changes including climate change, a rise in sea level, loss of biodiversity and changes in migration patterns and distribution of species.

B3 4.6

Biofuels

Learning objectives

- How can yeast produce fuel for your car?
- What is the environmental impact of biofuels?

∞ links

For information on ethanol, look back to B2 1.2 Bacteria and yeast.

∞ links

For information on deforestation, look back to B3 4.4 Deforestation and peat destruction.

Figure 1 In tropical regions plants grow fast, an important factor when they are grown for fuel

Everyone needs fuel of some sort but there is only a finite amount of fossil fuels to use. Around the world, we all need other, renewable forms of fuel. The production of **biofuels** has become increasingly important in both the developing and the developed world.

Biofuels are made from natural products by fermentation using yeast or bacteria. There are two main types of biofuels – ethanol-based fuels and **biogas**.

Ethanol-based fuels

Some of the land that is deforested is used for crops that grow very fast. The crops can then be used to produce biofuels. Sugarcane grows about 4 to 5 metres in a year and maize (sweetcorn) is another fast grower. The sugar-rich products from cane and maize are fermented anaerobically with yeast. The products are ethanol and carbon dioxide. You can extract the ethanol by **distillation**, and then use it in cars as a fuel.

Car engines need special modification to be able to use pure ethanol as a fuel, but it is not a major job. Many cars can run on a mixture of petrol and ethanol without any problems at all.

> **a** Why are sugarcane and maize used as crops for the production of ethanol?

The advantages and disadvantages of ethanol as a fuel

In many ways ethanol is an ideal fuel. It is efficient and it does not produce toxic gases when you burn it. It is much less polluting than conventional fuels, which produce carbon monoxide, sulfur dioxide and nitrogen oxides. In addition, you can mix ethanol with conventional petrol to make a fuel known as gasohol, which reduces pollution levels considerably.

Using ethanol as a fuel is known as a **carbon neutral** process. This means that in theory there is no overall increase in carbon dioxide in the atmosphere when you burn ethanol. The original plants remove carbon dioxide from the air during photosynthesis. When you burn the ethanol, you simply return the same amount of carbon dioxide into the atmosphere.

The biggest difficulty with using plant-based fuels for our cars is that it takes a lot of plant material to produce the ethanol. As a result, the use of ethanol as a fuel has largely been limited to countries with enough space and a suitable climate to grow lots of plant material as fast as possible. Scientists are attempting to find ways of producing economically viable quantities of ethanol from plants that grow fast and well in Europe. They have tried pine trees and beet but have not yet been very successful. Now they are looking at fast-growing grasses.

> **b** What is meant by the term 'carbon neutral'?

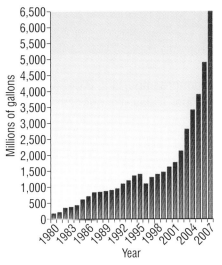

Figure 2 Increasing demand for gasohol in the US has lead to increasing production of ethanol from maize, as this data clearly shows

The latest biofuels

People around the world are worried about environmental problems such as global warming linked to burning fossil fuels. Interest in clean alternatives such as ethanol is soaring.

The main problem is finding enough ethanol. If Europeans added 5% ethanol to their fuel it would contribute to some reduction in Europe's carbon dioxide emissions. However, we would need 7.5 billion litres of ethanol a year, which would use a lot of plants.

The main methods of ethanol production use the edible parts of plants and leave large quantities of unused plant material. Many people are concerned about using plants for fuel that could feed hungry people. The aim is to make ethanol production work ethically and financially in the long term. To do this we need to find a way to use the waste, cellulose-rich biomass rather than the edible parts of plants.

The latest biofuel technologies use bacteria, enzymes and steam or chemical treatments to break down the cellulose in biomass. They use straw and woodchips as raw materials. The end-products of this breakdown are sugars. These can be respired by yeast to make more ethanol. We don't know exactly what the future will hold, but it seems likely that ethanol-based fuel will be part of it.

Figure 3 The latest biofuel plants like Longannet in Fife make ethanol from waste biomass

Summary questions

1 Make a table to summarise the advantages and disadvantages of ethanol as a fuel for cars.

2 Use the data in Figure 2 to help you answer the following questions:
   a What was the increase in ethanol production from maize in the USA between:
      i 1980 and 1990
      ii 1990 and 2000
      iii 2000 and 2007?
   b Graphs showing worldwide production of fuel ethanol follow a similar pattern. Explain what this suggests about the use of ethanol as a fuel.

Key points

● Some land has been deforested so that crops can be grown, from which biofuels based on ethanol can be produced.

● Biofuels can be made from natural products using fermentation by yeast.

B3 4.7

Biogas ⓚ

?!? **Did you know ... ?**

In the days before electricity, biogas was taken from the London sewers and used as fuel for the gas lamps that lit the streets.

Figure 1 Biogas generators have made an enormous difference to many families and communities by producing cheap and readily available fuel

Biogas is a biofuel that is becoming more and more important. Biogas is produced naturally in sewers and rubbish dumps. Today, it is becoming increasingly used as a fuel around the world.

What is biogas?

Biogas is a flammable mixture of gases. It is formed when bacteria break down plant material or the waste products of animals in anaerobic conditions. Biogas is mainly methane but the composition of the mixture varies. It depends on what is put into the generator and which bacteria are present (Table 1).

Table 1 Components of biogas

Component	Percentage in the mixture by volume
methane	50–80
carbon dioxide	15–45
water vapour	5
other gases including: hydrogen hydrogen sulfide	 0–1 0–3

a What is the main component of biogas?

Biogas generators

Around the world, millions of tonnes of faeces and urine are made by animals like cows, pigs, sheep and chickens. We produce our fair share of waste materials too! Also, in many places, plant material grows very rapidly. Both the plant material and the animal waste contain carbohydrates. They make up a potentially enormous energy resource – but how can we use it?

When bacteria decompose waste material in anaerobic conditions they produce methane. Methane is a flammable gas that can be used as a fuel for heating and cooking. We can also use it to produce electricity or as a fuel for vehicles.

The bacteria involved in biogas production work best at a temperature of around 30°C. So biogas generators tend to work best in hot countries. However, the process releases energy (the reactions are **exothermic**). This means that if you put some energy in at the beginning to start things off, and have your generator well insulated to prevent energy loss, biogas generators will work anywhere.

b What is an exothermic reaction?

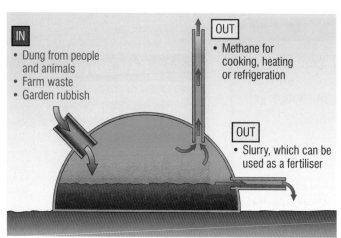

IN
- Dung from people and animals
- Farm waste
- Garden rubbish

OUT
- Methane for cooking, heating or refrigeration

OUT
- Slurry, which can be used as a fertiliser

Figure 2 Biogas generators take in body waste or plants, and biogas and useful fertilisers come out at the other end

How Science Works

Scaling up the process

At the moment most biogas generators around the world operate on a relatively small scale. They supply the energy needs of one family, a farm or at most a village.

What you put into your small generator has a big effect on what comes out. There are well over 7 million biogas units in China. These produce as much energy as 22 million tonnes of coal. Waste vegetables, animal dung and human waste are the main raw materials. These Chinese generators produce excellent fertiliser but relatively low-quality biogas.

In India, there are religious and social taboos against using human waste in biogas generators. As a result only cattle and buffalo dung is put into the generators. This produces very high quality biogas, but much less fertiliser.

The sizes and design of biogas generators will depend on local conditions. Many generators are sunk into the ground, which provides very good insulation. Others are built above ground, and are easier and cheaper to build. However, this offers less insulation so low night-time temperatures can cause problems.

Many countries are now looking at biogas generators and experimenting with using them on a larger scale. The waste material we produce from sugar factories, sewage farms and rubbish tips can be used to produce biogas. However, in the UK we have been relatively slow at starting to use biogas generators but a number of projects are now in place.

Vast herds of dairy cattle, containing several thousand cows, produce large amounts of slurry. This can be used to produce biogas which in turn can be used to generate electricity. This is already done in the US, Saudi Arabia and other countries, and may soon be set up in the UK.

Biogas could well be an important fuel of the future for all of us. It would help us to get rid of much of the waste we produce as well as providing a clean and renewable energy supply.

AQA Examiner's tip

Do not be put off by unfamiliar diagrams of biogas generators in the examination.
Remember, they all function in a similar way:

● anaerobic fermentation of waste carbohydrate, by microorganisms, to produce methane.

Figure 3 This commercial biogas plant in Texas uses the slurry from 10 000 cows as well as other agricultural waste as its raw material

Summary questions

1 Explain simply what biogas is and how it can be made.

2 Some types of biogas generators are set up with a large amount of plant material like straw and a starter mixture of bacteria, and left to produce gas. These batch digesters produce biogas very efficiently. Once gas generation begins to drop, the generator is emptied and cleaned out and the process starts again.
   a Using a generator like this, how could you be sure of a continuous supply of gas for cooking?
   b What are the advantages and disadvantages of a batch-type digester over the types shown in Figure 2, where dung and plant waste is fed in continuously?

Key points

● Biogas – mainly methane – can be produced by anaerobic fermentation of a wide range of plant products and waste materials that contain carbohydrates.

● Biogas generators can be small, to supply a single family, or large, to deal with the sewage from an entire city.

B3 4.8   Making food production efficient

Learning objectives

- Why do short food chains make food production more efficient?

- How can we manage food production to reduce energy losses?

⚭ links

For information on pyramids of biomass, look back to B1 5.1 Pyramids of biomass.

Figure 1 Reducing the number of stages in food chains could dramatically increase the efficiency of our food production. Eating less meat would mean more food for everyone.

⚭ links

For information on energy losses between trophic levels, look back to B1 5.2 Energy transfers.

Pyramids of biomass show us that the organisms at each successive stage of a food chain contain less material and therefore less energy. This has major implications for the way we produce food.

Food chains in food production

In the developed world much of our diet consists of meat or other animal products such as eggs, cheese and milk. The cows, goats, pigs and sheep that we use to produce our food eat plants. By the time it reaches us, much of the energy from the plant has been used up.

In some cases we even feed animals to animals. Ground up fish, for example, is often part of commercial pig and chicken feed. This means we have put another extra stage into the food chain. It goes from plant to fish, fish to pig, pig to people, making it even less efficient.

   a   Name three animals that we use for food.

There is a limited amount of the Earth's surface that we can use to grow food. The most energy-efficient way to use this food is to grow plants and eat them directly. If we only ate plants, then in theory there would be plenty of food for everyone on the Earth. Biomass produced by plants would be used to feed people and produce human biomass.

However, every extra stage we introduce results in less energy getting to us at the end of the chain. An example is feeding plants to animals before we eat the food ourselves. In turn this means less food to go around the human population.

   b   Why would there be more food for everyone if we all ate only plants?

Artificially managed food production

As you saw in B1 5.2, animals don't turn all of the food they eat into new animal. Some of the food can't be digested and is lost as waste. Energy is also used in moving around and maintaining a constant body temperature.

Farmers apply these ideas to food production to make it more efficient. People want meat, eggs and milk – but they want them as cheaply as possible. So farmers want to get the maximum possible increase in biomass from animals without feeding them extra food. There are two ways of doing this:

- Limiting the movement of food animals: then they don't use much energy in moving their muscles and so have more biomass available from their food for growth.

- Controlling the temperature of their surroundings: then the animals will not have to use much energy keeping warm or cooling down. Again, this leaves more biomass spare for growth.

Controlling these factors means keeping the animals inside with restricted space to move, and a constant ideal temperature. This is what happens in the massive poultry rearing sheds where the majority of the chickens that we eat are produced.

Birds kept in these sheds can be ready to eat in a matter of weeks. They always have plenty of food but there is not much room to move. There is a risk of disease spreading quickly through the animals as they are so close together. They need constant monitoring, which costs money, but they can be sold for meat very quickly. Animals reared in this way can appear more like factory products than farm animals. That's why these intensive methods are sometimes referred to as factory farming.

Intensive farming methods are used because there has been a steady increase in demand for cheap meat and animal products. This is the only way farmers can meet these demands from consumers.

On the other hand, these animals live very unnatural and restricted lives. In comparison, birds reared outside grow more slowly but have a better quality of life. It takes more space, the weather can be a problem and it is a slower process but there is no heating or lighting to pay for.

More people are now aware of how our cheap meat and eggs are produced. As a result there has been a backlash against the conditions in which intensively reared animals live. Increasingly, intensive systems are being developed with far greater awareness of animal welfare issues. Contented animals gain biomass more quickly than stressed ones, so everyone benefits.

Food miles

Another aspect of efficiency in food production is how far the food travels. Food produced around the world can travel thousands of miles to reach your plate. This uses fuel, which increases the amount of carbon dioxide in the atmosphere. People are more aware of these 'food miles' now and many people try to buy meat, fruit and vegetables which have been grown relatively locally.

Figure 2 Intensively reared chickens versus free-range chickens

??? Did you know …?

The biggest herd of dairy cows in the world is in Saudi Arabia, where 37 000 cows are all kept inside water-cooled buildings.

AQA Examiner's tip

Be clear about the ways in which the efficiency of food production can be improved to meet the needs of a growing human population. Make sure you have considered the advantages and disadvantages of each method before your examination.

Key points

- Biomass and energy are reduced at each stage of a food chain. The efficiency of food production is improved by reducing the number of stages in our food chains.

- If you stop animals moving about and keep them warm, they waste less energy, making food production more efficient.

Summary questions

1 Copy and complete using the words below:

movement food chain biomass material temperature energy efficiency

At each stage in a .... less .... and less .... are contained in the .... of the organisms. Farmers improve the .... of food production by limiting .... and controlling the ....

2 Why are animals prevented from moving much and kept indoors in intensive farming?

3 a What are the advantages and disadvantages for a farmer of rearing animals intensively?

b What are the advantages and disadvantages of less intensive rearing methods?

B3 4.9

Sustainable food production

As the human population keeps increasing, we are becoming more aware of the need for **sustainable food production**. This means producing food in ways that can continue for many years. It involves maintaining the health of the soil so plant crops grow well year after year. It also involves taking care of the fish stocks in our oceans so they do not run out.

Managing the oceans

People have fished for food throughout human history. However, in the past 60 years or so commercial fishing fleets of large factory ships have built up. These are capable of taking huge quantities of fish on a regular basis. The result of this uncontrolled overfishing is that stocks of edible fish are falling. In some areas, such as the North Sea, they are becoming dangerously low. That's because almost all of the breeding fish have been caught.

Figure 1 Many scientists think that only a complete fishing ban can save the bluefin tuna. It has been overfished almost to extinction in spite of net size control and fishing quotas.

It is important to maintain fish stocks at a level where breeding continues successfully. Otherwise certain species, such as cod and bluefin tuna, may disappear completely in some areas (Figure 1). People have been warning about the problems of overfishing for years. Numbers of some fish are so low they could disappear altogether. Finally, serious restrictions on fishing are being put in place.

Ways in which we can conserve fish populations include controlling the size of the holes in the nets. Then only the biggest fish are caught. There can also be bans on fishing in the breeding season and very strict quotas imposed on fishermen. This means they have a strictly enforced limit on the amount and type of fish they are allowed to catch.

Only with protection like this will we be able to conserve the fish stocks. Then we will be able to fish them sustainably for years to come.

a What is a fishing quota?

Mycoprotein production

Almost 30 years ago a completely new food based on fungi was developed. It is known as **mycoprotein**, which means 'protein from fungus'. It is produced using the fungus *Fusarium*. This grows and reproduces rapidly on a relatively cheap sugar syrup (made from waste starch) in large specialised containers called **fermenters**. *Fusarium* needs aerobic conditions to grow successfully. In optimum conditions it can double its mass every five hours! Because the fungi use cheap food and reproduce rapidly this is a very sustainable food source.

The fermenter is designed to react to changes, keeping the conditions as stable as possible (Figure 2). This means we can get the maximum yield. The fermenters have:

● an air supply to provide oxygen for respiration of the fungi

● a stirrer to keep the microorganisms in suspension. This maintains an even temperature and makes sure that oxygen and food are evenly spread throughout the mixture

● a water-cooled jacket, which removes the excess energy released by the respiring fungi. Any rise in temperature is used to heat the water, which is constantly removed and replaced with more cold water

● measuring instruments that constantly monitor factors such as the pH and temperature so that changes can be made if necessary.

b How quickly can *Fusarium* double its mass when conditions are right?

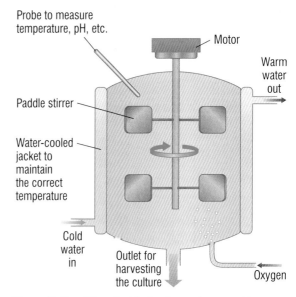

Figure 2 Conditions inside the fermenters used to culture microorganisms such as *Fusarium* are kept as stable as possible

The fungal biomass is harvested and purified. Then it is dried and processed to make mycoprotein. This is a pale yellow solid with a faint taste of mushrooms. On its own it has very little flavour.

However, mycoprotein is given a range of textures and flavours to make it similar to many familiar foods (Figure 3). It is a high-protein, low-fat meat substitute. The protein content of mycoprotein is similar to that of prime beef. So it is used by vegetarians and people who want to reduce the fat in their diet.

Figure 3 Mycoprotein can be made to look like meat, chicken, fish or burgers. It is very versatile.

When mycoprotein was first developed people thought a world food shortage was on its way. They were looking for new ways to make protein cheaply and efficiently. The food shortage never happened, but the fungus-based food continued. It is versatile, high in protein and fibre, low in fat and calories and very sustainable, so is widely used in the developed world.

AQA **Examiner's tip**

Make sure you understand the meaning of 'sustainable food production'. Humans need food now but also need to plan for feeding the next generation.

Summary questions

1 Copy and complete these sentences using the words below:

species declining conserve disappear stocks breeding

Fish .... in the oceans are .... It is important to .... fish stocks at a level where .... continues or certain .... may .... completely.

2 **a** How has the fishing industry reached crisis point?
   b How can fish stocks be protected?
   c Why do you think these measures were not put in place a long time ago?

3 Mycoprotein is an example of sustainable food production. Explain how it is similar to and how it differs from intensive farming.

Key points

● Sustainable food production means producing food in a way which can continue for many years.

● It is important to control net size and impose fishing quotas to conserve fish stocks, so breeding continues and the decline in numbers is halted.

● The fungus *Fusarium* is grown on sugar syrup in aerobic conditions to produce mycoprotein foods.

B3 4.10

Environmental issues

Learning objectives

- How do we affect the global environment?

- What sort of data have we got about environmental issues?

- How strong is the evidence for environmental change?

Figure 1 When the Aswan dam was built in Egypt, 60 000 people lost their homes as Lake Nasser was formed

Activity 1

Find out about the environmental impact of a single dam and reservoir. Then make a list of all the benefits and problems caused by that single project and decide if you think the dam was a good idea.

⃝⃝ links

For information on hard evidence for the build-up of greenhouse gases, look back to B3 4.5 Global warming.

Food and water – a vicious circle?

As the world population grows, we need ever more food and water. However, the way in which we get that food and water can affect the environment both locally and globally. You have already seen how food production can affect the environment. One example is deforestation. Others are the growth of crops, such as rice, and the rearing of livestock, such as cattle. These last two increase the production of the greenhouse gas methane.

Yet people need water as much as food. It isn't just people either – crops and animals also need water. One way of supplying water is to build a dam. A dam creates a reservoir, which can be used as a source of clean water for drinking and irrigating crops. Unfortunately there can be many environmental problems as a result:

- Dams destroy river ecosystems, particularly below the dam, where the rivers may be lost completely. This can cause huge areas to dry out.

- Flood plains with their fertile soil disappear, so people can no longer grow the crops they need.

- Environments are destroyed as the reservoir forms and animals, plants and people lose their homes (Figure 1).

- Reservoirs act as breeding grounds for the mosquitoes that carry diseases such as malaria.

- Dams and reservoirs may even add to methane in the atmosphere as eutrophication can occur.

How can we be sure?

The build-up of greenhouse gases cannot be denied, because there is hard evidence for it. The great majority of scientists now think the evidence shows that global warming is at least partly linked to human activities such as the burning of fossil fuels and deforestation, but not everyone agrees.

Some extreme weather patterns have been recorded in recent years. Yet throughout history there is evidence of other, equally violent, weather patterns. These occurred long before fossil fuels were used so heavily and deforestation was happening. Also, weather is not the same as climate. Weather can change from day to day but climate is the weather in an area over a long period of time.

How valid, reproducible and repeatable are the data on which the ideas are based? Scientists measure the daily temperatures in many different places. They also look at how the temperature of the Earth has changed over time (Figure 2). They collect many different types of evidence. For example, they use cores of ice that are thousands of years old (Figure 3), the rings in the trunks of trees and the type of pollen found in peat bogs.

Much of the evidence is published in well-respected journals, but there are some controversies. In 2009, it emerged that some scientists in the UK had hidden data that showed that global temperatures were falling slightly rather than rising. The scientists support the idea that human activities are causing global warming and did not want to publish data which might challenge that idea.

The evidence continues to be collected. At the moment, most people and governments are convinced that we need to change the way we live if we are to reduce the damage that global warming might do.

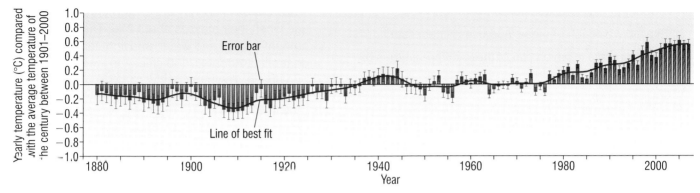

Figure 2 This graph shows how global surface temperatures have varied from the 1901–2000 mean over 130 years. These data are widely regarded as very reproducible and repeatable.

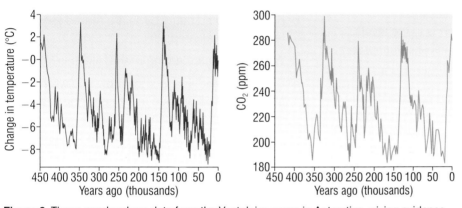

Figure 3 These graphs show data from the Vostok ice cores in Antarctica, giving evidence about temperature, carbon dioxide and dust levels over 420 000 years

Activity 2

Problems like greenhouse gas emissions, global warming and the management of food and water supplies for the world population can seem overwhelming. However, you can make a difference by the choices you make in everyday life.

● Research material on environmental problems.

● Carefully evaluate the evidence you find.

● Develop some web pages to be used by your school on environmental issues.

● Suggest ways in which individuals as well as governments can conserve resources and change attitudes.

Summary questions

1 Develop a spider diagram or flowchart to show how building a dam to produce water for people to drink can damage the environment.

2 Summarise the evidence shown on the graphs in Figures 2 and 3. Explain what they appear to show and how these data might be used as evidence for a human influence on global warming. What other data might you need to help confirm that conclusion?

AQA Examiner's tip

Media reports on environmental issues can be very confusing. If you are going to quote any in your examination, make sure that it is backed up by scientific evidence and not just an opinion.

Key points

● Methods used to produce food and water for people can have short- and long-term effects on the environment.

● There are a lot of data on environmental change. The validity, reproducibility and repeatability of all data must be evaluated before conclusions can be drawn.

Summary questions

1 a List the main ways in which humans reduce the amount of land available for other living things.

b Explain why each of these land uses is necessary.

c Suggest ways in which two of these different types of land use might be reduced.

2 a Draw a flowchart showing acid rain formation.

b Look at Figure 3 in B3 4.3 Air pollution.

   i What was the level of sulfur emissions in 1980?

   ii What was the approximate level of sulfur in the air in the year that you were born? (Make sure you give your birth year.)

   iii What was the level of sulfur emissions in 2002?

c What do these data tell you about trends in the levels of sulfur emissions since 1980. Suggest explanations for the trends you have observed.

3 In Figure 1 in B3 4.5 Global warming, you can see clearly annual variations in the levels of carbon dioxide recorded each year. These fluctuations are thought to be due to seasonal changes in the way plants are growing and photosynthesising through the year.

a Explain how changes in plant growth and rate of photosynthesis might affect carbon dioxide levels.

b How could you use the evidence of this data to argue against deforestation?

c How is the ever-increasing human population affecting the build-up of greenhouse gases?

d What type of evidence is used to investigate the effect of this build-up of greenhouse gases on the climate of the Earth? Which types of evidence are most valid, repeatable and reproducible?

4 a Suggest ways in which people might improve the quality of the biogas produced in their generators.

b Suggest reasons for and against the use of biogas generators and biogas in the UK.

5 Write a letter to your local authority, explaining why you think they should look into the idea of running all their vehicles – buses, emergency vehicles, etc. – on ethanol or gasohol. Explain the potential value of ethanol in helping to prevent the greenhouse effect and global warming.

6 Chicks grown for food arrive in the broiler house as 1-day-old chicks. They are slaughtered at 42 days of age when their mass is about 2 kg. The temperature, amount of food and water, and light levels are carefully controlled. About 20 000 chickens are reared together in one house. The table below shows their average mass:

Age (days)	1	7	14	21	28	35	42
Mass (g)	36	141	404	795	1180	1657	1998

a Plot a graph to show the average growth rate (gain in mass) per chicken.

b Explain why the temperature is so carefully controlled in the broiler house.

c Explain why so many birds are reared together in a relatively small area.

d Why are birds for eating reared like this?

e Draw a second line to show how you would expect a chicken reared outside in a free-range system to gain in mass, and explain the difference.

7 Human cells cannot make some of the amino acids that we need. We must obtain these amino acids from our diet.

The table shows the amounts of four of these amino acids present in mycoprotein, in beef and in wheat.

Name of amino acid	Amount of amino acid per 100 g in mg			Daily amount needed by a 70 kg human in mg
	Mycoprotein	Beef	Wheat	
lysine	910	1600	300	840
methionine	230	500	220	910
phenylalanine	540	60	680	980
threonine	610	840	370	490

A diet book states that mycoprotein is the best source of amino acids for the human diet.

Evaluate this statement. It may help to calculate the percentage of the daily amount of each amino acid found in the different foods. If there is obviously more than 100%, simply state that.

AQA Examination-style questions

1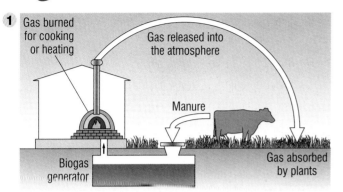

The diagram shows how the manure from a cow can be recycled.

a Choose the correct word to complete the sentences.

   i The gas used for cooking is .... (1)

      carbon dioxide   methane   nitrogen

   ii The gas released into the atmosphere is .... (1)

      carbon dioxide   methane   nitrogen

   iii The gas absorbed by the plants is .... (1)

      carbon dioxide   methane   nitrogen

b i Name the biological process that occurs in the biogas generator. (1)

   ii Name the organisms that are active in the biogas generator. (1)

c The biogas generator is built underground. Suggest two reasons for this. (2)

2 Humans need food, water and shelter. Large areas of land must be cleared to grow food or to build houses. Sometimes valleys are flooded in order to store water in reservoirs.

   a Land is usually cleared by cutting trees down. Give **two** disadvantages to the environment of removing trees. (2)

   b The cleared land may be used for rearing cattle or growing rice.
     i Name the **two** gases which increase in the atmosphere due to these activities. (2)
     ii Choose the correct answer to complete the sentence.

      These gases may contribute to .... (1)

      global warming   food production   deforestation

   c Water in reservoirs can sometimes be polluted by human farming activities. Explain how. (2)

3 *In this question you will be assessed on using good English, organising information clearly and using specialist terms where appropriate.*

Producing food efficiently to feed an increasing human population is a challenge for farmers.

Describe how farmers increase the efficiency of food production.

You should refer to food chains and reducing energy loss in your answer. (6)

1 Changes occur in the human body.

List **A** shows some causes.

List **B** shows some effects.

Match each cause with its correct effect.

List A	List B
blood is filtered	blood clots
platelets are released	glucose is reabsorbed
blood gets hot	skin looks red
	heart rate decreases

(3)

2 Choose the correct word or phrase to complete each sentence.

decrease   increase   stay the same

a When plant cells are transferred from warm water into cool water the rate of diffusion will .... (1)

b When a human gets hot the rate of sweating will .... (1)

c When humans sweat a lot the concentration of their urine will .... (1)

d When humans lie down to rest their rate of breathing will .... (1)

e When insulin is released into the blood the level of blood sugar will .... (1)

f Dialysis fluid contains sugar and ions so that the concentration in the blood will .... (1)

3 Flowering plants have transport systems.

Complete the following sentences.

a The tissue which transports water in a plant is .... (1)

b The tissue which transports sugar in a plant is .... (1)

c The organ which absorbs water from the soil is a .... (1)

4 Humans need food.

a Fishermen are not allowed to use nets that catch very small fish.

Explain why. (2)

b Some farmers keep their chickens in sheds.

Explain why. (2)

c Some people object to cutting down trees to clear land for food crops.

Give a reason why. (1)

5 Read the passage below about biogas production in Sri Lanka, which is a country with a much warmer climate than the UK.

Mr Ratnayake is a farmer. Using nothing more than cow dung, he has enough power to cook and provide heat and light for his home without using a single piece of wood. He collects the manure from his cows in their cattle shed. He then mixes the manure with water and leaves it to ferment in a large concrete pit. The gas produced is collected in a simple storage tank and is piped into his house for use. The dried manure left after this biogas is generated is richer than ordinary manure. It makes a good organic fertiliser for Mr Ratnayake's crops. He can then sell his crops at a higher price as they are organic produce.

http://www.i-sis.org.uk

a i What is the fuel gas present in biogas? (1)

ii Name the process that produces biogas. (1)

b i Give **two** ways in which Mr Ratnayake benefits from making biogas as described in the passage. (2)

ii This design of biogas generator works well in Sri Lanka. It would not work so well in the UK. Explain why. (2)

AQA, 2009

6 Microorganisms are often used in the industrial production of useful substances.

The fungus, *Penicillium chrysogenum*, can be used to make an enzyme that digests the sugar sucrose. When it is growing in a medium containing sucrose, the fungus releases this enzyme into the surrounding solution.

a Explain why it is useful to the fungus to release the enzyme into the surrounding solution. (2)

b Before setting up an industrial fermenter, laboratory-scale investigations are carried out to find the best conditions to use.

A manufacturer investigated the effect of changing several factors on the amount of enzyme produced by the fungus. The results are shown in the table.

Condition	Concentration of enzyme produced in arbitrary units		
	24 hours	72 hours	120 hours
Amount of fungus added as %			
1	9.0	28.8	44.4
5	7.2	54.0	60.0
25	6.0	66.0	62.4
Aeration rate in arbitrary units			
0.5	9.0	36.0	45.8
1.0	7.2	54.0	60.0
2.0	10.8	43.2	52.8
Sucrose concentration at start as %			
4	7.2	54.0	60.0
8	3.0	29.7	48.3
12	0	54.0	21.6

The manufacturer decided to use the following conditions:

- amount of fungus = 5%
- aeration rate = 1.0 arbitrary units
- time = 72 hours.

Suggest an explanation for each of the following.

i The manufacturer decided to add 5% fungus rather than 25%. (2)

ii The concentration of enzyme produced at an aeration rate of 2.0 arbitrary units was less than the concentration at an aeration rate of 1.0 arbitrary units. (2)

AQA, 2006

Glossary

A

Abdomen The lower region of the body. In humans it contains the digestive organs, kidneys, etc.

Accurate A measurement is considered accurate if it is judged to be close to the true value.

Acid rain Rain that is acidic due to dissolved gases, such as sulfur dioxide, produced by the burning of fossil fuels.

Active site The site on an enzyme where the reactants bind.

Active transport The movement of substances against a concentration gradient and/or across a cell membrane, using energy.

Adaptation Special feature that makes an organism particularly well suited to the environment where it lives.

Adult cell cloning Process in which the nucleus of an adult cell of one animal is fused with an empty egg from another animal. The embryo which results is placed inside the uterus of a third animal to develop.

Aerobic respiration Breaking down food using oxygen to release energy for the cells.

Agar The nutrient jelly on which many microorganisms are cultured.

Algal cells The cells of algae, single-celled or simple multicellular organisms, which can photosynthesise but are not plants.

Allele A version of a particular gene.

Alveoli The tiny air sacs in the lungs which increase the surface area for gaseous exchange.

Amino acids The building blocks of protein.

Amylase The enzyme made in the salivary glands and the pancreas which speeds up the breakdown of starch into simple sugars.

Anaerobic respiration Breaking down food without oxygen to release energy for the cells.

Anomalous result Result that does not match the pattern seen in the other data collected or is well outside the range of other repeat readings. It should be retested and if necessary discarded.

Antibiotic Drug that destroys bacteria inside the body without damaging human cells.

Antigen The unique protein on the surface of a cell. It is recognised by the immune system as 'self' or 'non-self'.

Aorta The main artery leaving the left ventricle carrying oxygenated blood to the body.

Artery Blood vessel which carries blood away from the heart. It usually carries oxygenated blood and it has a pulse.

Asexual budding A form of asexual reproduction where a complete new individual forms as a bud on the parent organism e.g. yeast, hydra.

Asexual reproduction Reproduction that involves only one individual with no fusing of gametes to produce the offspring. The offspring are identical to the parent.

Atria The small upper chambers of the heart. The right atrium receives blood from the body and the left atrium receives blood from the lungs.

Auxin A plant hormone that controls the responses of plants to light (phototropism) and to gravity (gravitropism).

B

Bacteria Single-celled microorganisms that can reproduce very rapidly. Many bacteria are useful, e.g. gut bacteria and decomposing bacteria, but some cause disease.

Bacterial colony A population of billions of bacteria grown in culture.

Bar chart A chart with rectangular bars with lengths proportional to the values that they represent. The bars should be of equal width and are usually plotted horizontally or vertically. Also called a bar graph.

Biconcave disc The shape of the red blood cells – a disc which is dimpled inwards on both sides.

Bile Yellowy-green liquid made in the liver and stored in the gall bladder. It is released into the small intestine and emulsifies fats.

Biodiversity The number and variety of different organisms found in a specified area.

Biofuel Fuel produced from biological material which is renewable and sustainable.

Biogas Methane produced by the fermentation of biological materials.

Biological detergent Washing detergent that contains enzymes.

Biomass Biological material from living or recently living organisms.

Bladder The organ where urine is stored until it is released from the body.

Blood The liquid which is pumped around the body by the heart. It contains blood cells, dissolved food, oxygen, waste products, mineral ions, hormones and other substances needed in the body or needing to be removed from the body.

Blood circulation system The system by which blood is pumped around the body.

Blood vessel A tube which carries blood around the body, i.e. arteries, veins and capillaries.

Breathing The physical movement of air into and out of the lungs. In humans this is brought about by the action of the intercostal muscles on the ribs and the diaphragm.

Breathing system The stems involved in breathing: the ribs, intercostal muscles, diaphragm as well as the lungs and the tubes which bring air into the body from the outside.

C

Capillaries The smallest blood vessels which run between individual cells. They have a wall which is only one cell thick.

Carbohydrase Enzyme which speeds up the breakdown of carbohydrates.

Carbon cycle The cycling of carbon through the living and non-living world.

Carbon neutral A process which uses as much carbon dioxide as it produces.

Carnivore Animal that eats other animals.

Carrier Individual who is heterozygous

for a faulty allele that causes a genetic disease in the homozygous form.

Catalyst A substance which speeds up a chemical reaction. At the end of the reaction the catalyst remains chemically unchanged.

Categoric variable See Variable – categoric.

Cell membrane The membrane around the contents of a cell which controls what moves in and out of the cell.

Cell wall A rigid structure which surrounds the cells of living organisms apart from animals.

Cellulose A big carbohydrate molecule which makes up plant and algal cell walls.

Central nervous system (CNS) The central nervous system is made up of the brain and spinal cord where information is processed.

Charles Darwin The Victorian scientist who developed the theory of evolution by a process of natural selection.

Chlorophyll The green pigment contained in the chloroplasts.

Chloroplasts The organelles in which photosynthesis takes place.

Chromosome Thread-like structure carrying the genetic information found in the nucleus of a cell.

Clone Offspring produced by asexual reproduction which is identical to its parent organism.

Combustion The process of burning.

Competition The process by which living organisms compete with each other for limited resources such as food, light or reproductive partners.

Compost heap A site where garden rubbish and kitchen waste are decomposed by microorganisms.

Concentration gradient The gradient between an area where a substance is at a high concentration and an area where it is at a low concentration.

Continuous variable See Variable – continuous.

Contraceptive pill A pill containing female sex hormones which is used to prevent conception.

Control group If an experiment is to determine the effect of changing a single variable, a control is often set up in which the independent variable is not changed, thus enabling a comparison to be made. If the investigation is of the survey

type (q.v.) a control group is usually established to serve the same purpose.

Control variable See Variable – control.

Core body temperature The internal temperature of the body.

Coronary artery An artery which carries oxygenated blood to the muscle of the heart.

Culture medium A substance containing the nutrients needed for microorganisms to grow.

Cuticle The waxy covering of a leaf (or an insect) which reduces water loss from the surface.

Cystic fibrosis A genetic disease that affects the lungs, digestive and reproductive systems. It is inherited through a recessive allele.

Cytoplasm The water-based gel in which the organelles of all living cells are suspended.

D

Data Information, either qualitative or quantitative, that have been collected.

Decomposer Microorganism that breaks down waste products and dead bodies.

Deforestation Removal of forests by felling, burning, etc.

Dehydrated Lacking in water.

Denature Change the shape of an enzyme so that it can no longer speed up a reaction.

Denatured Change the shape of an enzyme so that it can no longer speed up a reaction.

Deoxygenated Lacking in oxygen.

Dependent variable See Variable – dependent.

Depression A mental illness that involves feelings of great sadness that interfere with everyday life.

Detritus feeder See decomposer.

Diabetes A condition in which it becomes difficult or impossible for your body to control the levels of sugar in your blood.

Dialysis The process of cleansing the blood through a dialysis machine when the kidneys have failed.

Dialysis machine The machine used to remove urea and excess mineral ions from the blood when the kidneys fail.

Diaphragm A strong sheet of muscle that separates the thorax from the digestive organs, used to change

the volume of the chest during ventilation of the lungs.

Differentiated Specialised for a particular function.

Diffusion The net movement of particles of a gas or a solute from an area of high concentration to an area of low concentration (along a concentration gradient).

Digested Broken down into small molecules by the digestive enzymes.

Digestive juices The mixture of enzymes and other chemicals produced by the digestive system.

Digestive system The organ system running from the mouth to the anus where food is digested.

Direct contact A way of spreading infectious diseases by skin contact between two people.

Directly proportional A relationship that, when drawn on a line graph, shows a positive linear relationship that crosses through the origin.

Distillation A process which separates the components of a mixture on the basis of their different boiling points.

DNA Deoxyribonucleic acid, the material of inheritance.

DNA fingerprints Patterns produced by analysing the DNA which can be used to identify an individual.

Domed A curved, dome shape.

Dominant The characteristic that will show up in the offspring even if only one of the alleles is inherited.

Donor The person who gives material from their body to another person who needs healthy tissues or organs, e.g. blood, kidneys. Donors may be alive or dead.

Double-blind trial A drug trial in which neither the patient nor the doctor knows if the patient is receiving the new drug or a placebo.

Double circulation The separate circulation of the blood from the heart to the lungs and then back to the heart and on to the body.

Droplet infection A way of spreading infectious diseases through the tiny droplets full of pathogens, which are expelled from your body when you cough, sneeze or talk.

Drug A chemical which causes changes in the body. Medical drugs cure disease or relieve symptoms. Recreational drugs alter the state of your mind and/or body.

E

Ecology The scientific study of the relationships between living organisms and their environment.

Effective medicine A medicine that cures the disease it is targeting.

Effector organs Muscles and glands which respond to impulses from the nervous system.

Electron microscope An instrument used to magnify specimens using a beam of electrons.

Element A substance made up of only one type of atom. An element cannot be broken down chemically into any simpler substance.

Embryonic stem cell Stem cell with the potential to form a number of different specialised cell types, which is taken from an early embryo.

Emulsifies Breaks down into tiny droplets which will form an emulsion.

Endemic When a species evolves in isolation and is found in only one place in the world; it is said to be endemic (particular) to that area.

Environmental isolation This is when the climate changes in one area where an organism lives but not in others.

Enzyme Protein molecule which acts as a biological catalyst. It changes the rate of chemical reactions without being affected itself at the end of the reaction.

Epidemic When more cases of an infectious disease are recorded than would normally be expected.

Epidermal tissue The tissue of the epidermis – the outer layer of an organism.

Epithelial tissue Tissue made up of relatively unspecialised cells which line the tubes and organs of the body.

Error – human Often present in the collection of data, and may be random or systematic. For example, the effect of human reaction time when recording short time intervals with a stopwatch.

Error – random Cause readings to be spread about the true value, due to results varying in an unpredictable way from one measurement to the next. Random errors are present when any measurement is made, and cannot be corrected. The effect of random errors can be reduced by making more measurements and calculating a new mean.

Error – systematic Cause readings to be spread about some value other than the true value, due to results differing from the true value by a consistent amount each time a measurement is made. Sources of systematic error can include the environment, methods of observation or instruments used. Systematic errors cannot be dealt with by simple repeats. If a systematic error is suspected, the data collection should be repeated using a different technique or a different set of equipment, and the results compared.

Error– zero Any indication that a measuring system gives a false reading when the true value of a measured quantity is zero, e.g. the needle on an ammeter failing to return to zero when no current flows. Ethanol Chemical found in alcoholic drinks and biofuels such as gasohol, its chemical formula: C_2H_5OH

Errors Sometimes called uncertainties.

Eutrophication The process by which excessive nutrients in water lead to very fast plant growth. When the plants die they are decomposed and this uses up a lot of oxygen so the water can no longer sustain animal life.

Evaporation The change of a liquid to a vapour at a temperature below its boiling point.

Evidence Data which has been shown to be valid.

Evolution The process of slow change in living organisms over long periods of time as those best adapted to survive breed successfully.

Evolutionary relationship Model of the relationships between organisms, often based on DNA evidence, which suggests how long ago they evolved away from each other and how closely related they are in evolutionary terms.

Evolutionary tree Model of the evolutionary relationships between different organisms based on their appearance, and increasingly, on DNA evidence.

Exchange surface A surface where materials are exchanged.

Exothermic Releases heat energy.

Extinction Extinction is the permanent loss of all the members of a species.

Extremophile Organism which lives in environments that are very extreme, e.g. very high or very low temperatures, high salt levels or high pressures.

F

Fair test A fair test is one in which only the independent variable has been allowed to affect the dependent variable.

Fatty acids Building blocks of lipids.

Fermentation The reaction in which the enzymes in yeast turn glucose into ethanol and carbon dioxide.

Fertile A fertile soil contains enough minerals e.g. nitrates, to supply the crop plants with the all nutrients needed for healthy growth.

Fertiliser A substance provided for plants that supplies them with essential nutrients for healthy growth.

Fossil fuel Fuel obtained from long-dead biological material.

Fructose syrup A sugar syrup.

FSH Follicle stimulating hormone, a female hormone that stimulates the eggs to mature in the ovaries, and the ovaries to produce hormones, including oestrogen.

G

Gamete Sex cell which has half the chromosome number of an ordinary cell.

Gaseous exchange The exchange of gases, e.g. the exchange of oxygen and carbon dioxide which occurs between the air in the lungs and the blood.

Gene A short section of DNA carrying genetic information.

Genetic disorder Disease which is inherited.

Genetic engineering/modification A technique for changing the genetic information of a cell.

Genetic material The DNA which carries the instructions for making a new cell or a new individual.

Geographical isolation This is when two populations become physically isolated by a geographical feature.

Glandular tissue The tissue which makes up the glands and secretes chemicals, e.g. enzymes, hormones.

Global warming Warming of the Earth due to greenhouse gases in the atmosphere trapping infrared radiation from the surface.

Glucagon A hormone involved in the control of blood sugar levels.

Glucose A simple sugar.

Glycerol Building block of lipids.

Glycogen Carbohydrate store in animals, including the muscles, liver and brain of the human body.

Gravitropism Response of a plant to the force of gravity controlled by auxin.

Greenhouse effect The trapping of infrared radiation from the Sun as a result of greenhouse gases, such as carbon dioxide and methane, in the Earth's atmosphere. The greenhouse effect maintains the surface of the Earth at a temperature suitable for life.

Greenhouse gas Gases, such as carbon dioxide and methane, which absorb infrared radiated from the Earth, and result in warming up the atmosphere.

Guard cells The cells which surround stomata in the leaves of plants and control their opening and closing.

H

Haemoglobin The red pigment which carries oxygen around the body.

Hazard A hazard is something (e.g. an object, a property of a substance or an activity) that can cause harm.

Heart The muscular organ which pumps blood around the body.

Herbicide Chemical that kills plants.

Herbivore Animal that feeds on plants.

Homeostasis The maintenance of constant internal body conditions.

Hydrated With plenty of water.

Hydroponics Growing plants in water enriched by mineral ions rather than soil.

Hypothermia The state when the core body temperature falls below the normal range.

Hypothesis A proposal intended to explain certain facts or observations.

I

Immune response The response of the immune system to cells carrying foreign antigens. It results in the production of antibodies against the foreign cells and the destruction of those cells.

Immune system The body system which recognises and destroys foreign cells or proteins such as invading pathogens.

Immunisation Giving a vaccine that allows immunity to develop without exposure to the disease itself.

Immunosuppressant drugs Drugs which suppress the immune system of the recipient of a transplanted organ to prevent rejection.

Impulse Electrical signal carried along the neurons.

Independent variables See Variables – independent.

Indicator species Lichens or insects that are particularly sensitive to pollution and so can be used to indicate changes in the environmental pollution levels.

Industrial waste Waste produced by industrial processes.

Infectious Capable of causing infection.

Infectious disease Disease which can be passed from one individual to another.

Inheritance of acquired characteristics Jean-Baptiste Lamarck's theory of how evolution took place.

Inherited Passed on from parents to their offspring through genes.

Inoculate To make someone immune to a disease by injecting them with a vaccine which stimulates the immune system to make antibodies against the disease.

Insoluble molecule Molecule which will not dissolve in a particular solvent such as water.

Insulin A hormone involved in the control of blood sugar levels.

Intercostal muscles The muscles between the ribs which raise and lower them during breathing movements.

Internal environment The conditions inside the body.

Interval The quantity between readings, e.g. a set of 11 readings equally spaced over a distance of 1 m would give an interval of 10 cm.

Ion A charged particle produced by the loss or gain of electrons.

Isomerase An enzyme which converts one form of a molecule into another.

Isotonic Having the same concentration of solutes as another solution.

J

Jean-Baptiste Lamarck French biologist who developed a theory of evolution based on the inheritance of acquired characteristics.

K

Kidney Organ which filters the blood and removes urea, excess salts and water.

Kidney transplant Replacing failed kidneys with a healthy kidney from a donor

Kidney tubule A structure in the kidney where substances are reabsorbed back into the blood.

Kingdom The highest group in the classification system e.g. animals, plants.

L

Lactic acid One product of anaerobic respiration. It builds up in muscles with exercise. Important in yoghurt and cheese making processes.

Light energy Energy in the form of light.

Light microscope An instrument used to magnify specimens using lenses and light.

Limiting factor Factor which limits the rate of a reaction, e.g. temperature, pH, light levels (photosynthesis).

Line graph Used when both variables are continuous. The line should normally be a line of best fit, and may be straight or a smooth curve. (Exceptionally, in some (mainly biological) investigations, the line may be a 'point-to-point' line.)

Linear relationship The relationship between two continuous variables that can be represented by a straight line on a graph.

Lipase Enzyme which breaks down fats and oils into fatty acids and glycerol.

Lipid An oil or fat.

Liver A large organ in the abdomen which carries out a wide range of functions in the body.

M

Malnourished The condition when the body does not get a balanced diet.

Mean The arithmetical average of a series of numbers.

Median The middle value in a list of data.

Meiosis The two-stage process of cell division which reduces the chromosome number of the daughter cells. It is involved in making the gametes for sexual reproduction.

Menstrual cycle The reproductive cycle in women controlled by hormones.

Mesophyll tissue The tissue in a green plant where photosynthesis takes place.

Metabolic rate The rate at which the reactions of your body take place, particularly cellular respiration.

Methane A hydrocarbon gas with the chemical formula CH_4. It makes up the main flammable component of biogas.

Microorganism Bacteria, viruses and other organisms that can only be seen using a microscope.

Mineral ion Chemical needed in small amounts as part of a balanced diet to keep the body healthy.

Mitochondria The site of aerobic cellular respiration in a cell.

Mitosis Asexual cell division where two identical cells are formed.

Mode The number which occurs most often in a set of data.

Molecule A particle made up of two or more atoms bonded together.

Monitor Observations made over a period of time.

Motor neuron Neuron that carries impulses from the central nervous system to the effector organs.

MRSA Methicillin-resistant *Staphylococcus aureus*. An antibiotic-resistant bacterium.

Multicellular organism An organism which is made up of many different cells which work together. Some of the cells are specialised for different functions in the organism.

Muscular tissue The tissue which makes up the muscles. It can contract and relax.

Mutation A change in the genetic material of an organism.

Mycoprotein A food based on the fungus *Fusarium* that grows and reproduces rapidly. It means 'protein from fungus'.

N

Natural classification system Classification system based on the similarities between different living organisms.

Natural selection The process by which evolution takes place. Organisms produce more offspring than the environment can support so only those which are most suited to their environment – the 'fittest' – will survive to breed and pass on their useful characteristics.

Negative pressure A system when the external pressure is lower than the internal pressure.

Nerve Bundles of hundreds or even thousands of neurons.

Nervous system See Central nervous system.

Net movement The overall movement of …

Neuron(s) Basic cell of the nervous system which carries minute electrical impulses around the body.

Nitrate ion Ion which is needed by plants to make proteins.

Non-renewable Something which cannot be replaced once it is used up.

Nucleus (of a cell) An organelle found in many living cells containing the genetic information.

O

Obese Very overweight, with a BMI of over 30.

Oestrogen Female sex hormone which stimulates the lining of the womb to build up in preparation for a pregnancy.

Opinion A belief not backed up by facts or evidence.

Optic nerve The nerve carrying impulses from the retina of the eye to the brain.

Oral contraceptive Hormone contraceptive that is taken by mouth.

Organ A group of different tissues working together to carry out a particular function.

Organ system A group of organs working together to carry out a particular function.

Organic waste Waste material from living organisms, e.g. garden waste.

Osmosis The net movement of water from an area of high concentration (of water) to an area of low concentration (of water) along a concentration gradient.

Ova The female sex cells, eggs.

Ovary Female sex organ which contains the eggs and produces sex hormones during the menstrual cycle.

Overweight A person is overweight if their body carries excess fat and their BMI is between 25 and 30.

Ovipositor A pointed tube found in many female insects which is used to lay eggs.

Ovulation The release of a mature egg from the ovary in the middle of the menstrual cycle.

Oxygen debt The extra oxygen that must be taken into the body after exercise has stopped to complete the aerobic respiration of lactic acid.

Oxygenated Containing oxygen.

Oxyhaemoglobin The molecule formed when haemoglobin binds to oxygen molecules.

P

Pancreas An organ that produces the hormone insulin and many digestive enzymes.

Pandemic When more cases of a disease are recorded than normal in a number of different countries.

Parasite Organism which lives in or on other living organisms and gets some or all of its nourishment from this host organism.

Partially permeable Allowing only certain substances to pass through.

Pathogen Microorganism which causes disease.

Perfluorocarbon Chemical which can be used as artificial blood.

Period The stage in the menstrual cycle when the lining of the womb is lost.

Permanent vacuole A space in the cytoplasm filled with cell sap which is there all the time.

Pesticide Chemical that kills animals.

Phloem tissue The living transport tissue in plants which carries sugars around the plant.

Photosynthesis The process by which plants make food using carbon dioxide, water and light energy.

Phototropism The response of a plant to light, controlled by auxin.

Pigment A coloured molecule.

Pituitary gland Small gland in the brain which produces a range of hormones controlling body functions.

Placebo A substance used in clinical trials which does not contain any drug at all.

Plasma The clear, yellow liquid part of the blood which carries dissolved substances and blood cells around the body.

Plasmid Extra circle of DNA found in bacterial cytoplasm.

Platelet Fragment of cell in the blood which is vital for the clotting mechanism to work.

Polydactyly A genetic condition inherited through a dominant allele which results in extra fingers and toes.

Polytunnel Large greenhouse made of plastic.

Positive pressure A system where the external pressure is higher than the internal pressure.

Precise A precise measurement is one in which there is very little spread about the mean value. Precision depends only on the extent of random errors – it gives no indication of how close results are to the true value.

Predator An animal which preys on other animals for food.

Prediction A forecast or statement about the way something will happen in the future. In science it is not just a simple guess, because it is based on some prior knowledge or on a hypothesis.

Progesterone Female sex hormone used in the contraceptive pill.

Protease An enzyme which breaks down proteins.

Protein synthesis The process by which proteins are made on the ribosomes based on information from the genes in the nucleus.

Puberty The stage of development when the sexual organs and the body become adult.

Pulmonary artery The large blood vessel taking deoxygenated blood from the right ventricle of the heart to the lungs.

Pulmonary vein The large blood vessel bringing blood into the left atrium of the heart from the lungs.

Pyramid of biomass A model of the mass of biological material in the organisms at each level of a food chain.

Q

Quadrat A piece of apparatus for sampling organisms in the field.

Quantitative sampling Sampling which records the numbers of organisms rather than just the type.

R

Range The maximum and minimum values of the independent or dependent variables; important in ensuring that any pattern is detected.

Receptor Special sensory cell that detects changes in the environment.

Recessive The characteristic that will show up in the offspring only if both of the alleles are inherited.

Recipient The person who receives a donor organ.

Red blood cell Blood cell which contains the red pigment haemoglobin. It is biconcave discs in shape and gives the blood its red colour.

Reflex arc The sense organ, sensory neuron, relay neuron, motor neuron and effector organ which bring about a reflex action.

Reflex Rapid automatic response of the nervous system that does not involve conscious thought.

Rehydrate To restore water to a system.

Repeatable A measurement is repeatable if the original experimenter repeats the investigation using same method and equipment and obtains the same results.

Reproducible A measurement is reproducible if the investigation is repeated by another person, or by using different equipment or techniques, and the same results are obtained.

Resolution This is the smallest change in the quantity being measured (input) of a measuring instrument that gives a perceptible change in the reading.

Respiration The process by which food molecules are broken down to release energy for the cells.

Ribosome The site of protein synthesis in a cell.

Risk The likelihood that a hazard will actually cause harm. We can reduce risk by identifying the hazard and doing something to protect against that hazard.

Root hair cell Cell on the root of a plant with microscopic hairs which increases the surface area for the absorption of water from the soil.

S

Safe medicine A medicine that does not cause any unreasonable side effects while curing a disease.

Salivary gland Gland in the mouth which produces saliva containing the enzyme amylase.

Sample size The size of a sample in an investigation.

Secreting Releasing chemicals such as hormones or enzymes.

Selective reabsorption The varying amount of water and dissolved mineral ions that are taken back into the blood in the kidney, depending on what is needed by the body.

Sense organ Collection of special cells known as receptors which responds to changes in the surroundings (e.g. eye, ear).

Sensory neuron Neuron which carries impulses from the sensory organs to the central nervous system.

Sewage A combination of bodily waste, waste water from homes and rainfall overflow from street drains.

Sewage treatment plant A site where human waste is broken down using microorganisms.

Sex chromosome A chromosome which carries the information about the sex of an individual.

Sexual reproduction Reproduction which involves the joining (fusion) of male and female gametes producing genetic variety in the offspring.

Small intestine The region of the digestive system where most of the digestion of the food takes place.

Solar energy (light energy) Energy from the Sun or other light source.

Solute The solid which dissolves in a solvent to form a solution.

Specialised Adapted for a particular function.

Speciation The formation of a new species.

Species A group of organisms with many features in common which can breed successfully producing fertile offspring.

Stable medicine A medicine which does not break down under normal conditions.

Statin Drug which lowers the blood cholesterol levels and improves the balance of HDLs to LDL.

Stem cell Undifferentiated cell with the potential to form a wide variety of different cell types.

Stent A metal mesh placed in the artery which is used to open up the blood vessel by the inflation of a tiny balloon.

Steroid Drug that is used illegally by some athletes to build muscles and improve performance.

Stimuli A change in the environment that is detected by sensory receptors.

Stomata Openings in the leaves of plants (particularly the underside) which allow gases to enter and leave the leaf. They are opened and closed by the guard cells.

Sustainable food production Methods of producing food which can be sustained over time without destroying the fertility of the land or ocean.

Synapse A gap between neurons where the transmission of information is chemical rather than electrical.

T

Territory An area where an animal lives and feeds, which it may mark out or defend against other animals.

Thalidomide A drug that caused deformities in the fetus when given to pregnant women to prevent morning sickness.

Therapeutic cloning Cloning by transferring the nucleus of an adult cell to an empty egg to produce tissues or organs which could be used in medicine.

Thermoregulatory centre The area of the brain which is sensitive to the temperature of the blood.

Thorax The upper (chest) region of the body. In humans it includes the ribcage, heart and lungs.

Tissue A group of specialised cells all carrying out the same function.

Tissue culture Using small groups of cells from a plant to make new plants.

Trachea The main tube lined with cartilage rings which carries air from the nose and mouth down towards the lungs.

Transect A measured line or area along which ecological measurements (e.g. quadrats) are made.

Transfusion The transfer of blood from one person to another.

Transpiration The loss of water vapour from the leaves of plants through the stomata when they are opened to allow gas exchange for photosynthesis.

Transpiration stream The movement of water through a plant from the roots to the leaves as a result of the loss of water by evaporation from the surface of the leaves.

Transport system A system for transporting substances around a multicellular living organism.

Trial run Preliminary work that is often done to establish a suitable range or interval for the main investigation.

Tuber Modified part of a plant which is used to store food in the form of starch.

Type 1 diabetes Diabetes which is caused when the pancreas cannot make insulin. It usually occurs in children and young adults and can be treated by regular insulin injections.

U

Urea The waste product formed by the breakdown of excess amino acids in the liver.

Urine The liquid produced by the kidneys containing the metabolic waste product urea along with excess water and salts from the body.

Urobilin Yellow pigment that come from the breakdown of haemoglobin in the liver.

V

Vaccination Introducing small quantities of dead or inactive pathogens into the body to stimulate the white blood cells to produce antibodies that destroy the pathogens. This makes the person immune to future infection.

Vaccine The dead or inactive pathogen material used in vaccination.

Vacuum An area with little or no gas pressure.

Valid Suitability of the investigative procedure to answer the question being asked.

Valve Structure which prevents the backflow of liquid, e.g. the valves of the heart or the veins.

Variable Physical, chemical or biological quantity or characteristic.

Variable – categoric Categoric variables have values that are labels. For example, names of plants or types of material.

Variable – continuous Can have values (called a quantity) that can be given by measurement (e.g. light intensity, flow rate, etc.).

Variable – control A variable which may, in addition to the independent variable, affect the outcome of the investigation and therefore has to be kept constant or at least monitored.

Variable – dependent The variable for which the value is measured for each and every change in the independent variable.

Variable – independent The variable for which values are changed or selected by the investigator.

Variegated Having different colours, e.g. a green and white leaf.

Vein Blood vessel which carries blood away from the heart. It usually carries deoxygenated blood and has valves to prevent the backflow of blood.

Vena cava The large vein going into the right atrium of the heart carrying deoxygenated blood from the body.

Ventilated Movement of air into and out of the lungs.

Ventricles The large chambers at the bottom of the heart. The right ventricle pumps blood to the lungs, the left ventricle pumps blood around the body.

Villi The finger-like projections from the lining of the small intestine which increase the surface area for the absorption of digested food into the blood.

Virus Microorganism which takes over body cells and reproduces rapidly, causing disease.

W

White blood cell Blood cell which is involved in the immune system of the body, engulfing bacteria, making antibodies and making antitoxins.

Wilting The process by which plants droop when they are short of water or too hot. This reduces further water loss and prevents cell damage.

Withdrawal symptom The symptom experienced by a drug addict when they do not get the drug to which they are addicted.

X

Xenotransplantation Transplanting tissues or organs from one species to another, e.g. pig organs into people.

Xylem tissue The non-living transport tissue in plants, which transports water around the plant.

Index

Photo acknowledgements

H1.1 Science Source/Science Photo Library; H1.2 iStockphoto; H2.1 Steve Taylor/Science Photo Library; H3.1 John Kaprielian/Science Photo Library; H3.2 iStockphoto; H3.3 Martyn F. Chillmaid; H4.1 Matilda Lindeblad/Getty Images; H4.2 Cordelia Molloy/Science Photo Library; H7.1 CNRI/Science Photo Library; H9.1 NASA; H10.1 iStockphoto; H11 Q2 Martyn F. Chillmaid; H11 Q3 Photodisc 29 (NT); H11 Q5 Martyn F. Chillmaid; H11 Q8 Rubberball/Photolibrary; H11 Q10 Corel 21 (NT); B1 1.1.1 iStockphoto; B1 1.1.2 Christian Forchner/epa/Corbis; B1 1.1.3 Flip Nicklin/Minden Pictures/FLPA; B1 1.2.1 Getty Images; B1 1.2.2 iStockphoto; B1 1.2.3 Rex Features; B1 1.3.1 iStockphoto; B1 1.3.2 iStockphoto; B1 1.4.1 Eric Erbe/Science Photo Library; B1 1.4.2 Dr Harold Fisher, Visuals Unlimited/Science Photo Library; B1 1.4.3 Science Photo Library; B1 1.5.1 Kallista Images/CDC/Getty Images; B1 1.5.2 Eye of Science/Science Photo Library; B1 1.6.1 Tek Image/Science Photo Library; B1 1.6.2 Cordelia Moloy/Science Photo Library; B1 1.6.3 St Mary's Hospital Medical School/Science Photo Library; B1 1.7.1 Geoff Tompkinson/Science Photo Library; B1 1.7.2 CDC/Science Photo Library; B1 1.9.1 Jenifer Harrington/Getty Images; B1 1.10.3 iStockphoto; B1 1.10.4 Martin Lee/Rex Features; B1 2.1.1 Philippe Lissac/Godong/Corbis; B1 2.1.2 iStockphoto; B1 2.2.3 Anthony Bradshaw/Getty Images; B1 2.4.1 Saturn Stills/Science Photo Library; B1 2.4.2 Mirrorpix; B1 2.5.1 Gavin Rodgers/Rex Features; B1 2.5.2 Copyright 2010 Photolibrary; B1 2.5.3 iStockphoto; B1 2.6.1 Martin Shields/Science Photo Library; B1 2.7.1 Barcroft Media/Getty Images; B1 2.8 EQ1 Ann Fullick; B1 2.8 EQ3 FLPA; B1 3.1.1 Colin Cuthbert/Science Photo Library; B1 3.1.2 Andrew Dunsmore/Rex Features; B1 3.2.1 iStockphoto; B1 3.3.1 AP/PA Photos; B1 3.4.1 NASA/Science Photo Library; B1 3.4.2 Handout/Reuters/Corbis; B1 3.5.3 iStockphoto; B1 3.6.1 AFP/Getty Images; B1 3.6.2 Rex Features; B1 3.6.3 Sipa Press/Rex Features; B1 4.1.1 iStockphoto; B1 4.1.2 Norbert Wu/Minden Pictures/FLPA; B1 4.1.3 Ralph White/Corbis; B1 4.2.1 iStockphoto; B1 4.2.2(top) LANDOV/Press Association Images; B1 4.2.2(bottom) iStockphoto; B1 4.3.2 iStockphoto; B1 4.3.3 iStockphoto; B1 4.4.1 iStockphoto; B1 4.4.2 iStockphoto; B1 4.4.3 iStockphoto; B1 4.4.4 iStockphoto; B1 4.5.1 Lizzie Harper/Science Photo Library; B1 4.5.2 iStockphoto; B1 4.5.3 iStockphoto; B1 4.6.1 Silvestre Silva/FLPA; B1 4.6.2 James Cook, University of Reading; B1 4.6.3 Dembinsky Photo Ass./FLPA; B1 4.6.4 iStockphoto; B1 4.7.1 Copyright 2010 Photolibrary; B1 4.7.2 William Mullins/Science Photo Library; B1 4.8.1 Mike Lane/FLPA; B1 4.8.3 iStockphoto; B1 4.9 EQ1 Natural Visions/Heather Angel; B1 5.1.1 iStockphoto; B1 5.2.1 iStockphoto; B1 5.2.2 iStockphoto; B1 5.2.3 iStockphoto; B1 5.3.1 iStockphoto; B1 5.3.2 The Bridgeman Art Library/Getty Images; B1 5.4.1 Christopher Baines/Alamy; B1 5.4.2 iStockphoto; B1 5.5.1 Erica Olsen/FLPA; B1 5.5.2a iStockphoto; B1 5.5.2b Ian Wood/Alamy; B1 5.5.2c John Eveson/FLPA; B1 5.5.2d iStockphoto; B1 6.1.1 iStockphoto; B1 6.1.2 Steve Gschmeissner/Science Photo Library; B1 6.2.1 iStockphoto; B1 6.2.2 iStockphoto; B1 6.2.3 Allison Michael Orenstein/Getty Images; B1 6.3.1 Gary Roberts/Rex Features; B1 6.3.2 iStockphoto; B1 6.3.3 iStockphoto; B1 6.4.1 Copyright 2010 Photolibrary; B1 6.4.2 Nigel Cattlin/FLPA; B1 6.5.1 Press Association Images; B1 6.6.2 Nick Cobbing/Rex Features; B1 6.7.1(left) A & M University/Rex Features; B1 6.7.1(right) AP/EMPICS; B1 6.7.2 epa european pressphoto agency b.v.; B1 6.7.3 Courtesy Golden Rice Humanitarian Board. www.goldenrice.org; B1 7.1.2 Frans Lanting/FLPA; B1 7.1.3 English Heritage Photo Library; B1 7.2.2 Frans Lanting/FLPA; B1 7.2.3 Science Photo Library; B1 7.3.1 Scott Linstead/Minden Pictures/FLPA; B1 7.3.2 Brian Jackson/Fotolia; B1 7.4.1 iStockphoto; B1 7.4.2 Getty Images; B1 7.4.4(bottom) Pat & Tom Leeson/Science Photo Library; B1 7.4.4(top) Pat & Tom Leeson/Science Photo Library; B1 7.5 SQ4 Dr Jeremy Burgess/Science Photo Library; B1 7.5 EQ3 iStockphoto;

B2 1.1.4 iStockphoto; B2 1.1.1 Thomas Deerinck, NCMIR/Science Photo Library; B2 1.2.1(top) Hybrid Medical Animation/Science Photo Library; B2 1.2.1(bottom) Steve Gschmeissner/Science Photo Library; B2 1.2.4 Eye Of Science/Science Photo Library; B2 1.4.3 Dr R. Dourmashkin/Science Photo Library; B2 1.5.1 Eric Grave/Science Photo Library; B2 2.1.1 Cordelia Molloy/Science Photo Library; B2 2.3.1 iStockphoto; B2 2.3.2 Steve Gschmeissner/Science Photo Library; B2 2.3.3 iStockphoto; B2 2.3.4 Cordelia Molloy/Science Photo Library; B2 2.4.2 iStockphoto; B2 2.4.3 Noel Hendrickson/Getty; B2 2.5.1 iStockphoto; B2 2.5.2 iStockphoto; B2 2.5.3 Roberto Danovaro; B2 2.5.4 iStockphoto; B2 2.6.1 Edward Fullick; B2 2.6.4 Edward Fullick; B2 2.7.1 iStockphoto; B2 2.7.2 Imagebroker/Imagebroker/FLPA; B2 2.8.1 iStockphoto; B2 3.1.1 J.C. Revy, Ism/Science Photo Library; B2 3.1.2 Martyn F. Chillmaid/Science Photo Library; B2 3.2.2 Darwin Dale/Science Photo Library; B2 3.4.1 Martyn F. Chillmaid/Science Photo Library; B2 3.4.2 Dr P. Marazzi/Science Photo Library; B2 3.5.1 iStockphoto; B2 3.5.2 iStockphoto; B2 3.5.3 Stuart Howells/Rex; B2 3.6.1 allesalltag/Alamy; B2 3.6.2 Power And Syred/Science Photo Library; B2 3.6.3 iStockphoto; B2 4.1.2 iStockphoto; B2 4.2.1 Eye Of Science/Science Photo Library; B2 4.3.1 iStockphoto; B2 4.3.2 iStockphoto; B2 5.1.2 Ed Reschke, Peter Arnold Inc./Science Photo Library; B2 5.2.2 Eye Of Science/Science Photo Library; B2 5.3.2 Jan Sochor/Alamy; B2 5.3.3 PA Photos; B2 5.4.1 Corbis; B2 5.5.1 CNRI/Science Photo Library; B2 5.6.1 Zephyr/Science Photo Library; B2 5.7(left) Getty Images; B2 5.7(right) Brand New Images; B2 5.8.1 iStockphoto; B2 6.1.1 Millard H. Sharp/Science Photo Library; B2 6.1.2 AFP/Getty Images; B2 6.2.1 Fotolia; B2 6.2.2 Desmond Dugan/FLPA; B2 6.3.1 Norbert Wu/Minden Pictures/FLPA; B2 6.3.3 Martin Bond/Science Photo Library; B2 6.4.1 iStockphoto; B2 6.4.2 Art Wolfe/Science Photo Library; B2 6.4.3 Ulla Lohman; B3 1.1.3 Peter Arnold, Inc./Alamy; B3 1.2.4 iStockphoto; B3 1.3.1 Bryn Lennon/Getty Images; B3 1.3.2 Editorial Image, LLC/Alamy; B3 1.4.1 NationalGeographic/Getty Images; B3 1.6.1 Penny Tweedie/Science Photo Library; B3 1.6.2 BSIP Laurent/Trunyo/Science Photo Library; B3 1.7.1(top) Image Source/Getty Images; B3 1.7.1(bottom) Eye of Science/Science Photo Library; B3 1.9.1 iStockphoto; B3 2.2.3(left) Medical-on-Line/Alamy; B3 2.2.3(right) Steve Allen/Science Photo Library; B3 2.3.2 St Bartholomew's Hospital/Science Photo Library; B3 2.3.4 National Cancer Institute/Science Photo Library; B3 2.4.2 SSPL/Getty Images; B3 2.5.1 Volker Steger/Science Photo Library; B3 2.5.2 Power and Syred/Science Photo Library; B3 2.5.3 Martin Leigh/Photolibrary; B3 2.6 EQ2 Steve Gschmeissner/Science Photo Library; B3 3.1.1(left) iStockphoto; B3 3.1.1(right) iStockphoto; B3 3.1.2 Workbook Stock/Getty Images; B3 3.3.1 Life in View/Science Photo Library; B3 3.4.2 Geoffrey Robinson/Rex Features; B3 3.5.1(top) Robert Harding/Getty Images; B3 3.5.1(bottom) iStockphoto; B3 3.5.3 Martyn F. Chillmaid/Science Photo Library; B3 3.6.1 Cordelia Molloy/Science Photo Library; B3 3.6.2 iStockphoto; B3 3.7.2 Lea Paterson/Science Photo Library; B3 3.8.1 Scott Camazine/Science Photo Library; B3 3.8.2 Steve Gschmeissner/Science Photo Library; B3 3.8.3 Guy Somerset/Alamy; B3 4.1.1 NOAA/Science Photo Library; B3 4.1.3 Skyscan/Science Photo Library; B3 4.2.2 Wayne Hutchinson/FLPA; B3 4.2.4 Hans Schouten/FLPA; B3 4.3.1 Visuals Unlimited/Getty Images; B3 4.4.1 Gerry Ellis/FLPA; B3 4.4.2 ; B3 4.4.3 Ann Fullick; B3 4.5.3 Fotolia; B3 4.6.1 Gyro Photography/Getty Images; B3 4.6.2 Victor de Schwanberg/Science Photo Library; B3 4.6.3 John James/Alamy; B3 4.7.1 Martin Wright/Still Pictures; B3 4.7.3 NREL/US Department of Energy/Science Photo Library; B3 4.8.1 Fotolia; B3 4.8.2(top) National Geographic/Getty Images; B3 4.8.2(bottom) Image Bank/Getty Images; B3 4.9.1 Fotolia; B3 4.9.3 Gusto Images/Science Photo Library; B3 4.10.1 Dorling Kindersley/Getty Images.

edexcel
advancing learning, changing lives

BTEC National
IT Practioners

Book 1

Core units

Steve Farrell
Sue Jennings
Diane Sutherland
Jon Sutherland
Sharon Yull

A PEARSON COMPANY

Contents

Why choose a career as an IT Practitioner?

One of the biggest industries in the UK

- There are an estimated **1.2 million** jobs in the IT sector in the UK, made up of those working in the IT industry and IT professionals and practitioners working in other areas.

- There are almost 580,000 people working in companies in the UK whose primary function and business is IT; this accounts for approximately **2%** of UK employment.

- There are almost 590,000 IT professionals and practitioners working in other sectors in the UK, they often work in IT departments or as IT support staff within organisations

  [Source IT Insights: Drivers of Demand for Skills. e-skills UK/MRM Solutions, 2004]

- Four out of ten UK businesses employ IT professionals

  [ICT Inquiry issue 3 - Q2. e-skills UK. 2005]

Growing career opportunities

- Permanent IT salaries in the UK have risen by 5.5% in the last 12 months, and the average wage for an IT professional is now £32,965.

  [source. Computerweekly.com 2007]

Typical roles for IT professionals and practitioners:

IT/Telecoms managers

Technical support staff

PC support staff

Systems designers

Systems developersGames developers

Programmers

Software engineers

Operations staff

Networking staff

Internet professionals

Database staff

Games developers

[ICT Inquiry issue 3 - Q2. e-skills UK. 2005]

Did you know...

- Women make up less than 20% (one in five) of the IT workforce
  [source Quarterly Review of the ICT Labour Market Issue 14 - Q3. e-skills UK, 2005]

- 40% of IT professionals work in London and the South East; Northern Ireland, Wales and Scotland account for 11% of IT employment in the UK.
  [source: Labour Force Survey, Office for National Statistics, 2004]

The top five internet companies providing services via the web

- Google,
- Amazon,
- eBay,
- Microsoft
- Yahoo

The home of the IT industry

- Silicon Valley in San Francisco is home to the headquarters of some of the worlds largest and most famous IT companies including, Apple, Intel, eBay, Amazon and Hewlett-Packard, the company which is said to have started Silicon Valley 1970s.

The world's largest IT corporations

- Hewlett Packard is currently the world's largest information technology corporation (by revenue). Hewlett-Packard serves more than one billion customers in more than 170 countries on six continents and has approximately 156,000 employees worldwide.
  [source hewlettpackard.com]

- IBM is the largest information technology employer in the world with 355,766 employees worldwide who serves customers in 170 countries.
  [source IBM.COM]

How to use this book

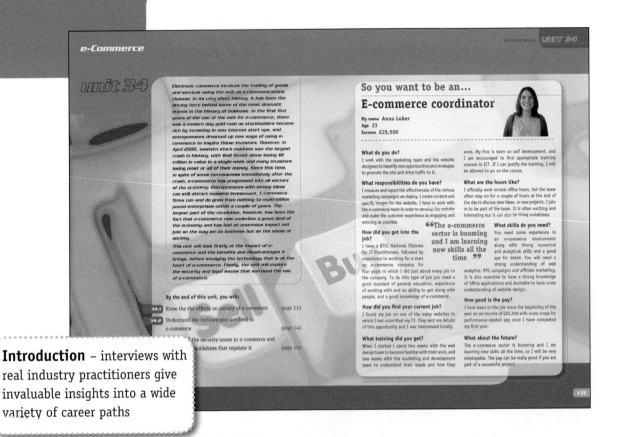

Introduction – interviews with real industry practitioners give invaluable insights into a wide variety of career paths

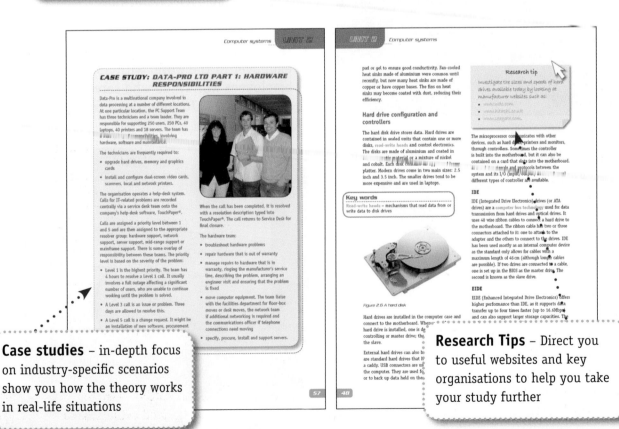

Case studies – in-depth focus on industry-specific scenarios show you how the theory works in real-life situations

Research Tips – Direct you to useful websites and key organisations to help you take your study further

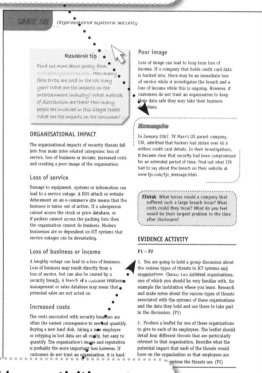

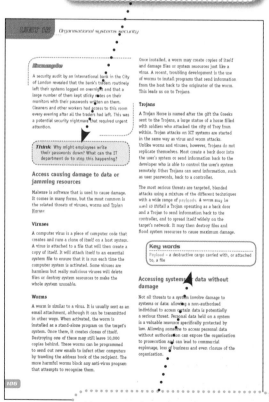

Track your progress

This master grid can be used as a study aid. You can track your progress
by ticking the level you achieve. The relevant grading criteria can also
be found at the start of each unit.

To achieve a pass grade the evidence must show that the learner is able to...	To achieve a merit grade the evidence must show that, in addition to the pass criteria, the learner is able to...	To achieve a distinction grade the evidence must show that, in addition to the pass and merit criteria, the learner is able to...
Unit 1		
P1 explain why employers value particular employee attributes	**M1** explain and use a specialist IT communication channel effectively	**D1** analyse interpersonal and written communications criticising or justifying particular techniques used
P2 describe potential barriers to effective communication	**M2** explain mechanisms that can be used to reduce the impact of communication barriers	**D2** independently use a personal development plan to undergo a process of identification of skill need and related improvement
P3 demonstrate effective communication-related interpersonal skills	**M3** proof read, review and amend both own and other people's draft documents to produce final versions	
P4 effectively communicate in writing technical information to a specified audience	**M4** explain how individuals can use a knowledge of their learning style to improve their effectiveness in developing new skills or understanding	
P5 use IT tools effectively to aid communications		
P6 describe ways of identifying and meeting development needs		
P7 create and maintain a personal development plan		
Unit 2		
P1 Explain the function of the system unit components and how they communicate	**M1** Explain and implement the installation and configuration of an additional or replacement device	**D1** Evaluate at least three specifications for commercially available computer systems and justify the one most suitable for use in a given situation
P2 Describe the purpose, features and functions of two different operating systems	**M2** Compare the features and functions of two different operating systems	**D2** Justify the considerations for selection in the upgrade of an existing computer system.
P3 Demonstrate the operation and explain the use of two different software utilities	**M3** Explain the effect of the software maintenance activities carried out on the performance of a computer system.	
P4 Describe the range of available utility software		
P5 Undertake routine maintenance tasks in relation to a PC.		

To achieve a pass grade the evidence must show that the learner is able to...	To achieve a merit grade the evidence must show that, in addition to the pass criteria, the learner is able to...	To achieve a distinction grade the evidence must show that, in addition to the pass and merit criteria, the learner is able to...
Unit 3		
P1 describe the characteristics and sources of information that an organisation needs	**M1** explain the importance to an organisation of effectively collecting, processing and using information	**D1** explain how an organisation could improve the quality of its business information justifying each of their recommendations
P2 describe how information is used for a range of purposes in a selected organisation	**M2** compare, using examples, the usefulness of different tools for processing information to support effective business decision-making	**D2** evaluate tools used for processing information with respect to their support in decision making
P3 describe how information flows between different functional areas in an organisation	**M3** explain the purpose and operation of data mining and predictive modelling	
P4 describe the features and key elements of a management information system, showing where it supports the functional areas of an organisation		
P5 identify the constraints that relate to the use of customer information in an organisation and describe how these may impact on the organisation		
P6 describe different tools used to manage and process information		
Unit 15		
P1 describe the various types of threats to organisations, systems and data	**M1** explain possible security issues which exist within a given system	**D1** describe the possible security issues which exist within a given system identifying the likelihood of each and propose acceptable steps to counter the issues
P2 describe the potential impact of four different threats	**M2** explain the operation and effect of two different threats involving gaining access to information without damage To information	**D2** justify the security policies used in an organisation
P3 describe the countermeasures available to an organisation that will reduce the risk of damage to information	**M3** explain the operation and use of an encryption technique in ensuring security or transmitted information	
P4 describe the countermeasures available to an organisation that will reduce the risk of damage to physical systems		
P5 describe different methods of recovering from a disaster		
P6 describe the tools and policies an organisation can adopt in managing organisational issues in relation to ICT security		
P7 describe how staff contracts and code of conduct can assist the task of ensuring secure systems		

To achieve a pass grade the evidence must show that the learner is able to...	To achieve a merit grade the evidence must show that, in addition to the pass criteria, the learner is able to...	To achieve a distinction grade the evidence must show that, in addition to the pass and merit criteria, the learner is able to...
Unit 34		
P1 describe the social implications, benefits and drawbacks of e-commerce	**M1** explain the potential risks to organisations of committing to an e-commerce system	**D1** evaluate the use of e-commerce in a 'brick and click' organisation that balances e-commerce with a continued high street presence
P2 describe three different and current e-commerce entities	**M2** compare two different payment systems used in e-commerce systems	**D2** justify the choice of security techniques used to protect an e-commerce system
P3 describe the hardware, software and networking technologies involved in e-commerce	**M3** explain how security issues in e-commerce can be overcome	**D3** predict and describe the potential future of e-commerce and its impact on society
P4 describe how e-commerce systems can be promoted and marketed		
P5 describe the security issues in e-commerce		
P6 describe what and how legislation impacts e-commerce systems		
Unit 35		
P1 describe new hardware and software technologies that impact on organisations	**M1** explain the impact of IT developments for an organisation	**D1** make reasoned recommendations about how a particular organisation can take advantage of IT developments
P2 identify the challenges posed to organisations because of IT developments	**M2** explain why organisations modify their activities in response to IT developments	**D2** assess the possible consequences for an organisation in implementing IT-based changes
P3 describe how the internal environment of an organisation has changed due to the changes the external environment brought about by IT developments	**M3** explain how employees and employers are affected by changes in IT	
P4 identify the changes in activity and performance that can arise from adapting organisational activities		
P5 describe ways that organisations can manage their risks when using new IT technology		

Research Skills

Before you start your research project you need to know where to find information and the guidelines you must follow.

Types of information

Primary Sources

Information you have gathered yourself, through surveys, interviews, photos or observation. This information is only as good as the questions and people you ask. You must get permission before you use someone's photo or include an interview in your work.

Secondary Sources

Information produced by somebody else, including information from the internet, books, magazines, databases and television. You need to be sure that your secondary source is reliable if you are going to use the information.

Information Sources

The Internet

The internet is a useful research tool, however, not all the information on the internet is accurate; anyone can set up a webpage, so when using the internet ask yourself if you can trust the information you find.

Acknowledge your source! When quoting from the internet always include author name (if known)/document title/URL web address/date site was accessed.

Books, Magazines and Newspapers

Information in newspapers and magazines is up to date and usually researched thoroughly. Books have a longer shelf life than newspapers so make sure you use the most recent edition.

Broadcast Media

Television and radio broadcast current news stories and the information should be accurate. Be aware that some programmes offer personal opinions as well as facts.

Acknowledge your source! When quoting from books, magazines, journal or papers, always include author name/title of publication/publisher/year of publication.

Plagiarism

Plagiarism is including in your own work extracts or ideas from another source without acknowledging its origins. If you use any material from other sources you must acknowledge it. This includes the work of fellow students.

Storing Information

Keep a record of all the information you gather. Record details of book titles, author names, page references, web addresses (URLs) and contact details of interviewees. Accurate, accessible records will help you acknowledge sources and find information quickly.

Internet Dos and Don'ts

Do ✓

- check information against other sources
- keep a record of where you found information and acknowledge the source
- be aware that not all sites are genuine or trustworthy

Don't ∅

- assume all the information on the internet is accurate and up to date
- copy material from websites without checking whether permission from the copyright holder is required
- give personal information to people you meet on the internet

Communication and employability skills for IT

unit 1

In today's society, employers require an increasing range of skills, including technical and non-technical abilities. Just being competent in a job role and able to perform the tasks required, for example designing a website, is no longer enough. Competition in certain employment areas demands a wider skills-base, which also needs to be supported by a knowledge base and effective communication skills. This means that a website, for example, can be designed, analysed, tested with end-users, evaluated and demonstrated across a range of users by employees at differing levels within an organisation.

Communication and employability skills are now integrated within job roles to ensure that future employees are capable of demonstrating social, professional, technical and personal effectiveness, all of which can be developed and demonstrated within the job role. This unit will introduce you to a range of concepts that will help you to understand and develop your own non-technical soft skills.

By the end of this unit, you will:

So you want to be a...

Helpdesk Support Analyst

My name Jamina Moore
Age 21
Income £17,500

What do you do?

I support a range of end-users with their computing needs. It could involve anything from helping someone carry out a task using a spreadsheet or database, checking out a system fault, changing the toner in a printer or training someone to use a new piece of software.

What does a typical day involve?

As I am 'first–line' support, any user queries come straight to me. I give them support over the telephone, by email or face-to-face. I have to make sure I provide a solution to their problem, either dealing with it myself or passing it over to another team member who may have more experience in that particular area.

How did you get into the job?

I have a BTEC National Diploma for IT Practitioners. I did the Systems Support pathway because I was interested in hardware and networking and knew that I wanted to get a job in this area rather than progressing on to higher education. I was able to do two weeks' work experience and I was very fortunate to be given a placement in this type of role. When I completed my course, the company offered me a trainee role in end-user support.

What training have you had?

The training that I was given was on-the-job practical training. I was given a 'buddy' and they helped me through my first month, introducing me to the systems and procedures. I was also given the opportunity to study a part-time HNC in Computing, which furthered my understanding of computers.

What are the hours like?

The hours are 8:30–4:30, but if we need to do a major upgrade or if there are network problems we occasionally have to do overtime at weekends or in the evenings.

> **"Your communication & interpersonal skills have to be top notch."**

What sort of person makes a good support analyst?

You need to have a genuine passion for computers and a liking and tolerance of end-users. Being in first-line support all day means that your communication skills and interpersonal skills have to be top notch. One minute you could be dealing with a sales advisor and the next it could be the finance manager or even the MD!

What is the pay like?

I started on £14,000 and have now progressed up the pay scale as I have been with the organisation for three years.

What about the future?

My HNC is nearly complete and I'm thinking about moving on to a more professional hardware route and becoming CISCO qualified. I am very happy where I am in this role and the people are always friendly, unless you can't solve their problem!

Grading criteria

The table below shows what you need to do to gain a pass, merit or distinction in this part of the qualification. Make sure you refer back to it when you are completing work so that you can judge whether you are meeting the criteria and what you need to do to fill in gaps in your knowledge or experience.

In this unit there are eight evidence activities that give you an opportunity to demonstrate your achievement of the grading criteria:

To achieve a pass grade the evidence must show that the learner is able to...	To achieve a merit grade the evidence must show that, in addition to the pass criteria, the learner is able to...	To achieve a distinction grade the evidence must show that, in addition to the pass and merit criteria, the learner is able to...
P1 explain why employers value particular employee attributes	**M1** explain and use a specialist IT communication channel effectively	**D1** analyse interpersonal and written communications criticising or justifying particular techniques used
P2 describe potential barriers to effective communication	**M2** explain mechanisms that can be used to reduce the impact of communication barriers	**D2** independently use a personal development plan to undergo a process of identification of skill need and related improvement
P3 demonstrate effective communication-related interpersonal skills	**M3** proofread, review and amend both own and other people's draft documents to produce final versions	
P4 effectively communicate in writing technical information to a specified audience	**M4** explain how individuals can use a knowledge of their learning style to improve their effectiveness in developing new skills or understanding	
P5 use IT tools effectively to aid communications		
P6 describe ways of identifying and meeting development needs		
P7 create and maintain a personal development plan		

1.1 Understand the attributes of employees that are valued by employers

Within the job market there is an ever-growing need for employees who can demonstrate a range of technical, social and transferable skills. The roles that individuals take at work have become more multi-faceted and complex. Employees are expected to be general 'all-rounders' so that they can plan and complete any skills-based tasks they are set, analyse and evaluate what they have done and then communicate this to other employees within the organisation, possibly at different levels.

Key words

Multi-faceted – more than just one. In a job you might be employed to do a range of tasks, such as take part in project work, support a colleague with the development of a website, be involved with general IT support and help train new users in a piece of software

SPECIFIC JOB-RELATED ATTRIBUTES

People are employed for the skills and attributes that they have or could possibly learn during their employment with an organisation. Most job descriptions identify specific skills that are required to meet the criteria of the role, as shown in Figure 1.1.

Think
What skills are required for this web developer's position? Why is it important that a candidate can demonstrate a competency in the 'essential' skills?

Specific job-related attributes can be divided up into a range of categories. Having a knowledge and understanding of these areas may provide a further advantage in terms of being attractive to an employer.

Junior Web Developer

Patterson and Co
16 The Elms
Liveredge Way
Norfolk

Patterson and Co. is a web-based marketing company with a strong client base throughout East Anglia.

We are looking to extend our team to include a junior web developer.

We are looking for an individual who has just completed a vocational qualification, such as a National Diploma or equivalent. We require a good understanding of website development and the use of commercial web page software. We also expect that the individual could demonstrate these skills through a portfolio of designs.

The individual should also be able to demonstrate good communication skills and feel that they could make a positive contribution to the team.

Starting salary of £14,500 to include training.

Please send a curriculum vitae and covering letter to Richard Henson at the above address.

Figure 1.1 Sample job advert

The following job-related attributes will be identified in many job descriptions.

Technical knowledge

- Software – this includes how to use application software, how to install new software and how to configure an operating system.

- Hardware – this encompasses knowing how to set up a new printer on the network, installing a new hard drive and setting up a range of peripheral devices.

- Security – you might be expected to know how to set up a firewall, monitor users on a network and set up passwords for new users.

Working procedures and systems

- Health and safety – this includes being aware of health and safety procedures and legislation, company policies and how to comply with first-aid basics.

- Data protection – you will need to be aware of the implications of the Data Protection Act and know how to keep paper-based and electronic data secure.

- Company policies – companies will expect you to be familiar with their day-to-day policies and procedures and to take responsibility for reading any company manuals or documents that impact upon working conditions.

GENERAL ATTRIBUTES

Alongside specific job-related skills, employers also expect employees to demonstrate a range of general attributes that will enrich their job role.

Planning and organisational skills

These skills are essential if the environment in which you work is very target-driven, and if it is expected that various tasks will be completed by a specific deadline.

Everybody makes plans, for example writing down a list to help you remember items to buy or drawing up an action plan in order to prioritise tasks. Assignment schedules involve identifying when assignments need to be completed and what has to be done to complete them, for instance by carrying out research.

Planning a project might involve collecting feedback from users or customers in order to improve a facility or service. You might also need to be able to look at sets of figures to see whether or not a project is financially viable.

In organisations, planning is crucial because it provides measurable progress steps for the future. Without planning you would not know where you are going or recognise when you have got there.

There are a number of techniques used by organisations to plan, but the way in which you plan will be dependent on a number of factors. These factors revolve around a TROPIC cycle as shown below.

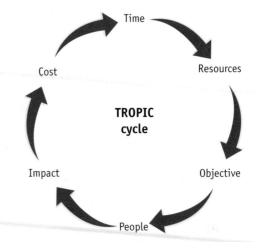

Figure 1.2 Tropic cycle of planning

This means that you need to consider:

- **T**ime – how long the plan is

- **R**esources – what is going to support the plan

- **O**bjective – what the purpose of the plan is

- **P**eople – who is involved with the plan

- **I**mpact – who and what will the plan effect

- **C**ost – how much it is going to cost to implement the plan.

Within an organisation, planning can be carried out over certain periods of time: the short-, medium- or long-term. The table below shows examples of these different types of plan.

Table 1.1 Examples of planning

Types of plan	Period	Example of plan
Short	1–3 years	Introducing computers into a single department
Medium	3–5 years	Ensuring that all departments within the organisation are computerised and networked
Long	5 years+	Expansion and acquiring new premises

As an employee, the ability to demonstrate good planning skills and to manage your own time and resources will be very desirable. An employer will value any experience that involves thinking about tasks, planning ahead and managing resources on an individual and team or group basis.

Time management

The ability to manage your own time is important in any aspect of daily life, but is especially so within an organisational context. Time management skills can range from:

- being able to draw up a schedule of tasks or events and allocate time slots to each

- being able to prioritise certain tasks or events in terms of urgency and pending deadlines

- being able to sequence a variety of tasks or events so that any tasks that are dependent on the completion of previous tasks are taken into consideration and addressed, and the impact of these not being completed is assessed.

Team working

The ability to work as part of a team is essential, as most organisations are very team or department focused. Projects will be set up on a team basis, drawing on the knowledge and skills of individuals. There are a number of studies that have been carried out about the way that teams work, team characteristics and leadership and motivation within teams, including the work carried out by Belbin and Tuckman.

Research tip

Find out more about studies by Belbin or Tuckman. Go to:
- www.belbin.com
- www.cognitivefitness.co.uk/ thinking_styles/articles.html
- www.businessballs.com
- www.chimaeraconsulting.com.

Think What qualities do you feel you could bring to a team situation? What difficulties might you have in working as part of a team? Do you think that it is important to have a plan of activities allocated to team members for any given project? Why do you think this is or is not important?

Verbal and written communication skills

Having good written and verbal communication skills is an essential attribute that is highly valued by employers. Being able to express your thoughts, findings and opinions orally either through a one-to-one conversation, debate, presentation or interview, for example, can demonstrate a level of understanding and confidence in the subject matter.

Written communication skills are also crucial as most employees will be expected to prepare written documents, such as letters, invoices, memorandums or reports. An employee may also be asked to contribute to a newsletter or website article, which would require a good level of written communication skills.

Numeric and creative skills

Some employers expect that employees will be able to demonstrate a certain level of numeric and creative skills. With numeric skills, this may be reinforced by a requirement to hold a GCSE in Mathematics at grade C or above or an equivalent Key Skills qualification in Application of Number.

For certain jobs, creative skills will be important, and these could be demonstrated through a portfolio of work demonstrating website design or illustrative contributions to projects that involve the manipulation of graphics, for example. Creativity is also a thinking skill, which could be demonstrated through the contribution of original thoughts and ideas to a specific project.

> **Think** What examples of your work could you use to demonstrate your creative skills?

ATTITUDES

Attitudes are very personal attributes, which are also very changeable. Your reaction in one situation may be completely different to your reaction in another, depending on the circumstances, the people involved, the task requirements and resources, for example. For an employer, having people with the 'right' attitude is essential to ensure that employees are happy, motivated and productive. Having a positive attitude can influence the people that you work with in a very positive way. On the other hand, a negative attitude tends to generate negativity throughout a team. Within an organisation it is expected that employees will adopt a very professional attitude that may encompass a range of qualities, some of which are outlined below.

Determination

Being able to demonstrate that you have a determined attitude is very important in an organisation. Employers value individuals who can show that they have enough stamina to complete a task and see things through to completion.

Independence

Many job descriptions now make reference to the need to demonstrate an independent approach to working. Although it is expected that you can work well within a team, it may also be necessary to work without supervision and to manage your own time effectively and independently.

Working with integrity

Integrity is an important part of any role, especially a professional one. In some environments it is critical that you can demonstrate how trustworthy you are. Being reliable in your job role is also valued and expected by employers, which means turning up for work on time, ensuring that you meet any deadlines set and being a reliable source of help for other colleagues to call on if needed.

Tolerance

Being able to show a certain level of tolerance of customers, end-users, students and clients is essential. Employers rely on these people to provide their income, so being tolerant of a customer who has a complaint, a student who has not handed work in on time or any other internal situation that requires a tolerant attitude is essential.

Dependable

It is very important that an employer feels that they can depend on you and your contribution to the organisation. Within your job role other people may depend on you within a team. You may have to carry out a task with an outcome that needs to be communicated to others. Meeting targets and delivering the solution on time will be critical to ensure that you meet others' expectations of you.

> **Think** How could you demonstrate attitudes like determination, integrity & dependability to prospective employers?

Problem-solving

Every job role comes with its share of problems. Having the ability to work through and demonstrate good, workable problem-solving techniques will help to ensure that any problems that arise are manageable.

Leadership skills

Are leaders born into the role or can they develop or evolve? Good leaders are inspirational and display visionary qualities, which come more naturally to some people than others. If you feel that you have these skills, try to exploit the qualities that you have for the benefit of yourself and others.

Confidence

Being confident and showing that you are confident is sometimes quite difficult. Confidence can be demonstrated through body language, stance and tone of voice. Employers value confidence as an asset, but being over-confident is not a quality that should always be displayed at work because it could be mistaken for arrogance.

Self-motivation

Motivation is a powerful tool, and being able to motivate yourself when work is getting difficult and tasks seem never-ending is an attitude employers value highly.

Although it may be difficult to display all of these attitudes all of the time, an appreciation that they are required at times and valued by employers will help your employment prospects and increase your effectiveness in being happy within a given task or job role.

ORGANISATIONAL AIMS AND OBJECTIVES

Organisations all function around certain aims and objectives based on their short-, medium- and long-term goals and achievements. The aims and objectives of an organisation vary according to the type of organisation: public, private and charity, for example. They are also dependent on the specific purpose of the organisation, such as to make a profit or to provide a service or product.

General – relevant to all employees

General aims and objectives affect all employees within an organisation and how their role contributes to the organisation's success in meeting these goals. Some of these aims and objectives might include:

- making a profit
- being more competitive in the market
- being more productive and efficient
- meeting sales and production targets
- being a 'greener' organisation
- becoming more ethically aware.

As an employee, you would be expected to support the organisation in meeting these aims and objectives.

Specific – relevant to the role of individuals

Specific aims and objectives are more individually focused and may be linked to specific job roles and tasks. These may be set down in a job description, project briefing, task or system-requirement document or as part of an appraisal/personal development plan.

Promoting organisational brand or image

Every employee has a responsibility to promote their organisation's brand or image. You should ensure that you represent your organisation professionally and positively at all times. This can include using the correct standard templates and letterheads/logos in all correspondence, adhering to company policy on uniform and dress code or simply representing the organisation favourably when enquiries are made by customers or third parties.

EVIDENCE ACTIVITY

P1

1. Produce a short report identifying a range of employee attributes and explain why employers value these. Think about skills, knowledge and interpersonal characteristics. (P1)

1.2 *Understand the principles of effective communication*

Communication is a way of expressing or exchanging ideas and thoughts between one person or group and another. To have effective communication there need to be three main elements: a source, a communication tool and a recipient, as shown below.

Figure 1.3 Elements to enable effective communication

The source generates or initiates the information that is to be sent. Sources of information include human resources (people) and electronic resources (computer systems). The recipient can also be a human or electronic resource.

The type of communication tool used to transmit the information will vary depending on a number of factors, some of which are identified in Figure 1.4. Some communication tools may be more appropriate than others in a particular situation, because of their convenience and/or flexibility. For example, the quickest way to get a response to a question from a person sitting next to you is to use the tool of speech to ask them. However, if this person had a hearing impediment the most effective form might be body language, sign language or a form of written communication.

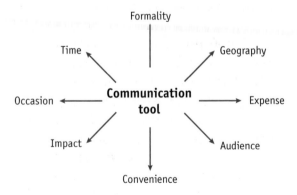

Figure 1.4 Factors determining communication tool use

When considering what communication tool to use, the following factors may be relevant:

- Formality – there are instances when a specific communication tool is required to match the formality of the situation. Written communication can provide more formality, and is suitable to make certain contracts and transactions legally binding, for example birth, marriage and death certificates, employment contracts and the guarantees offered by documents such as receipts.

- Geography – the distance over which the communication has to travel will influence the type of tool to be used. It would not be feasible to shout over a distance of ten miles, so the telephone or email will probably be used instead.

- Expense – different communication tools have different costs. Depending on the frequency and priority of the communication, costs could range from a few pence (the price of a stamp) to hundreds of thousands of pounds (setting up and coordinating global teleconferencing facilities).

- Audience – the audience or target group will influence the communication tool used to express information. Within an organisation you might chat informally to a colleague, email a team leader and send a memorandum to a whole department.

- Convenience – some communication tools are more convenient to use than others. Sending an email may be more convenient for you than writing and posting a letter; however, to a non-technical individual, sending a letter may be more convenient than trying to learn how to send an email.

- Impact – the impression that needs to be created can influence the choice of communication tool. It is unlikely that an employer would send an email to a potential employee offering them a contract of employment, for example.

- Occasion – this can determine the type of communication tool to be used, for example internal meetings are usually organised using email, rather than by writing and sending letters. A meeting with a business colleague might result in the use of physical communication, such as a handshake.

- Time – a communication tool may be selected based on how long it takes to transmit the information, for example it might be necessary to send a document by fax rather than post because of the urgency of the information.

GENERAL COMMUNICATION SKILLS

There is a range of general communication issues that should be considered to ensure communication is as effective as possible. Some of these issues are explored below.

Cultural differences

Across the world there is a whole array of different languages, delivery methods, cultures, customs and traditions that can impact on general communication. It is important that within organisations there is a general awareness and respect of cultural differences. This could be demonstrated by:

- acknowledging a range of festivals, ceremonies and important dates throughout the year from different religions and cultures

- being respectful of employees' religions and cultures, such as the wearing of head coverings or the need to pray at certain times of the day.

Figure 1.5 Respecting employees' religions and cultures is very important

Adapting content and style to audience

Being able to adapt and customise the way you communicate to meet the needs of your audience is an essential skill. Modulating your voice, using appropriate terminology (technical versus non-technical) and the format of the communication are all important features that should be considered when communicating with people.

Modulating your voice is very important, particularly when communicating with a large audience. By emphasising certain words and phrases and changing the speed and tone of your voice, key points can be emphasised. In addition, modulating your voice can help you to keep the audience's attention – people often switch off when something is delivered in a very monotonous tone!

The use of terminology should be considered to ensure that it is appropriate for the needs of your audience. Delivering a very technical presentation to non-technical users would create a barrier to understanding the content of the message being delivered. Delivering a very low-level presentation to highly technical end-users may also create a barrier as they might lose interest in the message being communicated.

The format of the communication should also be adapted to meet the needs of the audience. For example, some content might be best presented in a written format, such as a formal report to present sales figures to the sales director.

Providing accurate information

Relaying information that has relevance, validity and is current is essential, especially in certain situations, for example if you are delivering information of a statistical nature that reflects the current situation or finances of an organisation. Ensuring that all information is consistent (particularly facts or statistics) is important because it gives the audience confidence in what is being delivered.

Differentiating between facts and opinion

In some situations it is important to remain impartial when delivering certain information. This might mean differentiating between fact and opinion. For example, you might be asked to deliver some end-user training on a new piece of software. In terms of meeting the end-users' and the organisation's needs, you may believe that the software you are demonstrating is first-class. However, you may also believe that it is not the best value for money that the company could have purchased. In your presentation, you need to distinguish between:

- Fact – the software is user friendly, functional and has good built-in support tools.
- Opinion – after using the software, you think that, for the money spent, the organisation should have purchased a different brand.

As a trainer you would need to remain impartial and deliver the facts and not your personal opinions.

Techniques for engaging audience interest

There are a number of different techniques that can be used to capture audience interest, ranging from changing your intonation (the tone of your voice) to the use of technology to enhance the way that information is presented and delivered, for example by using multimedia elements or animations in presentations.

Figure 1.6 An interested audience: what you are aiming for!

Question and answer sessions

Question and answer sessions can be very effective in certain environments. If you want to gather a range of opinions from people following on from a presentation or demonstration, you could take questions from the audience. This would allow the audience to clarify certain issues, confirm the information and knowledge presented and also provide opportunities for further discussion. Question and answer sessions can also be used in very focused environments to establish facts and confirm understanding. A good example of this would be a lecturer asking a direct question in class relating to a topic just taught.

INTERPERSONAL SKILLS

Interpersonal skills are very important when people interact with each other. These skills include the use of body language, gestures and cues and the way that verbal exchanges are made in terms of tone of voice, types of question and expressions used.

Methods for communicating interpersonally

There are a number of ways of communicating interpersonally, including verbal exchanges, signing and lip reading. Verbal exchanges are any form of dialogue between two or more people. This method of communicating could be used when negotiating an agreement, enquiring about directions, debating a topic or simply greeting a friend, for example. If a person has an impairment such as a visual or hearing impairment, different methods of interpersonal communication may be necessary. For example, sign language is used to communicate with a person or people that have impaired hearing.

Techniques and cues

There are a number of techniques and cues that can be used as part of interpersonal communication. Body language conveys information and supports verbal communication: the way that you stand, move or fold your hands and arms during a conversation all provide clues about how you are feeling. For example, rubbing your chin during a conversation could indicate that you are thinking about what is being discussed. The tone of your voice can also emphasise an emotion or thought during conversation. A high pitched tone, for example, could indicate that you are shocked, surprised, angry or stressed.

In electronic communications, the use of 'smileys', as shown in Figure 1.7, or capitalisation of text in emails can be used to draw the attention of an audience or indicate your thoughts.

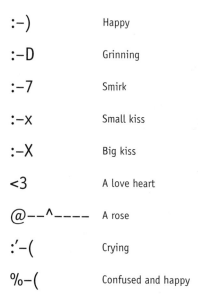

:-)	Happy
:-D	Grinning
:-7	Smirk
:-x	Small kiss
:-X	Big kiss
<3	A love heart
@--^----	A rose
:'-(	Crying
%-(	Confused and happy

Figure 1.7 Smileys

Positive and negative language

Language can be both positive and negative. Positive and negative effects can be conveyed through tone of voice, facial expressions or body language, for example, smiling when talking to someone contributes to a positive language. Word choice can also be positive or negative, as can the way in which feedback is given. An example of this is the way that messages might be communicated at an appraisal:

- Positive – You have contributed very well to the team over the year, showing excellent leadership qualities; to support you in this we feel that we should provide further management training to strengthen your people skills.

- Negative – Your people skills are not as good as they could be so we are going to send you on a management course to improve these.

Paying attention and active engagement

There are a number of ways to identify whether somebody is engaged in interpersonal communication. They may nod in agreement, smile and use their hands to acknowledge a point of information. Some people summarise or repeat key words to show that they have paid attention and it can be helpful to use these techniques to create an effective relationship with those you are communicating with.

Understanding barriers

There are a number of barriers to interpersonal communication, for example background noise that can block out what you are trying to communicate. Distractions of any type can also act as a barrier, for example, when a speaker does something unintentionally that distracts the audience and draws attention away from what they are saying. Think about the effect of a speaker tapping on a table, shuffling or generally fidgeting.

Types of question

Questions are a good way of gathering information from people. Questions can be categorised by type: open, closed and probing. An open question allows for an open-ended answer, rather than a simple 'yes' or 'no'. Examples of open questions include 'what do you think about …' or 'how did you find …' and these will encourage more descriptive responses. A closed question usually leads to a 'yes' or 'no' answer, for example 'Did you watch …. last night?' A probing question is structured to get as much detail as possible for an investigation or research.

Appropriate speeds of response

The appropriate speed of response will very much depend on the source of the initial communication – what was used and how it was delivered. For example, if you are communicating with somebody face-to-face the speed of response will be almost immediate, with further verbal exchanges or a nod to confirm agreement. With written communication, a wider range of speeds of response are open to you and it is important to judge what would be appropriate in terms of the particular situation.

EVIDENCE ACTIVITY

P3

You have been asked to attend an interview at TEY Industries for the post of Trainee Web Designer. As part of the interview process you have been asked to give a presentation on the importance of interpersonal skills in a technical role. In preparation for the interview you will have to prepare 15 slides with accompanying notes pages. In addition you will be delivering the presentation as part of your interview to the IT Manager and Web Design Team Leader.

You will be expected to engage in role-play for the interview situation and you may be recorded as part of the evidence to demonstrate your effectiveness in terms of communication-related interpersonal skills. (P3)

COMMUNICATION IN WRITING

Written communication is important for a number of reasons, including:

- to act as an instructional framework by providing direction to individuals, users, employees and organisations about policies, procedures and guidelines

- to allow people to convey messages in a variety of mediums such as letters, fax, email, agendas, reports, minutes, etc.

- to provide a warranty or assurance, in some cases formalising or legalising verbal consents. Filling in an application form identifies and provides assurances of the knowledge and skills of the applicant. Producing a curriculum vitae provides a written confirmation of ability and suitability for a particular task. A receipt is a warranty, verifying the sale of an item. Certificates verify an achievement in a particular area, such as qualifications, or simply birth, marriage or death

- to give a structure or framework to support other forms of communication. It promotes a more formal approach to conveying messages.

Following organisational guidelines and procedures

Within an organisation there are a number of organisational guidelines and procedures that need to be followed. To ensure that these are adhered to by employees they should be in a written format, such as a manual or file that can be easily accessed either electronically or as a hard copy. Typical guidelines and procedures could include:

- health and safety
- codes of conduct
- policies on using ICT or other working practices
- disciplinary procedures.

Identifying and conveying key messages in writing

Written documents vary in terms of style and layout. Each document type has its own set of criteria that makes it unique. Some documents that have their own unique styling include:

- letters
- faxes
- email.

Letters

Letters are one of the most common forms of written communication, although email is now used instead in many situations. The style of a letter will vary depending on the sender, recipient and subject matter. However, the overall framework of a letter will stay the same.

The identifier includes the details of the sender and recipient, such as name and address, date, reference codes and identification of who the letter is for. The introduction should provide a short overview of the content and also set the tone for the remainder of the letter. The main section of the letter contains the bulk of the information. The content should be set out clearly, ensuring that the subject matter is factual and relevant to the audience. The closure section signs off the letter and informs the recipient of any other documents that are also being sent. The recipient will expect additional documents if Enc. (Enclosure) appears at the end of the letter. In the example on page 26, the additional enclosure will be the £85.00 cheque.

Faxes

Faxes can be used to transmit information electronically from one destination to another. They are used when email is not available, if there is a need for a more formal method of transmitting information or the need for instant confirmation. Some fax messages are sent using a standard template that incorporates an organisation or user logo and standard letterhead, although a fax can just be a hand-written document, drawing, graphic, photograph or any other form of written communication.

Mr Richard Hawthorn   Identifiers
13 The Close
Hickering
NR1 234

Mr Martyn Crane
2 Dunn Square
Fleeting
IP21 345
19 April 2007

Reference: 2DD-YPO-1223

Dear Mr Crane

Application to join the East Anglia Interactive Computing Group   The introduction

After reading the advertisement in 'Buzz Computing' I would like to subscribe for a twelve-month period to your interactive computing group.

I feel that I could contribute to your group in a number of ways. Firstly I have an extensive knowledge of hardware and software. I am also a keen programmer and a software enthusiast.   Content

I enclose a cheque for £85.00 in respect of twelve months subscription to your computing group, and I hope that you accept my application.
I look forward to hearing from you in the near future.

Yours faithfully

Richard Hawthorn   Closure
Computing Enthusiast
Enc.

Figure 1.8 Framework of a letter

Using correct grammar and spelling

When you are communicating in writing it is important to make sure it is correct in terms of language, grammar, punctuation and spelling. Poor spelling and grammar can make it more difficult to understand what is being communicated, and do not create a good impression with the recipient.

Structuring writing into a logical framework

The appropriate framework for a piece of writing will very much depend on the type of document and the target audience. Some documents have their own unique style and layout, for example reports, agendas and memorandums as shown on the right.

Memorandum

To:

From:

CC:

Date:

Re:

Body of text would be displayed here

Figure 1.9 Memorandum structure

Identifying relevant information in written communications

There are a number of ways of identifying relevant information within a written document, depending on the type of document. References might be made to a specific page number within a contents page or summary document. Particular information may also be formatted in some way to distinguish it from other text, for example by changing the font style or size. Additionally, you could highlight or underline certain text or paragraphs, annotate or make comments to draw the user to key sections within the document.

Reviewing and proofreading own written work

Reviewing and proofreading is essential before submitting a completed document. This will give you an opportunity to amend the content, change the formatting, insert new or additional features and check the relevancy and accuracy of the material. This process can be supported by a range of tools offered within any word-processing or standard applications package.

Conveying alternative viewpoints

Depending on the context and purpose of a document, it might be essential to convey alternative viewpoints, especially if the document is research- or theory-based. To remain objective it is important to gather a range of viewpoints from different sources so that an opinion or justified reasoning can be applied to make a more informed decision. For example, if an organisation wants to upgrade its IT provision it might commission a report that considers a range of different suppliers and hardware and software options. The report would need to use a range of different sources to identify the best replacement.

Reviewing and editing documents created by others

This can be done in a number of ways. If the document has been created electronically, it can be highlighted, annotated, comments can be added and text can be crossed through using the strike-through function. If the document is being reviewed manually the same principles also apply, but hard copies of the document will need to be shared.

Note-taking

Note-taking is an important skill, which you will use at meetings, seminars and training sessions. You may later need to write up your notes so that they can be shared with other members of your team, so it is important that you make clear notes about the main points covered. You can also use notes to prepare the content of a document, for example by summarising the evidence that you want to include.

Research tip

The Cornell Note-taking System offers a format for taking notes. Use an internet search engine to find out more.

EVIDENCE ACTIVITY

P4 – M3

1. Produce a technical information leaflet that could be used by IT practitioners working within an end-user environment. The leaflet, which should include diagrams, should be based on different types of networks and network topologies. (P4)

2. When you have prepared a draft copy of your leaflet, print out a version that you can review. Annotate it to show amendments that you want to make and highlight any mistakes that need to be corrected, for example in spelling, grammar or punctuation. Work with other group members to help them check their work – you will need to show evidence of the suggestions you have made to other people. (M3)

**LEARNING ZONE
DEESIDE COLLEGE**

- Sharing data – information can be transferred to multiple users, giving people access to the same shared information, through attached files, graphics, hyperlinks and moving images.

- Ease of use – once familiar with some of the basic functions of an email package, it is very easy to send and receive email and user-friendly (because it is icon driven).

- Recording communication – users can keep a historical record of messages that have been sent and received. Messages can be saved into different formats, updated and printed out if required.

The disadvantages of using email are mainly related to technical and security issues, such as:

- Spamming – unwanted messages sent by advertisers, third parties and unknown users.

- Routing – email is not always sent directly from A to B; it can be routed to other destinations before it finally reaches the receiver/s. This can mean that more time is taken before the message reaches its destination, there are more opportunities for the message to be breached and intercepted by a third party, and a message can also become distorted or lost.

- Security – email can be intercepted easily unless some sort of encryption has been applied to the message.

- Confidentiality – because email can get lost, intercepted or distorted, it is often not appropriate to send confidential messages in this way.

Specialist channels

There are a range of specialist communication channels that can be used to relay information, including blogs, vlogs, podcasts and video conferencing. The development of these new technologies has provided opportunities for newer and more innovative ways of delivering information.

A blog (or web log) is an electronic account or diary that provides commentary on a particular topic or issue. Blogs are interactive websites that allow other people to read and leave feedback on the content the blog's author has created. A vlog (or video log) is essentially a blog that includes video footage.

Podcasts are digital media files containing audio and/or video that are broadcast over the internet, and can then be played back on portable media players and computer systems.

Figure 1.10 An internet podcast network [source: www.thepodcastnetwork.com]

Think There has been a growing trend for organisations and individuals to use podcasting. Find some examples of podcasts on the internet. What are some of their best and worst features?

Video conferencing has been in existence for a number of years, and has been used to connect academic and medical institutes across the world, as well as a whole range of other organisations that need to collaborate simultaneously. Video conferencing can be used to broadcast a range of types of information, either via a large screen that can be viewed by audiences or individual screens that can be viewed simultaneously by individuals.

EVIDENCE ACTIVITY

M1

You were offered the role of Trainee Web Designer at TEY Industries. Part of your job specification is to produce a weekly electronic newsletter that is posted on the company website. The topic for next week's newsletter is specialist IT communication channels.

You have been asked by your team leader to carry out some research on the following specialist IT communication channels:

- blogs
- vlogs
- podcasts.

As part of the research you are expected to engage with some of these technologies and demonstrate an understanding of how they work and how they can be created. In addition to the research you are expected to produce an electronic newsletter that explains some of the features and uses of each of the three specialist IT communication channels. (M1)

Benefits and disadvantages

There are both advantages and disadvantages of using ICT to communicate. In some situations, ICT can be more effective and efficient in communicating information. For example, an email can be received instantly and one message can be sent to multiple users, saving time as it avoids the need to retype and resend. Using ICT can also be more cost effective because a document can be sent for free or for the cost of a phone call if sending a fax. Information can also be created and sent more professionally using a standard template.

Some of the disadvantages of using ICT include the initial investment cost of purchasing the necessary hardware and software. In addition, there are time and cost issues in training users to use ICT effectively. There are also issues concerning security in terms of transmitting and storing the information.

SOFTWARE

The following are examples of some of the most commonly-used software today.

Word processing

Word processing software allows you to input text and numeric information, and to use this to create and format documents using a range of design functions and features, including a variety of fonts and formatting options. The software will allow you to use a predefined template, or to design and customise a document from the beginning. Most packages allow you to import other documents, graphics or pictures to enhance your documents.

Research tip

Microsoft produces some of the most commonly used communications software. Visit http://office.microsoft.com to find out more about their products.

Presentation package software

Presentation packages provide a whole range of features that allow you to create and edit professional presentations and slides, enabling the user to:

- customise slide backgrounds
- set the transitions between slides, determining the way content appears (e.g. dissolving in)
- control the speed of slide transitions
- automatically time the length that each slide stays on screen
- create links to other applications or the internet.

Presentations can be created from a blank slide, a design template or from the AutoContent Wizard, as shown in Figure 1.11.

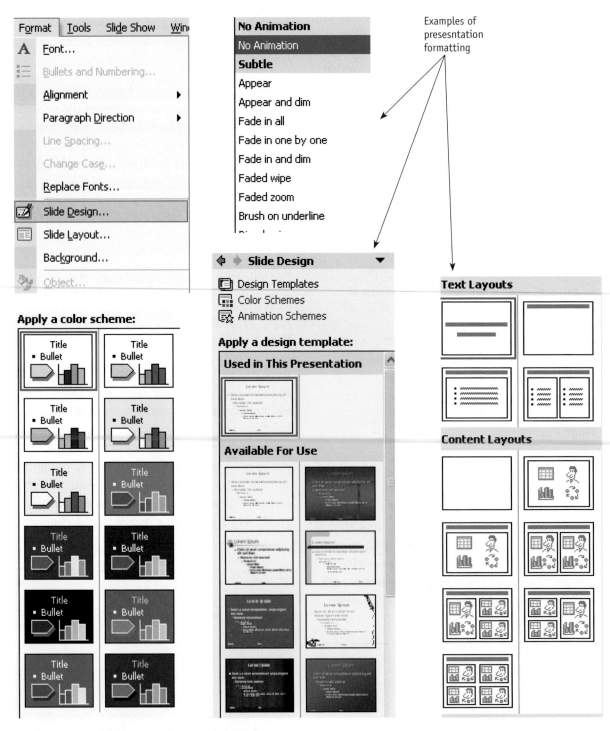

Fig 1.11 Ways of creating a presentation slide

There are a number of ways in which presentation slides can be formatted. The actual design of the slide can be changed and design templates can be added. Colour and animation schemes can be changed and applied.

In addition, the slide layout can be formatted to display other content in a variety of ways. Inserting text, pictures and charts can easily be achieved by using one of the many text and content layouts, where an individual slide can be divided into any one or all of these contents.

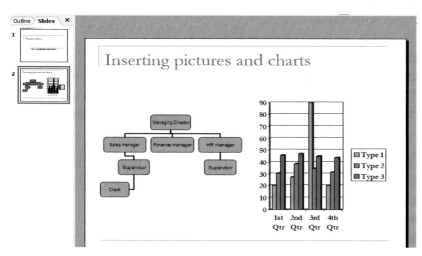

Figure 1.12 Using pictures and charts

Email software

The choice of email software will depend on the range of functions and features that a user requires and whether email is going to be used by an individual on a stand-alone machine, or by a number of users across a network.

Specialist software

There are a large number of people who require specialist hardware or software to interact with ICT. The range of ICT technologies available is extensive, and there are a number of organisations that are committed to providing either hardware or software to users with a sensory impairment, limited mobility or a language disability. In addition, certain people may have a particular need as a result of an illness, accident or general learning disability. These conditions can affect motor control, dexterity, use of limbs and attention span.

There is a range of specialist software available to support different learner needs, for example text to speech software to convert text documents into natural speech, such as NaturalReader, and software to support people with dyslexia, for example, Wordshark.

SOFTWARE TOOLS

There is a range of software tools available that can help people to communicate effectively. These include proofing tools, such as spellcheckers and thesauruses, as well as other tools that are integrated in software packages.

Proofing tools

There are a number of proofing tools that can be used to support users in the accurate design and presentation of documents. Word processing can save time and reduce the incidence of spelling, grammatical and formatting errors, as these tools are available to highlight mistakes and automatically make adjustments and corrections, for example by using the spellchecker and thesaurus.

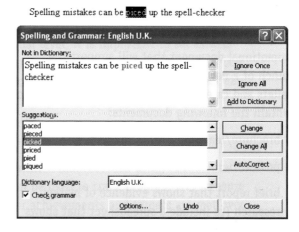

Figure 1.13 Using a spellchecker

A thesaurus can be used to find an alternative word that is more appropriate, for example the word 'support', as shown in Figure 1.14 overleaf, could be changed to any of the synonyms suggested by the thesaurus software.

METHODS OF ADDRESSING NEEDS

Once individuals' needs have been identified, the next step is to find ways in which these can be addressed. There are a number of ways of meeting needs, and the mechanism used will depend on the complexity of the need and what the individual's requirements are.

Job shadowing

This involves working alongside and observing the job role of another individual or individuals to gain a more practical understanding of how certain tasks are carried out and what procedures are involved in other people's roles.

Formal courses or training

To meet some development needs, it may be valuable for an individual to attend a specific course or programme of learning to develop their knowledge, skills base and understanding. These may either be external courses run by other organisations, or in-house training that the employee's organisation runs itself.

Team meetings

These provide the opportunity for information and good practice to be shared among individuals.

Attending events

Attending events and conferences allows you to learn from more experienced people, by attending seminars and meeting colleagues. You are likely to be expected to share your findings from the event with others in your organisation.

The mechanisms that will be used to address a particular need will be tailored to the requirements of the individual and also to what the identified need is. Sometimes a range of methods will be used over a period of time, but in other situations attending one training session or being involved in a single team meeting might be enough to address the need. The identified need might require on-going monitoring to ensure that, as various stages are reached and addressed, further needs are also recognised and mechanisms put in place to support them.

LEARNING STYLES

Personal development can be enhanced by the identification of an individual's learning style. Individuals all learn at different rates and demonstrate a range of traits and characteristics that can be classified as a particular learning style.

A number of studies have been carried out that recognise different ways and styles of learning. These studies help to identify why people learn in a certain way, how to encourage learning, categorisations of learning and how learning can be enhanced depending upon a particular learning style.

In addition, various studies and informal questioning techniques have been developed to allow individuals to identify what type of learner they are and what type of learning category they fall into.

Examples of systems

There are a range of systems that represent different learning styles, for example: active/reflective, sensing/intuitive, visual/verbal, sequential/global.

Active learners understand new information by doing something practical with it – they are keen to experiment and try new things. Reflective learners tend to ponder and think about the task in hand before acting. Sensing learners like to learn the facts and solve problems using established methods. On the other hand, intuitive learners are more innovative in their approach to discovering new information and do not like tasks that relate to lots of memorisation of tasks or routine calculations. Visual learners understand and relate to information that is presented in a visual or graphical format, as opposed to verbal learners who relate more to written down or spoken information. Finally, sequential learners prefer a stepped and logical approach to learning while global learners tend to gather information and absorb material more holistically.

Identification of preferred style

There are a number of ways that individuals can identify what their learning style is. There are a range of assessments and tests that can be taken to identify what type of person you are, how you learn and what characteristics dictate your own personal learning style. Through a series of questions and scenarios, a learning style can be identified based upon the individual's response.

Research tip

Visit www.support4learning.org.uk/education/learning_styles.cfm to find out more about your preferred learning style.

How to benefit from knowing your learning style

Knowing your learning style can support you in identifying your key strengths and weaknesses. For example, if you find that you are a visual learner you will know that you prefer information to be communicated to you in a graphical format, for example as a chart, graph or picture. This also helps you to play to your strengths, so when taking notes you could produce a mind-map instead of simply writing down notes.

Understanding how other people's learning styles impact on team working

Individuals may behave in a certain way because of their learning style. In a team situation this could impact positively or negatively. There might be a number of individuals within a team who display a range of characteristics, for example:

- manager – someone that takes charge to manage the group
- listener – sits back and takes on board other people's ideas
- organiser – arranges and organises the tasks and activities.

If people do not have an awareness of other people's differences and their learning styles, members of the team might feel resentful that activities and tasks have been organised for them, or that somebody has assumed the role of a team leader. On the other hand, in some situations, having a range of individuals with different learning styles in a group can be a good combination and motivate the team into action. However, having too many similar learning styles within a group could cause conflict, especially if there are only single-role responsibilities.

Research tip

Test your own learning styles at www.bbc.co.uk/keyskills/extra/module1/1.shtml.

EVIDENCE ACTIVITY

M4

You have been asked to deliver a personal development session for new employees that join the company. These sessions are designed to inspire and motivate new employees as they go off into their assigned jobs.

The session that you will be running is based on 'learning styles'.

Prepare and deliver a short presentation that covers a range of the following points:

- what learning styles are
- how to recognise your own learning style
- how to use your learning style to develop skills, knowledge and acquire a better understanding of tasks.

The presentation should contain at least 10–15 slides with notes pages and be delivered within a 15 minute time-frame. (M4)

Computer systems

unit 2

Most organisations use computer systems to help in the day-to-day management of their business. These systems need to be set up, configured and maintained. As computers have become more powerful, the complexity of computer systems has increased, so there is a need for knowledgeable IT practitioners to undertake this work.

This unit will help you to learn about setting up, maintaining and tailoring computer systems to meet a user's needs. Computer equipment may need to be upgraded or new peripherals, such as printers or scanners, added. Operating systems and application software may need patching to fix a problem or to add an enhancement. Latest versions of security software may need to be installed. The areas covered by the unit will be of value to all, regardless of whether you intend to become a desktop support technician, programmer, network engineer or systems analyst.

IT practitioners may be asked to advise on the purchase of new computer systems. Modern software makes increasing demands of the hardware needed to run it. Therefore, practitioners need to keep up to date with the latest developments in both hardware and software. They also need to be aware of the tools available to protect systems and keep them secure.

In this unit, you will:

So you want to be a...

Support Analyst

My name James Stimpson
Age 28
Income £24,000

What does a support analyst do?

I support the company's desktop computers, laptops and mainframe computer

What are your day to day responsibilities?

I set up all the new desktop computers and laptops. I maintaining them and I am, responsible for fault-finding if they develop problems. I do some software support, particularly spreadsheets. I also run SQL queries on the mainframe.

What qualifications did you need?

After completing my GCSEs, I went to college to complete a BTEC National Diploma in IT Applications. I wanted to take a practical route into the industry because I like to be 'hands on'. Some of my colleagues have degrees but there are a lot of IT certifications that can be taken and a lot of different routes into the industry.

What training have you had?

I got my first computer when I was ten years old. I have always upgraded and maintained my own PC and I enjoy using new gadgets and technology. My first job was as a mainframe operator. I did that for six years, and then moved into PC support. I have been on a number of training courses, but the most important training has been 'on the job'.

> **"Problem-solving abilities and an interest in new technologies are important"**

What are the hours like?

I usually work from 9am to 6pm, but sometimes the company needs me to work later into the evening. Sometimes we need to work at the weekend, when the office is quiet and we don't have to worry about taking the system down for a few hours. If I work extra hours I get paid overtime. It doesn't happen often but you have to be prepared to be flexible.

How good is the pay?

When I first stated work, pay was fairly low; about £12,000, but it has gradually improved and I now earn double that amount. I could earn a lot more if I was prepared to work in London or work as a contractor, but I like the company and the people I work with so for now I am more than happy top stay where I am.

What qualities do you think are important for your job?

You need a lot patience and good people skills. Obviously you need good technical knowledge as well as the ability to solve problems and prioritise your workload. It really helps to have an interest in new technologies, which luckily I do.

How do you see your career progressing?

I still have a lot to learn and with further training and after gaining some more on the job experience I would like to get more involved in the networking side of things.

Grading criteria

The table below shows what you need to do to gain a pass, merit or distinction in this part of the qualification. Make sure you refer back to it when you are completing work so that you can judge whether you are meeting the criteria and what you need to do to fill in gaps in your knowledge or experience.

In this unit there are three evidence activities that give you an opportunity to demonstrate your achievement of the grading criteria:

page 58   **P1, D1**

page 63   **P2, M2, P3, P4**

page 71   **P5, M3, M1, D2**

To achieve a pass grade the evidence must show that the learner is able to...	To achieve a merit grade the evidence must show that, in addition to the pass criteria, the learner is able to...	To achieve a distinction grade the evidence must show that, in addition to the pass and merit criteria, the learner is able to...
P1 explain the function of the system unit components and how they communicate	**M1** explain and implement the installation and configuration of an additional or replacement device	**D1** evaluate at least three specifications for commercially available computer systems and justify the one most suitable for use in a given situation
P2 describe the purpose, features and functions of two different operating systems	**M2** compare the features and functions of two different operating systems	**D2** justify the considerations for selection in the upgrade of an existing computer system
P3 demonstrate the operation and explain the use of two different software utilities	**M3** explain the effect of the software maintenance activities carried out on the performance of a computer system	
P4 describe the range of available utility software		
P5 undertake routine maintenance tasks in relation to a PC		

2.1 *Understand the hardware components of computer systems*

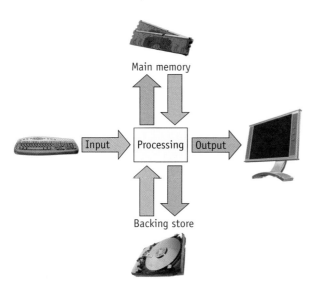

Figure 2.1 The components of a computer system

Regardless of their size, most computers perform similar basic functions:

- Input – data and instructions can be input into the computer using a number of different devices, such as a keyboard, mouse, scanner or microphone.

- Main memory – data and instructions are temporarily held in main memory before and after processing. This is sometimes referred to as 'temporary storage'.

- Processing – the central processing unit (CPU) takes the data and instructions from main memory and processes them in some way, for example, producing an image or a text document, generating a sound or opening a web browser.

- Output – once processing has taken place, data can be output, for example to a printer, as sound through speakers or to be viewed on a screen monitor.

- Storage – some information may need to be stored for use at a later date. This is sometimes referred to as 'auxiliary' storage. Common forms of storage include hard disks, USB memory sticks (sometimes known as pen drives) and CD-ROMs.

SYSTEM UNIT COMPONENTS

Processors and options

Computers contain a number of processors that perform different tasks, but the term 'processor' usually refers to the main processor, otherwise known as a microprocessor, CPU or chip.

The microprocessor is an integrated circuit (IC) that is located on the motherboard. It controls the activities of the computer by interacting with other components that are on or attached to the motherboard. The microprocessor executes a series of programmed instructions with four steps: fetch, decode, execute and write back. This process involves fetching program instructions and data from memory, decoding them, executing them and then writing the result back to memory. This process is covered in greater detail in Unit 9.

The speed of the processor is measured by a system clock as a number of operations or cycles per second. Modern processors normally operate at speeds measured in gigahertz (GHz). One gigahertz is 1,000,000,000 cycles per second!

> ### Key words
> Integrated circuit – a small electronic circuit
> Motherboard – the central circuit board of a computer

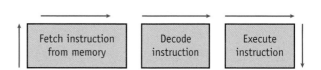

Figure 2.2 The fetch execute cycle

When building or upgrading a computer system, it is vital to ensure that the microprocessor is compatible with your motherboard.

Modern desktop processors

Two companies dominate the computer microchip market: Intel and AMD.

Table 2.1: Intel® and AMD microchips

Intel	AMD
Celeron® – this is a cost-effective processor using proven technology for home and small office applications.	Semperon™ – competes with Intel Celeron D.
Pentium® 4 – the series was launched in late 2000 and retired in 2006. It was the first major redesign since the launch of the Pentium Pro in 1995. It uses hyper-threading technology that allows the processor to operate more efficiently when multiple tasks are running.	Athlon™ 64 – competes with Intel Pentium 4.
Pentium® D – a series of chips was introduced in 2005 using two Pentium 4 processors on a single chip. This allows multiple tasks to be split across the two processors, giving improved performance over single processor chips.	Athlon™ 64 × 2 – first AMD dual-core processor.
Core™ 2 Duo – a new series of dual processors using several new technologies to save power and increase processor performance.	Athlon™ 64 FX – aimed at gamers. Dual-core from FX-60 onward.

Key words

Dual-core processor – a dual-core processor has two processors on the same chip handling data simultaneously, improving efficiency

Modern laptop processors

Some laptops contain desktop processors. These are likely to use more power, reducing battery life and generating more heat than processors designed specifically for laptop use.

Table 2.2 Laptop processors

Intel	AMD
Pentium® M	Mobile Athlon™ XP-M
Celeron® M	Mobile Athlon™ 64
Mobile Pentium® 4 and 4M	Mobile Semperon™
Core™ Duo and Core™ 2 Duo processors	Turion™ 64
	Turion™ 64 × 2 Duo Core

The system case

Most of the component parts of a computer system fit into a system case. There are a number of different styles of computer case available, including desktop, tower and mini-tower designs.

Figure 2.3 Different types of case – desktop and tower

It is important to consider the needs of the user when purchasing the case. Will the computer sit on a desk or under it? Some cases are designed to have a small 'footprint', meaning that they take up less space on a desk than a standard desktop computer. If you choose a small footprint case, you will need to consider carefully the form factor of the motherboard and ensure that all your components will fit in the case. The amount of equipment you need to house inside the case may determine the size of case you choose. It is also important to consider the position of the power button and the accessibility of USB connectors.

Key words

Form factor – the physical size and shape of a device. This term is frequently used in discussions about computer cases and motherboards

Cases are usually purchased with a power supply unit (PSU) and a pack of blanking plates, screws and mounts. The screws are used to hold devices, such as network cards or CR-ROM, drives in place. Mounts support the motherboard in the case. Blanking plates are used to cover holes in the rear of the case.

The motherboard

Figure 2.4 A motherboard

The motherboard (or system board) is situated within the computer case. All of the essential components that are involved in making a PC work correctly, including the processor, are either on the motherboard or connected to it. It performs a number of functions:

- provides connectivity between the components and the microprocessor so that they can communicate with one another

- distributes power at the correct voltages from the power supply to all devices that require it

- provides connectors for external devices, such as keyboards and mice

- contains external ports for connecting video, printers, etc.

- contains expansion slots for attaching additional devices, such as network interface cards, modems, soundcards, etc.

- has slots for RAM and an area for plugging in hard drives, CD-ROMs, etc.

Currently the ATX form factor is the most common form factor for PC motherboards.

Research tip

There are a large number of other form factors for motherboards. Familiarise yourself with the form factors that are available and have been produced in the past. A useful starting point for this research is www.motherboards.org.

Choosing a motherboard

Replacing the motherboard is a common upgrade that can be made to a computer. However, a number of questions need to be answered before making a purchase.

- What will the computer be used for? Will it need to do heavy-duty processing, such as game playing, scientific calculations or video editing?

- Are the processor and memory (RAM) compatible with the motherboard? This can be checked by going to the motherboard manufacturer's website. The purchase of both motherboard and processor need to be considered together.

**LEARNING ZONE
DEESIDE COLLEGE**

- What features are associated with the chipset (a component on the motherboard)? The chipset determines a number of essential features of the computer, such as the type and speed of the processor, the type and amount of memory that can be installed and additional features, such as whether integrated graphics and sound are included. Knowing these features may help to differentiate between otherwise similar motherboards.

- Is the computer to be used for multimedia applications? Many motherboards come with integrated sound. If it will be used for this purpose, it is important that the motherboard includes a PCI Express slot to take a graphics card.

- If you want to attach peripheral devices, how many USB2 ports are there? Do you need FireWire?

- Will the motherboard fit in your existing case?

BIOS

The BIOS (Basic Input and Output System) chip is situated on the motherboard of a PC and is vitally important to the computer's operation. It can usually be found by looking for a chip near to the processor with a sticker or text on it. It is usually a Flash memory chip (this means that the BIOS can be upgraded using software, rather than having to replace the chip).

The BIOS boots the computer. When the computer is switched on, its first action is to copy itself into memory. It always copies itself to the same location in memory. The processor then begins to run the BIOS instructions. This is known as the booting process. It completes a power-on test (POST) to ensure that all components are working. It checks to see that all the devices listed in CMOS are present and working. CMOS is a complementary metal-oxide semiconductor chip that contains a setup program that stores information about the date, time, hard drive and memory configuration. It has to be supplied with power constantly so that the information is not lost. A small CMOS battery (resembling a watch battery) is used. CMOS

provides a set of instructions that the processor executes until the operating system has loaded. It supplies routines that allow the operating system to interface with devices such as the keyboard, mouse and monitor. Once the operating system has loaded, peripherals use programs called device drivers to interface with the operating system.

Power supply

A computer needs a power supply to operate. The power supply unit (PSU) is usually, but not always, supplied when purchasing the computer case. The power supply unit converts AC current to the DC voltages needed to power a PC. The unit also contains a fan that is used to cool the inside of the case. The unit is able to regulate incoming power to reduce electrical noise and power surges. (Unfortunately the quality of the power we receive in our home, school and office varies.)

The external power supply can be subject to spikes or surges (higher than usual voltages), brownouts (lower than usual voltages), blackouts (sudden and entire loss of power), lightning strikes and electrical noise (when your computer shares its supply with other devices via an extension cable). Over time, any of these events may cause damage to your computer. Many organisations use surge protectors to protect their equipment and invest in uninterruptible power supplies (UPS) to avoid damage to computer systems and disruption to work in the event of a power blackout.

⚠ **Under no circumstances should you ever attempt to open the power supply unit. It contains capacitors and transformers that can supply a deadly electrical shock. (Note that there are also capacitors within monitors, which should be treated with the same caution.)**

Research tip

Investigate the range of uninterruptible power supply solutions and power surge protectors that are available.

The power supply unit has a number of connectors so that power can be distributed to the components of the computer.

Figure 2.5 The power supply unit and connectors

Currently there are two standards for connecting power to the motherboard of desktop computers. Older motherboards have 20-pin AXT power connectors. Newer motherboards have 24-pin AXT power connectors. It is possible to attach a 24-pin

Table 2.3 Power Supply Connectors

20-pin connector (older motherboards)	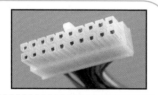
24-pin connector (newer motherboards)	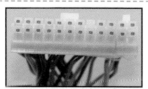
4-pin Molex connector (floppy drives, standard hard drives, CD-ROM drives, fans, etc)	
SATA connector (serial ATA hard drives)	

power supply to a 20-pin motherboard using an adapter, but you should not attempt to attach a 20-pin power supply to a 24-pin motherboard.

Fan and heat sink

Modern computer components, such as the microprocessor, graphics processors, the chipset and hard disks, can generate a build-up of heat. This heat must be reduced to within the range of safe operating temperatures. This is achieved through the use of fans and heat sinks.

Fans

Fans are used to disperse heated air, replacing it with cooler ambient air.

- PSU fan – this is a fan incorporated into the power supply unit, which blows cool air across the motherboard. If the power supply fan stops working, the power supply should be replaced immediately. It is important that the case is closed if this cooling is to be effective.

- CPU fan – a CPU cooling fan should be installed on any Pentium or higher microprocessor. It is attached either to the top of the processor or the top of the heat sink, depending on whether a heat sink is used. Most motherboards have a three-wire (power, earth and speed monitor) CPU fan connector. If the fan rotates too slowly, the processor could overheat and fail. The third wire on the connector allows the motherboard to monitor the speed. If it detects a problem, the computer will shut down or not boot, to protect the processor.

- Other fans – it may be necessary to add additional fans inside the case, particularly in tower cases where cards are mounted horizontally. Other components, such as graphics cards, may have their own fans to disperse heat.

Heat sinks

Heat sinks are machined blocks of metal, usually finned. The large surface area is used to disperse heat. An adhesive may be used to attach the heat sink to the top of the processor. Alternatively a clamp may be used, with a thermally conductive pad or gel to ensure good conductivity. Fan-cooled heat sinks made of aluminium were common until recently, but now many heat sinks are made of copper or have copper bases. The fins on heat sinks may become coated with dust, reducing their efficiency.

Hard drive configuration and controllers

The hard disk drive stores data. Hard drives are contained in sealed units that contain one or more disks, read-write heads and control electronics. The disks are made of aluminium and coated in ferro-magnetic material or a mixture of nickel and cobalt. Each disk contains an upper and lower platter. Modern drives come in two main sizes: 2.5 inch and 3.5 inch. The smaller drives tend to be more expensive and are used in laptops.

Key words

Read-write heads – mechanisms that read data from or write data to disk drives

Figure 2.6 A hard disk

Hard drives are installed in the computer case and connect to the motherboard. When more than one hard drive is installed, one is designated as the controlling or master drive; the other is known as the slave.

External hard drives can also be purchased. These are standard hard drives that have been encased in a caddy. USB connectors are used to connect it to the computer. They are used for additional storage or to back up data held on the computer.

The microprocessor communicates with other devices, such as hard disks, printers and monitors, through controllers. Sometimes the controller is built into the motherboard, but it can also be contained on a card that slots into the motherboard. It translates signals and protocols between the system and its I/O (input/output) devices. Several different types of controller are available.

IDE

IDE (Integrated Drive Electronics) drives (or ATA drives) are a computer bus technology used for data transmission from hard drives and optical drives. It uses 40 wire ribbon cables to connect a hard drive to the motherboard. The ribbon cable has two or three connectors attached to it: one to attach to the adapter and the others to connect to the drives. IDE has been used mostly as an internal computer device as the standard only allows for cables with a maximum length of 46 cm (although longer cables are possible). If two drives are connected to a cable, one is set up in the BIOS as the master drive. The second is known as the slave drive.

EIDE

EIDE (Enhanced Integrated Drive Electronics) offers higher performance than IDE, as it supports data transfer up to four times faster (up to 16.6Mbps) and can also support larger storage capacities. The technology can support other devices, such as CD-ROMs and CD Writers. A later development of EIDE, called Ultra-ATA, can support data transfer rates of 33Mbps.

Key words

Computer bus technology – a collection of wires through which data is transmitted from one part of a computer to another

SCSI (Small Computer System Interface)

The SCSI standard has been around since 1986, but further improvements have been made since then. It has traditionally been used for attaching multiple hard drives to high-end workstations and servers. It is also used because of the device's speed at transferring data.

An adapter card is used to connect the SCSI devices to the motherboard. An adapter can support up to fifteen devices. Each SCSI device has its own controller. These are intelligent and handle data transfer operations, freeing up other system resources, including processor time, that would otherwise be used for this purpose.

SCSI devices may be internal to the computer or external. If they are external, they use a thick shielded cable with Centronics-50 or DB-25 connectors to connect the devices. Multiple SCSI devices can be daisy-chained (wired) together. If the device is internal to the case, it uses a 50-pin ribbon cable. Other SCSI devices include printers, scanners, optical and tape drives.

SATA (Serial Advanced Technology Attachment)

SATA has been developed as a replacement for older ATA standard. Data can be transferred much faster using serial transmission. The connectors and cabling used are very different to ATA ribbon cables. Each drive has its own thin cable and it is possible to hot-swap drives, which was impossible to do using ATA. The connectors are grooved, ensuring that they can only be connected one way. SATA transfers data at speeds from 150Mbps and there are plans to increase this up to 600Mbps.

Key words

hot swap – the ability to remove and replace components while the computer is operating

Example

There is continued rising demand for small, high capacity hard drives. In January 2007, Fujitsu announced a breakthrough in magnetic storage technology that could enable storage capacities of a terabyte per square inch to become a reality.

Ports

Parallel and serial ports

A parallel port is a type of connector found on older PCs. They were mostly used to connect printers, zip drives and some scanners, but have been largely superseded by USB ports. Another form of connector found on older PCs is a serial port. These were used to connect mice, joysticks, keyboards and other peripherals to a PC. They have also mostly been superseded by devices using USB connectors.

USB (Universal Serial Bus)

USB is a connection technology that can be used to connect up to 127 devices to a computer. It is primarily intended for slow devices, such as keyboards, mice, joysticks and external hard drives. USB is designed to be Plug and Play: it should be possible to attach and detach USB devices while the computer is running. The standard specifies two types of connectors and receptacles: series-A and series-B. Series-A connectors are designed for devices such as mice and keyboards; series-B connectors are designed for scanners, and printers.

Think There are two standards for USB: USB1.1 and USB2.0. Find out what the differences are.

Firewire is a high-speed technology that allows data to be transferred between digital devices, such as digital camcorders and some digital cameras. It was developed by Apple, but is also used with PCs. Many new desktop computers and laptops come with Firewire ports built in, but Firewire cards can be purchased for older systems.

Peripherals

Peripherals are pieces of optional hardware that can be added externally to expand the functionality of the computer. Common peripherals include printers, scanners, plotters, webcams and digital cameras, and will be looked at in more detail in the following section.

Printers

Three main types of printer are available: dot matrix, inkjet and laser printers.

- Dot matrix printers – these have a print head that moves back and forth across a sheet of paper and print by striking an inked ribbon against the paper. The letters are formed from a matrix of dots. Some models can be very noisy and they vary greatly in quality of output, speed and price. Very fast dot matrix printers are often used when reports containing large amounts of data processing need to be printed quickly and regularly.

- Inkjet printers – these are very popular as they are relatively inexpensive to purchase, easy to use, quiet and produce good quality output. Most work by producing pulses of current which propel heated droplets of ink onto the page. The ink is water-based and can smudge if handled too quickly after printing or if exposed to water. They contain one or more disposable cartridges of ink, which hold only small amounts of ink and need to be replaced frequently, which can be expensive, particularly for colour printing. Print heads can clog with ink if the printer is not used regularly.

- Laser printers – these produce high-quality output. They used to be much more expensive that inkjet printers, but there are now many cheaper models developed for the home market. A laser printer temporarily saves print-job data to its own memory. Some models are able to make use of the memory within an attached computer. The printer contains a drum made of photoconductive material. The drum receives a positive electrical charge from either a corona wire or a charging roller. As the drum rotates, a laser passes across its surface, drawing (as a pattern of negative electrical charges) the letters

or images to be printed. Toner (a fine positively charged black powder) coats the drum, adhering to the negatively charged areas. A sheet of negatively charged paper rolls under the drum. The toner is transferred to the paper, which then passes between two hot rollers, known as the fuser. The toner melts and bonds with the paper. After the toner has been removed, the drum passes a discharge lamp. This removes the electrical charge from the drum, so that the process of printing the next page can begin.

Example

The development of new printer technologies tend to be evolutionary rather than revolutionary, involving improvements in existing types of printer. Ricoh have recently developed a range of gel-based printers. The gel dries instantly on contact with paper, reducing smearing and bleeding that can occur with inkjet printers. Revolutionary new products are less common. Xerox is presently developing an inkless printer that uses reusable paper.

Scanners

Scanners are devices that can analyse an image or text and save it as an image. The most commonly used type is a flatbed or desktop scanner, but hand-held and rotary scanners are also available. To scan a document, it is placed face down onto a glass plate. The scanning program needs to be opened and selected, such as the area to be scanned. When the scan is completed, the image is saved. When installing a scanner, accompanying software, including drivers, needs to be installed.

Plotters

A plotter is a device used to create line drawings by means of a pen or pencil attached to a mechanical arm. Plotters are frequently used in engineering and architecture to produce very precise drawings, which can be very large. The colour of pens can be changed to produce multi-coloured drawings. Many are being replaced with very large format inkjet and laser printers. In some plotters, other tools, such as cutters, can replace pens on the mechanical arm and vinyl can replace paper. Patterns can then be cut by the device.

Webcams

A webcam is a camera that is able to capture and send real-time images across the internet. The webcam is attached to a computer, usually facing the user so that images of the user can be sent to another computer. This will require additional software, some of which is freely available as a download. Webcams may also be used for other purposes, including security. Software is available that will activate and record sound and movement when it is detected. Webcams are often positioned over busy roads, allowing internet users to check road conditions before travelling. Webcams are also used to show the weather in different locations.

Digital cameras

Many digital cameras use flash memory cards to store the pictures taken. It is easy to transfer images taken by most modern digital cameras to a computer using a USB cable. Once saved on the computer, image manipulation software can be used to edit the images, if required, before printing. Alternatively, memory card readers can be purchased for PCs, removing the need to connect the camera to the PC via a cable. Some photo printers have memory card readers built in.

Internal memory

Computers need to be able to store data and instructions temporarily while processing takes place. In PCs, three types of memory need to be considered: RAM, ROM and cache.

RAM (random access memory)

This memory is situated on the motherboard, close to the processor. It consists of modules that are inserted into slots on the motherboard. They can be removed or replaced as necessary. At the time of writing, most PCs have 512MB or 1GB of RAM.

Figure 2.7 RAM module

Instructions and data are read from and written to RAM from the processor. RAM is sometimes known as 'primary or main memory' and is vital to the operation of a computer. It is volatile, meaning that when the computer loses power or is switched off, the data held in RAM is lost.

Data held in RAM can be accessed quickly using its memory address. This is much faster than serial access, such as from tape, or access from a hard-disk drive (which requires read/write heads to move to the location where the data is stored before it can be accessed). However, with the development of faster processors, the time taken to access data stored in RAM has become an issue: it has created a performance bottleneck.

At the time of writing, the most common types of RAM are DDR and DDR2 memory.

- DDR SDRAM (double data rate synchronous dynamic random access memory) – these memory modules operate at twice the speed of the earlier SDRAM. They had 168 pins and are not interchangeable with the newer DDR modules with 184 pins. DDR RAM cannot be installed on motherboards designed for SDRAM.

- DDR2 SDRAM – this is superseding DDR SDRAM. It operates in a similar fashion, but with higher bus speeds, reducing system latency time. It has lower power consumption and operates at a lower temperature than DDR SDRAM.

> ### Key words
> --
> System latency time – the length of time between transmitting and receiving data

ROM (read-only memory)

ROM is a hardware chip used to store BIOS information. It is sometimes known as 'firmware'. ROM is non-volatile, so it maintains the information it holds, even when the computer is turned off. It consists of permanent instructions used when a computer is booted.

Cache

This is very fast RAM that operates in conjunction with the processor. It temporarily stores the most frequently accessed data and instructions. When the processor operates, it looks for data in the cache prior to looking in RAM. Cached data and instructions can be accessed more quickly than data and instructions that have to be fetched from main memory.

Memory caches built into the microprocessor are called Level 1 (L1) caches. They are usually 32KB in total, divided into two 16KB memory caches: one for data and one for instructions. (AMD K6 processors use 64KB of L1 cache). Many modern PCs also have a further cache, called Level 2 (L2). L2 cache is usually 256KB or 512KB, and is located on a separate chip. If the processor cannot find the data it is looking for in L1 cache, it will look in L2 and then in main memory.

Specialised cards

Cards (also known as expansion boards), are printed circuit boards that can be added to provide increased functionality.

Network interface cards (NICs)

Networks can now be found in many different locations, including the home. A network can range from two computers linked together to networks of large numbers of computers.

Figure 2.8 A network interface card

An NIC allows a computer to communicate with others on a network. It slots onto the motherboard, although some motherboards have NIC circuitry built in. An NIC converts the parallel data stream used by the computer to serial data packets used by a network. It comes with either PCI or ISA connectors, depending on the type of slot it is to be positioned in on the motherboard. It also comes with either BNC or RJ45 connectors, depending on the cabling being used. Software drivers need to be installed on the computer to complete the installation.

NICs can also be used to network printers. Without an NIC, if you want two or more computers to share a printer, one computer needs to act as a host. This computer would have to be switched on for the other to be able to use the printer. Some modern printers come with network capability (NICs) built in. These are slightly different from the NICs discussed above, as they have a processor built in to manage the tasks that the software drivers perform on a computer. The NICs tend to be proprietary (the property of a company) and are usually manufactured by the maker of the printer.

Graphics cards

For high-end gaming and processor-intensive 3D graphics rendering, separate graphics cards are usually required. A graphics card performs three main tasks: geometry, lighting and rendering images. Geometry involves the computation of shapes, lighting involves the creation of shadows, and so on, and rendering involves adding textures to surfaces.

There are two sorts of graphics cards – AGP or PCIe. AGP is slower and is being phased out. Motherboards come with either an AGP slot or PCIe slot(s). An AGP card cannot be installed in a PCIe slot, so it is essential that you check that you have a matching motherboard and graphics card. For high-end processing, it is possible, using PCIe slots, to install two different graphics cards in a PC. This allows complex processing to be shared across both cards. This also allows up to four monitors to be attached to a PC (an operating system that supports multi-monitors, such as Microsoft Windows® XP is also required).

Graphics cards have a number of components:

- A GPU (graphics processor unit) – this dedicated processor is designed to process complex graphics algorithms quickly. It therefore reduces pressure on the main processor.

- Memory – a graphics card has its own dedicated memory.

- RAMDAC – this is an additional chip found on graphics cards that converts digital signals from the GPU to analogue signal to be output to the monitor.

BACKING STORE

Different technologies have been used to develop devices that can store programs and data on a more permanent basis than the expensive and volatile main memory allows.

From the early days of computer systems, the use of magnetic storage systems, such as hard disks, floppy disks and tape, has been common. More recently, mainly due to the development of pen drives, most new computer systems have stopped shipping with floppy disk drives.

Types of backing store

Disks

A floppy disk is a portable storage device. It is a circle of Mylar, encased in a plastic rectangular sleeve. The most common version is the 3.5 inch floppy disk, which can store 1.44MB of data.

Most new desktop computers and laptops now ship without floppy-disk drives as many computer users now use much higher capacity USB pen drives to move files from one computer to another.

Pen drives

These devices, sometimes known as USB Flash Drives, have largely replaced floppy disks as the portable storage device of choice. At the time of writing, they can be purchased in a wide variety of sizes from 128MB to 8GB.

These devices use Flash memory. This is non-volatile, erasable and rewritable memory. It offers fairly quick access times and is more resilient to

Figure 2.9 A pen drive

knocks than disks. The number of times you can erase and then rewrite to the device is limited, however. Data is erased in blocks (blocks of data make up files). Most available Flash memory devices are guaranteed to last for at least one million rewrites. Chip firmware or system drivers spread the rewrites between sectors so that certain areas of the device do not wear out before others. This is called wear levelling. Bad blocks, ie corrupted data, are also rempved from use.

Optical media

A CD-ROM (Compact Disk Read-Only Memory) is a disk composed of a polycarbonate, covered with one or more very thin layers of reflective metal, usually aluminium, which is then coated with lacquer. CD-ROMs are designed to store text, images and stereo sound. Data is encoded onto the CD starting at the centre and finishing at the outer edge. A CD can hold 650MB or 700MB of data.

The data held on a CD-ROM is read by a drive using laser light to read the pits and lands on the CD as it rotates. (Pits are etched onto the CD when it is produced. Lands are the areas on a CD between the pits). The reflection of the laser light away from the surface of the disk is detected by a sensor. The sensor converts the signal into digital signals that can be interpreted by the computer.

A DVD is another type of optical storage disk and can store between 4.7 and 17GB of data. The disks resemble CDs, but store data using a different format and at a much higher density. DVD drives are backwardly compatible with CD-ROMs.

There are a number of different recording standards and you need to ensure that you purchase disks that are compatible with your DVD drive and/or DVD player. The most commonly used formats are:

- DVD-R and DVD-RW – DVD-R was the first format (non-rewritable) that could be played on DVD

Evidence activity

P1 – D1

You have been employed by a college to support their computer systems.

1. Your line manager has asked you to produce a presentation that explains the function of system unit components to new computing students. It is important that the use of jargon is kept to a minimum and that all terms are defined. The presentation could include diagrams with hotspots or hyperlinks to slides containing details and examples. You must ensure that you include details of how the components communicate. (P1)

2. The college has asked you to specify three different computer systems for the college:

- a computer to be used to run Office applications, web browser and email

- a computer to be used by the media studies department for video editing

- a computer to be used by the engineering department to run a CAD program.

Produce a report making three different recommendations for each of the computer systems required, with an appropriate output device also selected. Decide which system is most suitable for each situation, considering cost and technical requirements, and justify your choice. (D1)

2.2 Understand the software components of computer systems

OPERATING SYSTEM SOFTWARE

The operating system (OS) of a computer is a program, or suite of programs, that controls the operation of the computer. It acts as an interface between the hardware and software applications.

Operating system examples

There are a number of different operating systems available for computers. The most common are:

- Microsoft Windows® – this is a very widely used operating system. The latest version is Vista. Previous versions include XP Professional and Home, 2000, 98, NT, ME and 95. Microsoft Windows® is designed for use on home and business PCs and laptops. Historically, it was designed for use on single-user systems. Microsoft Windows® XP is a multi-tasking operating system developed from the earlier NT kernel. It incorporates both a graphic user interface (GUI) as well as a command line interface (cmd.exe). Microsoft Windows is thought to be easy to learn to use.

- UNIX® – Unix is a multi-tasking, portable multi-user operating system. It has been developed since the 1960s by many different corporations and individuals. It has a hierarchical directory structure. The operating system consists of a kernel that manages hardware and data access, schedules tasks and enforces security. It has a shell that supports custom environments for users and executes user commands. A large number of utilities are available for process, user, print and file management. Unix has traditionally been viewed as more difficult to learn to use than Windows, due to its command line interface. Many Internet servers are UNIX-based.

Key words

Portable – can be used on a computer system that is different from the one for which it was designed

- Linux – Linux is a multi-user OS that will run on a number of different computer architectures, including PCs. It is similar to UNIX, but requires less hardware resources to run. It is Open Source software, which means that anyone can have access to the source code. Examples include Red Hat and Fedora.

- Mac OS – This GUI OS was developed for use with Apple Macintosh computers. Early versions operated only with Motorola 68000 systems, but later versions were compatible with PowerPC. The latest versions are compatible with Intel x86 architecture.

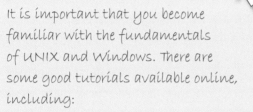

Research tip

It is important that you become familiar with the fundamentals of UNIX and Windows. There are some good tutorials available online, including:

- www.ee.surrey.ac.uk/Teaching/Unix/
- www.microsoft.com/windows/using/windowsxp/default.mspx.

Command line and GUI operating systems

Command line interface

The command line interface is text-based and relies on users typing commands onto the screen from the keyboard. UNIX shells and DOS both use this type of interface.

It is possible to access the command line in Microsoft Windows® XP by clicking the Start button, clicking Run and typing **cmd**. This opens a window with the DOS prompt. To see a list of files and folders, type **dir** at the command prompt (where the cursor is flashing). If there are too many folders and files to fit on one screen, type in **dir/p**. This will allow you to view the first screen, and then press the spacebar to see the next screen until you have viewed all the files and folders. Alternatively, you could type in **dir/w** to see the files and folders using a wide format. At any point, you can go to the root of the C drive, by typing **cd**.

The command line interface is very quick to use when the correct commands are known, because the user does not have to work their way through menus or click through a number of selections with a mouse. It does not require Windows, uses less memory than a GUI and will run on a very basic PC and monochrome monitor. However, it relies heavily on a user's typing skills and knowledge of commands.

Batch files

It is possible to write multiple commands into a text file. This is very useful, particularly for procedures that need to be repeated frequently. The file is saved with a .bat extension. It can be scheduled to run at specific times of day, or when specific events occur, such as when a PC boots or shuts down.

Graphical user interfaces (GUIs)

This interface allows users to interact with the computer using **w**indows, **i**cons, **m**enus and a **p**ointing device (WIMP). Microsoft Windows®, Mac OS and X Windows (Linux) all use variations of this type of interface.

The interface consists of 'widgets' that allow the user to interact with the program, including windows, scroll bars, buttons and menus. Large widgets, such as windows, are containers for content. One of the features of a well-designed GUI is that the widgets are customisable, allowing the user to adjust the layout of the interface to suit their method of working. GUIs are described as intuitive or easy to use (although some might disagree!). Once a user can interact with the interface in one application, that knowledge can be applied in other applications designed using the same widgets.

> **Think** List a number of GUI widgets that are customisable in a common application such as a word processor or spreadsheet.

Some GUIs are designed for very specific requirements, such as ATMs (Automated Telling Machines), self-service checkouts and touch-screen point-of-sale systems.

Operating system functions and services

The operating system performs a number of vital functions:

- File and disk management – the transfer of data and program instructions from a backing storage device to main memory and back again are functions of the OS. The OS also enables users to create folders and move, copy and delete files. It keeps a database of where all the files are stored so that they can be retrieved.

- Memory management –the OS manages the allocation of memory to programs, so that they can operate. Many operating systems can run several programs at once, enabling users to switch quickly from one program to another. When a computer is booted, part of the OS, called the kernel, is loaded into main memory. This sits in memory while the computer is turned on.

- User interface – the OS provides an interface for the user to interact with the operating system. For example, in the Microsoft Windows® OS, users can use Windows Explorer to move files. They can use the Control Panel to add and remove programs and printers, optimise and configure multimedia devices and much more.

- Scheduling and peripheral management – the OS assigns priorities for different operations involving processor time. It also manages input and output, using queues and buffers. Buffers are required to store data temporarily as many devices within the computer system operate at different speeds. For example, data can be sent to a printer faster than the printer can process it, so data is stored in a buffer allowing the printer to operate in the background and freeing computer resources to get on with other tasks.

- System tools – the operating system often contains a number of additional programs called utilities, which are used to monitor and maintain elements of the system. It is usually necessary to keep the operating system patched. A patch is a program that will fix a problem, such as a software bug or a security issue, or add extra features to improve usability or performance. They are usually small programs, but can in some cases be large. It is important to keep the OS patched to avoid viruses.

Operating system software also helps to guard against security issues:

- Logins and passwords – user IDs and passwords can be set on individual computers (a feature of the OS) or on networked computers (as part of the network OS). Network administrators can set a minimum password length, set complexity of the password and force users to change passwords at regular intervals. They can also control the areas of the network that users have access to and on what days and times the user can access the network. Rights to particular files can also be set, for example read-only access, read and write access, create new files and folders and delete files and folders.

- Encryption – this is the conversion of data into a cipher with the aim of stopping the data from being read by others. A 'key' is required to translate the data back into readable form. There are a great many different methods of encryption. To protect data from hackers, private and public key systems are sometimes used. These systems require two different keys to be used. One key is used to encrypt the data and another is used to decrypt it.

- Audit logs – these can be used to record information about activities on the network, for example about who accesses data and when they access it. Do they edit, copy, move or delete data? Logs can be useful to track down any unauthorised activity.

Device drivers

A device or software driver is a software program that allows operating systems and other programs to interact with a hardware device. One example is printers' drivers, which convert data to a format that printers can understand. Drivers are specific to certain operating systems and devices. If a device does not function correctly, it is worth going to the manufacturer's website to see if there are any newer drivers available for your model. Other devices that need drivers are modems, CD-ROMs, webcams and monitors.

SOFTWARE UTILITIES

Software utilities are programs that perform a task or tasks that help to manage a computer system. They are frequently, but not always, small programs that are bundled with the operating system.

Virus protection

It is important to protect computer systems from virus attacks. The installation of scanning software and a schedule of regular updating can reduce the risk of a successful virus attack occurring. A number of other actions can be taken by users to reduce the risk of infection, including not opening unsolicited email or attachments, avoiding pirated software and backing up data regularly.

System profilers

This software can provide information about a computer's configuration and properties. It can be used to display a list of all hardware and software, including version numbers, on a computer. It can also be used to assist in the detection of hardware and software problems.

Firewalls

A firewall is used to protect a network from unwanted internet traffic. It exists between your computer(s) and the internet. Some firewalls are software programs that are installed on your computer, others are built into hardware, such as a broadband router. The firewall allows you to access websites and download files while ensuring that hackers cannot access your computer resources.

Clean up tools

- Cookies and internet history – when web pages are visited, copies of these files are stored temporarily on the hard disk of your computer. It is possible to control the amount of disk space that is allocated to storing these files. A list of pages and sites visited is also stored and it is possible to set how many days this list is kept for.

- Anti-spyware – spyware is software that is able to collect personal information without the user's knowledge. It may do this by recording keystrokes made by the user, scanning documents on the computer or recording the Internet history. A number of software applications can be installed to prevent the use of spyware. Anti-spyware can also scan a system for the presence of spyware and remove it.

- Defragmentation – as files are saved to a hard drive, then edited, resaved, and deleted, parts of a file may be saved to several different physical locations on the hard disk. This fragmentation of files leads to longer times taken to read data into memory. Many operating systems have a defragmentation utility, which attempts to move files into contiguous sectors, thereby reducing data access time.

> **Key words**
>
> Cookie – a cookie is data that some internet sites download onto your computer. In some cases a cookie collects information about the websites you visit; in others, it may contain auto-login information that will enter your login and password automatically for a website you visit regularly

Drive formatting

IT practitioners are usually only required to perform high-level formatting of hard disks. The disk is low-formatted at the factory to prepare the surface of the disk for data and it is rare for this procedure to be repeated. High-level formatting might include:

- scanning the disk for problems and marking bad sectors

- creating magnetic tracks and 512-byte sectors

- creating areas between the sectors to keep error correction information

- creating a file allocation table to record the location of files stored on the disk.

On newer operating systems, such as Microsoft Windows® XP, the format commands are run as part of the OS setup procedure. On older operating systems such as Win95, the FORMAT command would be run prior to the installation of the operating system.

It should be noted that formatting a disk does not mean that the data is irretrievable, although the process of recovering it is complex. If you need to ensure that the data is gone forever, which you may need to if the information is confidential or financial, then you should either destroy the hard drive or use a utility that has been created specifically for that purpose.

CASE STUDY: DATA-PRO LTD PART 2: SOFTWARE RESPONSIBILITIES

Software is installed using imaging or cloning software to deploy standard builds. Different builds are required to meet the software needs of different departments and some departments require more that one build. Additionally, each different model of PC or laptop will require an individual image to maintain hardware and software compatibility, which means that bulk purchases of new PCs and laptops are preferred to reduce the need to create new images, which take two days to complete.

An image is created by installing all software and patches required onto a PC and then using a utility provided by Microsoft called Sysprep to remove the machine's unique identity. The imaging software is used to create a copy of this PC. On image restore, the Microsoft setup wizard automatically runs to recreate the PC's unique stripped (SID) identity. Once an image has been created, a final machine configuration can be completed in less than an hour. One-off custom builds and server builds are always done from scratch.

Quality control of work done is maintained using checklists.

Requested one-off installations of software are done manually.

A software licensing database is kept up to date. This is done automatically via auditing software. Reports are run manually every three months and compared against licensing records. Any unauthorised software found is removed. Spare licenses are identified for future allocation.

Patching of software from Microsoft is achieved automatically using Microsoft SUS server. Other patches may be deployed manually or via group policies.

Virus protection software is installed onto PCs via login scripts. They run an agent that looks to a central database on the network for updates. The central database updates from the vendor's site, thus minimising internet traffic.

Evidence activity

P2 – M2 – P3 – P4

1. Questions have been asked about what operating system should be used by the college. Create a table with two columns that describes the purpose, features and functions of two different operating systems, such as Mac OS, Unix® or Microsoft Windows®. (P2)

2. Identify the differences and similarities between the two operating systems and summarise each one's strengths and weaknesses in terms of their features and functions. (M2)

3. Your line manager has asked you to create a step-by-step guide to the use of two different software utilities. The guide should include screenshots of the steps taken to operate the software. (P3)

4. There have been arguments in the department about how to define a software utility. Describe four different software utilities, including one from each of the following categories: virus protection, firewall, clean up and drive formatting. (P4)

2.3 *Be able to undertake routine computer maintenance*

SOFTWARE MAINTENANCE

Upgrade software

It is worth checking manufacturers' websites for the latest device drivers for installed peripheral devices, such as graphics cards and printers. These sometimes include bug fixes or provide improved functionality.

It is vital to ensure that anti-virus protection software is kept up-to-date to protect computers from new viruses. It is usually possible to configure the virus protection software so that it automatically checks the anti-virus manufacturer's website every time the computer connects to the internet and automatically downloads the latest files.

Installation of patches

Many software companies release patches for their programs. Because software programs can contain millions of lines of code, it is almost inevitable that there will be some errors in it. These errors, or holes, can be exploited by rogue program writers. To correct the errors, the operating system or software manufacturer will issue a patch. Patches are also released to add additional features to a program. These can be downloaded from software manufacturers' websites. Microsoft Windows® XP can be configured to automatically check for and download updates. Instructions for the installation of updates are usually supplied in a text file or on the website.

Example

Microsoft has a number of different types of patches, to deal with different issues. These include 'critical updates', which provide fixes for issues in software; 'feature packs' which include additions to software programs; and 'driver updates', which update software that supports or controls hardware.

Scheduling of maintenance tasks

Some organisations maintain a schedule of preventative maintenance. This includes tasks to be completed daily, weekly, monthly, six monthly and annually, which might look like the example shown below.

Table 2.4 A maintenance schedule

Daily	• Backup data • Check computer case ventilation is not blocked.
Weekly	• Check power cables are in good condition • Wipe over the exterior of equipment with a damp cloth • Check that anti-virus software is updating correctly.
Monthly	• Clean inside the system case • Reseat any expansion cards that are working loose • Clean the keyboard and mouse.
Six monthly	• Use a diagnostic package to check system • Scan the disk • Defragment the hard drive.
Annually	• Check warranties, maintenance contracts and licensing.

Utility software aimed at users

Defragmentation

To defragment a disk in **Microsoft** Windows® XP:

▶ go to Start > All Programs > Accessories > Disk Defragmenter

▶ or: click My Computer, then right-click on the hard drive icon

▶ select Properties > Tools > Disk Defragmenter

▶ click the Defragment Now button.

Clean up

To clear temporary internet files, cookies and internet history on a computer, in IE7

▶ go to Tools > internet Options > Browser History > Settings

▶ choose the settings you require

To clear temporary internet files in IE7:

▶ go the Tools menu > internet Options > Browser History > Delete

▶ A number of options exist:
  • temporary internet files
  • cookies
  • history
  • form data
  • passwords.

System Profilers

To access system hardware and software information in Microsoft Windows® XP:

▶ go to Start > All Programs > Accessories > System Tools > System Information

▶ the right-hand pane of the Information window allows you to select the following information:
  • hardware resources
  • components
  • software environment
  • internet settings.

Other third-party utility software

Compression utilities

Compression software is used to reduce the size of files for storage, download or for sending as an email attachment. A popular format is .zip. A software program is required to compress the data and to uncompress it. A number of free compression utilities are available on the Internet, but Microsoft Windows® XP has its own compression utility.

To compress a file or folder in Microsoft Windows® XP:

▶ right-click on the file or folder and select Send to

▶ choose Compressed (zipped) folder from the fly out menu

▶ to unzip a file or folder in Windows XP, double-click the zip file.

▶ click Extract all files.

Spyware Removal

A number of free software utilities are available for download from the Internet. These can be configured to detect and prevent spyware from being downloaded onto your computer. Alternatively, a program called Microsoft Windows® Defender, a free download from Microsoft for Win2000 and XP, can be used. It is built into Vista.

To scan your computer:

▶ start > All programs > Windows Defender

▶ click the down arrow next to Scan

▶ select Full Scan.

Diagnostic tools

Many software tools, some of which are free, can be used to run a series of tests on your computer to aid in the diagnosis of problems. An internet search will find a number of these programs.

HARDWARE MAINTENANCE

It is usually preferable for computer equipment to be stored off the floor. Carpet and dust can reduce the flow of air around the computer case, which can lead to the temperature within the case being hotter than desirable, which will shorten the life of the computer.

The computer case should always be kept closed when in operation. The fans inside the case are designed and positioned to maximise cooling of the components.

Example

There are many companies that offer professional computer cleaning sevices.

Capital Computer Care offers cleaning services of equipment including desktops, laptops, printers and scanners. Their clients range from small businesses to major national organisations.

Think Why might some businesses choose to employ professional computer cleaning services?

Cleaning equipment

To avoid problems developing with a computer system, you should take preventative measures. This can be as simple as having a simple cleaning regime. Computer systems attract dust and dirt, which shorten their efficiency and life. It is important that the right products and methods are used when cleaning to avoid damage. A range of products will need to be used, including soft cloths, screen wipes, anti-static spray, a small paintbrush, compressed air (usually in an aerosol), a vacuum cleaner (special attachments such as fine crevice tools can be purchased), cotton swabs, flat-headed and Philips screwdrivers and a grounding strap.

⚠ **Always check manufacturer's instructions for cleaning their equipment and ensure that the computer is unplugged before undertaking cleaning.**

• Computer cases – use soapy water on a squeezed soft, clean cloth. Ensure that no excess moisture is able to penetrate into the case.

• Computer screens – avoid the use of solvents as they may cause discolouration. Screen wipes are useful for removing general dust and finger marks. Anti-static spray may be applied.

- Keyboards – the keyboard should be unplugged, then turned upside down to shake out loose dust or crumbs. A vacuum can also be used. To loosen a sticky key, use a flat-headed screwdriver to gently remove the key. Clean the key socket as well as possible (using computer cleaner or distilled water), then, when dry, snap the key back in place.

- Mouse – the inside can become clogged with dust. Unplug the mouse, remove the cover and release the mouse ball. A damp cloth can be used to clean the ball. Three rollers are located inside the mouse. Dust will need to be removed from them, using a pair of tweezers or your fingernails.

- Inside the computer case – only compressed air should be used to clear dust. It is extremely easy for static electricity to permanently damage the inside of a computer, so avoid touching any components in the process.

- Inkjet printers – these are prone to developing clogged nozzles, especially when the printer has not been used for some time and the ink dries. Most printers have an automatic cleaning program, which may need to be run a couple of times to clear the nozzle. Many manufacturers advise against manually cleaning the printer heads.

- Laser printers – general dust and bits of paper can cause poor print quality and paper jams. Check the printer manual and warranty before cleaning. Turn off the printer, unplug it and allow it to cool down first. Remove the toner cartridge and use compressed air to remove dust and general debris. Use a disposable soft cloth to remove residual toner from the inside of the printer.

Install and configure new peripherals

IT practitioners may be called upon to install new computer devices, particularly printers. Most new printers come with manuals and installer programs. If so, you should always read the documentation for any special instructions. You will probably need to install toner or ink-jet cartridges and you should follow the instructions on the packaging.

If instructions aren't available, the following procedures can be used:

USB printers

▶ if you have an installation program, install the printer drivers before you connect the printer to the computer. Follow the instructions given

▶ if you do not have an installation program, attach the USB cable to the computer and printer. The 'Add New Hardware' window should appear on your screen

▶ click next, then click 'Search for the best driver for your device'. Click Next again

▶ browse to locate your printer drivers, then click OK

▶ click Next a further two times and then click Finish

▶ turn on your printer and print a test page.

Parallel port Printers (Microsoft Windows® XP)

▶ go to Start > Printers and Faxes > Add Printer

▶ select Local printer OR Printer connected to this computer, then click Next

▶ select the LPT port and the make and model of printer

▶ otherwise, click Have disk, and browse to the location of the driver

▶ click Open, then OK

▶ select Yes to make the printer the default printer, then select Do not share this printer, then Next

▶ turn the printer on, then print a test page by selecting Yes. When the page has printed, click Finish.

Install and configure additional or replacement device

You need to be able to install or upgrade a hard drive, graphics card, optical drive or a network interface card.

⚠ **Remember to always turn off the computer and unplug from the mains before opening the computer case. Use a grounding strap when touching components within the case.**

Replacing a hard drive

Hard drives are mechanical devices, and therefore may fail, necessitating a replacement. Alternatively, a user may find that the disk is no longer large enough to store all their programs or data in which case a new hard drive will be needed. Replacing a hard drive may be a way of extending the working life of a computer.

To replace an IDE drive:

▶ backup any data you will want to copy to your new disk

▶ turn off the computer. Unplug the power lead

▶ remove the old drive. Note where cables connect to power supply and the motherboard

▶ set the jumpers for master, slave or cable. Select the replacement hard drive. Check the original drive settings, and do the same

▶ install the drive in the mounting frame, reusing the screws from the previous drive

▶ attach the cables to the motherboard and to the power supply

▶ most modern BIOSs will auto-detect the new hard drive. If not, go into the BIOS to change the drive settings.

Installing a sound card

▶ install the card into a free slot. Avoid touching the components on the card. Ensure that the card seats itself firmly

▶ connect the cable from the CD/DVD drive to the soundcard

▶ screw the card in place, if a screw hole exists on the card

▶ close the case and reattach the keyboard, mouse, monitor, speakers, etc

▶ on startup, Microsoft Windows® should recognise the soundcard. Follow the onscreen instructions to install software drivers.

Upgrading a graphics card

▶ Uninstall existing card drivers.

▶ Remove card.

▶ Install new card.

▶ Install new drivers.

▶ Configure display settings.

Adding a CD/DVD drive

▶ remove the drive slot cover on the case.

▶ set the IDE drive mode to Master if it is the only device attached to the cable.

▶ install the drive in the case.

▶ attach the audio cable to the drive. The other end of the cable attaches to the motherboard or a PC audio card.

▶ attach the IDE cable into the motherboard and one of the other connectors of the cable into the CD/DVD drive.

▶ insert a 4-pin molex connector from the power supply into the CD/DVD drive.

Key words

4-pin molex connector – a commonly used power connector for disk drives and other components

Adding and configuring a Network Interface Card

If you wish to attach your computer to a local area network (LAN), a network interface card (NIC) will need to be installed unless the computer already has onboard networking. The user manual that comes with the card contains vital information related to installing and configuring the NIC.

▶ Ensure that the card has connectors that are compatible with the cabling used by the network. Many Ethernet cards come with both BNC and RJ45 connectors so that they will work with both thin Ethernet and CAT5, CAT5e cabling.

▶ Check the User Manual to determine the required jumper settings

▶ Install the card into an expansion slot on the motherboard of the computer. Secure it to the back plate of the computer using a screw

▶ Microsoft Windows® XP should detect the card and load the drivers, otherwise install drivers when prompted. Install the NIC drivers onto your computer. This software allows the computer to manage communication between itself and the NIC

CASE STUDY: DATA-PRO LTD PART 3: MAINTENANCE RESPONSIBILITIES

When a piece of equipment comes into the department for work it is given a surface and internal clean before being returned.

Backups are taken every night of all servers and data areas. A full backup is taken on a Friday night. This takes approximately 15 hours to complete and spans multiple tapes. These are autoloaded using a robotic tape device. Incremental backups are taken on weekdays. These complete in eight hours. A 30-day cycle is used, with tapes being sent off site for storage every day.

The team is involved in a yearly BCP test (Business Continuity Plan). The company pays for floor space and hardware in a DR (disaster recovery) centre located in a different part of the country. Once a year, all systems, including desktops, servers, and network connectivity, are implemented according to the plan using only backups and pre-supplied machine images to emulate a loss of site. This process takes three days.

The team are responsible for day-to-day administration, such as setting up user accounts and logins, maintaining group memberships for email and security, granting of access to server areas, general maintenance of user details, password resets, account lockouts and account deletion. They are also responsible for the procurement and installation of printers, configuring network printers, user access to the printers and management of repair calls under warranty and post-warranty. Laser printers are not repaired by the team due to the hazardous nature of the equipment.

The team:

- is responsible for keeping an inventory of all PCs, laptops, printers, scanners and servers

- set up training and meeting rooms with any PC-connected equipment that is required

- is responsible for reporting IT-related risks to management. Identified risks are added to a risk database

- is responsible for the procurement or maintenance agreements on software and hardware where required

- supply a limited amount of user support for software. Generally, training is dealt with by the HR department

- maintain a knowledge base of unusual and reoccurring issues and procedures.

A third-party company comes in to clean the computer equipment. This is done overnight. The company use specialist cleaning materials.

Disposal of old and broken equipment is also handled by a third-party company.

- Differential backup – This creates a cumulative backup of modified files only. The archive attribute is not updated. This method is useful when only the latest version of an altered file is needed.

Example

There is a growing market for data storage. Sun Microsystems, a US-based software and computer server maker, bought a data storage firm called Storagetek for £2.3 billion in 2003. Whereas Sun produces primary data storage systems, Storagetek provides secodary storage services, e.g. data archiving and back-up systems. Sun's move into the market reflects a growing recognition by businesses of the potential threat posed by data loss, and the need to put in safeguards to minimise the risk.

Even though there is an increased awareness of the need to manage risk, computer failures can still cause massive disruption for businesses and other organisations. In July 2007, there were severe flight delays on US East Coast routes when the computer system that manages part of the air traffic control system failed. When the back up computer became overloaded, flight controllers were forced to enter information manually, resulting in lengthy delays.

Evidence activity

P5 – M3 – M1 – D2

1. Identify the maintenance activities that are needed for a PC. Produce a checklist (plan) for each activity. Carry out each maintenance task, take photographs as evidence and/or obtain signed observation sheets. (P5)

2. Explain how the activities you carried out for P5 have improved the performance of the computer. (M3)

3. Install and configure a printer and one of the following: a hard drive, graphics card, sound card, CD-ROM drive or a network interface card. Produce supporting notes, explaining the process you followed, to show understanding. (M1)

4. In a short report, justify the considerations for selection of your upgrade. (D2)

Information systems

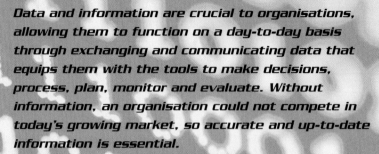

Data and information are crucial to organisations, allowing them to function on a day-to-day basis through exchanging and communicating data that equips them with the tools to make decisions, process, plan, monitor and evaluate. Without information, an organisation could not compete in today's growing market, so accurate and up-to-date information is essential.

With advances in information technology, the methods used to capture, process and output this valuable information have also become more sophisticated. An information system is a combination of hardware, software and communication networks that can meet an organisation's needs. Information systems enable organisations to collect, manipulate and store data and information that can then be used to obtain a competitive advantage within the market and operate as an efficient and profitable business.

This unit will give an overview of information systems, how they work, their benefits and what they are used for. In addition, you will also explore how organisations use information and the constraints that exist in the use of business information.

By the end of this unit, you will:

So you want to be an...

Information Systems Manager

My name Richard Cowell
Age 29
Income £34,500

What does an information systems manager do?

I maintain the management information systems (MIS) that we use in our company. I also oversee a team of support officers who work on data entry and processing tasks.

What are your day-to-day responsibilities?

I manage a team of six support officers and data entry clerks. I have to ensure that they carry out their roles effectively and accurately, as we support four other departments in the company. I'm also responsible for ensuring that the MIS is operating correctly and I analyse the reporting data that comes through from the finance department.

How did you get into the job?

This job was a trainee support role, and I applied just after leaving college, I've been here ever since.

What training did you get?

When I first started I was given the opportunity to train in a number of areas all linked to support. To begin with I was expected to be involved with small-scale support roles – nothing too taxing. After six months I was put on an intensive training programme on the company's MIS system and as we were then introducing new software everybody had to get used to the new methods. Since that time I have been on a number of varied

training programmes designed at preparing me for my management role and also technical MIS training.

What are the hours like?

We have flexi-time so as long as you work 37 hours a week between the hours of 8 am and 8 pm it's up to you, although I am expected to support my team during normal working hours (9-5).

> "When I started I was given the opportunity to train in a number of areas"

What skills do you need?

Patience – working with data all day can be quite tedious at times, especially if the MIS isn't behaving. As a manager, I also have to have good people skills and be able to motivate others. I also have quite an extensive knowledge about information systems and data processing.

How good is the pay?

I started on £16,000, which went up to £17,500 after a year. Once I started on my fast-track management programme my salary increased to £21,000 and over the years I've managed to get various pay and incentive awards to take me to my current salary of £34,500.

What about the future?

I've been with the same organisation for almost 10 years and have never worked anywhere else. It's quite a large company and there are opportunities to move into other areas, but I'm happy here.

Grading criteria

The table below shows what you need to do to gain a pass, merit or distinction in this part of the qualification. Make sure you refer back to it when you are completing work so that you can judge whether you are meeting the criteria and what you need to do to fill in gaps in your knowledge or experience.

In this unit there are five evidence activities that give you an opportunity to demonstrate your achievement of the grading criteria:

page 81	P1, M1
page 84	P2, M2
page 88	P3, D1
page 89	P5
page 96	M3
page 100	P4, P6, P2, D2

To achieve a pass grade the evidence must show that the learner is able to...	To achieve a merit grade the evidence must show that, in addition to the pass criteria, the learner is able to...	To achieve a distinction grade the evidence must show that, in addition to the pass and merit criteria, the learner is able to...
P1 describe the characteristics and sources of information that an organisation needs	**M1** explain the importance to an organisation of effectively collecting, processing and using information	**D1** explain how an organisation could improve the quality of its business information justifying each of their recommendations
P2 describe how information is used for a range of purposes in a selected organisation	**M2** compare, using examples, the usefulness of different tools for processing information to support effective business decision-making	**D2** evaluate tools used for processing information with respect to their support in decision-making
P3 describe how information flows between different functional areas in an organisation	**M3** explain the purpose and operation of data mining and predictive modelling	
P4 describe the features and key elements of a management information system, showing where it supports the functional areas of an organisation		
P5 identify the constraints that relate to the use of customer information in an organisation and describe how these may impact on the organisation		
P6 describe different tools used to manage and process information		

3.1 *Know the source and characteristics of business information*

Information can be categorised in many ways depending on how, where and in what context it is being used. It comes from different sources, both primary and secondary, and can be data-rich (quantitative) or detail-rich (qualitative). It is important that the information used for business purposes is valid, reliable, timely, fit for purpose and accessible, especially in a large organisation, or if it is being communicated over a networked system. Cost-effectiveness is also an important consideration for businesses when thinking about how data is captured, stored, processed and outputted. In addition, a business also has to consider the accuracy and relevance of information, especially if it is to be used for marketing or financial purposes.

Any business also has to consider the source of its information: whether it has been gathered from a direct customer or client base, inherited from a third party or indeed purchased, as the sources may raise issues of data security, confidentiality and overall confidence in the information.

CHARACTERISTICS OF BUSINESS INFORMATION

The difference between data and information

Data is a set of random, unprocessed facts that have little or no value until they have been processed in some way. A piece of data could be a date, for example, 17/04/2007, or a customer account number, for example, P072-100-4555. The processing activity converts the data into information, as shown below.

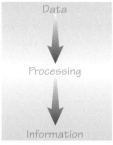

Figure 3.1 Conversion of data into information

Data Processing Information

Within a given data set, there are a number of different levels that can be accessed, as shown in Figure 3.2.

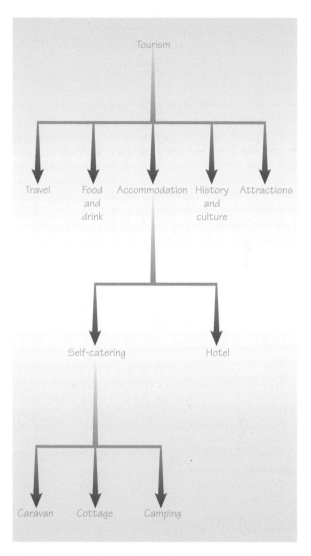

Figure 3.2 Levels of data within a given data set

Without any knowledge of the data or the statistics, a string of numbers or characters is quite meaningless and can be classed as a random data set, for example:

```
SCA/456/IH0000
- - - - - - - - - - - - - - - - - -
NET/678/PY0000
- - - - - - - - - - - - - - - - - -
CON/294/KL0000
```

Figure 3.3 A random data set

This is a data set, however it is unclear what the data set refers to. If additional data was provided to complement the set, this could transform the data into meaningful information as shown here.

Part number	Part description
SCA/456/IH0000	Scart lead
NET/678/PY0000	Network cable
CON/294/KL0000	Connector

Figure 3.4 Meaningful data set

Types of information

Information is a set of meaningful data. This meaningful information can be used to support people and organisations in day-to-day tasks and decision-making.

Qualitative information

Qualitative information provides depth and details. Qualitative information can give a much greater insight into a subject than quantitative information. The basis of qualitative information is to probe and question in order to gain an understanding of the subject matter. The best ways to extract qualitative information are through interviewing, questionnaires, feedback forms and surveys.

Statistics might have been generated to identify retention and achievement rates of students studying for a BTEC National qualification at a college as a percentage based on similar conditions across the country. However, qualitative information could be acquired through a course feedback form about which modules students enjoyed and how they felt about assessments, support and resource issues that may have helped them to achieve.

Quantitative information

Quantitative information is based on facts and statistics and provides key information that can be used, for example, for finance planning and modelling. Examples of this type of information include sales figures, control measurements and test data for an experiment.

There is a great need for quantitative information if you work within mathematical, scientific, medical or logic-orientated environments where calculations and experimentation play a dominant role in day-to-day tasks.

> **Think** Why might it be important to have both qualitative and quantitative information?

Primary and secondary information

Information can be classified as either primary or secondary according to its source, how it was derived and the reliability of the source. For example, information that came from interviewing a customer first-hand about their shopping patterns is data that came from a primary source. Observing what shoppers buy in a particular shop or conducting a survey would also give you information that came from a primary source. Information that comes from a third party, such as information from a website or newspaper report, would be classed as a secondary source.

Characteristics of good information

Valid

Information should be valid, as misinterpretations, inaccuracies and misinformation could impact negatively on decisions that need to be taken. For example, if you were making a train journey you would need to ensure that the timetable you have is valid for the date you want to travel on, otherwise you may miss your train.

Reliable

Information should be obtained from a reliable source to ensure that it is correct, especially if the information is to be used as the basis for decision-making. For example, information about sales of a product over the last month might be used as the basis for decisions about whether to extend or reduce the product range or change the price, so reliable sales information is critical.

Timely

Ensuring that information is captured, processed and delivered at the appropriate time can be critical to an organisation. Having timely information might mean that you are able to launch a product before your competitor, because you have all the facts in advance, allowing you to prepare for an early launch.

Fit for purpose

Information that is fit for purpose means that it is appropriate for the audience that it will be communicated to. For example, providing full information about current student enrolments might be fit for purpose if decisions about which courses to run in the new academic year are to be made.

Accessible

Good information should be accessible to everybody who needs to view, process or use it in some way. With the growth of networked environments, information has become more accessible as the network allows a range of users to access it at any one time.

Cost-effective

It can be very expensive to capture, process, store and present information. This means that it is important to consider the degree of benefit that can be gained from having the information before sourcing it.

Sufficiently accurate, relevant and having the right level of detail

Good information can also be defined in terms of whether it provides sufficient detail, accuracy and relevance for the target audience. For example, if you were giving a presentation on the current market share of a company that produces games consoles, you would have to conduct sufficient detailed research into the other types of consoles available, possible prices and market share in order to ensure that your presentation was both sufficient and relevant.

From a source in which the user has confidence

Information should be obtained from a source in which you have confidence. If you are researching internet usage for recreational purposes, you might use recognised and established websites that have conducted surveys on this subject, or try to find articles in respected computer magazines or journals. You could not rely on any old website that you happened to find!

Understandable by the user

Information needs to be presented in a format that is easy for the target audience to understand. It is important to ensure that the content is pitched at the correct level, for example not too technical, and that it is presented in a clear format, either in a written, visual or verbal way, that is understandable and transparent.

> **Think** Why is it important to make sure that your information has come from a reliable source?

Transformation of data into information

There are a number of stages involved in the transformation of data into information:

Stage 1 Data collection/capture

Stage 2 Data storage

Stage 3 Data processing

Stage 4 Manipulation and retrieval

Stage 5 Presentation

Depending on the activity or organisation some of the stages may occur in a different order. Each stage can be broken down further into individual elements that may be unique to certain functional departments, for example, the accounts department may capture data in a different way to a sales department.

Data collection

Data collection involves gathering information from a variety of sources and saving it using a manual or electronic resource. Once data has been gathered, it can be saved by transferring the data into another format manually, or by entering the data onto a computer.

Data storage

Data storage is essential to ensure that saved data is kept secure. The storage of data also allows for easier access, transference, updating and monitoring. The benefits of electronic storage include:

- it is permanent storage that remains after the system has shut down

- it is easy to update, make changes and save

- it provides easy access to multiple users if the data is stored in a specified location

- it can be stored in a secure format if data is coded or password mechanisms are used.

Electronic data storage can generate problems, however, if certain security protocols or standard ways of working are not enforced. If users are not aware of backup procedures then data can be lost or become corrupt.

Data processing

Data processing involves some activity that will convert the data into information. Some of the more common processing activities are described here:

- Calculating – such as using a spreadsheet to add up two columns of data automatically and present a final value. In the spreadsheet below, two columns are being multiplied together to present a final total for each week.

Monthly motherboard sales

	A	B	C	D
1	Month ending March 2007	Total sold	Unit price (£)	Value
2	Week 1	83	79.2	=PRODUCT(B2:C2)
3	Week 2	69	79.2	=PRODUCT(B3:C3)
4	Week 3	78	79.2	=PRODUCT(B4:C4)
5	Week 4	113	79.2	=PRODUCT(B5:C5)
	Total			=SUM(D2:D3)

Table 3.1 Spreadsheet adding two columns of data

- Merging – two or more pieces of data can be merged together, e.g. using mail merge (see Fig. 3.7), to make a combined document. This is a common function in word processing packages, where a standard letter template can be produced to suit a general purpose, and information, such as names and addresses, is retrieved from another document and merged with the template to create a customised letter.

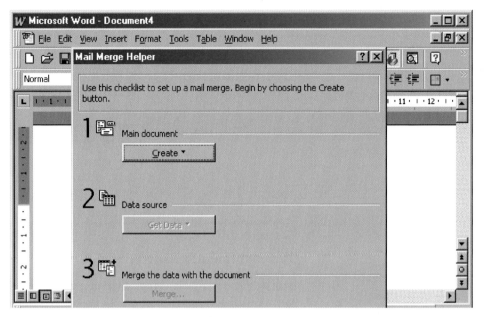

Figure 3.5 Overview of mail merge facility

• Sorting – this allows users to sort through information using specific criteria, for example sorting information alphabetically in ascending or descending order.

Figure 3.5 Three stages of sorting customer account numbers alphabetically by surname

Customer account number

Surname	First name	Account number
James	Stewart	SJ/12670P
Harrison	Charlotte	CH/5374LP
Michaels	John	JM/2900GL
Davids	Rebecca	RD/6729HN
Smyth	Pippa	PS/2773BN
Peterson	Jack	JP/7002LS
Morris	Joan	JM/3544NM
Jacobs	Mary	MJ/1003RT

Figure 3.5a Stage one: Unsorted

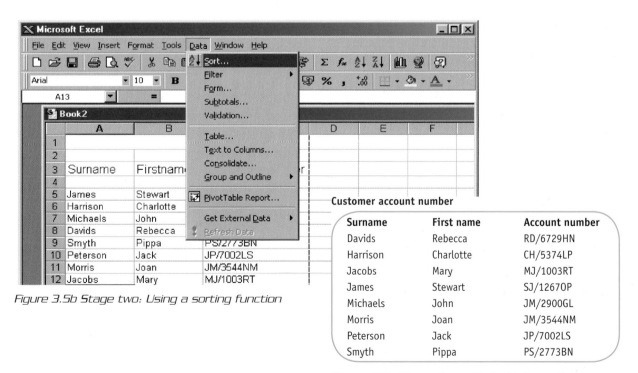

Figure 3.5b Stage two: Using a sorting function

Customer account number

Surname	First name	Account number
Davids	Rebecca	RD/6729HN
Harrison	Charlotte	CH/5374LP
Jacobs	Mary	MJ/1003RT
James	Stewart	SJ/12670P
Michaels	John	JM/2900GL
Morris	Joan	JM/3544NM
Peterson	Jack	JP/7002LS
Smyth	Pippa	PS/2773BN

Figure 3.5c Stage three: Sorted information

Table 3.2 Types of processing activity

Manual activity	Processing method	Computerised activity	Processing method
Completing an assessment	• Read through tasks • Carry out research • Produce a draft copy • Proofread • Submit final copy.	• Search for customer information	• Access a central resource such as a database • Search through information • Set up search/sort criteria parameters • Select and collate customer details.

• Selecting and interrogating – data can be fetched and retrieved so that it can be used for another purpose. An example of this would be using a query to generate a report in a database to retrieve information that is stored in a table(s).

The type of processing activity that will be used will depend on the type of system or processing requirement. Some activities are manual and others use computerised processing methods, as shown in Table 3.2 above.

Some data processing activities can be carried out manually or using computerised systems, for example:

• accessing information, physically from a resource or digitally from a file

• sorting information, physically using files and alphabetical ordering, or digitally using a tool or wizard

• performing a calculation, physically using a calculator, or digitally using a macro or a program.

Data manipulation and retrieval

Manipulating involves using, changing or updating data. An example of this would be applying a filter to a data set in order to extract specific data types, for example, only customers that lived in Norwich.

Once data has been processed it may still require further refinements in order to make it accessible and user friendly. This could involve transferring the data into more practical documents that already exist on the system, to allow for easier retrieval.

Presentation of data

The last stage in the data conversion process involves presenting or outputting the information to produce evidence, which might be a hard copy, such as a report or other business document. This evidence can then be distributed and used to get feedback. In turn, the feedback can be filtered back into the system to make it more dynamic, efficient and reliable.

To complete the data conversion process, the original model can now be extended and updated to reflect these stages as shown in Figure 3.6.

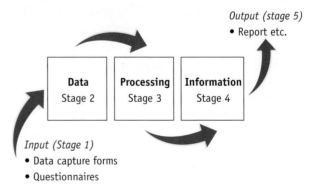

Figure 3.6 Completed conversion process: data into information

Key words

Wizard – a program within a program that helps you perform a particular task e.g. 'letter wizard' within a word processing program helps users to produce letters

Evidence activity

P1 – M1

You work as an information support analyst for TEY Insurance Group, a large insurance company with branches across the United Kingdom. The company specialise in motor, home and life insurance. Each of these three specialist areas have their own teams of managers, team leaders and call centre representatives. All of the key functional areas such as Finance, IT, Human Resources, Marketing and Promotions however are located in their head office in Canterbury.

The range of information and the sources of information that the organisation has to manage on a daily basis include:

- customer queries regarding a quotation
- new policy, renewal and policy cancellations
- underwriter queries regarding special claims or enquiries
- information that is derived internally from Head Office, other branches or other departments
- statistics and data that are released concerning changes to motor, life or home policies
- Regulatory and Statutory institutes to ensure that they are acting in compliance to certain rules, regulations and legislation.

All information that is collected by TEY Insurance is stored on a database and a MIS (management information system) that is used by the senior managers to predict trends in the market and establish patterns of trading.

You have been asked to prepare a presentation about the use of information in the company. You should prepare 10–15 slides with accompanying notes pages to remind you of the detail you will need to include when delivering the presentation.

1. Describe the characteristics and sources of information that the insurance company needs. (P1)

2. TEY Insurance use a range of information on a day-to-day basis. Explain the importance to the company of effectively collecting, processing and using information. (M1)

SOURCES OF INFORMATION

Information can be derived from a number of different sources, both internal and external

Internal sources of information

Within an organisation information can be obtained from a number of functional departments for various purposes, including:

- Finance – information on profit and loss, salaries, costs and expenses
- Human resources – information about employees, skills, CVs and training
- Marketing – details of new campaigns and launches, what products are going to be promoted over a given period and whether there are special offers available
- Purchasing – information regarding products and services purchased from suppliers and third parties, as well as analysis of facts and figures about stock and purchasing trends within the organisation
- Sales – information about the products and services that have been sold or sales that are pending, including sales sheets, forecasts and targets for a given period
- Manufacturing – might provide information about the physical production of products, examining the cost, productivity and efficiency of resources used during the manufacturing process
- Administration – administrative information largely takes the form of the day-to-day paperwork that exists within a functional department or the organisation as a whole.

External sources of information

Organisations also make use of information from a range of third-party sources, including:

- Government – the information available from government and local authorities is wide-ranging. Information from these sources includes government White Papers about proposals for new policies, guidelines on taxes, electoral data and new legislative procedures.

Research tip

You can find government white papers for the IT industry at www.knowledgestorm.co.uk or you can search all white papers at www.direct.gov.uk.

- Trade groupings – these are associations that represent the interests of organisations that work in a particular industry. The information they provide includes general leaflets and information sheets, about protecting your rights as an individual, working practices and procedures.

- Commercially provided – commercial information can be bought from organisations that specialise in data collection. Credit rating agencies are one such source, as they gather information to sell on to other organisations.

Research tip

You can check your own credit rating and see and compare information held about you at each credit reference agency at www.checkmyfile.com and www.Experian.co.uk/creditreport.

- Databases – databases can be used to provide a wide range of different types of information, about all sorts of resources. Once information has been supplied by a database, further analysis or research can be conducted to identify trends and patterns within it.

- Research – research information can come from a number of sources, including the internet, books, magazines, television, and through various fact-finding techniques, such as interviews, questionnaires, investigation of documents and observation.

Reliability of data sources

The more varied the sources of information an organisation can draw on, the more likely the information obtained is to be reliable and authentic. This is because information from different sources can be analysed and compared for accuracy. Using information from just one source may lead to bias. It is important for organisations to consider what the provider of the information might have to gain or lose as a result of the decisions taken on the basis of the information being presented, and whether it is likely that the provider may not be offering reliable information.

Example

The British Crime Survey for England and Wales uses two key sources of data to provide information about crime: the British Crime Survey (BCS) and Police-recorded crime figures. The Government believe that together they provide a better picture of crime than just one source alone. The Police-recorded crime figures provide information on well-reported crimes and can be used for local crime pattern analysis but they often under-estimate petty offences which go unreported and sexual and domestic crimes. This is because people are sometimes unwilling to report crimes to the Police which they believe are too small or commonplace or because they are afraid or distrust the Police. The BCS surveys the public and covers unreported and unrecorded crime and as a result it provides a more reliable indication of trends in crime as it is unaffected by changes in levels of reporting to the police, or in police recording. Taken together the two sources of data are a more reliable source of information as they provide a clearer picture of what is actually happening and not just what is officially reported.

3.2 Understand how organisations use business information

Business information can be represented in a number of different ways and can be derived from a range of different sources. The function of information within an organisation is to serve the needs of the functional departments, support their key activities and tasks and provide a source of reference from which they can plan, make decisions, monitor, analyse, identify trends and patterns, provide feedback and evaluate.

PURPOSES

Business information serves a number of different purposes. It can be used to support users at all levels of an organisation in their everyday operational activities, analysis and decision making. Business information can also be used at higher levels as the basis for strategies to achieve competitive advantage through increased market share, reduction in prices and diversification of a product range or to make efficiencies in operational procedures.

Operational support

At an operational level, information can be used to support the monitoring of various tasks and control of various activities in an organisation.

Example

Supermarkets make use of sales information to monitor the quantities of fresh fruit and vegetables purchased to see how much stock is required and when. Using this information, control mechanisms are put in place to notify the stock supervisor when more stock needs to be ordered. If there is an abundance of stock with a short shelf-life, through monitoring the quantities surplus stock can be put on promotion, perhaps with a 'buy one, get one free' offer.

Figure 3.7 Supermarket special offer

Analysis

The analysis of business information can be used to identify trends or patterns within a particular system or sector.

Example

In the fresh fruit and vegetable department of a supermarket, an analysis of buying patterns, customer demand and seasonal trends could be used to determine the quantities of stock required at certain periods during the year. During the Wimbledon tennis tournament, supermarkets know from previous years that there will be an increased demand for strawberries, for example.

Decision-making

Business information can be used to support users in making decisions at all levels within an organisation.

Figure 3.8 Strategic, tactical and operational decision-making

Operational decisions relate to day-to-day tasks and the mechanics of the organisation. This level, at the base of the organisational structure, involves the majority of the workforce at sub-management levels. The tactical level represents middle management, including heads of departments and assistant directors. Decisions at this level are generally about project plans, resource issues and financing. The strategic level represents the highest levels of management: the managing director, chief executive and other senior managers. Decisions at this level encompass planning for the future, strategy decisions, including mergers and takeovers, and forecasting market trends.

Gaining competitive advantage

Certain types of information give an organisation tools and knowledge that give them competitive advantage. This means having the 'upper hand' by being more cost effective, having a more diverse target audience, a larger market share or a more well-known brand or presence within the market. The type of information that would be required to gain competitive advantage includes the prices, products, customer base and possibly sales and marketing strategies of competitors within the market. Having an advantage over your competitors is very important because ultimately it will determine how much you sell, how many customers you retain and how much profit you can make.

Example

Each week people are employed by the large supermarket chains to visit competitors' shops and price check a range of items. Decisions can then be made about whether to alter prices to be the cheapest or offer the best deals.

Figure 3.9 'Buy one, get one free', offers help supermarkets stay competitive

Evidence activity

P2 – M2

TEY Insurance group generates a large amount of information on a daily basis. This information is used at all levels of the organisation.

At an operational level, the call centre representatives use information to advise and support customers on the policies for motor, home or life insurance. Team leaders use information within the organisation to make decisions and set targets to monitor whether or not the call centre representatives are meeting their sales targets on a daily and weekly basis. Managers use the MIS to identify and analyse trends within the market – a good example of this is at the end of each month when demand for motor policies increases because the push for manufacturers to sell new cars before the month end when targets are being assessed is greater. The MIS also allows data to be gathered about the market as a whole and whether or not targets being set are realistic. From this information senior managers can then decide whether or not to reduce policy prices to gain them a competitive advantage within the market.

1. Produce a report that describes how information is used for a range of purposes in the TEY Insurance group. (P2)

2. Using three examples, compare the usefulness of different tools, for example a database and an Artificial Intelligence or Knowledge Based system for processing information to support effective business decision making. Present your findings in the form of a table as shown. (M2)

Tool	Environment and examples of use	Ability to process information to support effective decision making	
		Benefits	Limitation
Example 1			
Example 2			
Example 3			

FUNCTIONAL AREAS OF AN ORGANISATION

Organisations are built around a collection of functions, each of which provides support for the operations of the business. Functional departments each serve a specific purpose within an organisation and work together to enable the organisation to achieve its objectives. The most common functional areas of an organisation are discussed below.

In large organisations, each of the functional departments may be separate, whereas smaller organisations may have integrated departments. Smaller organisations may carry out the tasks and responsibilities of each functional department, but without the dedicated resources to support it. For example, a small kiosk selling refreshments would need to sell, promote, purchase stock, distribute stock and finance it, but all of these roles may be carried out by a single person.

Figure 3.10 This man is the sales, promotion, purchasing, distribution and finance dept all rolled into one

Departments within an organisation need to communicate with each other to ensure that they share information and good practice. To ensure that this happens effectively, a number of measures need to be taken. The first is ensuring that a good organisational structure is in place with appropriate levels. Secondly, steps need to be taken to ensure that the flow of information between the levels of an organisation is open and fluent.

Sales

The sales team deal with customers and generate orders. The techniques used to generate sales varies between organisations, but some of the most common are telephone, door-to-door sales, advertising and direct sales through representatives. The sales department may also provide supporting functions to other departments, particularly if the organisation does not have a dedicated marketing or customer service department.

The sales function is critical to the success of an organisation because it provides the direct link to customers and generates income.

Purchasing

The purchasing department is responsible for monitoring how many products or stock is required at any one time and buying accordingly. The purchasing department may also be responsible for buying in consumable products, such as stationery, to support the other functional departments within the organisation.

Manufacturing

Depending on the type of organisation, one of the functional departments may be manufacturing, who would deal with all of the processing of products or services.

Large national or multi-national organisations offering a diverse range of products or services would certainly need a manufacturing department to spearhead product developments.

Whistle-blowing

Other ethical issues that may be identified include 'whistle-blowing'. What is the policy on informing colleagues or peers about the practice and behaviour of another individual? In some organisations there may be an informal communication channel providing access to a line manager. Other organisations may use a more formal written procedure for recording this information that can then be used as part of any disciplinary action required.

> **Think** Do you think that it is ethical to whistle-blow on a colleague? If you do not think that it is, what about if this colleague came into work late every single morning and you had covered for them on more than one occasion?

Organisational policies

Organisational policies can be quite wide-ranging, some of which may carry a penalty if not adhered to. There may be policies on using the IT resources, email and the internet. For example when you log-in to a computer at work the first screen might be a policy document outlining the conditions of use of IT resources. This could make reference to accessing certain sites, downloading information, spamming other users and inappropriate use of email. Users may be required to accept the conditions of use prior to accessing the system.

> **Example**
>
> In 1999 the UK saw its first 'sacked for surfing' case when Lois Franxlin, an office manager from Cheshire, was dismissed after bosses found out she had arranged a holiday over the internet during office hours.

Information ownership

Information ownership is also a consideration in terms of who owns the right to materials produced or software written, is it the individual or the organisation? In addition, what are the policies on sharing information among colleagues?

OPERATIONAL ISSUES

Information within an organisation costs money, time and numerous other resources to support its existence. Some of these issues can be classified as being operational.

Security of information

Keeping information secure is a very important operational issue that costs time and money. The Data Protection Act provides legislative procedures about the security of information and organisations must adhere to this. In conjunction, the loss of information can cost an organisation a huge amount of money, if the information has not been protected or backed up in some way. Certain organisations retain more sensitive information than others, especially in the medical profession where data about a patient's health and well-being is available at the touch of a button.

Information is at risk both internally, from users (authorised or unauthorised) who may accidentally overwrite or intentionally cause sabotage; and also externally, from hackers, viruses, Trojans or worms. Therefore backup procedures, passwords, anti-virus software, firewalls, encryption services (and additional administrators) may be required. Information also needs to be physically secure, so ensuring that the hardware and storage mechanism is secured and locked is essential.

> **Key words**
>
> Trojans – a program in which malicious data is contained inside an apparently harmless attachment
> Worms – similar to a virus, worms clone themselves once inside a system and travel the address book to send infected emails to other computers

Backups

The consequences of an organisation losing data can be very severe and the disruption to processing activities costly and time consuming. There are a number of backup options available to an organisation. These include:

- simple backup

- stack backup

- advanced stack backup

- incremental backup

- grandfather, father, son backup.

Simple backup is the elementary backup type. Each time an archive is created, the oldest version of the backup file is replaced with the newly created one.

Stack backup consists of the last created backup and previous versions – the previous versions being organised into a stack format.

The advanced stack backup procedure differs in that it does not permit unchanged or unedited files in the old backup version copies to be stacked.

An incremental backup provides a much faster method of backing up data than a full backup. During an incremental backup only the files that have changed since the last full or incremental backup are included. As a result, an incremental backup may take a fraction of the time it takes to perform a full backup.

The grandfather, father, son technique is probably the most common backup method that uses a rotation set of backup disks or tapes so that three different versions of the same data are held at any one time.

Health and safety

The best measure for health and safety in the workplace is to use common sense and adhere by standard ways of working. Organisations also offer guidelines and procedures for maintaining good working practice. In conjunction with these the Health and Safety at Work Act 1974 provides clear instruction as to the responsibilities of an employer with regards to the health and safety of it's employees.

Organisational policies

In any organisation there could be a number of organisational policies that range from 'professionalism and behaviour at work', through to 'use of ICT' and 'health and safety'. Depending upon the type of environment that a user is working within there may also be very specific policies relating to the way in which a user engages with ICT in terms of how long they can sit in front of a computer before they have to have a break. Policies relating to ICT security could ensure that no external devices are plugged into the network, that all plug-in devices are tested prior to use and that nothing is downloaded onto the network.

In terms of security there may also be very strict policies relating to what you can and cannot do with data held on a system, especially if this data is sensitive and refers to customer or client details.

Business continuance plans

Business continuance plans or disaster recovery plans should be considered and implemented by all organisations. Continuance plans can be used to combat potential and actual threats to a system. The majority of organisations will have an adopted security policy that employees should be aware of, the plan and policy being open to continuous review and updating.

The structure of a continuance plan will be unique to an organisation and their requirements. Some organisations are more at risk than others, depending upon:

- size

- location

- proximity to known natural disasters and threats – flood areas, etc.

- core business activity.

A strategy based on recovery recognises that no system is infallible. As a result, a number of companies have emerged providing 'disaster recovery' services if no internal organisation continuance plan has been drawn up. These companies will maintain copies of important data and files on behalf of an organisation. Some large organisations may have a 'backup site' so that data processing can be switched to a secondary site immediately in the case of an emergency. Smaller organisations might employ other measures such as RAID or data warehousing facilities.

Key words

RAID – redundant array of inexpensive disks. Identical copies of important files are kept in a number of different storage devices

Costs

There are a number of cost issues to consider in relation to the use of information within organisations; these can range from additional resource support in terms of hardware and software, increased storage mechanisms and additional users to manage the information. The development costs involved with capturing, processing, storing and outputting information is also a major consideration to organisations.

Impact of increasing the sophistication of systems

Systems require updating and replacing periodically, as hardware and software becomes inefficient or obsolete. As a result of this, more sophisticated and dynamic systems are required to replace them. The implications of changing a system can be quite minor if the process is managed efficiently in terms of training users on the new system or possibly employing users with a more specific system skill-base. However, if no thought is given to the complexity of introducing new hardware and software and ensuring that there are no compatibility issues across different systems/platforms or functional departments and users, the impact can be very negative and ultimately cost the organisation more than originally anticipated.

3.4 Know the features and functions of information systems

Information systems are systems that have been set up to manage and support the day-to-day activities of an organisation and also management. Almost every organisation will have information systems ranging from quite a basic system relying on simple application software to process, store and deliver information required, through to quite complex, integrated systems that support the entire organisation.

Information systems can provide support for all levels of user within an organisation. There are specific information systems that can be used by specific categories of user such as strategic, management, knowledge level and operational level. This section will address the following areas:

- information system tools
- information system examples
- management information systems (MIS)
- key elements of information systems
- information system functions.

INFORMATION SYSTEM TOOLS

Information systems can be classified in terms of their tools, function and complexity. General information systems use application software tools to process, store and deliver data and information such as databases. More specific information systems are used to support a very specialist function or need within an organisation. These can include artificial and expert systems, the Internet and a range of other information systems such as data mining or predictive modelling.

Databases

A database is one example of a general information systems tool that can be used to assist organisations in their pursuit of manageable and supportive data systems.

Databases carry out a range of functions to support all types of users. Their primary function is to store volumes of data and specific formats to allow for easy processing and access. Data that is input into a database can be formatted into meaningful and useful information.

Databases offer a range of features and tools to support an organisation. Some of these are standard across a range of database software and some are more specific. Examples include: menu systems tools, input and output tools, query and manipulation tools, validation and analysis tools.

Artificial intelligence and expert systems

Artificial intelligence and expert systems represent an advanced level of knowledge and decision support systems. Artificial intelligence systems can be used to automate certain tasks and procedures that require a certain level of 'intelligence' or 'intelligent behaviour'. Expert systems encapsulate the experience and specialised knowledge of experts in order to relay this information to a non-expert, so that they too can have access to the specialist knowledge.

Artificial intelligence systems are used in a number of different environments to provide scheduling, control or planning tools and provide the ability in cases to diagnose certain problems and give a task-based solution.

Expert systems are based on a reasoning process that resembles human thought processes. This process is dependent upon rules and reasoning, and has been extracted by experts in the field. The primary function of an expert system is to provide a 'knowledge base' that can be accessed to provide information, such as a diagnosis for a patient, to assist non-experts in their own decision-making process.

Research tip

Honda's ASIMO Robot is an artificially intelligent humanoid robot that is able to walk and carry objects. To find out more go to www.honda.com/ASIMO/new/.

Internet

The Internet is probably one of the most widely available and used information systems available. The knowledge base that exists within the Internet can provide an organisation with a wealth of data-rich information. This information can be used at all levels of an organisation to support operational functions such as buying and selling products and services, aspects of trading and e-commerce. At a tactical level, the Internet can be used to analyse different markets and competitors and monitor what they are doing.

At a strategic level, the Internet can be used to support senior managers in their decision making by providing data on other organisations that could be used if a merger or take-over was planned. At this level, data about emerging worldwide markets and locations can also be accessed to support any decisions about diversifying a product range or entering new markets on a European or global scale.

Other information systems

Data mining

Data mining is a generic term that covers a range of technologies. The actual process of 'mining' data refers to the extraction of information through tests, analysis, rules and heuristics. Information will be sorted and processed from a data set in the hope of finding new information or data anomalies that may have remained undiscovered.

Data mining embraces a wide range of technologies to include: rule induction, neural networks and data visualisation all working to provide an analyst with a more informative and better understanding of the data.

Predictive modelling

Predictive modelling uses applied reasoning to give a predicted outcome or the probability of an outcome. Predictive modelling is built upon a foundation using mathematics and equations to estimate a given outcome. For an organisation, this can be very important, especially if you want to predict 'how much a customer will spend on a particular product' or 'when they are likely to buy a particular product'.

Evidence activity

M3

You have also been asked by the senior management team at TEY Insurance if you could offer any guidance on the purpose and operation of data mining and predictive modelling. They would like to research this area as they feel it might help them to predict more accurate trends in the market. Research and deliver a short presentation (10–15 minutes) that provides guidance on the purpose and operation of data mining and predictive modelling and how it could possibly be used by the organisation. (M3)

Executive support systems (ESS)

Executive support systems support strategic personnel within an organisation, their function being to provide the support and guidance needed to carry out long-term forecasting and planning. These systems use data and information collected from the current environment in order to establish trends or anomalies, which can then be used for future planning. For example, an organisation that may wish to transfer production to Europe over the next five years may look at a range of available data sources to include:

- cost of manufacturing (labour, transportation, premises)
- import and export issues (cost, initiatives, barriers to trade)
- existing businesses already trading in Europe and their profitability
- current financial status and whether there would be enough capital to finance such a venture in the future
- existing competition in Europe.

In order to identify specific trends, ESS may also rely on historical data to identify what has been done in the past and if it was successful.

Decision support systems (DSS)

Decision support systems support the management levels within an organisation, helping them to make dynamic decisions that are characterised as being semi-structured or unstructured. These systems have to be dynamic in order to support

the demand for up-to-date information, enabling a fast response to the changing conditions of an organisation.

These information systems are complex analytical systems designed explicitly with a variety of analysis and modelling tools to process, enquire and evaluate certain conditions.

Transaction processing systems (TPS)

These systems exist to support the operational level of organisations and assist in providing answers to structured routine decisions. The systems are pivotal to any organisation because they provide the backbone to day-to-day activities and processing. Examples of TPS include: a holiday booking system, customer ordering system and payroll system.

Office automation systems (OAS)

These systems are set up to identify and increase levels of efficiency and productivity among the workforce. To assist in this role, various tools and software are available to schedule, monitor and improve workforce activities. These systems will enable the workforce to:

- communicate more effectively
- promote collaborations and group synergy
- structure daily tasks and activities
- track and schedule appointments and activities
- increase productivity by reducing repetitive workload
- assist with the automation of repetitive tasks.

Process control systems

Process control systems monitor, support and control certain process activities within a manufacturing environment. Applications, which are used to support process control systems, can help an organisation in the following ways:

i)   Improve quality control
ii) Assist with project planning of the product
iii) Assist with physical design
iv) Identify resource requirements
v)   Identify development status or stage in the product life cycle.

INFORMATION SYSTEM EXAMPLES

Information systems can be used to support a range of business functions, examples of which include marketing, financial and human resources.

Marketing information systems

Within this functional area, an information system can be used to support a wide range of activities. These can include:

- examining sales performance figures and targets to identify peaks and troughs in sales and possibly to predict when sales will be at their highest and lowest throughout the year

- analysis of competitors to identify who they are, market shares, profits, customer base and product ranges

- promotions to identify when the best time is to launch a new promotion depending upon the season and possibly stock levels.

Figure 3.15 Information systems help organisations analyse competitors' market share

Financial information systems

Financial information systems are very important as they can control and monitor on a day-to-day basis the profitability of an organisation, financial costs and possible investments made. In some environments, financial information systems are deemed to be critical as the tracking of worldwide markets, stocks and shares can change every second.

At an operational level, financial systems can be used to support users in the preparation of wages and salaries, they can assist in price-setting and target-setting, and they can also link into third-party systems to ensure that transactions are conducted in a more timely and efficient way.

Human resource systems

Information systems can be used to support the monitoring of staff, skills base, recruitment campaigns and also professional development in terms of training opportunities, attendance at development events and ensuring that staff members are equipped with the skills that they need to carry out their job role effectively.

MANAGEMENT INFORMATION SYSTEMS (MIS)

The primary role of a MIS is to convert data from internal and external sources into information so that it can be communicated to all levels within an organisation. Management, however, will use the information produced to enable them to make more effective decisions.

Management information systems are used to support tactical and strategic decision-making and are therefore associated with use by managers at these levels. MIS clearly embraces a range of information systems including:

- information reporting systems

- decision support systems

- executive information systems.

Features and benefits

The most important feature of a MIS is the role it plays in supporting managers in their decisions, based on fact and figures taken internally from the organisation.

In order to assist managers in their decision making, data and information needs to be made available in an appropriate format. Another main feature of an information system is the reporting system that it provides. Reports can be generated periodically at predetermined intervals, for example, every hour, every day, week or month, on demand – as and when required or by exception when an event triggers the need for a report.

The report will be the result of data collected internally and possibly externally at an operational level – on the shop floor, processed and output through the information reporting system. Typical report types are shown in Table 3.4.

The benefits of a MIS can therefore include having fast and reliable information, access to an extensive knowledge base, access to data that can support managers in their decision-making role and having information that can be used to improve the efficiency, productivity, cost-effectiveness and overall competitiveness of an organisation.

Effectiveness criteria

A good MIS meets the requirements of the user; this can be measured through certain effectiveness criteria that can analyse the accuracy, sustainability, response time and confidence in the system by end users.

Accuracy

As the purpose of MIS is to support management in their decision making, it is essential that any input data and the processing that takes place is accurate.

Errors in the data caused by information and knowledge that has been derived from an inaccurate MIS could result in major flaws in decisions that are made.

Sustainability

To be effective, a MIS has to sustainable and robust. The design and implementation of a MIS takes times and costs money and valuable resource input, therefore it has to have a prolonged shelf-life to justify this expense.

Response times

The response times of a MIS can be critical in the decision-making process for managers. Some information such as financial reporting may indeed be required at specific times within a set period; therefore it is critical that the MIS can meet this demand.

Confidence

Finally having overall confidence in a MIS ensures that users want to embrace the technology and the knowledge that it provides. If the MIS is unreliable, then a user may look to alternative methods to capture and process certain information that could raise issues about the need for a MIS and overall justification of the initial and day-to-day costs of maintaining it.

Table 3.4 Typical report types

Report type	Internal data	External data
Stock requisition	Current stock levels & stock prices (generated by warehouse or stock personnel	Availability and pricing of stock item (suppliers)
Productivity	Amount of widgets made in a set period, amount of personnel making the widgets and cost of production.	Competitor widget output levels, market share information

KEY ELEMENTS OF INFORMATION SYSTEMS

There are a number of key elements that can impact upon the success or failure of an information system. Some of these elements can include: data, people, hardware, software and telecommunications.

Data

The source of the data and information that feeds into an information system will have a direct impact on the quality and reliability of the output data.

To ensure that the output data is delivered at the correct level and in the appropriate format, the source data needs to be clear, concise and easily accessible.

People

People are required to assist with the design, information input, manipulation and maintenance of information systems. Information systems are only as good as the expert that the knowledge has been drawn from. If management have not been involved with the design of the information system, the completed system may not meet the requirements of the end user. The design may be flawed and inadequate to meet the demands the organisation. People are also required to interrogate the information system and ensure that the correct information is output.

> **Think** In what other ways can people have an impact on the success or failure of an information system?

Hardware and software

An information system should be flexible enough to cope with current and future demands made upon it. The hardware and software provisions used to support an information system should therefore be dynamic enough to meet this demand.

The hardware needs to robust enough to ensure that data can be processed quickly and stored in large volumes. In conjunction, the software needs to be able to cope with a range of analytical and possibly predictive and intelligent tasks and requests, and above all, the software should be user friendly.

The hardware and the software need to be sophisticated enough to process data at all levels and draw upon the knowledge base created to make informed value judgements that can then be presented in an appropriate format.

Telecommunications

The ability to communicate the data and knowledge from an information system is crucial. The use of ICT and telecommunication tools is essential to ensure that information is delivered in a secure, reliable and speedy format. It might also be necessary to distribute the information to a wide audience simultaneously. This is where telecommunications can play an integral role in providing easy access and a synchronous format of delivery.

> **Key words**
>
> Synchronous – a synchronous signal on a computer is one in which the time between one BIT and the next is the same. In telecommunications terms a synchronous format of delivery refers to a fast method like email or instant messaging

INFORMATION SYSTEM FUNCTIONS

Information systems perform a range of tasks and serve a number of functions/purposes within an organisation. Some of these functions can be quite specialist, others are more general. However the basic function of an information system is to create an environment that facilitates input, storage, processing, output, control and feedback. These functions can then be applied to different system formats, for example open and closed systems.

Input

The inputs for an information system or the 'triggers' can be captured from a range of sources; these can include data that is sourced directly from a particular target audience, such as customers, students or patients. The data can then be input by a user through the use of an 'input device' such a keyboard, scanner, optical reader, point and click device, and so on.

Storage

Once data had been input, the function of an information system is to store, process and output the information in a suitable format. The storage mechanism can vary between a range of internal and external devices depending upon the need for portability. By storing the data, it can then be retrieved at a later date for processing.

Processing

The processing of the data is where information develops as possibly meaningless facts are processed into meaningful information and a knowledge-base.

Output

Information can then be output in the form of a report or other required document that the user can then use to support their job role or a specific organisational task.

Control and feedback loops

Control and feedback is essential as part of this looped process to ensure that certain measures are implemented to provide guidelines as to the 'effectiveness' of the information system in delivering both quantitative and qualitative information. These controls and feedback tools can be devices that are built into the system and can be hardware- or software-based. Alternatively, the end user can provide the control and feedback instruments required to measure the effectiveness of the system.

Closed and open systems

All of these combined information system functions apply to both open and closed systems. An open system provides the opportunity for interaction with other systems outside of its environment, for example a college system interacting with a local government system. A closed system is more insular in that it only operates within its own internal environment and rarely interacts with other systems outside of these boundaries.

Evidence activity

P4 – P6 – D2

In your role as an information support analyst for TEY Insurance, you have been asked to carry out some research on information systems. The company would like to use your research to present to the finance director. Hopefully your findings will show that there is a need to expand the current management information system and allow access to a general information system that will support users at all levels.

1. Describe the features and key elements of a management information system, showing where it supports the functional areas of an organisation. Use a table to relate the features and key elements to the different functional areas. (P4)

2. Use any records of practical work that you have gathered throughout the course of this unit to describe the different tools used to manage and process information. (P6)

3. Evaluate tools used for processing information with respect to their support in decision making. (D2)

CASE STUDY: INFORMATION SYSTEMS

Silver Books is a book publishers specialising in fiction books for children and young adults. They employ 50 members of staff and publish around 25 books a year. Staff are employed in a number of departments including Editorial, Production, Design, Marketing, Sales and Finance. In order to manage the book production process across the different teams, it is important that all the departments are kept up to date and that information is shared freely between departments.

The information system Silver Books use is called Book Project Management (BPM). BPM tracks and logs the progress of a book from proposal (initial idea) stage through to publication and it also monitors sales after publication.

One of Silver Books bestselling authors, Eleanor Browning, has an idea for a new children's book. The editorial team use BPM to run off a report showing the annual and lifetime sales of the author's previous titles. They can use this information to make a judgement about how well the new title is likely to sell. Once the editorial team has decided to proceed with the book, a contract is signed and the details of the book (such as the manuscript delivery date and format of the book) are entered onto the BPM system by the BPM administrator, the only person in the company who can add or alter data on BPM. Eleanor Browning agrees to deliver the final manuscript within six months and by using the information on BPM each department can now create a schedule within BPM. Each team can refer to the schedule, enabling them to plan for their part in the production process. For example, Marketing can plan a marketing campaign, for example printing promotional

material with details of the price and book publication date for distribution to customers and arranging a book launch for the day of publication. BPM is also used to manage the publication process. The warehouse manager allocates space in the warehouse for the book and organises deliveries to retailers around the country. The company's sales representatives are briefed about the new book and regularly check BPM to make sure that they have the most up to date information about the publication date and price of the book.

BPM also links to external contacts such as bookshops and internet retailers like Amazon. When Amazon receives information about the forthcoming book via BPM it can begin advertising it to users of their site. They can take orders and commit to delivering ordered copies on the day of publication.

QUESTIONS

1. Why do you think only one member of staff can add and alter data on BPM?

2. The BPM administrator makes an error when inputting the manuscript delivery date; this has a knock-on effect for other departments as it means their schedules are now incorrect. What systems could be put into place to ensure that data input errors are caught as soon as possible?

3. The author will miss her deadline and the book will be 6 months late. Her Editor tells the BPM administrator who updates BPM. How should this update be communicated to the rest of BPMs users? Is simply expecting people to check the system regularly enough?

Organisational systems security

unit 15

Computer systems and the information on them are under constant attack. Hackers, crackers and cyber-criminals are testing the defences of systems 24 hours a day. Viruses and worms break through the outer walls of the system, and an army of Trojan horses are sent in to transmit information back out. Natural disasters, human error and system failures are also a constant worry. Above all, the members of an organisation are themselves the largest potential threat to systems security.

When establishing a system's security, the ICT team has many measures at their disposal. They build strong rooms, and use bigger and better locks. They have ways to establish that users are who they say they are, including secret passwords and biometric controls. They use virus and worm killers, and put the system behind firewalls, proxy servers and content filters. They lock down resources and restrict what users can do. Web pages viewed and the messages sent and received are monitored and unbreakable encryption, fireproof safes and blast-proof data centres are all employed. ICT teams have fully rehearsed disaster recovery plans.

There is a tension between the need for security and personal rights. if security is too rigid, individual liberty is sacrificed. If every email is read, every web page viewed, every keystroke monitored, what is the impact on the rights of the individual?

By the end of this unit, you will:

So you want to be an...
IT Support Technician

My name Richard Bennicot
Age 24
Income £20,500

What do you do?

I am part of a small team that supports the PC LAN (local area network) and the users of the network and ensures the security of the system.

What responsibilities do you have?

I am responsible for users and their security. I set up new accounts, help users set up strong passwords and advise them on how to use the network safely. I troubleshoot problems on users' workstations in response to help desk incidents. I am part of the team that deals with back ups and upgrades. I have also just recently been part of the team that conducted a major internal security audit.

> 66 **I am hoping to try for network administration and network management posts within a couple of years** 99

How did you get into the job?

I have a BTEC National Diploma for IT Practitioners, which was a first step to the job. Colleagues have Applied GCEs in ICT or a BTEC Higher National Diploma in Business IT - I believe one of the team also has a degree. You need a good standard of general education, the ability to get along with people, and an interest in computers and networks.

How did you find your current job?

I found my job in a national newspaper (the Guardian), though I have also seen similar jobs in local papers and on internet job sites.

What training did you get?

When I started I did an on-the-job induction course, which familiarised me with the company, policies and procedures, and the company network. I have been on a number of training courses, and I am currently working toward being a Microsoft Certified Systems Engineer.

What are the hours like?

I work normal office hours most of the time. Occasionally a large upgrade or a security problem can mean that I have to stay on and work overnight to ensure the network is secure and back up again as soon as is possible.

What skills do you need?

You have to develop solid technical skills, but you can usually gain these as you learn. You must be willing to listen and to learn. Most of all you should be able to get on with people regardless of their ages or backgrounds. You need to be a good communicator: confident and outgoing, but also polite and tactful.

How good is the pay?

I started on £17,000 two years ago. The pay and the responsibilities vary between companies – the top rate's about £26,000 unless you move on to become a Senior Engineer or Network Manager in which case it can be a great deal more.

What about the future?

I'm taking more responsibility as I become more experienced and take more training courses. I am hoping to try for network administration and network management posts within a couple of years.

Grading criteria

The table below shows what you need to do to gain a pass, merit or distinction in this part of the qualification. Make sure that you refer back to it when you are completing work so that you can judge whether you are meeting the criteria and what you need to do to fill in gaps in your knowledge or experience.

In this unit there are six evidence activities that give you an opportunity to demonstrate your achievement of the grading criteria:

page 112	P1, P2
page 117	M3
page 121	P4, P5, M1, M2, D1
page 127	P6, P7
page 129	P3, D2

To achieve a pass grade the evidence must show that the learner is able to...	To achieve a merit grade the evidence must show that, in addition to the pass criteria, the learner is able to...	To achieve a distinction grade the evidence must show that, in addition to the pass and merit criteria, the learner is able to...
P1 describe the various types of threats to organisations, systems and data	**M1** explain possible security issues which exist within a given system	**D1** describe the possible security issues which exist within a given system, identify the likelihood of each and propose acceptable steps to counter the issues
P2 describe the potential impact of four different threats	**M2** explain the operation and effect of two different threats involving gaining access to information without damage to information	**D2** justify the security policies used in an organisation
P3 describe the countermeasures available to an organisation that will reduce the risk of damage to information	**M3** explain the operation and use of an encryption technique in ensuring security of transmitted information	
P4 describe the countermeasures available to an organisation that will reduce the risk of damage to physical systems		
P5 describe different methods of recovering from a disaster		
P6 describe the tools and policies an organisation can adopt in managing organisational issues in relation to ICT security		
P7 describe how staff contracts and code of conduct can assist the task of ensuring secure systems		

15.1 *Know potential threats to ICT systems and organisations*

Organisations must be aware of potential threats to ICT systems in order to protect the security of their systems and the information they manage. The most common threat is unauthorised access to resources by members of staff or by people outside of the organisation. Other threats include: natural disasters, malicious damage, failures and theft. An organisation's data can be stolen, corrupted or mismanaged, its websites can be attacked and goods and services can be stolen. In this section you will learn about these threats and the impact they could have on an organisation's services, profit and reputation.

UNAUTHORISED ACCESS

'Phone phreaks' were the first to cause breaches of network security, by using tones to control the routing of telephone calls across automated telephone networks. Hacking is now a huge movement causing problems for organisational security. Any opening hackers find is an invitation to thieves so a large part of the ICT team's job is protecting against unauthorised access.

A Who's Who of unauthorised access!

Hacker – rewrites (hacks) parts of programs or systems. The name is now used as a generic term for hackers and crackers, but early on hackers were seen as clever maverick programmers.

Cracker – tries to break into (crack) protected programs or systems.

Phreak – explores and attempts to control phone systems.

Pirate – copies and distributes software and media illicitly.

Virus author – writes worms, viruses, Trojan horses and logic bombs.

Internal and external threats

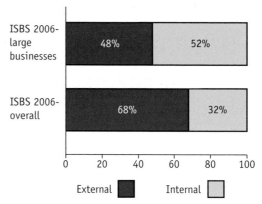

Figure 15.1: Internal and external security breaches
[Source: DTI/Pricewaterhouse Coopers, 2006]

The immediate threats to systems security come from within. Employees are able to access systems legitimately. They can see how the systems work and can plan more sophisticated attacks that involve knowledge of the system and its security. For example, they can place password cracker and keylogger programs on systems inside the network security.

Key words

Password cracker – a program that attempts to find a user's password by trying a list of common programs and then doing a brute force search

Keylogger – a program that logs every keystroke made at the keyboard. This can then be used to find passwords, logon details, bank account details, etc.

Employees can also commit simpler security breaches like reading the passwords stuck onto colleagues' monitors or guessing passwords using knowledge of people's football teams and children's names. As a result a lot of the security measures in the system have to be directed at internal threats.

External threats include attempted theft and vandalism, attempts to flood the organisation's systems with messages, attempts to trawl for customer details in phishing and pharming attacks Turn to page XX to learn more about phising and pharming), and the possible spread of viruses, worms and Trojans. People who work within the premises but do not have the same access as employees are also a potential threat.

A security audit by an international bank in the City of London revealed that the bank's traders routinely left their systems logged on overnight and that a large number of them kept sticky notes on their monitors with their passwords written on them. Cleaners and other workers had access to this room every evening after all the traders had left. This was a potential security nightmare that required urgent attention.

Think Why might employees write their passwords down? What can the IT department do to stop this happening?

Access causing damage to data or jamming resources

Malware is software that is used to cause damage. It comes in many forms, but the most common is the related threats of viruses, worms and Trojan Horses.

Viruses

A computer virus is a piece of computer code that creates and runs a clone of itself on a host system. A virus is attached to a file that will then create a copy of itself. It will attach itself to an essential system file to ensure that it is run each time the computer system is activated. Some viruses are harmless but really malicious viruses will delete files or destroy system resources to make the whole system unusable.

Worms

A worm is similar to a virus. It is usually sent as an email attachment, although it can be transmitted in other ways. When activated, the worm is installed as a stand-alone program on the target's system. Once there, it creates clones of itself. Destroying one of these may still leave 10,000 copies behind. These worms can be programmed to send out new emails to infect other computers by trawling the address book of the recipient. The more harmful worms block any anti-virus program that attempts to recognise them.

Once installed, a worm may create copies of itself and damage files or system resources just like a virus. A recent, troubling development is the use of worms to install programs that send information from the host back to the originator of the worm. This leads us on to Trojans.

Trojans

A Trojan Horse is named after the gift the Greeks sent to the Trojans, a large statue of a horse filled with soldiers who attacked the city of Troy from within. Trojan attacks on ICT systems are started in the same way as virus and worm attacks. Unlike worms and viruses, however, Trojans do not replicate themselves. Most create a back door into the user's system or send information back to the developer who is able to control the user's system remotely. Other Trojans can send information, such as user passwords, back to a controller.

The most serious threats are targeted, blended attacks using a mixture of the different techniques with a wide range of payloads. A worm may be used to install a Trojan operating as a back door and a Trojan to send information back to the controller, and to spread itself widely on the target's network. It may then destroy files and flood system resources to cause maximum damage.

Key words

Payload – a destructive cargo carried with, or attached to, a file

Accessing systems or data without damage

Not all threats to a system involve damage to systems or data: allowing a non-authorised individual to access certain data is potentially a serious threat. Personal data held on a system is a valuable resource specifically protected by law. Allowing someone to access personal data without authorisation can expose the organisation to prosecution and can lead to commercial espionage, loss of business and even closure of the organisation.

Specific examples of unauthorised access

Phishing

Phishing is a method of trying to discover users' authentication details. It is called Phishing because it is similar to a fisherman laying out a lure to catch fish. Official looking emails are sent asking a customer to confirm their bank account details. The email will direct the customer, via a hyperlink, to a clone of the bank's official website, where they will be asked to input passwords and log in details.

The Anti-Phishing working group reported that the average number of new phishing websites in existence during the last quarter of 2005 was around 33,000.

Identity theft

Identity theft occurs when someone takes on the identity of another person to obtain goods, services or access to information. The cost to the UK economy is estimated to be over £1.72 billion per annum. The cost to individuals who have had their identity stolen can be devastating. The thief uses an individual's name to take out loans, credit cards and to buy goods. The individual affected will have to prove that they did not build up these debts themselves and were not party to the fraud.

Piggybacking

Piggybacking is a method of accessing networks without authorisation. Wireless networks are piggybacked by finding an unprotected wireless hotspot and accessing the internet using this connection. In the worst cases intruders may access someone's personal network by piggybacking on their connection. An AOL survey revealed that nearly one in six people have piggybacked off someone else's wireless connection.

Another form of piggybacking is the use of someone else's network authorisation to access services or to visit sites they would not visit using their own identity. Piggybacking also occurs when someone gains access to a secure area by following someone else in before a secure door or gate closes.

Example

Some local authorities in New York and California are making it an offence to permit unsecured access to Wi-Fi networks because they are worried about access to confidential data through an open connection.

In the UK, Channel Five's Gadget Show is spearheading a campaign to bring free wireless hotspots to the whole of the UK.

> **Think** Would you be happy to allow unsecured wireless access to any home network or corporate network that you establish?

Figure 15.2 Home Office Identity Fraud website
[source: www.identity-theft.org.uk]

Hacking

Hacking is now a generic term for almost any illegal activity that involves breaking into ICT systems. Hacking includes a range of activities, including:

- programming designed to test the security and intelligence of the ICT industry

- children running cracking programs they find on the internet to crack passwords for fun

- teenagers using codes found on the internet to crack the copy protection on an expensive piece of software that they could not otherwise afford

- organised criminals doing the same for massive profit

- terrorists attempting to break into military and other systems to gain intelligence.

All hackers, even those without criminal intent, can cause enormous problems for ICT security staff.

> **Think** Do you think hacking is essentially a fun activity or is it always potentially dangerous?

DAMAGE TO OR DESTRUCTION OF SYSTEMS OR INFORMATION

Natural disasters

In the UK, dramatic natural disasters like earthquakes are unlikely, although they do occur from time to time so need to be planned for. It is more likely that organisations will be affected by fire, flooding or loss of power.

Malicious damage

Malicious damage to systems or data can be caused by vandalism or sabotage, but is more likely to be the result of damage from an electronic cause, such as viruses. According to a survey by the Department of Trade and Industry/Price Waterhouse Coopers, 52 per cent of all businesses and 84 per cent of large businesses suffered incidents of malicious damage in 2006.

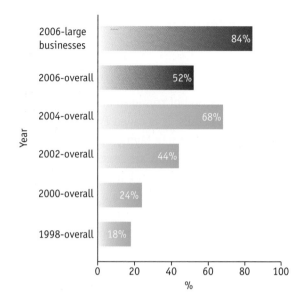

Figure 15.3 Graph showing the percentage of businesses experiencing information security breaches, by year
Source: DTI/Pricewtaerhouse Coopers, 2006

Technical failures

All equipment fails at some point and some technical failures are more drastic than others. A broken monitor may be inconvenient, but is not a great risk. A failed domain server could result in a whole organisation being out of action while it is being restored.

Human errors

Human error is inevitable. If a network manager forgets to change the default password, hackers could gain access to the system's resources using what is, in effect, an open door. If a user who is logged on with a guest account leaves a machine logged on then the consequences will probably be minimal.

> **Example**
>
> Over the August bank holiday in 2005, the Argos website advertised a deal that bundled a TV and DVD player for 49p. A large number of users snapped up the deal. Argos declined to accept the orders however, stating that it was a genuine mistake caused by human error in entering the price.

Theft

In addition to the theft of equipment or software one of the biggest threats is theft of the information that an organisation holds. A network may be secured against hackers, but an employee can still load company data onto a USB flash memory device and walk out, or steal a laptop containing valuable information. Theft of personal data held on devices that are being transported or stored insecurely is a major problem.

Examples

In May 2006, an employee of the US Department of Veterans Affairs took a laptop and small external hard wireless disk home. These contained personal information about all the military veterans discharged from the services since 1975, a total of over 26 million people. These devices were subsequently stolen, exposing the veterans to potential ID theft.

In the UK, in November 2005, three laptops containing personal data on Metropolitan Police officers were stolen in a burglary of the firm that handles their pay and pensions payments.

In Autumn 2006, a laptop containing the records of 11 million Nationwide Building Society customers was stolen in a domestic burglary.

Research tip

Look at the Chronology of Data Breaches website to find out how many data breaches there are per month on average: www.privacyrights.org/ar/ChronDataBreaches.htm.

INFORMATION SECURITY

The information that systems hold is often extremely valuable. There are legal requirements for organisations to keep personal data secure. Other information has a commercial value to companies, so it must be held securely to ensure that it is not corrupted in any way.

Confidentiality

Organisations are obliged to store personal data securely so that it cannot be accessed by others. Marketing and customer data and profit forecasts would be useful to competitors or criminals if they could access it.

Example

One threat to confidential data is posed by the employees of an organisation. In February 2007, a research scientist called Gary Min, who had worked for DuPont for ten years, was found to have stolen trade secrets worth more than $400 million from his employer when he gained a job with a competitor.

Email poses a threat to confidential information. SurfControl, a content monitoring software organisation, found that 39 per cent of people surveyed had received confidential information intended for others via email. Fifteen per cent of respondents said that they had sent out confidential information to the wrong addressee.

When storage devices are decommissioned, sold or recycled, confidential data can be put at risk. Recycled hard disks from discarded PCs sent to Nigeria have been found to contain confidential information.

Integrity, completeness and availability of data

Data can lack integrity, it might not be complete or it may not be available when needed. A data entry clerk may not enter data correctly and if the errors are in a supermarket's price look-up database, for example, the prices at the till will be wrong and customer confidence could be shaken. People in charge of security must consider this threat to data alongside the more high profile threats.

THREATS RELATED TO E-COMMERCE

Websites are subject to a number of specific risks. To a home user these can cause inconvenience and frustration but to an e-commerce business these risks threaten the organisation's business website.

Website defacement

All organisations with websites face the threat of website defacement. Some defacers like to write obscene messages; others may attempt to attack sites for political reasons. Animal rights activists have targeted sites of companies associated with animal experimentation.

Figure 15.4 Simulated defacement of a website

Research tip

Read the information about website defacement on the Cybercrime website at http://library.thinkquest.org/ 04oct/00460/defacement.html. What are the motives behind defacement attacks? What are the potential impacts on a personal home page and on an e-commerce site?

Control of access to data via third-party suppliers

ICT staff spend a lot of time ensuring the security of the systems and data held onsite; it is not uncommon for mission critical data to be managed offsite by third-party suppliers. Website hosting is also often preferred to managing a website internally.

Key words

Mission critical – data which is crucial to the operation of the organisation

The decision to outsource is usually taken on security grounds. The web host will provide state-of-the-art network security and monitoring with excellent back-up facilities. In some cases, however, it is not clear how good their physical security is. If they routinely allow people access to manage their own servers or only own part of a building the potential threat is great. An organisation's ICT staff must be very aware of all aspects of security at any outsource centre they use and ensure that it is at least as good as the security at their own site.

Other threats related to e-commerce

E-commerce sites are vulnerable to other forms of threat, such as denial of service (DOS) attacks, which take a variety of forms. The simplest form of DOS attack might be cutting a cable to disable the main network. The classic form of DOS attack is flooding the network by sending lots of messages, but a DOS attack is more likely to be created by exploiting a software or network flaw to get a network interface to pump out signals continually. The impact of this type of threat is usually short-lived as these attacks can usually be dealt with quite simply, but while the attack is ongoing the effects are very serious.

COUNTERFEIT GOODS

Most branded goods have been counterfeited. In the ICT industry the threat is even greater because of the ease of cloning. The equipment used can be as simple as a CD rewriter, or as complex as a complete factory making counterfeit goods. The main impact of this threat is the loss of revenue to the genuine business, and the extra costs in enforcing the copyright.

Products at risk

The main products at risk in the ICT and media industry are software, music, DVDs and games. Software products are counterfeited in a number of ways. Professional business software is often cloned in factories and distributed through websites and the post, usually from overseas addresses. A particular hate of the software industry is the CD compendium, which bundles together a large amount of pirated software, worth thousands of pounds, as legal software on a single optical disk.

CDs and DVDs are counterfeited and sold illegally in similar ways, ranging from shrink-wrapped clones to poor, obviously illegal copies. Recorded music is available almost universally in digital format and takes almost no effort to copy. Live concerts can be recorded using DAT, minidisk and then copied and sold on. Good quality copies of films are harder to create, they are often poor quality, and some are recorded using a hand-held video camera in a cinema.

Distribution mechanisms

Counterfeit shrink-wrapped products are sold alongside genuine products, on foreign-based websites or auction sites. Inferior copies are often sold at boot sales, markets and on auction sites where they cannot be viewed before purchase or are cheap enough for buyers to overlook the moral position.

Example

A raid at a boot sale in Wombourne in Staffordshire in 2005 uncovered nearly half a million pounds worth of counterfeit goods, including 20,000 fake DVDs, copies of the game Doom 3 and Game Cube software.

The main channel of distribution for counterfeit software and entertainment is the Internet, through peer-to-peer file-sharing sites.

Key words

Peer-to-peer file sharing – a file sharing system where computers that download data also serve that data to other downloaders

The software industry, through the Federation Against Software Theft, and the entertainment industry, through the Federation Against Copyright Theft, are very concerned about counterfeit goods and have both had successes in chasing pirates.

Some less reputable shops and other dealers, known as hard-disk loaders, tempt buyers to purchase their hardware by loading on copied software, without valid licences. People with an OEM (Original Equipment Manufacturer) licence have the rights to distribute bundled software with the machines they sell, but these licences are sometimes abused by selling software without a licence, which means that they don't pay the software manufacturer, or selling the OEM software without hardware, thus enabling the customer to avoid paying the correct price.

Some companies have been known to copy software they already have onto new machines without purchasing new licences. Others put one copy of licenced software on a server and allow anyone in the organisation access. These are forms of copyright theft and could expose an organisation to massive law suits and prison sentences for those responsible.

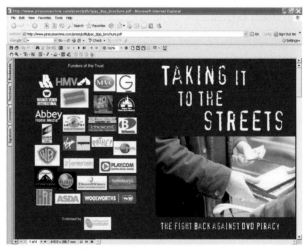

Figure 15.5 A brochure from www.piracyisacrime.com

ORGANISATIONAL IMPACT

The organisational impacts of security threats fall into four main inter-related categories: loss of service, loss of business or income, increased costs and creating a poor image of the organisation.

Loss of service

Damage to equipment, systems or information can lead to a service outage. A DOS attack or website defacement on an e-commerce site means that the business is taken out of action. If a salesperson cannot access the stock or price database, or if packers cannot access the packing lists then the organisation cannot do business. Modern businesses are so dependent on ICT systems that service outages can be devastating.

Loss of business or income

A lengthy outage can lead to a loss of business. Loss of business may result directly from a loss of service, but can also be caused by a security breach. A breach of a customer relations management or sales database may mean that potential sales are not acted on.

Increased costs

The costs associated with security breaches are often the easiest consequence to see and quantify. Buying a new hard disk, hiring a new employee or retyping in lost data are all costly, but easy to quantify. The organisation's image and reputation is probably the more important loss however. If customers do not trust an organisation, it is hard to do business at all.

Poor image

Loss of image can lead to long-term loss of income. If a company that holds credit card data is hacked into, there may be an immediate loss of service while it investigates the breach and a loss of income while this is ongoing. However, if customers do not trust an organisation to keep their data safe they may take their business elsewhere.

Example

In January 2007, TK Maxx's US parent company, TJX, admitted that hackers had stolen over 45.6 million credit card details. In their investigations, it became clear that security had been compromised for an extended period of time. Find out what TJX had to say about the breach on their website at www.tjx.com/tjx_message.html.

Think What losses would a company that suffered such a large breach incur? What do you feel would be their largest problem in the time after disclosure?

EVIDENCE ACTIVITY

P1 – P2

1. You are going to hold a group discussion about the various types of threats to ICT systems and organisations. Choose two different organisations, one of which you should be very familiar with, for example the institution where you learn. Research and make notes about the various types of threats associated with the systems of these organisations and the data they hold and use these to take part in the discussion. (P1)

2. Produce a leaflet for one of these organisations to give to each of its employees. The leaflet should detail four different threats that are particularly relevant to that organisation. Describe what the potential impact that each of the threats would have on the organisation so that employees are clear about how serious the threats are. (P2)

15.2 Understand how to keep systems and data secure

Data is subject to a large number of risks so a variety of different methods are used to keep data systems and data secure.

Figure 15.6 Physical data centre security

PHYSICAL SECURITY

The physical security is one of the first areas that must be looked at. Hacking into a system from the outside is a danger but more damage can be done from within a system. It is important to identify the points within a system that are most open to damage. The servers of a large local area network (LAN) are one such point. Access to a server gives limitless access to accounts, files and security logs. The physical security system will need to take account of the potential risks and damage, and balance the measures taken to prevent this with the need for access to the system.

Locks

Servers and mass storage devices are often kept in locked rooms that are only accessible to authorised personnel. Racks containing the communication devices (the routers, switches, hubs and the patch panels used to connect the individual workstations to these devices) should be locked away securely

to prevent accidental or malicious disruption of the network. Administrative workstations should be locked away in a secure office.

There are a huge variety of locks available, from latch locks to key code locks; magnetic keys, in which an ID card is used to open the lock; and biometric keys, in which some measure of the user's biology is matched to a known record.

Visitors' passes and sign in/sign out systems

One security procedure is to ensure that every person on the premises is logged. This can involve all members signing in and signing out at reception, accompanied by some form of ID card. In an integrated system, ID cards will be used to allow particular people access to more secure areas.

Visitors should sign in and out and be issued with a visitor's pass that they must display clearly while on the premises.

Other physical security measures

A secure area will use perimeter alarms, CCTV and security patrols. Access to main areas will be controlled by swipe cards or a PAC (Proximity Access Card) and visual identification by security staff. In the most secure areas there may be biometric sensors and electronic locks.

BIOMETRICS

Biometric systems use some measure of an individual's biology. Biometric security is increasingly being used in everyday security situations. There are a whole range of biometric recognition methods, ranging from fingerprint recognition to DNA sampling.

The main advantage of biometric methods is that they give improved security. Because they are based on human characteristics, they provide a link to an individual that is not subject to theft, error, or fraud. Biometric measures are better for the user because they do not have to remember or carry anything. Once a biometric system is set up, it is easy and inexpensive to maintain.

e-Commerce

Electronic commerce involves the trading of goods and services using the web as a communications channel. In its very short history, it has been the driving force behind some of the most dramatic events in the history of business. In the first five years of the use of the web for e-commerce, there was a modern day gold rush as stockholders became rich by investing in new internet start ups, and entrepreneurs dreamed up new ways of using e-commerce to inspire these investors. However, in April 2000, western stock markets saw the largest crash in history, with Wall Street alone losing $2 trillion in value in a single week and many investors losing most or all of their money. Since this time, in spite of some nervousness immediately after the crash, e-commerce has progressed into all sectors of the economy. Entrepreneurs with strong ideas can still attract massive investment. E-commerce firms can and do grow from nothing to multi-billion pound enterprises within a couple of years. The largest part of the revolution, however, has been the fact that e-commerce now underlies a great deal of the economy and has had an enormous impact not just on the way we do business but on the whole of society.

This unit will look firstly at the impact of e-commerce and the benefits and disadvantages it brings, before studying the technology that is at the heart of e-commerce. Finally, the unit will explore the security and legal issues that surround the use of e-commerce.

By the end of this unit, you will:

So you want to be an...

E-commerce coordinator

My name Anna Luker
Age 23
Income £25,500

What do you do?

I work with the marketing team and the website designers to identify new opportunities and strategies to promote the site and drive traffic to it.

What responsibilities do you have?

I measure and report the effectiveness of the various marketing campaigns we deploy. I create content and specify images for the website. I have to work with the e-commerce team in order to develop the website and make the customer experience as engaging and enticing as possible.

How did you get into the job?

I have a BTEC National Diploma for IT Practitioners, followed by experience in working for a start up e-commerce company for four years in which I did just about every job in the company. To do this type of job you need a good standard of general education, experience of working with and an ability to get along with people, and a good knowledge of e-commerce.

How did you find your current job?

I found my job on one of the many websites to which I had submitted my CV. They sent me details of this opportunity and I was interviewed locally.

What training did you get?

When I started I spent two weeks with the web design team to become familiar with their work, and two weeks with the marketing and development team to understand their needs and how they work. My firm is keen on self development, and I am encouraged to find appropriate training courses in ICT. If I can justify the training, I will be allowed to go on the course.

What are the hours like?

I officially work normal office hours, but the team often stay on for a couple of hours at the end of the day to discuss new ideas, or new projects. I join in to be part of the team. It is often exciting and interesting but it can also be tiring sometimes.

> **"The e-commerce sector is booming and I am learning new skills all the time"**

What skills do you need?

You need some experience in an e-commerce environment along with strong numerical and analytical skills and a good eye for detail. You will need a strong understanding of web analytics, PPC campaigns and affiliate marketing. It is also essential to have a strong knowledge of Office applications and desirable to have some understanding of website design.

How good is the pay?

I have been in the job since the beginning of the year on an income of £25,500 with some scope for performance-related pay once I have completed my first year.

What about the future?

The e-commerce sector is booming and I am learning new skills all the time, so I will be very employable. The pay can be really good if you are part of a successful project.

Grading criteria

The table below shows what you need to do to gain a pass, merit or distinction in this part of the qualification. Make sure you refer back to it when you are completing work so that you can judge whether you are meeting the criteria and what you need to do to fill in gaps in your knowledge or experience.

In this unit there are eight evidence activities that give you an opportunity to demonstrate your achievement of the grading criteria:

To achieve a pass grade the evidence must show that the learner is able to...	To achieve a merit grade the evidence must show that, in addition to the pass criteria, the learner is able to...	To achieve a distinction grade the evidence must show that, in addition to the pass and merit criteria, the learner is able to...
P1 describe the social implications, benefits and drawbacks of e-commerce	**M1** explain the potential risks to organisations of committing to an e-commerce system	**D1** evaluate the use of e-commerce in a 'brick and click' organisation that balances e-commerce with a continued high-street presence
P2 describe three different and current e-commerce entities	**M2** compare two different payment systems used in e-commerce systems	**D2** justify the choice of security techniques used to protect an e-commerce system
P3 describe the hardware, software and networking technologies involved in e-commerce	**M3** explain how security issues in e-commerce can be overcome	**D3** predict and describe the potential future of e-commerce and its impact on society
P4 describe how e-commerce systems can be promoted and marketed		
P5 describe the security issues in e-commerce		
P6 describe what and how legislation impacts on e-commerce systems		

34.1 Know the effects on society of e-commerce

SOCIAL IMPLICATIONS

Changing customer perspective

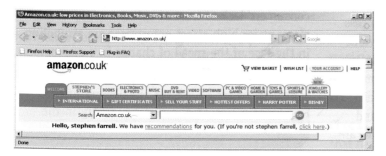

Figure 34.1 Amazon's customer focused storefront
[source: amazon .co.uk]

E-commerce allows businesses to operate in a more customer-focused manner, which, if done well, can create better relationships with customers and greater profits. A good e-business is built around information and automation. This means that an online retailer can easily offer its customers additional services and/or a more personalised service, as shown in Figure 34.1. This can make the shopping experience more fulfilling for customers.

In order to minimise the risk of large quantities of returned goods, online stores have to provide a lot of information about their products to customers. Good stores will make this necessity into a virtue.

Another major change in the relationship with customers is that an online store can be available 24 hours a day, 7 days a week, all year round. Of course, customers can shop at a competitor's store just as easily. The best stores will therefore use techniques to entice and engage customers, giving them added value, passing on some of the savings they make as a result of having lower overheads.

Impact on business and society as a whole

The impact of e-commerce on business and society has been wide-ranging. E-commerce can potentially open up a global market for goods, expanding the potential customer base and reducing barriers to trade. It has also enabled completely new markets to be created, especially in the sale of digital products, such as MP3s, MPEG movies, software and information. E-commerce not only provides a business with more potential clients, but also with more sources of supply. This form of global trade has a number of impacts. Firstly, there is more readily accessible information about what else is available in the marketplace. This can lead in some cases to large firms swallowing up smaller rivals, but can also allow small niche services to survive where a small local service could not.

It is in the business to business (B2B) sector where the impact of globalisation is largest. Firms can source and control their supply much more easily across the globe. Orders can be sent automatically and instantly using EDI over an extranet from a distribution centre in the south of England to a manufacturing facility in Ireland or even Taiwan. Using e-commerce means that even smaller organisations can in effect be multinational. This usually leads to more direct competition in the market and more efficient services. This combination will usually lead to lower prices. Some companies, especially in the travel industry, have managed to use e-commerce technology to provide differential and fluid pricing opportunities.

Key words

EDI (Electronic data interchange) – the exchange of information electronically between two or more organisations using agreed standards. It is often used to automate purchasing

Extranet – a private network over the internet, accessible by two or more organisations

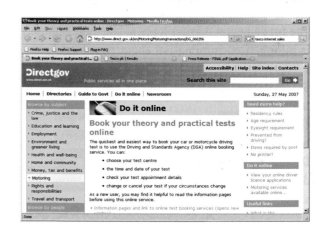

Figure 34.2 Booking your driving tests online
[source: www.direct.gov.uk]

Larger e-commerce sites use multiple servers arranged in clusters, usually rack-mounted, known as a web farm. This means that there are multiple computers available in case of the failure of one, and that load balancing can take place so that web requests can be sent to the least loaded server closest to the location of the web request. The largest sites employ hundreds or even thousands of servers in their clusters.

Figure 34.9 A Google web farm

Research tip

Visit the Web Traffic site www.itfacts. biz, then select 'web traffic' from the categories menu to research the amount of traffic different sites have to handle.

Browsers

A browser is a software application that allows a user to request and view web pages. A web page is a text file that is marked up so that it will display text, images and multimedia laid out as designed on a page. Text and images are used to hyperlink to other related pages.

There are a number of popular browsers, as is shown in the chart below. By far the most common is Internet Explorer, with around 58 per cent of the market. Mozilla Firefox is also very popular, with around 33 per cent share.

Browser market share April 2007

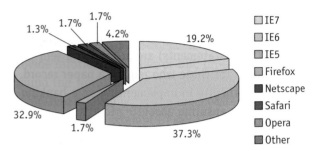

Figure 34.10 Data showing usage of different browsers. [Source: www.w3schools.com/browsers/browsers_stats.asp]

In e-commerce applications, it is the browser that allows the customer to interact with the web server. It requests a page from the server and the server then sends the page, along with any files referenced on that page. Typically these will include style sheets that tell the browser how to lay out and style the page, images (which are always kept separately from the main page), multimedia files and any scripts that allow dynamic interaction with the user. The browser will then assemble these and lay them out as specified by the web page author.

Server software

The server software receives a request from a client, usually a web browser. It will then load and transmit the file requested along with all of the files referenced within it. The file sent may be a static page stored on the web server. More typically, in an e-commerce system, it will be a page that is created dynamically using a mixture of static elements and database queries.

The web server software will also manage a range of other services connected with managing websites. It will manage identification and authorisation to control access to the site. It will create logs to show the events on the site to administrators. It may deal with multiple websites on the same host. It will execute server side scripts and manage the merging of HTML from special web pages included on the server, called server side includes. Critically on an e-commerce site, the software will also manage the encryption of web pages for secure areas of the site, such as the login and checkout using SSL/TLS.

The web server software most commonly used has traditionally been the Apache server, provided by the Apache Software Foundation. This is extremely stable open source software that will run on Unix® and Microsoft Windows® operating systems and is popular across the whole market, from small websites to the largest e-commerce sites. Apple use Apache at the heart of their web sharing services and to host their website. Microsoft's own server software, Internet Information Server, is another extremely popular and reliable product. It is a growing force in the market and is now thought to be used by the majority of top public companies on the USA stock exchange, whereas Apache is thought to be used by less than a quarter of these.

Research tip

Visit the Port80 website source: www.port80software.com/surveys/top1000webservers and investigate the trends in web and application servers within the major corporations.

ey words

ver side scripts – scripts run on the website server
dynamically generate web pages

/TLS (Secure Sockets Layer/Transport Layer
urity) – protocol for providing secure transmission
establishing an authenticated and encrypted
nection

Web authoring tools

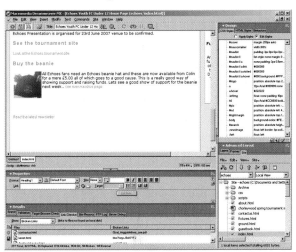

Figure 34.11 A site being edited in Dreamweaver MX showing some of the variety of tools available

The web pages that make up an e-commerce site are designed and built using web authoring software. There are a range of different applications available, depending on the budget and how the development is planned.

Text editors are the simplest web development tools. They allow the developer to write HTML pages and scripts using only text. This is a quite viable task for anyone with some knowledge of HTML and scripting. Text editors vary from general purpose editors, such as the Microsoft Windows® accessory Notepad, to programmer's editors, which can spot errors in the code as it is typed.

Some e-commerce sites are created by customising templates provided by a specialist commerce house. This allows the site to be built without any specialised knowledge. A database is loaded with information and images of the products to be sold and the categories they are to be sold in. A front end, or interface, is also created by customising fixed elements of a pre-written design, such as the name of the shop and the colours and styles of the headings and sub-headings on the pages. When a web page is requested, a template engine (or set of scripts) will merge the information from the database with the web template to create the online shop.

Site editors were developed from text editors. They have a number of additional features that enable the user to manage a whole website as well as individual pages. Most are graphical editors that present the page in the editor as close as possible to how it will be viewed, and a preview can be viewed in a browser. Typically site editors will feature WYSIWYG editing, editing in code with auto completion and code checking; easy hyperlinking; image and multimedia management; style sheet support; built-in scripts and customised scripting; automated uploading to remote servers and additional features like global search and replace across the whole site; automated moving of links on multiple pages, and a great deal more. Among the most popular of these applications are Adobe Dreamweaver® and Microsoft FrontPage®. Site editors are used as authoring tools for many e-commerce sites, in combination with server scripting to manage the product and back-office database.

Application server and software development framework

Very large e-commerce sites will be managed by programs running on the server interacting with the product and back-office database. The client-side web pages will merely be an interface to these programs. The authors of these programs can and do write them from scratch in Java or C++ but it is more common to use a software development framework. The framework will provide a number of fundamental interface elements and web services, including dynamic form builders, database connectivity, search tools, security handlers and XML handlers. The result is a customised shopping application delivered over the web. It is possible to author these using some of the more sophisticated site editors, such as Adobe Dreamweaver, which has support for a great deal of the scripting required. It is common however to use authoring tools such as Adobe Cold Fusion, ASP.NET and Java Enterprise Edition to achieve this.

Research tip

Visit www.dartmouth.edu/~webteach/articles/tools.html to view the variety of web authoring tools available to a developer.

Key words

WYSIWYG editing (What You See Is What You Get) – a system in which content being edited appears in a way very similar to how it will appear in the final product

Database system

A database is fundamental to any e-commerce site. It will hold details of the products sold, the items stored in the shopping basket and the back-office processes such as orders, payments, deliveries and returns. There are a wide variety of databases available. It is possible to use Microsoft Access®, but it is much more usual to use heavy duty databases that can handle much larger volumes of data. Commonly used relational databases include MySQL on Unix platforms, SQL Server on Microsoft platforms and Oracle, Ingres and DB2 on either.

Programming requirements

Most e-commerce stores require some programming as part of their operation. The programs can be written in a traditional programming language such as C++, but it is more common to write in a scripting language that is interpreted as the script is run. There are two main varieties of scripts used in web stores:

- Client-side scripts are programs that are run by the client's browser. These may be used to validate data entry fields prior to being submitted to the server or enable some event handling, such as dealing with a click or load event to make the page a little more interactive and dynamic. They may implement simple applications, such as an exchange rate calculator or mortgage repayment calculator for the client to use. The most common of these scripts is Javascript, though it is also common to use Vbscript. It is also possible to write applets in Java, a fully object-oriented programming language, to give more functionality on the client's side. For multimedia sites, Flash is often used, along with Actionscript to provide full integration of web pages, movies, videos, sounds and images. Clients can, however, turn off these technologies in their browser so e-commerce organisations have to be aware of losing functionality with some clients. The percentage of users of e-commerce sites who do disable these is not known for certain, but is believed to be around 5 per cent.

- Server-side scripts are those that are run on the server to implement the database driven e-commerce solution. These will be responsible for the vast majority of the user's experience. They usually dynamically generate web pages, fetch product pictures and information from the database to display in the pages, manage adding to, editing and deleting from the cart and manage the security for the checkout, along with the checkout processes and payment authorisation. They also manage the back-office processes of accounting, picking, delivery and returns. There are numerous means of creating server-side scripts. If site editors are the main tool used then ASP, server-side Javascript, PHP and Perl are typically used. If a software development framework is used then Cold Fusion, ASP.Net, and Java Enterprise are commonly used. In heavy duty programming environments traditional programming may also be used.

Storage size

When an e-commerce site is established, the amount of storage required for the site must be calculated, and this must be reviewed regularly. If there is too little space, the application may fail as the database fills up with transactions, or the space fills up with log files. If the site is hosted externally, calculating the required storage size accurately for the present and future is absolutely vital as the first indication of problems may occur when the site fails to operate. At that stage, it is too late as some loss of service, and accompanying loss of trust, will have occurred.

The amount of storage space required for an e-commerce site will depend very much on the quantity of products sold, the size and quality of product images used, the amount of information stored about products, the quantity of multimedia and other components deployed, and the development method used. In addition to this, it is important to factor in the size of the log files, which will grow more quickly with a larger volume of transactions. A sensible manager will add in a factor for future growth and then monitor the site to ensure that there is still some leeway.

Portability

Opera   *IE 6.0.2*

Figure 34.12 Browser incompatibilities

A major issue when designing websites is portability. While the majority of people use Internet Explorer (IE), a significant and growing number use Firefox, Safari, Opera or one of the Gecko browsers. Different browsers do not display the mark up in exactly the same way. Figure 34.12 above shows the same simple web page viewed in different browsers. The pages look similar at first glance, but there are significant differences.

This situation will improve for web developers as XHTML and CSS web standards become more widely used and the different browsers are implemented more closely to web standards. At present, if a customer is using a pre-version 5 browser (IE4 or early versions of Netscape) there may be significant problems as these do not understand standards at all. Good web designers currently work to the standards, with occasional workarounds to ensure that the site can be viewed more or less identically in alternate browsers. The valid XHTML mark shown in Figure 34.13 is often displayed on websites that are developing to standards.

Figure 34.13 Valid XHTML mark
[source: http//:validator.w3.org]

EVIDENCE ACTIVITY

P3

Create a leaflet for a networking company to use as briefing material to go alongside their marketing literature. It should describe the hardware, software and networking technologies that are required to run an e-commerce store. (P3)

PAYMENT SYSTEMS

In order for a website to conduct e-commerce, it needs to be able to accept payments in some way. Most solutions involve accepting payment by credit or debit card, although prepay smart cards and electronic bill payment are other alternatives.

There are a number of ways of integrating payment systems into an e-commerce site. A simple method is to collect and calculate the shopping basket data so that when the customer selects the checkout button, the total amount owing is sent to a payment gateway. A secure server at the bank's end of the gateway then deals with the payment, taking care of the security issues. The e-commerce site has no dealings with the customer's credit card, but receives payment direct from the bank. The main drawback of this approach is that, although the bank's server can be customised to look similar to the main site, it is obvious to the customer that the transaction is being undertaken by a third party. Some very successful sites do use this model and a number of banks, including WorldPay, a Royal Bank of Scotland company, operate a scheme that works in this way. PayPal merchant accounts work in a similar way to this, although the fee structure is different and usually more suited to small e-commerce sites.

A full merchant system involves an e-commerce website taking full responsibility for all payments, storage of credit card details and SSL/TLS security alongside the shopping basket. When a payment is taken from a customer, the e-commerce site transmits a request for authorisation to a payment gateway, which returns an authorisation code or a rejection. The card payments are then periodically relayed to the merchant's bank for payment. The bank collects the payments from the various cardholders' banks and forwards a payment to the company, minus commission and chargebacks (customer refunds due to disputed transactions).

Research tip

Research the payment processing provided by the following companies:
Nochex: www.nochex.com
WorldPay: www.worldpay.com
PayPal: www.paypal.com/uk/cgi-bin/webscr?cmd=_merchant-outside

EVIDENCE ACTIVITY

M2

Echoes Youth Football Club (www.echoesyouthfc.co.uk) is considering selling items on their website, including photos and small memorabilia. They also want to take payments for subscriptions and tours using the website. They want you to recommend a suitable payments system for this small business.

Compare the use of PayPal as a payment system with the service provided by one other system of your choice. The website has no shopping cart software and they want a secure and easy-to-use solution. The webmaster does know how to customise HTML. (M2)

PROMOTION

The major obstacle to becoming a really successful web store is customers either not knowing about or not trusting the store. There are a number of steps that e-commerce organisations can take to overcome this issue.

Effective use of search engines

Most potential customers will look for a suitable store using a search engine. If someone wants to buy a new guitar they may type 'guitar shop' into a search engine, which will in turn provide them with a number of pieces of information.

Figure 34.14 Search for a guitar shop on Google

```
<title>Mansons Guitar Shop. Number ONE for
service.</title>
<meta http-equiv="Content-Type" content="text/
HTML; charset=iso-8859-1">
<link rel="stylesheet" href="style/style.css"
type="text/css">
<meta name="keywords" content="mansons,
manson, manson guitar,mansons uk guitar shop, uk
guitar shop">
<meta name="description" content="Mansons
Guitar Shop supply guitars, basses, amps and effects
to the music industry and the public.">
```

In the main area of the page, the main results are shown. Most potential customers will only look at the first few entries, and hardly anyone will look past the first page of results. It is therefore important for companies to have a good search engine placement. This is not easy to arrange for general keywords. Changing the search slightly to 'buy guitar' would yield totally different results.

A simple, and almost no-cost, way of achieving this is to make effective use of titles and metatags on the company's web pages. The top entry for Guitar Shop on the date this search was undertaken was Mansons (www.mansons.co.uk). The title of the index page of this web store is 'Mansons Guitar Shop. Number ONE for service'. Search engines use the title for indexing, to some extent, and for the entry in the results page. Search engines also use the keywords supplied as metatags by the web designer in building the indexes, although this is now less relevant, because of the practice of adult sites overloading their pages with keywords. Search engines also use the description metatag in building indexes and in supplying the text for the results page. You can see this by comparing the source code shown overleaf with the search results page.

These simple measures should be taken, but they will not in themselves guarantee a high ranking in search results. It is useful to submit the site to the most popular search engines, which can usually be done free of charge. Search engine robots will 'spider' the site to index it and they expect some degree of consistency.

Key words

Spider – a program that automatically fetches web pages. Spiders are used to feed pages to search engines and are so-called because they 'crawl' over the web. Another term for these programs is webcrawler

If the site is a guitar shop, it may be ranked higher if there are references to the word guitar. Search engines also take account of many other factors, including the number of links to the site from other sites (often known as backlinks), although less reputable sites have manipulated these results by creating masses of fake blogs each with a link to their site.

In Google, the coloured area at the top of the window and down the right side of the page shows paid for, or sponsored, links. These can be customised by the company to say exactly what is required. The customer sets a budget and Google places the adverts. The company pays Google when a client clicks through to their site using this link.

Research tip

Visit https://adwords.google.com/ select/Login to find out how adwords works and see some success stories.

Newsgroups and forums

Newsgroups and forums are an effective way of promoting certain types of website. Many allow users to post links back to their site for free, preferably accompanied by a useful or interesting post. Creating a blog and filling it with interesting content has a similar effect. Ezine articles (http://ezinearticles.com) allows users to submit an article related to their product or service, which, if accepted, can be accompanied by a back link to drive traffic directly to the site. Listing here will also build more credibility for search engines. However, posting promotion material to masses of news groups and forums without saying anything relevant could be considered spamming and will annoy people as much as entice them to a site.

Banners and pop-ups

Banners and pop-ups allow companies to advertise on popular websites. Some sites make good use of these tools as the quality and low impact of the adverts make them attractive and useful marketing aids. In many other cases, banners, and especially pop-ups, detract from the browsing experience and turn potential customers away.

Spam and direct marketing

Unsolicited email, or spam, is used to contact huge numbers of potential clients. However, if the email does manage to get past spam filters, customers are often annoyed by this.

Direct marketing, in the form of a targeted email to existing customers or registered users of the e-commerce site, will be much more acceptable and more likely to successfully promote the business. Other direct marketing techniques include leaflets delivered through the post, mailshots and telephone sales. As with spam, there is a danger that if these techniques are not targeted carefully, they will annoy potential customers, but used sensitively they can have a role in promoting a website.

Site name

One of the best means of promoting a site is to register an effective site name. An existing business should have a site name that is effectively the same as that of the business. Web store names should suggest the nature of the product or service being marketed, such as shoeshop.com. Such a name is instantly identifiable with the product and can also help with search engine placement. The best site names are memorable, easy to spell and easy to search for. A good example is 'I Want One Of Those' (www.iwoot.com and www.iwantoneofthose.com.) This is a particularly useful name as its uniqueness means that virtually all front page results in search engines will be references to that store. When choosing the name, trademarks should also be considered, to ensure that there is no conflict with another site and also to begin to build a strong brand with a good trademark.

Ensuring an effective user interface

The most important page on any e-commerce website is the home page. This is the storefront and shop window. It must immediately engage customers and invite them in. Most e-commerce sites use their front page to set a style for the site, to advertise their most attractive deals and to show the range of products and services available. It can be difficult to strike a balance between masses of detail and a unified style that is suited to the target audience.

It is also very important to consider the interface as this affects how the user navigates and searches the site. A good site will allow fast and effective browsing using clearly defined routes and a search facility that brings up what is required without too much extraneous detail.

CASE STUDY: I WANT ONE OF THOSE

Figure 34.15 An example of an interface that meets various demands successfully

www.iwantoneofthose.com (IWOOT) is an example of a really successful e-commerce site that uses multiple promotion techniques in a very engaging manner. It started as a small venture to sell cool stuff over the web in January 2000, survived the big clear out in the e-commerce industry later that year and has grown to become a very large multi-channel retailer indeed. It is now part of the Findel Plc group.

QUESTIONS

1. How effective are IWOOT in utilising search engines?

2. What is it about the name that is so good in promoting the business?

3. How do they attempt to use colour and font to help create a brand image?

4. What features of the IWOOT interface make it so successful?

5. How do they try to involve the customer in the website?

Establishing customer loyalty in a virtual environment

Traditional measures of customer satisfaction are based on factors such as the friendliness, responsiveness and product knowledge of employees, and the style and quality of the store's physical appearance. In a virtual environment, these factors are not at all relevant. Web marketers must think about the relationship with the customer differently. The key to a successful relationship is customer data. A great store will personalise the shopping experience so that the shopper can shop more efficiently and be made to feel special.

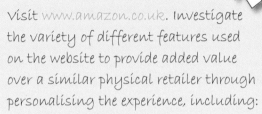

Research tip

Visit www.amazon.co.uk. Investigate the variety of different features used on the website to provide added value over a similar physical retailer through personalising the experience, including:
- Favourites list
- Recommendations
- Personalised store
- Independent reviews.

EVIDENCE ACTIVITY

P4

You are a new employee at a website development company. Create a short presentation to potential clients describing the various methods that can be used to promote and market their e-commerce applications. (P4)

CUSTOMER INTERFACE

Usability issues

It is important that a site performs well and that visitors can use it from their very first visit without difficulties. The visitor must be able to browse in a natural manner, and the content should be laid out logically and in a way that is easy to find and view. There should be a search function that works effectively, finding the products required without showing too many irrelevant ones.

The speed of the site is another important issue. Detailed images and 3D views of products are helpful, but if they take too long to load the user will give up and may not return. A user should always be warned when a large or slow resource is about to be viewed and given the option of not following that path.

Contact information

In order to build customer loyalty and trust, it is important to provide contact information to allow visitors to get in touch with the company using their preferred method. Most users will just require information, which can be provided through online manuals, online communities and bulletin boards, answers to FAQs, help and support centres, help pages and interactive tours. Where this is not sufficient, a good website will provide another option for contacting the company. Email and online forms are the most common methods, as these are relatively straightforward to manage in a 24/7 environment. Some customers will not deal with sites unless they offer traditional methods such as phone, fax and ordinary mail. Some very customer-focused sites offer live chat, along with free (0800) or local (0845) phone numbers. Some companies, however, see phone calls as an opportunity to make additional income and charge a premium rate phone line for customer service.

> **Research tip**
>
> To see an example of a live chat facility go to Evans cycles at www.evanscycles.com/contactus.jsp;jsessionid=1B2E1B3371C23EA4A90EA1 0AC584CEBD.tc7.

Providing customer account/profile

Many e-commerce sites allow customers to register an account. This involves setting up a record with a user ID, password and personal details. In return, the store will usually offer some benefits. The most common is a faster checkout, which can be provided if the store already has the delivery details and even the payment details. In this case, all a registered customer needs to do is sign in and confirm details rather than re-entering them. This is a great benefit to the store as it removes an obstacle to purchasing, and also allows the store to build a better profile of the customer, without this being obvious. Many stores also send account holders reminders to buy, newsletters, special offers and promotions, often tailored to the customer. Having an account also allows companies to provide order histories, favourites lists and a more personal service for customers. This gives the customer an obvious benefit and is another useful method of building loyalty.

Order tracking

Figure 34.16 Royal Mail's track and trace service

Online order tracking is a very useful facility that improves interaction with customers. It allows customers to check the progress of their orders instantly and saves the company time and expense in answering enquiries. Royal Mail and Parcelforce, along with other couriers, offer this facility, on a number of their services. They also allow integration of the tracking from within client websites, which provides a better interface for the customer and gives a sense of confidence in the efficiency of the vendor.

Dealing with complaints

Things go wrong. Even on the best websites, mistakes and misunderstandings occur. A good web store therefore needs to have a strategy for dealing with complaints. There are a number of methods that can be used:

- dealing with the complaint as a technical issue and providing step-by-step instructions about what to do to put it right. This is the first step adopted by established etailers such as Amazon

- using a call centre to deal with enquiries. This works well if staff are well trained and have the ability to deal with complaints. If they are not, they can be counter productive, especially if calls are charged at a premium rate

- providing a web form to enter details of the complaint

- allowing customers to contact customer services using any method of their choosing.

Whatever strategy is employed, all complaints should be addressed within a reasonable timeframe because it will increase customer confidence to know that problems are not ignored. A prompt response also allows the business to identify and put right any ongoing, systematic failures in its processes.

34.3 Understand the security issues in e-commerce and the laws and guidelines that regulate it

SECURITY

Prevention of hacking

Hacking is a particular danger to e-commerce sites as they store vital business and customer information. It is important to remember that hackers can be employees or contractors, as well as those who may break in from outside. This means that a multi-layer approach to security is essential, protecting the physical environment, the web server and any ancillary devices (including database servers, domain servers and routers), data, the network and all transmissions:

- The physical environment where the e-commerce hardware is housed can be protected by conventional security, including locks, CCTV and sign-in procedures, to help ensure that only authorised users can gain physical access to the hardware.

- The server can be protected through solid authentication systems requiring user IDs and strong passwords, backed up by access control lists and policies about which users can access which services. Sensible administrators will disable all unwanted services on the server, such as finger, netstat and telnet, to prevent hackers using these as a way in. They will also ensure that routers are properly configured to withstand denial of service and other attacks.

- Firewalls can be installed to examine all traffic between networks and deal with suspicious packets. The administrator can set up ports on the server for specific purposes. Any traffic that is directed to an incorrect port is inherently suspicious and can be ignored or monitored. A firewall can prevent all access to back-end databases, and prevent FTP access to the website from outside the local network, or indeed allow it only from specified devices.

- To protect data, reliable anti-virus and anti-spyware solutions should be installed. The

Impact of the use of IT on business systems

unit 35

This unit looks at the impact of new technologies and the reasons why organisations have to respond to these changes. You will look at how IT developments have had an impact on organisations and how IT is now shaping the business environment. Technology has affected almost every business activity and has brought with it a wealth of jargon and buzz words. You will discover the ways in which technology has impacted on employers and employees, including employment patterns and the requirements for businesses, managers and employees to display even greater flexibility than ever before.

By the end of this unit, you will:

So you want to be an...

IT Project Manager

My name Keith Routledge
Age 42
Income £41,000

What do you do?

It varies weekly. I manage the installation of new systems, upgrade telephone networks for the call centre, manage a team of IT technicians, prioritise work, undertake risk assessments, monitor progress, manage budgets and sign off tasks when they are completed.

How did you get the job?

I finished school with 8 GCSEs, then I did an Access to Higher Education course, then I did a degree in IT and joined the Association for Project Management (APM). I worked as an assistant project manager for a large food processing company, then I saw this job and applied, got short-listed and obviously impressed at interview.

How did you find your current job?

It was advertised in the regional paper, and in the Guardian as well. There were about 60 applications, and I got down to the last three in the shortlist. The interview was pretty tough, and they made me do a role-play and a written test.

What training have you had?

Plenty. I've done all my Microsoft training, management training and other short courses.

> **"I'll be a senior project manager in the next 18 months and moving towards £48K"**

I'm studying for an MA in Global E-commerce Applications. The firm's paying; they are good like that.

What are the hours like?

Theoretically it's a 37-hour week. Practically, well it's probably twice that sometimes if a big project is having problems or near the end. That means coming in at the weekend and getting things done when nobody is messing about with the network. I don't mind the extra hours, but my partner isn't too keen.

How good is the pay?

Pretty good for this area. I started on £32,000. This is my fifth year here and the pay has gone up each year, as long as I hit my performance targets. The ceiling at the moment is around £48,000. I could get more if I moved jobs, but I'm settled.

What about the future?

I'll be a senior project manager in the next 18 months and moving towards £48K. After that I'm angling for a seat on the board. That's a functional directorship, with shares and profits. They need a 'techie' on the board; most of the directors haven't got a clue how complicated things are these days.

Grading criteria

The table below shows what you need to do to gain a pass, merit or distinction in this part of the qualification. Make sure you refer back to it when you are completing work so that you can judge whether you are meeting the criteria and what you need to do to fill in gaps in your knowledge or experience.

In this unit there are five evidence activities that give you an opportunity to demonstrate your achievement of the grading criteria:

To achieve a pass grade the evidence must show that the learner is able to...	To achieve a merit grade the evidence must show that, in addition to the pass criteria, the learner is able to...	To achieve a distinction grade the evidence must show that, in addition to the pass and merit criteria, the learner is able to...
P1 describe new hardware and software technologies that impact on organisations	**M1** explain the impact of IT developments for an organisation	**D1** make reasoned recommendations about how a particular organisation can take advantage of IT developments
P2 identify the challenges posed to organisations because of IT developments	**M2** explain why organisations modify their activities in response to IT developments	**D2** assess the possible consequences for an organisation in implementing IT-based changes
P3 describe how the internal environment of an organisation has changed due to the changes the external environment brought about by IT developments	**M3** explain how employees and employers are affected by changes in IT	
P4 identify the changes in activity and performance that can arise from adapting organisational activities		
P5 describe ways that organisations can manage their risks when using new IT technology		

35.1 *Know the information technology developments that have had an impact on organisations*

HARDWARE AND SYSTEMS

Computer hardware and systems are the means by which calculations, processes and the storage of data is achieved. People have been using varieties of hardware since the abacus, dating back to at least 500 BC. The first programmable machines came into existence in the nineteenth century, however the early digital computers were not developed until after World War Two. Since then, there have been never-ending developments in computer hardware and systems. Each successive generation has improved on the previous one. This has meant smaller and smaller machines, a reduction in cost to the user and generally far more robust products.

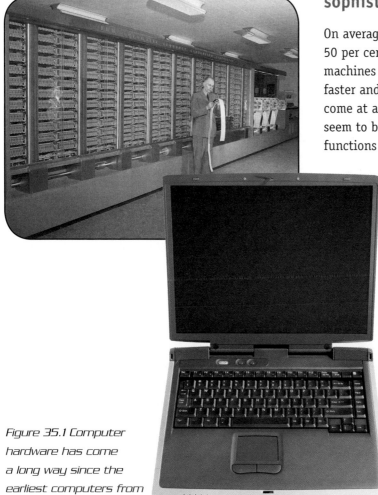

Figure 35.1 Computer hardware has come a long way since the earliest computers from WW2

Alongside the technical developments of hardware there have also been developments in operating systems software. This provides a set of functions that are required by application software and the links for control and synchronisation of the hardware.

Mini-computers, or computers as we know them today, did not come into existence until the late-1960s and the development of the microprocessor brought about standard operating systems in the 1980s. Now just a handful of operating systems dominate the market and most are proprietary, branded operating systems, such as those owned by Microsoft.

> **Key words**
> ---
> Proprietary – a product that is marketed under a registered trade name

Increasing power, capacity and sophistication of computer platforms

On average, hardware and operating systems get 50 per cent faster than the previous generation of machines every two years. Hardware has become faster and memory has increased, but this has come at a time when many software applications seem to be lazier and are not created with faster functions to achieve faster applications. The net result is that some applications appear to be running more slowly.

There are gradual moves towards ensuring proper design and optimisation, not just of hardware or operating systems, but also of the software that is run on them. One of the major developments in this area is the creation of dual core processors, which essentially have two chips in one. These have improved computation power and reduced power requirements. Importantly, they are also less prone to overheating and, as a result, need less cooling than previous generations of chips or processors.

Example

The Taiwanese business Via Technologies announced in April 2007 that they have created a motherboard the size of a playing card. It has a single chip and a single memory slot and is likely to appeal particularly for smaller mobile applications.

Almost at the same time, Intel announced no fewer than twenty new microprocessors and semiconductor technologies. Their new 'system-on-a-chip' designs are 45 per cent smaller. Intel hopes that this will make laptops even more powerful and that it will improve performance and graphics on desktop PCs.

Source: adapted from www.technewsworld.com

Research tip

For more information on mobile communications, look at www.informatm.com/newt/l/mobilecomms/index.html.
For networks try http://networks.silicon.com and the International Journal of Computer and Telecommunications Networking at www.elsevier.com.
For email developments have a look at www2.btbroadbandoffice.com.
For EDI developments see www.edibasics.co.uk.

Availability of new communication technologies

The workplace, human interaction and financial transactions are being revolutionised by the availability of new communication technologies. Managing the effects on businesses is becoming increasingly more complex, and the pace of change has been very fast moving. Many businesses in the UK have been slow to adapt to or even to adopt new communication technology, which has caused some communication problems for British businesses. This has had a particularly negative impact on British businesses operating in the global marketplace.

There have been countless rapid developments, a selection of which are outlined on Table 35.1

Think Why do you think UK businesses, in particular have been slow to adopt new communication technology? Why might countries like Australia have been keen to embrace it?

SOFTWARE

Application software is a subclass of computer software. It directs the computer to perform a task designated by the user. It should not be confused with operating systems software, which aims to integrate the computer's capabilities.

Increasingly, however, the boundaries between operating systems and application software are becoming blurred. Windows is an operating system, but an integral part of that system, and bundled with it by Microsoft, is the web browser, Internet Explorer, which is a piece of application software.

Most people will be familiar with the software applications that are used universally throughout businesses in the form of spreadsheets, databases, word processors and media players. Many software applications are bundled, such as Microsoft Office.

Some industries also use specific application software. An accounts department is likely to use Sage; travel and tourism organisations will use booking and reservation software. Other businesses need more tailor-made software applications to enable them to streamline particular aspects of their operations.

Table 35.1 New communication technologies

Communication technology	Development	Implications
Mobile communication	3G, telephone networking and audio conferencing, as well as new routing technology, have all improved the coverage, reliability and quality of mobile phone technologies.	Many British businesses have focused on landline operations, but developments now require them to shift their attention to new mobile phone developments.
Networks	One of the primary developments has been the migration from wired to wireless networks. This improves the speed, resilience, extent and facilities of networks. It requires major reorganisation, although this will actually simplify networks.	Businesses that have not switched over to wireless networks are still constrained in terms of network expansion and reliability. Wired networks are not as efficient or reliable. They also restrict the number of users that can be on the network and the general speed of applications and the transfer of data.
Email	There have been many developments in email, notably webmail services, filtering to reduce junk mail and email forwarding and auto replies. There has also been a general increase in email delivery rates, which, according to the National Email Benchmarking Report, has now reached 90 per cent for three quarters of email service providers.	Many businesses have effective email marketing campaigns, much improved by removing inactive email addresses from their mailing lists. Businesses can create many hundreds of email sub-accounts, with a dedicated email address for every employee. Email also facilitates home and teleworking.
Electronic data interchange (EDI)	EDI is now an affordable and straightforward way to implement electronic trading. Standard business data, including orders, invoices and payments, can be sent direct from computer-to-computer.	Many businesses have moved towards a fully integrated electronic commerce business environment. EDI facilitates this, allowing the business to move to new and improved ways of working, which have better controls and are paperless.

Generally speaking, application software falls into a number of different categories:

- software that assists the organisation's processes and dataflow, often referred to as enterprise software

- databases, email servers, security and network management, commonly known as infrastructure software

- word processors, spreadsheets, information and resource management systems are usually known as information worker software

- software with the ability to create and use digital content, including digital entertainment, therefore covering media players, help and web browsers. This is known as web and entertainment software

- educational software, which facilitates the delivery of tests and tracking

- media development software, which has the ability to generate print and electronic media, either in a commercial or education environment, incorporating desktop publishing, graphics arts, html editors, animation editors, digital and video composition

- project engineering software, including computer-aided design, computer-aided engineering, computer language editing and compiling and other application interfaces.

Think To what extent do you think that the development of software is limited by the advances in hardware?

LEARNING ZONE DEESIDE COLLEGE

Increased sophistication and integration of application software

The previous list alone suggests the increasing sophistication and the integration of application software. Application software is primarily designed to increase accessibility and productivity for all types of users of computers. The creation of application software is driven by both demand and the abilities of software developers. It has permeated all areas of business. Many of the software applications are common and are used with little or no adaptation by the widest variety of different businesses and organisations. This is particularly true of databases, word processors, spreadsheets, presentation packages, email, desktop publishing, imaging, product management and web browsers.

One of the major problems with many commercially available application software packages is that they are released prematurely and are not bug free. The intense demand for new products and the competitive nature of the industry requires developers to release partially completed software applications packages. The practice of releasing products prematurely means that the user is required to update the software with a series of patches over the life of the software. These patches deal with major or minor problems, which have either been encountered by the developers post-release, or have caused other users particular problems. This has certainly been a policy adopted by large application software companies, such as Microsoft.

Key words

Bug free – software that does not contain faulty programming or code and is largely immune to any crashing caused by the activities of a user

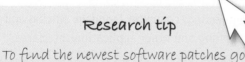

Research tip

To find the newest software patches go to www.softwarepatch.com.

Example

In Spring 2007, it was alleged that there were three major bugs in Microsoft's latest product, Office 2007. One of the bugs made computers unusable until they were rebooted, while another had a problem with the execution of a code. Microsoft was roundly criticised when they produced Word 2000 and Word 2002. They failed to include patches to deal with bugs in their monthly updates to registered users. Such patches would have dealt with some serious problems with the two previous versions of the application software. According to an Israeli security researcher, Word 2007's bugs also leave users open to remote attack codes.

Specialised support software

There is an enormous range of specialised support software, some of which is generally available off the shelf, which can then be adapted or modified for personal or business use. Software applications encompass almost any area of business; however, there are common types of support software aimed at facilitating the storage and use of information and decision-making.

A typical educational establishment is likely to rely on a management information system. They may also use suites of programs that help to create, test and maintain help files, packages such as Adobe Acrobat Pro to create PDFs and optical character recognition software to transfer images and texts from printed sources, so that these can be manipulated in either graphics or word processors.

Management Information Systems

Management information systems collect, manipulate and disseminate data. They require the inputting of data, the processing of data into information, and the storage and production of outputs, including management reports. Management information systems are designed to provide a business with up-to-date information on performance, such as sales or stock levels. The purpose of the systems is to produce reports in formats that are usable by managers at various levels of the organisation. They can provide financial statements and performance reports, which aim to assist in the planning, monitoring and implementation of strategies and policies.

Many businesses have an enormous volume of data, which would be almost completely useless to the organisation and its decision-makers on its own. Management information systems use this raw data and manipulate it so that it can reveal trends and patterns. The systems can also be used to answer what-if scenarios, should strategy be changed. They are therefore useful for making predictions and decisions. They can save the business an enormous amount of time as the data does not have to be manually processed. This dispenses with the need for manual filing and analysis. Overall, management information systems allow the business or organisation to react quicker and make decisions that are both based on actual data and predicted information.

Key words

What-if scenarios – these are designed to show the net outcomes of slight or major changes in policies or situations in the future. They allow the business to create models and create workable solutions should the future not be precisely as is predicted

Decision Support Software

Decision support software or systems (DSS) are computerised information systems created to support organisational decision-making. They are interactive software systems, allowing decision-makers to compile information from raw data, documents, personal knowledge or information and business models. Businesses would routinely use a DSS to gather and present comparative sales figures, projected revenue, different decision alternatives and current information assets.

There are in fact five different types of DSS:

- communication-driven DSS – designed to facilitate collaboration and communication
- document-driven DSS – for storage, processing, retrieval and analysis of documents, images, sounds and video
- knowledge-driven DSS – designed to suggest or recommend actions to managers
- web-based DSS – delivers decisions to support information and tools using web browsers
- data-driven DSS – allows access and manipulation of company data by accessing the systems by query and retrieval tools.

Expert systems are a derivative of knowledge-driven DSS. They have specialised problem-solving expertise and are often known as 'suggestion DSS'. The first major program of this type was used in 1965 to assist doctors in diagnosing blood diseases. Expert systems are really a form of artificial intelligence. They can be used for scheduling manufacturing and for providing advisory systems. In recent years, they have come to incorporate relational databases.

Think What standard application software might be required to be compatible or compliant with a DSS in order for the business to make full use of this system?

Key words

Relational databases – store information in tables in a number of fields and records. This allows the system to quickly pull from thoussands of records contained in many different tables just the data nedded to create a useful report or small table

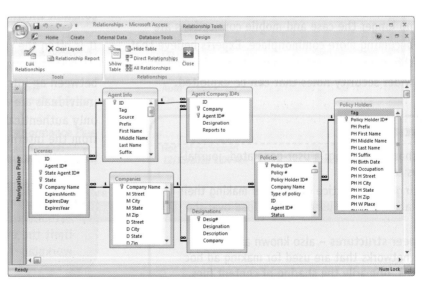

Figure 35.2 A relational database [source: www.jegsworks.com]

EVIDENCE ACTIVITY

P1 – M1 – D1

A recent review of internal communication systems has highlighted that the organisation that you work for is not making the best use of information technology developments. Most of the key concerns seem to revolve around a lack of efficient communication systems.

Routinely, information is passed to the relevant individuals at work, but from a recent questionnaire circulated to all employees the following results were discovered:

	% Admitted:
Poor communication	43%
Managers not listening to each other	40%
Saying one thing and doing another	33%
Continual reorganisation	32%
Ineffective reward and recognition	29%
Unwillingness to take tough decisions	21%
Looking inward	15%

Currently, the organisation utilises the following internal communication systems:

- typed and duplicated paper-based memoranda
- notice boards
- monthly team meetings
- bi-annual meetings for all employees
- management briefings (weekly)
- stand-alone computers (which are not networked)
- one in five computers have internet access
- paper-based manual filing systems
- analogue switchboard.

As the designated IT specialist for the organisation, you have been asked by the owners to either write a report or prepare a presentation, with supporting notes, which looks at the potential impact of new hardware and software technologies.

1. Describe new hardware and software technologies that impact on organisations. Your report must cover increased power, capacity and sophistication, new communication technologies, sophisticated and integrated application software, specialist support software, and the internet and intranets. (P1)

2. The organisation is seriously considering a major upgrade in terms of the use of IT. It wants to make use of the latest technology developments. The owners have asked you to follow up your initial report and to comment and explain the following:

a. How the current internal communication systems could make use of IT developments.

b. How the developments might affect the organisation.

c. How the developments could be rolled out for use in external communications. (M1)

3. As a final part of your work on IT developments and their impacts, the owners have also asked you to make specific recommendations as to which IT developments should be taken up and explain how they might be beneficial to the organisation. (D1)

35.2 *Understand why organisations need to change in response to information technology developments*

ORGANISATIONAL CHALLENGES

Theoretically, information technology is an invaluable tool for businesses and other organisations. In fact, it is not so much an invaluable tool as an absolute necessity! The greatest problem for many organisations is that IT presents unfathomable and constantly changing requirements. As a result, many organisations are using inefficient systems. This leads to employee frustration, loss of customers and profit and a host of other issues.

Constant changes needed for re-engineering of systems

One of the major problems that faces all businesses and organisations is the re-engineering of their systems. This poses enormous problems, as there is a considerable amount of hardware, software and stored data that is related to and reliant upon the existing IT system. The greatest fear for organisations is that re-engineering will cause far greater problems in the short- to medium-term than the problems it will resolve for the organisation in the longer-term. Some businesses resist modification and evolution of systems because of this fear, meaning that they are unable to meet constantly changing business requirements.

It is important that those proposing the re-engineering approach the problem in a careful and considerate manner, whether they are employees of the organisation or external consultants, or freelancers working for the organisation.

The process of re-engineering can be likened to the relocation of a business to a new site. The ideal situation for any business is to move to what is known as a greenfield site – a blank canvas that has no construction on it. This type of site affords the business the opportunity to build premises that are ideal for their needs. The reality, however,

is that when most businesses relocate they move to a brownfield site, or at least premises that were previously occupied by another organisation. The configuration of the buildings and the rooms within it will never be ideal, hence there is considerable disruption as walls are torn down and extensions built. This is the situation facing those companies re-engineering their systems. For a time both systems have to work alongside one another, then at some point all users and applications have to be switched over to the new system.

> **Think** How might an organisation installing an entirely new computerised system ensure that none of its activities or operations is adversely affected during the changeover period?

Ensuring that management is IT aware

The 'Digital Divide' refers to the gap between the benefits and advantages available to people and businesses that understand and use up-to-date IT developments and those who don't.

In business, technological advances have become synchronous with business development and a lack of knowledge and understanding could mean a business is at a serious disadvantage to its competitors.

As strategic decision-makers of organisations, it is vital that managers are aware of the latest technology developments and the relevant applications to their type of business.

Managers need to be well-informed themselves if they are to be able to make decisions about the use of IT in their organisation, in consultation with the highly-qualified technical advisors that are often contracted in to review and update IT systems.

IT education is widely available from basic to advanced levels and local Chambers of Commerce also provide valuable sources of information in the form of free or low cost seminars.

Need for reduction in complexity and for integrated systems

Theoretically, each successive IT development makes hardware, software and the processes and usefulness of IT systems easier. Technologically, there may be complexities, but immediate access to and use of technology is becoming ever simpler.

Organisations have to make decisions about when is the right time to invest in technology. It is important for them to prioritise how new IT developments could affect their activities and operations. For most organisations the priorities tend to revolve around reducing complexity and bringing together applications or activities that were previously discrete into an integrated system. As with many business-related investments, it is about making the correct choices and making those investments at the right time.

Example

Until relatively recently, many businesses used Microsoft Excel to store key facts and figures. Many have now moved on to using PDAs and Microsoft Outlook to store customer information. Some others now use ACT! to manage customers, this application being a prime example of an integrated approach.

Ensuring payback on the internet in IT systems

Websites, and the necessary supporting IT infrastructure, can be a costly and confusing prospect for many organisations. Clearly they are useful, in terms of promoting and advertising products and services. Increasingly they are vital for taking orders, selling access to information and a host of other e-commerce possibilities. However, there are significant costs in terms of cash, time and effort in establishing an online presence. It is also notoriously difficult for businesses to make any reasonable judgement as to how long it might take to see a return on their investment.

Example

Oxfordshire County Council, the Department for Education and Skills, various Oxfordshire schools, the Southeast Museum Library and the River and Rowing Museum, all based around Henley-on-Thames, were joint stakeholders in establishing a website for use with secondary schools. It was not proposed that this be a profit-making venture. The website development costs were £7,000. In addition, £2,000 was paid to a project officer and evaluation and trials cost a further £2,500.

Purchasing the domain name is a minor consideration in terms of cost, as is hosting. Businesses can achieve a basic web presence for less than £200. Basic structures of up to ten pages can cost anything up to £800. The more sophisticated the website, the higher the costs, particularly when shopping cart facilities are incorporated along with secure payment facilities. Most small- to medium-sized businesses, therefore, budget up to £3,500 for sites selling a hundred different products or services.

As with any developmental cost, businesses will be looking for a return on their investment. In other words, they will want a system by which they can monitor and calculate additional income that the business would not have otherwise attracted, but which has been stimulated solely by a web presence.

Developing technical infrastructures

Alongside any implementation of new IT, organisations need to develop a coherent technical infrastructure in order to support it. This has implications, both in terms of training users and continuing to support them, and acquiring the skills and expertise to deal with ongoing potential infrastructure issues.

Without a technical support infrastructure, IT businesses can neither make adequate use of the IT development, nor can they assess its impact on their activities. As importantly, they are not in a position to assess the need to either re-engineer their systems or bring in timely upgrades and changes.

CASE STUDY: JOINED UP COUNCILS

Suffolk County Council, Mid-Suffolk District Council and BT announced a ten-year partnership in 2004 to offer residents, and businesses better, more cost-effective and easily accessible council services.

Suffolk County Council will invest around £30 million a year and Mid-Suffolk around £3 million in the partnership. This comes from existing budgets allocated to service delivery, so there will be no additional financial burden on council taxpayers. BT will invest more than £50 million over the course of the contract in resources and new systems.

BT will bring its expertise to a rural area where the county council has already earned a good Comprehensive Performance Assessment (CPA) rating. BT has chosen CGI Group Inc. as its strategic technology partner, a company that specialises in IT and business process outsourcing services.

In the future, people will no longer need to be passed between several departments, or even from one council to another when they phone in.

Improving access to public services by providing choice and convenience is one of the first areas being addressed by the joint venture. Among the improvements to service will be:

- a single customer service centre that will manage all public access points across the county, joining up County and District services for enquirers

- a series of 'one-stop-shop' centres for Council services, within 15 minutes travel of 99 per cent of Mid-Suffolk's population

- a website where customers can both access service information and carry out transactions, such as paying bills or applying for licences online

- a single point of access to District and County services and joined-up health and social care services.

Source: Adapted from www.bt.com

QUESTIONS

1. Why are the changes necessary? How will the IT systems need to be re-engineered?

2. Why is it important for the project to have the full backing and understanding of all management groups from the four organisations involved in the project?

3. Why have the councils recognised that their systems need a radical overhaul and that they need to be fully integrated?

4. How will the councils, in particular, and the residents of the area benefit in the medium- to long-term by the implementation of the project?

5. What is the role of the four organisations in making collaborative decisions regarding the development of technical infrastructures to support the project?

EXTERNAL ENVIRONMENT

No business or organisation operates in a vacuum. The external environment will affect it in a range of ways. Organisations are continually affected by changes in business partners, competition, fashions, trends, technology, regulation and the economy. Many businesses that, until relatively recently, could adequately operate and run their activities with little concern beyond their immediate region are now faced with influence and interference on a global scale. Not all external influences are negative or constraining, however; some actually provide businesses with greater opportunities.

Increasing globalisation

Globalisation has been gathering momentum since the end of World War Two. It is driven by advances in technology, in particular information and communication technology. Globalisation has a number of key features:

- economic interdependence

- increased influence from dominant cultures

- significant advances in IT

- geo-political challenges.

Globalisation has caused a convergence in terms of products, prices and profits. Its continued development is driven by the migration of workers, the free movement of money, integration of the financial markets and, of course, international trade.

On the one hand, globalisation is an enormous advantage for all businesses, as it frees trade between countries around the world. It provides access to a wider range of technologies and developments. On the other hand, it brings increased competition and alternate technologies, which may be more efficient, cost-effective and faster than the IT systems currently used by an organisation.

Significant investment may be needed to adopt or adapt to these new methods in order to remain competitive.

Research tip

For more information on globalisation, visit www.opendemocracy.net or www.worldbank.org.

> **Think** For many, globalisation is a two-edged sword. Try to list three advantages and three disadvantages of globalisation in terms of IT development.

Potential for outsourcing and geosourcing

Outsourcing became a trend in the 1980s. Companies attempted to lower their business costs by delegating non-core operations and activities to an external organisation. It is sometimes referred to as off-shoring, as the non-core activities are often outsourced to organisations and individuals in other countries.

Many businesses have outsourced their customer support by using call centres in other countries. Others have focused on the conservation of energy and labour costs by outsourcing their manufacturing and engineering.

Figure 35.4 Many UK businesses outsource their call centres to India

There can be considerable problems with outsourcing, especially the quality of the service. There has been the beginnings of a backlash against outsourcing, with companies bringing back many of the services in-house (known as in-sourcing).

Geosourcing is a version of outsourcing, which involves identifying and subcontracting to partners abroad who can carry out IT-based requirements, either development work or the running of systems. Geosourcing can be very practical in IT, providing the cost and quality is assured. By extending the working day across three time zones, it is possible to carry out IT development projects with three 12-hour days in one 24-hour period. Typically the cost savings are up to 30 per cent.

The biggest risk with outsourcing and geosourcing is that there are often major cultural differences. However, with outsourcing and geosourcing specialists operating in the overseas locations, transitions are becoming less and less difficult.

Research tip

For more information on outsourcing, visit the website of the Outsourcing Institute at www.outsourcing.com.

Changing regulatory and legal frameworks

As the UK is a member of the European Union, businesses and organisations must comply with EU regulations and legal requirements, in addition to any national ones. However, in practice, most EU regulations and directives have already been accepted to a greater or lesser extent by the British government.

With IT developments and businesses, there are many straightforward health and safety issues involved. These encompass the use of display screens, regular medical checks for heavy users of IT and risk assessments of the workplace.

Through improved communication of information, businesses are now rarely faced with changes in the regulatory and legal frameworks without prior notice. It is also important to be aware that additional regulations and legal requirements are not necessarily restrictive, as they apply industry- or Europe-wide. They are often designed to protect the business's interests as much as they protect the employees and the business's customers.

Reduced costs of business start-ups

Until recently, businesses setting up for the first time had one or both of the following requirements:

- premises that were suitable for the organisation's operations and based in an area with sufficiently trained or experienced potential employees. (In addition, the location would have to be convenient for suppliers and making deliveries to customers)

- a visible presence for customers to make personal visits to the business's premises.

The development of the internet and secure online purchasing and payment systems now means that relatively small businesses can, without a great deal of ready investment, easily begin trading and directly compete with larger, more established businesses.

These online organisations can be located in smaller premises than more traditional organisations. Many rely almost exclusively on IT to replace some of the manual functions still retained by their older competitors.

Even new start-up businesses that sell physical products rarely require premises large enough to hold stock. Fulfilment of orders is outsourced, so the new business simply acts as an intermediary between the customer and the actual supplier of the product. As these organisations are online businesses, they do not require a high-street presence as there is no expectation to have face-to-face interaction with customers. All interaction takes place either via the internet, by email or by telephone.

This means that start-up costs are considerably lower for what are known as 'clicks' organisations, as opposed to 'bricks and mortar' businesses. Many traditional organisations are now known as 'clicks and mortar' businesses as they retain their original physical presence in the high street, while offering an alternative, or complementary, service online.

Example

HMV, the music and home entertainment chain, is a prime example of a clicks and mortar organisation. They retain their high-street presence in the form of traditional 'record shops'. They also have a very successful online presence and their warehouse in Jersey fulfils orders made by British customers.

Figure 35.5 HMV have a high-street presence as well as an internet business

Increased competition from global companies

Each year, e-commerce competition grows fiercer. The success of global organisations in any particular marketplace is largely dependent on their ability to deliver products or services to that marketplace at a reasonable cost.

For service-based global companies, using e-commerce to deliver their services over the internet is relatively straightforward. It is more difficult, however, for global companies with overseas manufacturing and fulfilment centres to offer products at a competitive rate that covers transportation costs, compared to businesses that are local to the marketplace. Now, typically, global companies run their primary operations in their home countries, but find partners in other markets to fulfil and deliver orders and provide customer support.

It is very difficult to make any kind of judgement in financial terms about the percentage of products and services supplied directly by global companies. In fact, the British government and World Trade Organisation are looking at ways in which these figures can be measured and monitored. Potentially there are enormous implications for almost every type of British business. It now means that it could be considerably cheaper to purchase the same product direct from China and pay for the shipping, compared to purchasing it from a high-street store.

Research tip

For more information about e-commerce trade, visit the website of the Department of Trade and Industry at www.dti.gov.uk and the World Trade Organisation at www.wto.org.

INTERNAL ENVIRONMENT

The previous section looked at the external influences on business organisations and systems. In this section, our focus is the impact on the activities and operations of organisations as they seek to respond to developments in IT. The main impact, of course, is on the ways in which work is carried out and the skill requirements of employees.

Need for constant upskilling of the workforce

Upskilling is the process of increasing the overall range of skills of employees, usually demanding that they develop more technical and varied skills. This is usually achieved through training, either in the workplace or using external training courses.

Upskilled workers are considered to be more employable, but this does not necessarily mean that they are better paid or that they have better prospects for promotion. In fact it is the employer who sees the main benefits, rather than the employee.

It is important to distinguish between upskilling and reskilling. Upskilling reinforces, extends or updates employees' current range of skills to match new employer requirements. Reskilling requires the employee to acquire new skills, perhaps to deal with a new job role.

Redundant skills and employees

Just as outdated hardware and software might eventually reach a point where it simply cannot be upgraded, IT developments can also have the same effect on employees. This is not a new process or phenomenon. In the past, particularly in manufacturing, many skilled people were required to produce products, but over time machinery and then robots have replaced manual skills, making generations of employees redundant.

Employees are sometimes made redundant when their skills are no longer required. It does not mean that the employee has been replaced by a better-trained individual, but simply that their job as it once was no longer exists. Some employers

will take the view that, although the skills of particular employees are now redundant, the inherent quality of that employee suggests that it is a worthwhile to invest in retraining or reskilling them to do an alternative job. The process of replacing humans with machine-based processes is one that is unlikely to stop and has in fact become more common in some areas of work.

Home and remote working

Improvements in the field of IT and communications technology have allowed people to develop alternative work patterns. As it is no longer an absolute requirement for a business to maintain expensive business premises that can house a supervised and managed workforce, employees can, in fact, be based almost anywhere. Assuming that the business's IT systems are sufficiently developed and integrated, seamless operations can continue to take place, regardless of the location of the workforce.

There are two distinct trends:

- home working – this is also known as teleworking or telecommuting. The employee operates for most of the working week at home. Their work patterns, workload and behaviour can be monitored by simple checking systems, such as counting keystrokes. Webcams and permanent communication links can replicate the supervisory and management processes

- remote working – this involves employees working in a range of locations, essentially having a mobile office. Individuals can operate from anywhere, while fully interacting with the headquarters of the organisation, with the requirement only to be physically present for particular events and meetings. By using wireless technology, work can be transmitted and received via the internet, using laptops, PDAs and mobile phones. This also means that employees or representatives can operate in overseas locations, regularly liaising and feeding back information, as well as receiving instructions from the employer.

Research tip

The British government website www.direct.gov.uk provides specific advice about flexible working and employees' rights.

Impact of regular restructuring

Restructuring means reorganising an organisation to make it more efficient. Any form of restructuring will be disruptive to both the organisation's operations and activities and its employees, as it causes a period of uncertainty. Clear restructuring plans may be in place, but they rarely go through without considerable unforeseen difficulties and delays.

As far as employees are concerned, restructuring is often accompanied by reductions in employment. Restructured organisations incorporating IT developments are usually described as being leaner. They are said to be more efficient, better organised and to have a greater focus.

Key words
- -
Leaner – the organisation operates with just the number of employees needed to carry out necessary work and in times of additional demand, they will usually outsource

Example

In 2005, Hewlett Packard announced that they were going to restructure their entire operation. Some 14,500 employees (10 per cent of the workforce) lost their jobs. The business had been losing money in certain areas of operations, so management and shareholders demanded a restructuring exercise to deal with these problems and to save the business an estimated $1.9 billion per year in wages. The then Chief Executive, Mark Hurd, said 'the objective is to create a simpler, nimbler HP with fewer matrices.'

Source: adapted from *www.infoworld.com*

Managing change

For the management of an organisation, there are four key factors for success when managing change:

- The actual pressure for change – the management's commitment to making the change.

- A clear and shared vision – an agenda that will benefit the entire organisation.

- The capacity for change – whether the organisation has the necessary time, finance and other resources required to implement the change.

- Action – whether the organisation has systems in place to check on the progress of the change and how it is affecting operations, activities and employees.

There are also four factors that can lead to failure when managing change:

- a lack of consistent leadership

- uninformed and de-motivated employees

- a lack of capacity, which leads to budget cuts, stressed employees and spending money to save money later

- a lack of initiative to consider a different way of doing things.

According to a study carried out by Changefirst, 65 per cent of senior IT executives believed that change management is a specialist area of expertise. Despite this, only 20 per cent of executives assigned a specific change management specialist to handle the implementation of a major IT project.

Whenever IT developments are being implemented, there are likely to be conflicts of interest. Some people will see the implementation of the IT as a solution. Others will see it as a distinct threat, while another group might view it solely as a disruptive exercise that prevents them from carrying out their normal work. In order to successfully implement complex IT changes, the following measures are advisable:

- predict the impact of a major IT project on users and take these people into account in the implementation decisions

- ensure that line managers have the tools and ability to lead all users through the IT change process

- ensure that there are tracking and accountability mechanisms, which cover employee-related, financial, technical and logistical considerations

- build in the capacity for the IT department to support line managers in planning and executing the transition over to the new systems.

Think To what extent do you think most businesses consider the adoption of IT developments to the extent listed above?

Balance of core employees with contractors and outsourced staff

In most modern organisations there are three main types of employee or staff:

- Core employees – these are considered to be essential members of the workforce, who may tend to be senior management, supervisors and project managers. It is thought to be absolutely essential that these individuals are directly employed by the organisation.

- Contractors – these are individuals who are brought into the organisation on an as-needed basis. Usually contractors have a yearly contract and a financial relationship with the organisation. The contractor undertakes to provide essential services as required by the organisation, in return for a regular retainer, paid by the organisation. Contractors will take responsibility for clearly defined areas of operation. These can either be regular activities, such as the fulfilment of call centre or customer support operations, or simply the servicing and repair of IT related hardware and software.

- Outsourced staff – as we have seen there has been a trend to outsource the operations of entire departments, functions, activities or operations. Outsourced staff are essentially subcontractors, employed by an organisation that is contractually obliged to provide an agreed level of service in return for payment by the client organisation. Outsourced staff are not directly employed by the client organisation and it is the responsibility of the outsource organisation to ensure sufficient coverage, quality, training and other issues.

Organisations need to think carefully about the balance between these three different groups of individuals who together provide what the business needs. Employing core members of staff directly allows organisations to keep key operations, decision-making and problem-solving in-house, which helps to prevent problems that could arise from poor levels of service or conflicts of interest by contractors or outsourced staff.

Other internal changes in organisational structures

Traditionally, the organisational structure of many businesses looked like a pyramid. A handful of key decision-makers would be at the top. These would then be supported by successive layers of management and supervision, through which instructions are passed down the organisation to the bulk of employees at the bottom of the structure.

The pyramid structure can be viewed as a visual representation of the levels of authority, as well as illustrating how information passes up and down the organisation, being filtered, amended and implemented at various levels.

As businesses have tended to become more reliant on IT, they have shed staff, functions and operations and so become leaner, with layers of middle management stripped out of the pyramid. In most cases, there is now much less of a gulf between the senior management of a business and the employees at the bottom of the pyramid. These functional employees are usually organised into work teams, managed by a supervisor. The supervisor is answerable to a functional or departmental manager, who in turn reports to senior management.

This is a far more flexible structure, which allows instructions and ideas to pass down to the frontline workforce without becoming diluted. It also allows those at the frontline to inform the senior management of problems in a far more meaningful way and to offer solutions to those problems.

The pyramids that existed for many decades were proven to be quite inefficient and not cost effective. Organisational structures are far flatter now. In most cases, dedicated specialist departments that provide essential services, such as accountancy, human resources and administration, support these flat organisations.

EVIDENCE ACTIVITY

P2 – P3

You are a researcher for a county council and have been asked to investigate the experience of Suffolk County Council and Mid-Suffolk District Council. In 2004, these organisations entered into a partnership with British Telecom and the CGI Group Inc to revolutionise the way in which their services to Suffolk residents, visitors and businesses are delivered. (See page 173 to read the full case study).

The councils recognise that IT developments offer them an opportunity to deliver their services in a radically different way. The key is the way in which the services are delivered. The councils have asked for a report in three parts:

1. A specific identification of IT developments that could be used by the councils in the delivery of their services. (P2)

2. An identification of any specific issues that could arise in transforming current service provision over to new IT-based solutions. (P2)

3. What organisational changes may be necessary (or desirable) once the service provision has switched over to being IT-based? (P3)

35.3 *Understand how organisations adapt activities in response to information technology developments*

ACTIVITIES

Different organisations will have a variety of alternative responses to IT developments, dependent on their size and areas of activity. This section looks at typical adaptations, but it must be appreciated that not all organisations will be required to make all of these adaptations, as the area of activity may not be relevant to their operations.

Adapting sales and marketing strategies

Businesses are constantly seeking new opportunities. The development of IT offers new opportunities to a business and requires them to adapt their sales and marketing strategies. Broadly speaking, there are two key components to sales and marketing:

- product – existing products and new products

- markets – existing markets and new markets.

The combination of these factors creates a range of different scenarios in which different strategies can be adopted:

- Existing product, existing market – the business is already selling products into this marketplace, but IT developments may mean that this process can become more widespread and efficient. For example, it may allow more targeted marketing and a closer relationship between the sales force and customers.

- Existing product, new market – this is a typical opportunity that presents itself to a business that has implemented an IT development, such as the establishment of an online store. The new market may still be in their home country, but a type of customer that may have been unaware of the business's products until they were available online.

Alternatively, the products may now be available in a new country, bringing with it a radically different series of challenges in terms of sales and marketing. Marketing may have to incorporate the translation of sales literature and advertisements, adaptation to the country's customs and laws and may require the physical presence of a sales force or distributor

- New product, existing market – there may be an opportunity for the business to introduce in a new or adapted product, perhaps selling a next generation product to existing customers. IT developments may make it easier to demonstrate the product, for example by using a website, with the possibility of including audio-visual content. Sales can be achieved using the existing customer database and pointing those customers towards the website for further information, sales and payment. Marketing can revolve around promoting the website as a contact point for both information and for sales.

- new product, new market – traditionally a difficult area for sales and marketing, as it requires the business to make a standing start, and sell an unproven product into an unproven market. There is still a great reliance on market research, coupled with considered product development. However, IT can streamline this process and support the interaction between the intended type of customer and the product's benefits and features. The process should produce a product that is more in tune with the needs or demands of the market.

> **Think** Which of the above scenarios is the easiest for a business to develop in terms of its sales and marketing strategies and why?

Adopting new purchasing opportunities

E-commerce is not restricted to the business-to-consumer field. It is also a necessary and efficient system for transactions between businesses. Primarily this means electronic data interchange (EDI). This requires the purchasing company to adopt electronic data capture, so that it can monitor its stock levels and then, once the minimum stock level has been reached, create an order, which can be sent using EDI to its suppliers.

Businesses rely on these systems, as they will only hold enough stock to cover a short period of time. They rely on their suppliers to act as a forward warehouse facility. This is often known as Just-in-Time, as they will only hold sufficient stock for the anticipated immediate demands of their customers.

> ### Example
>
> Most supermarkets chains use automated ordering systems. Each product has a unique barcode. When a sale is made the barcode is scanned, automatically reducing the stock level on the database by the appropriate number of items. Once the stock level has reached the minimum re-order quantity, an automated order will be sent to the supplier or warehouse. There are no manual ordering processes but the system is periodically checked by manual stocktaking exercises.

Figure 35.6 Computerised tills help shops to monitor stock levels

Using new technology in customer support

There have been three key advances in the use of IT to facilitate and streamline customer support functions for most organisations and businesses:

- Smart online help pages – this technology revolves around a searchable database. Customers are prompted to type in either key words or phrases. The database then searches for appropriate documents, statements or instructions related to the key word or phrase. A series of options is offered to the customer, who can then read the advice online. Prompts are given for the customer to confirm whether the information helped them to solve their problem. If this was not the case, they are asked to type in additional key words or phrases or to contact the customer support line.

- Automated voice recognition systems – it is now possible to make telephone enquiries by calling a telephone line that has voice recognition software. The software can recognise key phrases and responds to numbers entered using the telephone key pad, such as strings of figures in the case of automated banking. The customer can make enquiries and be passed through various filter levels, so that gradually the enquiry is dealt with without human intervention.

- Semi-automated and supported customer service – in order to facilitate outsourced customer service centres, searchable databases are made available via computer networks to live call-centre employees in remote locations. The employees are able to access data and interrogate the database to provide solutions to customer enquiries. This is a hybrid system, which incorporates a live human response to queries, coupled with the flexibility of a searchable database.

> **Think** The three different options or approaches outlined above are very commonly used in business today. Try to identify at least one business that uses each of them.

Secure funds transfer

Theoretically, secure funds transfer reduces the occurrence of error and fraud. However, many customers and businesses have serious concerns about entering their credit or debit card details for payment on websites, regardless of encryption. A number of proprietary hybrid transfer systems now exist, such as Paypal or Nochex. If customers can be convinced that funds transfers are secure, online payments can be facilitated, which has a positive benefit on the cash flow of the organisation.

Supply chain management, logistics and integration with partner businesses

Supply chain management covers the movement and storage of products and services from raw materials through to the end user. It incorporates logistics, which is the primary movement or flow of products and services.

Developments in IT have made the entire process of supply chain management more responsive and streamlined. Businesses can now operate solid supply networks, with key business partners focusing on particular aspects of the entire operation. The network is a series of complicated interactions between different businesses, all of which mutually support one another, and share risks and profits from the overall supply chain.

IT has been instrumental in integrating and formalising these relationships, as the following advantages indicate:

- it is easier to plan and control
- it is straightforward to organise work responsibilities and structures of organisations
- product and information flows are instantaneous
- management methods can be shared
- there is a shared culture and attitude throughout the supply chain.

Research tip

For up-to-date information on the application of IT to the supply chain, visit www.supplymanagement.co.uk.

Establishing an internet presence

As we have already seen, the vast majority of customers, competitors and suppliers, as well as business partners, have access to and regularly use the internet. It has therefore become essential for most businesses to have an Internet presence. However, different businesses respond to this need in different ways:

- passive brochure ware – some companies simply put an electronic copy of their current product catalogue and/or price list up on a website. The site has limited functionality, but provides customers with background information and information about ways to contact the business, either by email, fax or telephone

- semi-functional extended information point – this is something of a halfway house, as additional information, beyond what is normally included in a brochure or catalogue, is put on a website. Sometimes this is augmented by audio-visual content, case studies and customer endorsements of products. Slightly more sophisticated communication opportunities may be provided, such as forms that allow enquiries to be sent directly from the website

- fully functional web stores with secure payments – this is the ultimate opportunity and adaptation, as it provides the business with an alternative point of contact, marketing and sales with their customers. For many businesses this has become the means by which the bulk of sales are achieved, as these web stores have eclipsed the sales of their traditional bricks and mortar outlets.

Automated manufacturing processes

Automated manufacturing is an ideal solution for businesses that wish to combine component parts in different ways to provide customised products. By creating products as and when they are ordered, rather than stocking separate lines of each product type, this gives the business a great deal of flexibility. It also allows them to make products that exactly match the customers' requirements.

Such businesses use systems that can locate an item, and identify its status and identity. Theoretically, the production time is reduced by automating many of the processes, but this mass customisation process does require enormous investment by the manufacturing business.

Research tip

For further information about automated manufacturing, visit the website of the Society of Manufacturing Engineers at www.sme.org.

Reducing intermediation

Intermediation is a term used to describe the number of businesses or organisations involved in a supply chain between the original supplier of the raw materials and the end user of the finished product.

IT has enabled businesses within a supply chain to streamline this process. In particular, it has allowed manufacturers to deal directly with the end users of products. In the past, it was not economically viable for them to have a sales presence in the marketplace or to deal with individual orders. It was also not economically advisable to accept individual orders, as each product would need to be customised.

The establishment of an internet presence, coupled with automated manufacturing processes, has facilitated mass customisation. This means that traditional intermediaries or partners in the supply chain, such as wholesalers and high-street vendors, can be bypassed and direct sales achieved.

> **Think** Dell is an ideal example of an organisation that has reduced intermediation. Visit their website at www.dell.co.uk to find out more about the company. How are their processes designed to cope with individual orders from consumers?

EVIDENCE ACTIVITY

M2

Revisit the Suffolk County council case study on page 173. You are a researcher for another county council that is interested in their experiences. The council is keen to understand the implications that IT developments may have on the ways in which they deliver services and carry out their necessary activities. They have asked you to look more closely at the impact on the two councils, particularly in terms of the range of activities that they are involved in and how these are delivered.

Specifically you have been asked to:

1. Explain any necessary changes in processes.

2. Explain any subsequent changes in staff roles and functions.

3. Explain any longer term requirements as far as the organisation is concerned. (M2)

PERFORMANCE

For all organisations, the ultimate test of any investment in new systems is whether it results in an improvement in their overall performance. This can be measured in terms of real time and cost savings, increased returns to investors, more streamlined decision-making and problem-solving or customer service provision.

Productivity, costs, profitability and efficiency

Productivity measures the amount of goods an organisation produces, and the rate at which they are produced, compared to the work, time and money invested. The implementation of IT can result in a productivity gain. This is invariably achieved by the automation of systems, as machines can work 24 hours a day without a break and with minimum human support or intervention.

Although the initial investment needed to introduce automation will be high, if the business looks towards the medium- to long-term they will see major cost reductions. In fact, even from the outset, cost reductions will be seen, as the cost per unit of production will decrease. Each unit produced is carefully costed out in terms of components, raw materials, human wage costs, overheads and the cost of running machinery. Each unit of production is expected to make a contribution to these costs, which is a major part of the pricing structure established by the organisation.

Once the cost of each unit has been calculated, and the contribution derived, the business will then add a calculated additional percentage, or flat fee figure, to the sale price of the product. This difference between the actual cost of the product to the business and the final sale price to customers represents the profit.

Clearly, if the business can reduce its overall costs, but retain its sale price to customers then increased profits will result. Usually, though, to make the business more competitive and to pass on a percentage of the cost savings, sale prices are slightly reduced to encourage a higher sales volume.

Taken together, productivity, cost reduction, increased profitability, and the additional benefit of reduced wastage that results from using machinery, improve the efficiency of the business. Collectively these are all performance measurements and the success of investment in IT will be determined by whether performance improvements in these areas have been made.

> **Think** As far as the owners or shareholders of an organisation are concerned, which of the above performance measurements would be the most important? Why?

Improved management information and control

Management information systems should provide managers with the necessary tools to access and use data, which would previously have been manually manipulated. When raw data is input into a management information system, it can produce valuable outputs that can be digested by managers. This means that they can have real-time information, enabling them to control the activities and operations of the business on a minute-by-minute basis.

At a stroke, management is able to view current production levels, peaks and troughs in sales, the deployment of human and machine-based resources, stock levels and any other information necessary to solve problems or make decisions.

Customer service

As we have seen, IT developments have enabled businesses to adopt more accessible and efficient customer service provisions. If a business is producing more products and services, attracting a wider range of customers and operating in a number of different markets, then it needs to invest in its customer service provision.

Customer service is, of course, not simply related to the sales function of a business. It involves a period before sales are made, during the sales process and the vital period after purchase, which aims to

Figure 35.7 Amazon are able to recommend products to customers based on previous purchases

ensure that customers remain loyal and stimulate new customers through recommendations.

Businesses will routinely measure their customer service performance levels in terms of whether they are able to deal with volume enquiries, satisfied outcomes, feedback from customers and the level of complaints.

Synergy and integration of systems

Synergy occurs when systems are integrated in a way that means the efficiencies and performance achieved are greater than the sum of all of the individual parts. In fact this is a dynamic state, where all of the components of a business's activity are brought seamlessly together to provide a fully integrated and efficient set of systems.

Synergies require cooperation and the willingness to compromise in order to make the organisation and its systems work in closer harmony with one another. Using IT allows information, control and direction to be far more efficient than in manual or traditional systems.

Synergy is an ultimate performance measurement, where all parts of the organisation operate together, in order to improve productivity, reduce costs and increase profitability. Additional benefits would include job satisfaction for employees and greater flexibility and manoeuvrability for the business and management.

EVIDENCE ACTIVITY

P4

Revisit the case study on page 173. You are a researcher for another county council that is interested in the experiences of Suffolk County Council. It is clear to your council that both Suffolk County Council and Mid-Suffolk District Council have had to make significant changes to their activities. Your council is also interested to see the impact on performance levels through the implementation of the project. By investigating these areas, the council hopes to better understand the implications of such a strategic partnership and use of new information technology.

The council recognises that there will be a period of time that could be problematic as the systems are transformed from paper/people-based to IT-based. It is concerned that performance levels will drop in this time and that there may well be a transition period as staff and clients adapt to the new systems. The council is hoping that you can identify possible problems and coping strategies.

1. What might be the likely reasons for a downturn in service provision and performance during the transition?

2. What steps could be taken to ensure the disruption is minimised?

3. How might staff and systems be better prepared for the transition?

4. How might new problems be anticipated and dealt with before they adversely affect customers? (P4)

MANAGING RISK

Potentially, computer-based or computer-related crimes could affect all businesses. The main problems revolve around:

- hacking

- fraud

- theft

- copyright abuse

- obscene content

- harassment.

A great many of the crimes can actually be dealt with within the existing justice system, but others are now covered under the Computer Misuse Act 1990. There are increasing moves to both combat and prevent these types of computer crime, although the criminals are often one or two steps ahead of the systems, groups and specialists seeking to protect, prevent and prosecute the perpetrators of the crimes.

Research tip

To read a full version of the Computer Misuse Act, visit www.opsi.gov.uk or for a shorter version with examples visit www.computerevidence.co.uk/cases/CMA.htm.

Cyber-crime

CASE STUDY: POLICE STRUGGLE TO COPE WITH RISE OF CYBER-CRIME

The police are finding it almost impossible to deal with the massive rise in cyber-crime. London's Scotland Yard admitted that the problem has become so large that it is now unlikely that all of the allegations of crime will be investigated.

Chief Constables want a national e-crime unit to help them deal with the ever-growing number of cases. Identity theft alone costs the country some £1.7bn a year. In a report by the Metropolitan Police, the force admitted: 'It is widely recognised that e-crime is the most rapidly expanding form of criminality, encompassing both new criminal offences in relation to computers (viruses and hacking, etc.) and 'old' crimes (fraud, harassment etc.), committed using digital or computer technology. The Metropolitan Police Service assessment is that specialist e-crime units can no longer cope with all e-crime.'

Detective Inspector Charlie McMurdie wrote the report, and concluded: 'The ability of law enforcement to investigate all types of e-crime locally and globally must be "mainstreamed" as an integral part of every investigation, whether it be specialist, or murder, robbery, extortion demands, identity theft or fraud. Hackers and virus writers have evolved from largely enthusiastic amateur "criminals" to financially motivated, organised global criminal enterprises. Prosecutions of virus writers and hackers in the UK have been infrequent up to now. However, the motivation of such offenders has now migrated from the curious adolescent to the profile of the financially motivated professional, often with organised crime links.'

Source: Adapted from www.independent.co.uk

QUESTIONS

1. How could an organisation be involved in identity theft cases if its systems are not secure?

2. What does the report mean when it suggests that cyber-crime be mainstreamed?

3. Why might cyber-crime have changed from being committed by enthusiastic amateurs to hardened professional criminals?

Computer-related crimes can be classified into three different categories:

- content-related crime, such as pornography and criminal copyright infringement

- traditional crimes committed using a computer, such as harassment, fraud and theft

- straightforward attacks on computers and computer systems by unknown individuals, such as hackers.

Taken together, all of these types of crime are referred to as cyber-crime, e-crime or hi-tech crime.

Cyber-crimes fall into the following categories:

- Diverting financial assets – this is fraud that takes place on the Internet. The criminal steals debit or credit card details, clones the card and then makes illegal transfers or withdrawals, usually in countries where chip and pin facilities are not yet available.

- Sabotaging communications – typically these are attempts by hackers to access computer systems using malicious code. They can bombard servers and email accounts with messages. These are generally known as intrusion crimes.

- Stealing intellectual property – piracy and the theft of intellectual property is considered to be widespread on the internet. The term intellectual property encompasses patents, trademarks, designs, copyrights and domain names.

- Denial of service attacks – this is an attempt to make a computer's resource unavailable to its users. Hackers on root servers make attacks by saturating the target machine with communications requests to such an extent that it cannot deal with legitimate information requests.

- Halting e-commerce transactions – this is achieved by breaking into a business's website and compromising the security of online ordering and payment systems.

Example

In 1995 Vladimir Levin, a Russian University graduate, hacked into the Citibank system and transferred more than £6.2m out of Citibank accounts all over the world. The bank recovered £250,000 but could not find the rest.

In April 2007 there was a wave of denial of services attacks against websites in Estonia. The attacks crippled websites for Estonia's prime minister, banks and some school sites. Analysis of the malicious traffic pinpointed the attacks as coming from the US, Brazil, Canada and Vietnam.

Research tip

For more information on the fighting of cyber-crimes and to read about specific cases, visit the website of the Federal Bureau of Investigation at www.fbi.gov.

Preventive technologies

Preventive technologies are designed to combat cyber-crime by adapting software and creating hardware that is more resilient to attack. In reality, however, many of the preventive technologies are reactive rather than proactive. A notable exception to this is Microsoft Vista, which is specifically designed to prevent external attacks on the system and is self-protecting and healing.

The key preventive technologies are:

- Firewalls - these are designed to block potentially infected communications or attempts to access a computer system. Firewalls can block outgoing as well as incoming traffic.

- Access control methods - these systems have been used for many years to control who can enter a building and when. They have been adapted for use on computers and networks, requiring the user either to use a swipe card and/or a user name and password. The system is only as good as its weakest link, though, and in order to prevent the system from being compromised user names and passwords need to be periodically changed.

Disaster recovery

In some cases, there may be the total destruction or loss of an organisation's information and databases, or a loss of all website content. The primary means of dealing with this threat is to make sure that there is regular backup of all data. It is a comparatively straightforward task to store a real-time mirror copy of data, including all web pages, which can then be uploaded back onto the systems once the cause of the disaster has been located and dealt with.

Think Can you think of any ways for preventive technologies to proactively deal with potential cyber-crimes before they have happened?

EVIDENCE ACTIVITY

P5 – M3 – D2

Revisit the Mid-Suffolk County Council case study on page 173. You are a researcher for another county council; your council wants you to focus on risks and impacts on the two councils, both during and after the implementation of the information technology project. The council feels that it will be in a better position to respond and deal with potential problems if it can learn lessons from the experiences of the two councils.

Clearly any such implementation puts a massive strain on both employers and employees, as they both have vested interests in making sure that the investment works. Ultimately they are answerable to the elected councillors, who in turn are answerable to those that elected them – the customers of the services.

As the last part of your report you have been asked to focus on the following:

1. How could the council seek to offset or avoid any potential risks involved in implementing new information technology? (P5)

2. What are the likely affects on employees, in terms of their working patterns?

3. What new management systems would have to be put in place by the employers? (M3)

4. Assess the short term and long-term effects on the council as a result of the IT changes. (D2)

Index